S0-AEL-535

EX·LIBRIS

SERVING

THE WORD

Also by Vincent Crapanzano

The Fifth World of Foster Bennett:
A Portrait of a Navaho Indian

The Hamadsha: An Essay in Moroccan Ethnopsychiatry

Tuhami: Portrait of a Moroccan

Waiting: The Whites of South Africa

Hermes' Dilemma and Hamlet's Desire:
On the Epistemology of Interpretation

SERVING THE WORD

*Literalism in America
from the Pulpit to the Bench*

VINCENT CRAPANZANO

THE NEW PRESS   NEW YORK

© 2000 by Vincent Crapanzano

All rights reserved.
No part of this book may be reproduced in any form
without written permission from the publisher.

Library of Congress Cataloging-in-Publication Data

Crapanzano, Vincent, 1939–
    Serving the word : literalism in America from the pulpit to the
bench / Vincent Crapanzano.
            p.   cm.
    Includes bibliographical references and index.
        1. Fundamentalism — United States.   2. Bible — Criticism,
interpretation, etc. — United States.   3. Constitutional law — United
States.   4. Law — United States — Interpretation and construction.
I. Title.
BT82.2.C73   2000
306.44 — dc21   99–22220

Published in the United States by The New Press, New York
Distributed by W. W. Norton & Company, Inc., New York

The New Press was established in 1990 as a not-for-profit alternative to the large, commercial publishing houses currently dominating the book publishing industry. The
New Press operates in the public interest rather than for private gain, and is committed
to publishing, in innovative ways, works of educational, cultural, and community value
that are often deemed insufficiently profitable.

www.thenewpress.com

Printed in the United States of America

9 8 7 6 5 4 3 2 1

For
Wicky

Contents

SERVING

THE WORD

Acknowledgments

There are a great many people whom I should like to thank. To protect their identity I have chosen not to acknowledge them by name. Many spent hours patiently describing either religious beliefs or the intricacies of the law. They accepted my project in good faith, and, though I know I will have disappointed many of them, I trust they will recognize the effort I have made to be as true as possible to their beliefs and understanding. I hope they will take my criticism as a challenge, as it is meant to be, and not simply as a disparagement to be dismissed. The issues we have raised are too important for that.

I do want to thank my several research assistants, Saul Anton, David Goldfarb, and Andrew Libby as well as Luiza Chwialkowska, Jared Holt, and Radu Popa, for their help. I have discussed my work with many colleagues across the country and in Europe and Brazil. I want to thank the Center for Transcultural Studies, the New York Institute of the Humanities, the Ecole Française de Rome, the participants in the Anthropology and Literature Conference at Le Louverain in Switzerland, the anthropology and literature research program at the University of Konstanz in Germany, the Museu Nacional in Rio de Janeiro, the Frobenius Institut in Frankfurt am Main, the anthropology departments at the universities of Southern California, Rio de Janeiro, Brasília, Heidelberg, and Montréal, as well as those at Harvard, the CUNY Graduate Center, and the Ecole des Hautes Etudes en Sciences Sociales in Paris, for giving me the opportunity to present my research and offering me countless suggestions. I am indebted to the California Institute of Technology for having appointed me a Sherman Fairchild Distinguished Scholar. This enabled me to carry out much of my research on Christian Fundamentalism in southern California. I would particularly like to thank Daniel Keveles for his continued interest in my work and for facilitating my stay at Cal Tech. My research was also supported by a BSC-CUNY Research Award Program at the City University of New York.

I am of course deeply grateful to André Schiffrin and Jessica Blatt at the New Press who did so much to make this book possible. Finally, and above all, I would like to thank my wife, Jane, who listened patiently and critically to my endless discussions of the intricacies of Fundamentalist and legal hermeneutics and still had the fortitude to read through the manuscript with her red pen.

To protect their identity, I have changed the names of the people I interviewed.

A Note on Bible Translation

U nless otherwise indicated, I have quoted from the New American Standard Bible, which is the preferred translation in many of the seminaries where I worked. The New International Version is also popular among Fundamentalists and Evangelicals.

Preface

"You'd want me not to hire a good waggoner, 'cause he'd got a mole on his face," [Mr. Tulliver said to his wife].

"Dear heart!" said Mrs. Tulliver, in mild surprise, "when did I iver make objections to a man because he'd got a mole on his face? I'm sure I'm rather fond o' the moles; for my brother, as is dead an' gone, had a mole on his brow. But I can't remember your iver offering to hire a waggoner with a mole, Mr. Tulliver . . ."

"No, no, Bessy; I didn't mean justly the mole; I meant it to stand for summat else; but niver mind — it's puzzling work, talking is. . . ."

George Eliot, 1860[1]

Talking is surely "puzzling work," as are understanding and interpreting. Mrs. Tulliver is a literalist; Mr. Tulliver is not. Nor is he a particularly articulate philosopher of language — but he knows better than to try to explain his use of figurative language to his literal-minded wife. Mrs. Tulliver's literalism is no doubt a function of her intelligence. It is also a source of George Eliot's humor. Literalism has been a source of humor since Aristophanes. It can be taken seriously, too.

In the American movie *Forrest Gump*, the eponymous hero is also a literalist, but unlike poor Mrs. Tulliver, whose life begins and ends on the Floss, Forrest becomes a national hero. Stupid is as stupid does, Forrest's mother tells him, and he repeats it. He does exactly what he is told, without much understanding but with good heart, and he achieves enormous success. Forrest is an innocent, like Parsifal, another literalist. But, unlike Parsifal, Forrest has no quest. When his friend and former commanding officer Lieutenant Dan, whom Forrest saved when the lieutenant's legs were blown to pieces in Vietnam, maliciously asks him if he has found Jesus, Forrest, clearly puzzled, answers simply, "I didn't know I was supposed to be looking for Him."

Forrest's literalism is comic, but unlike Mrs. Tulliver's, it is dis-

turbing because of its contemporary—satiric—relevance. It parodies a style of interpretation that appears to be increasingly
predominant in the United States today. This literalism does not
result from dull wit, though it is often taken to, even by those of us
who are sometimes, despite ourselves, caught in it. It demands
discipline—not Forrest's mindless discipline, though to the outsider it often seems just as mindless, but a strict commitment to
what is taken to be "literal" or "true" meaning. It is associated with
a set of assumptions about the nature of language, language's relationship to reality, its figurative potential, its textualization, and its
interpretation and application. It is the object of considerable philosophical reflection among Fundamentalist Christians, for example,
and certainly among those legal scholars who interpret the Constitution in terms of what they claim to be its "plain meaning." It encourages a closed, usually (though not necessarily) politically
conservative view of the world: one with a stop-time notion of history and a we-and-they approach to people, in which *we* are possessed of truth, virtue, and goodness and *they* of falsehood,
depravity, and evil. It looks askance at figurative language, which,
so long as its symbols and metaphors are vital, can open—
promiscuously in the eyes of the strict literalist—the world and its
imaginative possibilities.

When most people think of literalism in America, they think of
Christian Fundamentalism. Since its origins in the late nineteenth
and early twentieth century, Fundamentalism has been associated
stereotypically with poor, marginalized, and ignorant Southern
"hillbillies." Hence it has been explained as a product of poverty
and ignorance, as offering a transcendental escape from the grim reality in which these backcountry people find themselves. There is
little truth in this stereotype. To be sure, Fundamentalism is widespread in the rural South and no doubt related to the poverty there,
but its origins were in the urban North, and today Fundamentalists
of all classes and backgrounds are found all over the country. Many
of them have college and even advanced degrees. Their icon is the
white middle-class family living in a safe, carefully groomed development and attending a church like Jerry Falwell's Thomas Street

Baptist Church. Though the Fundamentalists were traditionally one of the least politicized groups in the United States, many of them, like Falwell, the founder of the Moral Majority, became politically concerned, if not actively engaged in politics, in the seventies. As Falwell puts it, they became aware of the moral and spiritual crisis that was destroying the fiber of the country and its ability to fight communism and other degenerate ideologies like "secular humanism." As evidence of this parlous state, Falwell provides us with a now-familiar litany of symptoms: a 40 percent divorce rate; rampant pornography, sexual promiscuity, and drug addiction; abortion; feminism; the gay rights movement; the notion of children's rights; sex education; the teaching of evolution; the interdiction of school prayer; easy welfare; and a weak foreign policy.[2] Today, the Fundamentalist is identified with the Christian Coalition and the religious right. They have a voice and, making use of the latest technologies, they broadcast it widely, giving the impression that they are more numerous than they are in fact.

However, Christian Fundamentalism is only a part of the story. Literalism in the United States is far more widespread than most realize or are even prepared to accept. It occurs, with obvious modification, in conservative understandings of the law, particularly those concerned with the interpretation of the Constitution; in popular approaches to psychoanalysis and psychotherapy, especially those that aim to liberate the patient by retrieving "real" traumatic events long buried in memory; in popular accounts of genetics that stress "a gene for" you name it—homosexuality, baldness, or adultery—without considering the role of environment, even genetic environment, in the actualization of genetic potential; in current identity politics in which a racial, ethnic, or some other social characterization is taken at face value, as an essential feature of whoever is being labeled; in mechanical Marxisms that do not question their categories; and in positivist philosophies of language that believe in the possibility of a pure, unambiguous language of science.

In *Serving the Word*, I will examine literalist styles of interpretation in two of its main expressions: Christian Fundamentalism and

the legal thinking that gives interpretive priority to "plain meaning," "original meaning," or "original intent." I have chosen to focus on these two domains because of their real and symbolic
significance in American social and cultural life. They exemplify literalism. They illustrate its range, its pervasiveness, its effect on everyday life. They point to the moral implications of interpretation,
which are generally ignored in secular society and even in many
philosophical circles. Although neither the Fundamentalists nor the
legal literalists—I shall call them, for lack of a better term,
"originalists"—are numerically significant, they have very considerable moral and political influence today. The Fundamentalists,
who, with some exaggeration, say they number as high as twelve
million, have been called the conscience of American evangelicals.
They challenge both directly and indirectly the liberal Protestant
churches, which have been losing membership for most of the century.[3] Even the Roman Catholic church has not been immune to
their influence, particularly among its charismatics. The originalists
have held enormous sway in law and politics since America's turn
to the right. Ronald Reagan succeeded in placing them in all Federal courts, and they have, wherever possible, succeeded in undo-
ing, or at least eroding, many of the decisions of the Warren and
Burger courts that preceded them. Their greatest influence, like
that of the Fundamentalists, is, I suspect, less through direct
accomplishment—the overturning of a decision they find
obnoxious—than by indirection: by forcing their opponents to
frame a problem in their terms. Although it has been argued by
many legal historians that literalism in the law is rooted in American
evangelicalism, I make no such claim.[4] Nor do I look to the religion
of the legal literalists for an explanation for their approach to interpretation. Some, like the former Supreme Court justice, Hugo
Black, come from Fundamentalist backgrounds, but others, the majority, do not. My concern is neither with historical influence nor
with sociological or psychological explanation. My aim is to delineate a mode of interpretation, whatever its source, which has very
considerable—and, in my view, potentially dangerous—purchase.

I hope, thereby, to offer a critical perspective on it and its relationship to more open modes of interpretation.

———

My interest in literalism began in the early eighties when I doing research for a book on the white South Africans.[5] I was working in a small village in the wine district just north of Cape Town when, to my surprise, the villagers were suddenly caught up in a wave of evangelical fervor. They were both Afrikaners and English-speaking whites whose relations were traditionally inimical. The Afrikaners were members of the highly conservative, pro-apartheid Dutch Reformed Church, and most of the English-speaking whites were at least nominal members of the more liberal Anglican church. (Though there were nonwhites in the Anglican church, there were none in the Reformed church, which was divided according to apartheid's racial categories.) What surprised me about the revival was its extreme literalism. The Reformed church was quite literal, particularly among its laity, but it did not insist that every word in the Bible was inerrant. It did assume the Bible's truth. The Anglicans—many of them charismatic—were given to figurative and even allegorical readings. The evangelicals were critical of their symbolic interpretations and even frowned upon the Reformed church's tolerance for error in the Bible.

When I returned to the United States, I began following the rise of evangelical Christianity and even attended a few services. I noticed the same allegiance to the literal word, the same intolerance of figurative understanding, the same denial of any possible error in the Bible, and of course the same—or at least similar—political conservatism I had found in South Africa. Like the white South African evangelicals, the Americans were committed Calvinists. They insisted on their chosen status—the fact of being reborn, of being saved—and divided the world accordingly into the saved and the unsaved. There was an unbridgeable gap between them. The "Christians," as the evangelicals call themselves, with what often seems a calculated exclusion of all other Christians, had truth and salvation on their side and, accordingly, evangelical responsibility—to "witness," or convert, the unsaved. Pagans, Muslims, Buddhists, and the members of other "cults" were thought to be worshippers of Satan. (The Jews, at least some of them, were an exception, for the Bible speaks of their salvation.) I found that the American evangelicals did not try to integrate their theology with social and racial differences as did some South Africans, who even went so far as to say that God had marked the saved and the unsaved by the color of their skin. I detected at times among the Americans a morally and theologically inadmissible sense, but a sense nevertheless, that the "Christians'" well-being, their family life, and material success (or indeed their impoverishment and marginalization) was a sign of their salvation. I could not help thinking that this was reflected in the often brutal social policies of the religious right. There was, it seemed to me, an intolerance built into the conservative evangelical's literalism, perhaps into every literalism, because that literalism can admit no deviance from a single, unambiguous meaning.

I soon realized that the literalism I was seeing among the Fundamentalists was in fact a widespread characteristic of American thought. It is always easier to distinguish patterns of thought and value in foreign cultures than in one's own, where they are simply taken for granted. We discover ourselves, our assumptions, through contrast or, as Martin Heidegger remarked, when a breakdown occurs and we have suddenly to rethink what we have been thinking and doing all along.[6] It was Ronald Reagan's nomination of Robert Bork to the Supreme Court in 1987 that called my attention to similarities between the literalism I was observing among Evangelicals and the originalism that Bork was preaching. I had not been particularly interested in jurisprudence, but, like most educated Americans, I was suddenly caught in its implication. I was troubled by the narrowness of Bork's vision, his allegiance to what seemed to me to be a very simplistic understanding of meaning, and the way he manipulated that sense of meaning for precisely the political ends he claimed his originalism avoided. At the time, I saw Bork simply as a hypocrite who was using a particular, moralistic stance toward the law as a way of fulfilling his political agenda. I was too involved in the immediate consequences of his nomination to consider the features of his interpretive stance, which facilitated his ambition, manipulation, and hypocrisy. That came later, after the 1994 Congressional elections, when it was no longer possible to ignore the close relationship between conservative evangelicalism, legal originalism, and the religious right.

It was then that I decided to write about literalism. Rather than view it in terms of particular social and political issues, as so many commentators had, I chose to look at it as a system of interpretation—to write a critical ethnography. To this end, I focused on the play between what Fundamentalists and originalists have to say about interpretation and how they actually carry it out. Most of my research on Fundamentalism was carried out in Southern California where I interviewed students and faculty at various conservative evangelical seminaries, went to some of their classes, and attended innumerable church services and Bible study groups. I also did research in other parts of country—New York City, Chicago, northern Washington State, upper New York State, and rural Massachusetts—and covered still other areas by listening to evangelical television and radio programs. A study like this cannot be limited to a single research site—or even multiple ones—if only because the people involved are connected in complex ways by the media, telecommunications, the Net, and travel. My work on the law was even less site-specific. Although I interviewed lawyers, judges, and legal scholars, most of my work was textual—the analysis of law review articles, books, and court decisions. Given the priority that Fundamentalists and the lawyers give to the written word, it is impossible not to pay close attention to what they have written or read. In my interviews, I was continually referred not only to the Bible and the Constitution but to commentaries, cases, and articles.

Although the rise of Christian Fundamentalism has been compared to the dramatic increase in religious fundamentalisms around the world, I have chosen not to generalize. Most generalizations about these fundamentalisms—Islamic, Jewish, Hindu, and of course Christian—have tended to ignore doctrinal differences, such as the belief in more than one god or the degree of God's involvement in the world, which are central to the believers' faith. These doctrinal differences affect the evaluation of sacred texts. Are they God-given? Of ancient but unknown authorship? They influence the way in which a text is interpreted. Can there be any variation in its meaning? Some religious texts play on ambiguity and exalt figurative language; others do not. Can their readings be dissociated from prevalent interpretive practices in other domains? Should interpretation focus on a single text? Or multiple texts? Are comparisons of texts valid? Is correct interpretation the result of debate? Or is it vested in a single authority like a pope or an ayatollah? To what extent should one give authority to traditional understanding? To commentary? To derivative, para-sacred texts such as the Islamic hadith (traditions) or the Jewish Talmud? Given these important differences, it seems premature to generalize religious fundamentalisms. We risk creating ethnocentric stereotypes that do justice to none of them and impede our understanding of all of them. What we *can* say is that all these "fundamentalisms" are reacting, often self-consciously, to modern, and now postmodern, conditions—to disturbances in the way we understand the world and, perhaps even more important, the way we do not understand it.

There is a certain arrogance in the task I set myself. I like to think of it as a professional hazard. Anthropologists always presume to write about more than what, from their subjects' perspective, they can know. Their expertise is never sufficient. I am neither a theologian nor a believing Christian (though I confess to a certain troublingly sentimental respect for the Episcopalians); I am neither a lawyer nor a specialist in the anthropology of law. I am an outsider, and I have to recognize both the limits and the advantages this position gives me. Outsiders see differently, both more and less, than insiders. Despite our greatest empathetic projections, as every lover knows deeply, we can never enter fully the world, the mind, of another. Our vision is always askew, our hearing never perfectly pitched. We are always about to transgress, to blaspheme. We see rhetoric, plays of power, unacknowledged desire, and rationalization, where the insider sees substance, concern, cause, reason, and logic. (I am referring not just to the insider's unreflected-on experience but also to his critical reflections on that experience, for as an insider he can never be an outsider, not really.) This is why any social or psychological description is bound to fail if it claims, as many do, to be an inside view. Of course, in the flow of everyday life, in the heat of argument, and even in a discipline's reflective moments, this view is intolerable. We cannot sustain in social life a rigorous epistemology. The lover has even more deeply to deny what he knows deeply.

It is the open-to-argument stance of even the most literalist approaches to the law that most dramatically distinguishes them from Christian Fundamentalism. Though Fundamentalism is as prone to apologetics as any church—and though, given its debased status in mainstream America, it is probably more defensive than most other churches—it has tended to retreat from any active, critical engagement with other Christianities, certainly other religions. Fundamentalist theologians argue among themselves. For the most part they do not argue with theologians from non-evangelical churches. They tend to dismiss these other theologies in a name-calling way, with easy stereotypes. Their understanding of other religions, indeed, other value systems, is limited and judgmental. They have the truth, they have Jesus, they have been chosen—why bother to engage? Engagement, as many of them see it, is always corrupting. This inward-turning has had, in my view, a devitalizing effect on Fundamentalism. It has turned its interpretative activities into gestures of confirmation of what is already postulated—the Fundamentalists would say, revealed—rather than into a means of discovery and expansion. It has prevented them from making what (critical) contribution they can to ongoing debates in Christianity and other areas of life. When I asked one elderly professor of theology at one of the more conservative seminaries in Los Angeles about his relations with ministers in liberal Protestant churches like the Episcopalian, he told me he hadn't talked to an Episcopal priest in more than twenty-five years. Many Fundamentalists had nothing good to say about the evangelical historian Mark Noll, who advocates intellectual participation in what he calls America's "first-order discourse." For them, Noll has succumbed to worldly philosophy and secular humanism.[7]

It was the law's argumentative stance that caught me: I had no choice but to accept its challenge. (As I write this, I see Ted Winter, a Fundamentalist pastor with whom I often met, smiling sadly. How, he asks, can you see yourself having to engage in legal argument and not having to accept the single most important challenge in your life—your accepting Jesus and the salvation He offers you?) I felt at home with the law, its style of argument, the kind of questions it posed and the answers it demanded. To engage in argument, which I took mistakenly for openness, came as a relief after my encounter with Fundamentalism. (I did most of my research on Fundamentalism before turning to the law.) I say "mistakenly" because, as I made my way though books and articles by legal academics, I was overwhelmed by the repetitiveness. Niceties of distinction seemed to paper over repetition. The same arguments in different guises appeared again and again in the law reviews—there are more than 700 published in the United States—no doubt giving their authors a certain satisfaction, perhaps even a moment of fame, salary and consulting fee increases, and the possibility of moving to more prestigious law schools.

What I have said about repetition in academic law (which applies in different ways to the practice of law) can be said about all academic disciplines, including my own. What seems repetitive to the outsider does not necessarily appear so to the insider, who is perhaps more sensitive to the consequences of the new angulations that occur with each "repetition." What is fascinating to the outsider is the way in which these repetitions articulate with changing circumstances, as they betray the novelty of these circumstances by encouraging a sense of continuity. When I began my research, I thought of it not in temporal but only in semantic terms. I did not realize that literalist understanding gives at least the illusion of stopping time and history by projecting (a notion of) meaning that transcends time. Of course, it stops neither time nor history, for however diligently we try to divorce our literalist understanding from the circumstances in which we understand, we can never fully separate it from these circumstances. When the literalists impress on us the importance of distinguishing meaning from significance—the one resistant to interpretive circumstances, the other determined by them—they fail to realize that meaning is always porous, always susceptible to contemporary significance and application. It is perhaps for this reason that they stress original meaning and so privilege its moment of origin that it takes on a sacred or near-sacred aura. It is God who inspired Scripture. Its writers—Moses, Mark, Paul, and Peter—have heroic stature; the texts themselves are treated with an at times fetishizing respect. The Constitution is, of course, man-made. It is supported, however, by the Declaration of Independence, in which authoritative appeal is made to the "Creator," "the Supreme Judge of the world," and to "Divine Providence." It situates itself in both divinely and politically measured time. Article Seven, the last article of the unamended Constitution, reads: "Done in Convention by the Unanimous Consent of the States present the Seventeenth Day of September in the Year of our Lord one thousand seven hundred and Eighty seven, and of the Independence of the United States of America the Twelfth." The Framers are taken as heroes, and the original, autographed text in Washington is a site of pilgrimage. The originary moments become, as it were, transhistorical, giving to the texts produced in that moment a timeless, authentic, and authoritative meaning. The task of interpretation is to lay bare that meaning so that it may be truly projected forward into the present and become determinative of that present.

The organization of *Serving the Word* mirrors my own research and, no doubt, reflects changes in my understanding which accompanied that research. I began my study at various Bible seminaries in Los Angeles and then went on to study conservative approaches to the law. The Introduction generally is concerned with theories of interpretation and language. Chapters One, Two, and Three are devoted to Christian Fundamentalism. The first, Election, focuses on the history and theology of Fundamentalism. The second, Sanctification, is concerned with practice—with the application of biblical truth to everyday life. It discusses conversion and sanctification—the process of making one's life as biblical as possible—and biblical counseling, the therapy by which the Fundamentalists and other evangelicals attempt to straighten out those who have gone astray. Chapter Three, History, looks at how Fundamentalists and other literalists understand time and history. Chapter Four, The Constitution, introduces the U.S. Constitution, its history, and interpretation. Chapter Five, Foundations, is concerned with the foundational role of the Constitution. It centers on the textualism of Raoul Berger and Antonin Scalia. In Chapter Six, Intention, I consider critically those approaches to the law, like Robert Bork's, which insist on the need to determine original intent in the interpretation of the Constitution and other legal texts. Chapter Seven, Precedent, examines the weight of previously adjudicated cases on the reading of Constitution. In all the law chapters, I am particularly concerned with the way in which legal argument, any argument I suppose, has to deny its own rhetoric if it is to be successful. Literalism comes then to promote what can be called a structural hypocrisy. Despite its aim to be true to some "letter of the law," it verges on semantic nihilism, for the letter, the word, has (at the expense of its own meaning) to mask its rhetorical usage. The Conclusion is a personal reflection on my findings. I ask how extensive the literalism I have described is. I note how easy it is for serving the word to become subservience to the word.

Introduction

"When I use a word," Humpty-Dumpty said, in a rather scornful tone, "it means just what I choose it to mean—neither more nor less."

"The question is," said Alice, "whether you can make words mean so many different things."

"The question is," said Humpty-Dumpty, "which is to be master—that's all."

Lewis Carroll, Alice in Wonderland[1]

Any society, even the most primitive, can be seen as a field of competing interpretive styles, the relations among which are governed by a set of more or less conventional strategies. These strategies serve, if not to reduce conflict, then to determine expectations about how encounters between competing interpretations will (or ought to) work out. They are, as such, always implicated in the structures of power. The expectations figure strategically in the relations between the different interpretative styles and their advocates. We see this in the United States today in our tendency to symptomatize interpretations in terms of some social characterization like African-American, gay, or white middle class. We avoid the challenge posed by another's interpretation or understanding by "knowing where it comes from" and acting in accordance with that knowledge. If we are Asian-Americans, for example, we know, or think we know, the appropriate way to respond to the views of an African-American. If we are African-Americans, we know the way to respond to someone from the white middle class. This etiquette of response is for the most part deadening, preserving traditional social distance, stereotypic knowledge, and complacent expectations. It is often carried to extremes by separatists like those Fundamentalists who divide the world between the saved and unsaved and never really explore the world of the unsaved. They know; they know better; they know the dangers of knowing.

The strategies for managing different interpretations may become the source of reflection and systematization—particularly, I would argue, where there are not only important differences in style but a breakdown in the conventions that govern the relations among different styles. Such breakdowns occur with dramatic social realignments when, for example, the worldview of a marginal people—the Christians of the late Roman Empire—becomes dominant; or with prolonged engagement with new and alien cultures, as occurred during the Age of Discovery; or in America today where for whatever reasons—economic and cultural globalization, rapid development in technology and communications, new patterns of immigration, the dramatic redistribution of wealth, and the voicing of those who only a few years ago had no voice—there is a pervasive sense of the loss of values, if not bearings. Though reflection and systematization may open up new possibilities, they can also promote closure and closed-mindedness by reaffirming traditional views and values and—more important—the frames in which we articulate these views and values. The uncritical reaffirmation of frames of knowledge plays an important role in the literalisms I treat in this book. It is particularly striking in the law, whose argumentative pretense suggests an openness that is not found among the Fundamentalists but is, in its way, quite limiting. Often, this openness, whether to different views and values or to ways of construing these views and values, is arrested by the fear of relativism that has had considerable purchase among conservatives in recent years. Openness and indeed relativism are frequently contested, not in terms of the issues at stake, but in assertions of simplistic interpretive modes, like the literalist. An arid hermeneutics comes to substitute for live moral, political, and intellectual debate.

By literalism, I mean, roughly, a style of interpretation that shares the following ten features:

1. It focuses on the referential or semantic dimension of language—more specifically on the word—rather than on its rhetorical or pragmatic (that is, its context-relating) dimensions.
2. It assumes a simple, unambiguous correlation of word and thing.

3. It insists on the single, the essential, the "plain, ordinary, commonsense" meaning of the word.

4. It believes that the meaning of a text, at least a sacred or otherwise exceptional text, is ultimately decidable.

5. It finds figurative understanding distorting, even corrupting. Or it contains such figuration in special genres, like "poetry" or "parable," which limit its extension.

6. It stresses authorial intention—"original intention"—as an indicator of right meaning.

7. It views certain texts as fundamental—as grounding meaning.

8. Its practitioners are given to quoting or citing such texts on all manner of occasions.

9. It gives priority to the written—the text—over the spoken and in the case of sacred texts like the Bible, at times over experience.

10. Its proponents argue for the most part that a text must be interpreted in its own in terms before it can be applied to a particular situation. In other words, they tend to separate exegesis, interpretation, and application from one another rather than conjoin them in a single, mutually enriching movement.

Of course all of these features are not necessarily present in all literalist interpretation They are united by what the philosopher Ludwig Wittgenstein called family resemblance.[2] They form a constellation rather than a list of essential features shared by all.

I realize that in distinguishing the literalist from other, more figuratively sensitive styles I am simplifying both literalism and those other styles. Styles of interpretation are never pure or without contradiction. They are always engaged with other interpretations—with other interpretive styles. *And* they respond, defensively, to the authority of these other styles. Even the most powerful of them are always apologetic (in the theological sense) and, therefore, porous.

For the Fundamentalists, the originalists, and other literalists, it is the written word, the text, that gives them at least the illusion of a secure reference point. Though they may argue over the niceties of meaning, and they may recognize at some level the problematic of literalist interpretation, they cling to their literalism if only because it gives constancy to the texts they privilege. Indeed, interpretation can be dangerous if it gives way to irresponsibly figurative understanding, to self-interest, to personal desire, to uncontrolled flights of the imagination, and to the allure of power. It undermines the text and the stability it offers. The stakes are high. Flawed interpretation, if it is thought to be true to God's Word, risks toppling the Fundamentalist's world. It may not topple the originalist's world (for their commitment to literalism is, as we shall see, never so consummate as it is for the Fundamentalists), but it betrays the intentions of the Framers of the Constitution (and statutes) and mutilates the polity they created. It affronts nation, national pride, and tradition. That a text is nothing more than an occasion for interpretation, as the French literary critic Roland Barthes suggests, is anathema to both the Fundamentalist and the originalist.

Our conventional understanding of the written word gives to the texts we write and read an illusory stability and independence. Echoing this understanding, Barthes speaks of writing as "hardened language" and of the monumentality and autonomy of the written word.[3] This contrasts with the effluence, flexibility, immediacy, context-dependency, and ephemerality of the spoken word. Its meaning is less transparent, always deferred, demanding interpretation. In its continuance, it is subject to the vicissitudes of history: changes in understanding, evaluation, and significance. There is an ever present tension between a text's original meaning (its assumption at some level always an artifice) and the meanings given at later dates. The givenness, the materiality, of the text can give it such symbolic weight that its being a site of interpretive strife is lost or easily ignored. Some Fundamentalists appear to take comfort in the presence of the material word—the Book. They never seem to go anywhere without their Bible. Hugo Black, one of the most literalist members of the Supreme Court in this century, always carried a copy of the Constitution with him. When the commentator Eric Sevareid asked him why, he answered that as his memory was not good enough to know the Constitution by heart, "When I say something about it, I want to quote it precisely."[4] Clearly, Black did not want to depart from the corporeal word any more than he wanted to depart from its literal meaning.

The monumentality and autonomy of the written word encourage our ignoring the complex interlocution—the arguments, assertions, accommodations, seductions, and surrenders, perhaps the echoes of text-silenced voices still sounding somewhere—in the unconscious—which lies behind and gives support to the written text. They are not, however, intrinsic qualities of the written word. We can imagine—in fact we *know* of—societies that evaluate the written word differently. In Yemen, for example, as elsewhere in the Arab world, the written is never considered as trustworthy as the spoken. Given that Arabic scripts are usually strings of unvoweled consonants, there is, as the anthropologist Brinkley Messick observes, "an identifiable physical loss in 'reducing' something in Arabic to writing."[5] Reading a text aloud, then—or better still, memorizing and reciting it orally—restores, as if by magic, its full meaning. Since the string of written consonants is ambiguous, voweling or reciting a text is always an act of interpretation. Our simple contrast between writing and speech can never do justice to the complex relationship between them. They are always in a complicit relationship. The spoken sounds through the written, as the written inscribes itself in the spoken. No clearer example of the latter can be found, I suppose, than in the Scripture-penetrated speech of the Fundamentalists, but it certainly occurs among lawyers, and indeed throughout our literate and semi-literate society.

Despite the monumentality of texts, their interpretation is always contestatory, for interpretation always assumes an interlocutor's challenge. This contestatory dimension of interpretation is more pronounced in the law, because one is always arguing the law in one institutional context or another, but it can be found in all interpretive endeavors, even where they are understood, as among the Fundamentalists, as simply revealing divine truth. What is always at stake is the control of meaning and the power that comes with that control. It is frequently masked by the theory of interpretation itself, one which stresses its objectivity or, for that matter, its divine inspiration. Of course, given its commitment to truth, the effect of control and power on an interpretation cannot be acknowledged in the practice of interpretation.

The Bible and the Constitution play similar though by no means identical roles for the Fundamentalists and the originalists. They are documents of ultimate authority. The Constitution is paramount in the complex, hierarchical structure to which it has given rise. It provides for a tribunal of final recourse—the Supreme Court—whose authority is (ideally) unquestioned. All laws, from municipal to federal, have to be in accord with the Constitution. However, the courts normally decide on the constitutionality of a law or statute not when it is promulgated but only later when it is brought into question in a legal preceding. There is, then, in the law both a text of final appeal and a tribunal of final authority for determining meaning.

This tribunal is, in fact, a highly organized arena in which there are definite rules of procedure (for the admissibility or non-admissibility of evidence, for example), highly defined roles, and a rigid, ceremonial etiquette. It is not just the seriousness of cause but the social, ritual, and material accoutrements of cause that give what transpires in the court near-sacred gravity. Although most of what lawyers and judges do does not take place in the courtroom, the courtroom is the law's symbolic locus. It is here, at a remove, in a sort of liminal space-time, the kind anthropologists like to attribute to ritual, that the law displays its authority. The courtroom is like a sacred hall, a temple, a church, removed from the ordinary give and take of everyday life in which that life, its structures and values, the conflicts they generate, are submitted (with the force of allegory, I am tempted to write) to the law's measure, judgment, and comment—to its imposing narrative. It is within the law's precinct—which extends well beyond the courtroom, partaking of in diminishing fashion yet never fully relinquishing that room's sanctity—that interpretations are made and argued. They are constrained by the court's procedures, by the weight of law, its past, precedent, including not only a body of decisions but a way of articulating and framing cases. And, paradoxically, they are freed by this constraint: the judge, as final arbiter, permits, demands, and restricts argument. It is he or she who decides, and that one fact gives a transitory freedom to those who argue before the court. Their interpretations, which may well be about life, but are not about *their* lives, are never life-committing for them. The case ends with the decision and proceeds thereafter to a new independent status, that of precedent. The decision may affect the moral and spiritual condition of the lawyers who argued it and the judges who decided it, but that condition, be it of satisfaction or regret, is outside the law. So, at least, we are told.

For the Fundamentalists (for Protestants generally) the Bible has not given rise to—nor been integrated into—a formal hierarchical structure. There is no tribunal, like courts of law, in which meaning can be argued according to stipulated procedures and finally determined. (Whatever their ceremonial trappings—they are minimal in the evangelical church—meetings, synods, and academic conferences are only fora for debate and recommendation.) Unlike the Constitution, the Bible is said to be perspicuous; its meaning is open to all. Within certain limits, everyone is able to make of Scripture what he or she will. Unlike the judge or the clergy in more formal churches like the Episcopal or the Roman Catholic, evangelical preachers and pastors—they are usually called by their first name—are treated with little formality and are not distinguished, even during religious services, by dress. Interpretive authority may be enhanced by scholarship (though in some evangelical churches scholarship is treated with suspicion) or by force of personality, but, ultimately, having no secure institutional support, it rests on the perceived moral and spiritual condition of the interpreter. The result is inherent instability in each church and a seemingly exaggerated but no doubt functionally necessary dependency on the personal quality of the preacher and his deacons and elders. Meaning then is always in question, though for the Fundamentalists at least this questioning of meaning is sacrificed to the assertion of singular, unambiguous meaning.

What is always at stake is the control of meaning and the power that comes with that control. It is frequently masked by the theory of interpretation itself, one that stresses its objectivity or, for that matter, its divine inspiration. Of course, given its commitment to truth, the effect of control and power on an interpretation cannot be acknowledged in the practice of interpretation.

The modern study of interpretation, or hermeneutics (from Hermes, the Greek messenger god) finds its roots in the study of classical texts during the Renaissance and of the Bible during the Reformation and Counter-Reformation, as well as in the renewed interest in Roman law in Italy that began in the twelfth century. As the German philosopher Hans-Georg Gadamer notes in his magisterial study of interpretation, *Truth and Method*, both classical and biblical studies involved "a revival of something that was not absolutely unknown, but whose meaning had become alien and unavailable."

Both treated texts in languages foreign to the scholars' medieval Latin and demanded philological investigation. Both were confronted with a gap in understanding that had to be bridged if the original meaning was to be uncovered. Interpretation became an historicizing gesture. The interpreter, the hermeneut, was likened to Hermes, who (etymologically "he of the stone heap") was associated with border stones.[6] He had to cross boundaries—of space and time and between cultures. He had to translate "messages" from the past. He had to be convincing, to preserve the authority of the message.[7]

During the Reformation, Martin Luther and other Protestant theologians challenged the Roman Catholics' reliance on the role of tradition in the interpretation of Scripture. As is well known, the Catholics held that "tradition" had binding doctrinal authority, for, like faith and morals, the Holy Spirit protected Scriptural exegesis from error.[8] Luther argued that tradition has to be measured against its fidelity to Scripture. Scripture has a clear sense, he maintained, and is interpretable in and of itself. It is *sui ipsius interpres*. Its meaning, though not always clear, is in fact literal. Its discovery does not require external support—the support of tradition and (papal) authority—but careful study, especially of the ancient languages in which it was written, and the inspiration that comes with faith. It is the whole of Scripture that guides the understanding of individual passages, but the understanding of the whole can only come through the understanding of the individual passages.[9]

Luther's stress on the circular relationship between the whole and its parts is an early formulation of the notion of the "hermeneutical circle" which has played a central role in interpretive theory. It was not an entirely new idea, as Gadamer points out, for it was already known to classical rhetoric, which compared perfect speech to the organic body.[10] Luther extended the notion from the art of speaking to that of understanding.[11] It was the German theologian, the "father of hermeneutics" Friedrich Schleiermacher (1768– 1834) who made the "hermeneutical circle" the centerpiece of his own, distinctly romantic, approach to interpretation.

Although Schleiermacher was not a systemic thinker, his influence on subsequent theorists of interpretation, most notably on the historian Wilhelm Dilthey, on Heidegger and Gadamer, and on the Protestant theologians Karl Barth and Rudolph Bultmann, has been enormous. Most of Schleiermacher's writings on interpretation are in the form of lecture notes, which he delivered at the universities of Halle and Berlin in the second two decades of the last century. Unlike his predecessors, whose hermeneutics were determined by the content of the texts they wanted to understand, Schleiermacher was interested in elaborating a universal theory of interpretation whose principles, or procedures, were of so general a nature as to be applicable not only to any written text but to speech as well.[12] Gadamer suggests that this move to a universal hermeneutics resulted from Schleiermacher's rejection of the Enlightenment's assumption that "rational ideas" are in the nature of humanity. In other words, he was forced to examine critically the principles of interpretation, since no agreement on the meaning of a text could be arrived at on either scriptural or rational grounds.[13]

For Schleiermacher, every act of understanding always involves two equal and contemporaneous moments: the "grammatical," which is concerned with the language of the text to be understood, and the "psychological," which focuses on its author's subjective state.[14] The interpreter must understand the language of the text he is interpreting in a historically sensitive fashion. He must also put himself in the position of its author. A text can never be understood immediately, Schleiermacher insists. Just as the interpreter moves from the particular to the whole so must he move from the grammatical to the psychological. Interpretation involves, then, a continual movement, which later writers understood dialectically or in terms of a dialogue. There are times when Schleiermacher seems to be saying that there is no definitive interpretation—unless we command full grammatical and psychological knowledge, which is of course impossible.

Many of the issues that concern contemporary hermeneutics are adumbrated in Schleiermacher's writings. Among these are the role of the gap or breakdown in initiating interpretation; the movement of interpretation, its expectation, its projective nature, its circularity, its metaphorization as dialogue; the priority of the text, its link to speech and writing, its framing, its (historical) contextualization; the "psychology" of the author, his perspective, his intention, and that of the interpreter, his empathy, his expertise. Issues like these have been questioned and reformulated, often radically, particularly by postmodernists. Is there ever understanding? Can there be a definitive interpretation? Is the determination of meaning conventional? The result of the plays of power and desire? Is the circle of understanding impenetrable? Is the circle an appropriate metaphor for interpretation? Is reference to a whole illusory? Is the model of the dialogue for describing the relationship between the text and the interpreter misleading? Can we give priority to the text? Is context—historical context—always a pseudo-objective prop for a desired, empowering interpretation? Does the author's psychology have any relevance to interpretation? Is looking to the author's intention for the meaning of a text a fallacy?

———————

Central to all interpretive theory is language—more accurately, or at least in addition to language per se, a theory of language. Philosophers in the German hermeneutic tradition speak of the *Sprachlich-*

keit, or the linguistic endorsement of the world in which we find ourselves. They stress, romantically, the experience of language. They say that man dwells in language, that he would not be man (or woman) without language, that it is only through language that his possibilities for action are revealed. Language, Heidegger says, "is the foundation of the human being."[15] This existential-hermeneutic approach to language contrasts sharply with scientific approaches and those of analytic philosophy, which look at language instrumentally, as a system of signs.[16]

In his *Course on General Linguistics*, Ferdinand de Saussure, the founder of modern, scientific linguistics, differentiates traditional grammar, which prescribes rules of correct usage, from modern linguistics, which is concerned with simply "recording the facts" of usage.[17] Saussure released the study of language from the shackles of prescriptivism, which had characterized it at least since the ancient Greeks, and laid the foundation for a study of language that looks to the ways languages are used rather than to the ways they ought to be used.[18]

Prescriptivism is one of the many ways in which people speak about their own language and about language in general. It may take a form as crude and unreflected as a series of dos and don'ts or as elaborate and abstract as our treatises on grammar and style. It may have formal institutional support: classes in which correct usage is taught, editorial rooms in which it is determined, and academies, such as the French and Portuguese, in which it is legislated. Most often, it is implicit in what we say when we talk about what a particular utterance or text means. However elaborated, prescriptivism reflects the assumptions a people makes about language: it is an aspect of their linguistic theory, or ideology.[19]

By assuming an objective stance toward language, scientific linguists have been able to uncover the structures of language and the dynamics of speech with extraordinary success. They have been rather less successful in relating language—particularly speech—to its setting. I would argue that this results in part from their tendency to isolate language from other social phenomena with which it is intimately related. Language—and here my conception of "language" reflects my own theorizing—constantly overflows its own systemic limits. It refers to, relates to, indeed evokes, that which is outside it. It "creates" an exterior—which, paradoxically, folds in on it, creating an "interior." The relationship between what is inside and outside language is one area of very considerable philosophical and linguistic debate. One need only think of all the speculation about denotation, signification, symbolization, and reference. How does the sign relate to its referent? What is the relationship between the symbol and the symbolized? The signifier and the signified? Are they both "interior" to language? Are they both mental, as Saussure maintained? Is it not more accurate to understand signification as a triadic relationship between the sign, its meaning, and that which it denotes? Are there special languages, poetic languages, as the Symbolist poets believed, in which the distance—the split—between the symbol and the symbolized is obliterated? Are there rituals (like the Eucharist in the Catholic Church) that bring about the coalescence, the identification, of the symbol and the symbolized (the transformation of the wine and wafer into the blood and flesh of Christ)?

These questions relate to a series of concerns about language that arise in part from two contradictory attitudes we take toward it. Plato already described these attitudes in the *Cratylus* when he asked if there is a natural agreement between a word and its object, one that can be described in terms of correctness, or if their relationship is simply conventional. Plato opted, as has linguistics generally, for the second. With the exception of a few onomatopoetic words such as "tintinnabulation," "splash," "moo," and "roar," which have received far more attention in our speculations about language than they merit in terms of their frequency and importance, there is no immediate mimetic or iconic relationship between a word and the object for which it stands: the relationship is arbitrary. We may refer to a female dog as a "she-dog" or a "bitch"; neither word relates in any ostensible way to a quality inherent in a female dog. The conventionality of language, of words, becomes even clearer when we look at different languages. A female dog in French is *chienne*, in Italian *cagna*, in German *Hündin*, in Russian *suka*, and in Moroccan Arabic *kelba*. Clearly, there is no sound-symbolic relationship between any of these words and a female dog. To say, however, that the relationship between a word and its object is arbitrary does not mean that the relationship is free. Words are positioned in complex grammatical and semantic structures that govern, in part, their meaning and application.

To the layman, however, meaning is generally understood in terms of the relationship between word and thing—and not in terms of a word's position in a complex language system. When asked what a word means, we generally point to an object or give an example. The relationship seems "perfectly natural." Naturalization is, of course, one of the ways in which speakers speaking or thinking about their language avoid considering the moral—the obligatory—dimension of signification.[20] Such "contractual understandings" call attention to the minimum obligations speakers of a language have. Language—or, at any rate, its usage—must accordingly be situated in a moral field, a field of obligation and responsibility, which is precisely the prescriptive field that linguistics, in its quest for a pure, descriptive science, has bracketed.

The notion of the contract between individuals calls our attention to the etiquette of communication and its moral basis. We know that totalitarian regimes have often used seemingly innocent statements as evidence to incarcerate or destroy their enemies. One has only to think of how Claudius, Gertrude, Polonius, and other courtiers at Elsinore took Hamlet's often obscure words. They were taken as a convenience—to justify all sorts of power politics. We are, of course, haunted by the possibility of not being understood or, worse, not being allowed to be understood. We watch such occasions on television, for example, on *Law and Order* and Court TV. We are fascinated as well as terrified by the way the law can refuse, on procedural grounds, to acknowledge the validity of interpretations that depart from the literal meaning of the words actually used, even when it's obvious to everyone that they were not meant to be taken literally. I am reminded of a British law case, *National Society for the Prevention of Cruelty to Children v. Scottish National Society for the Prevention of Cruelty to Children*, which is familiar to all students of Wills and Trusts.[21] A Scotsman left a legacy to the National Society for the Prevention of Cruelty to Children rather than to the Scottish National Society for the Prevention of Cruelty to Children. The first society, apparently unknown to the testator, was based in London; the second, to which he had shown considerable interest during his lifetime, was in Edinburgh where he had lived. Though there were a number of indications that he had intended his legacy for the Scottish society, the Law Lords ruled that, because the will contained no indication other than the name of the Society, his legacy had to go to the one in London.

Up to now, I have stressed, as the literalists do, what linguists call the "referential function" of language. Words refer to things out there—they name them. Sentences are primarily propositions about reality, or they can be so construed. However, words do many other things beside naming and designating: they point to, highlight, evoke, and even create the contexts in which they occur. They are said to have a pragmatic function. The meaning of some sentences (for example, "Water is composed of two hydrogen atoms and one oxygen atom") are nearly context-independent: their meaning does not depend upon where or by whom they are uttered, whether by a professor in chemistry class or by a caged parrot on a Brazilian porch. Others—for example, "Yesterday, I saw my neighbor slouching past that woman's house"—can only be understood in terms of the context in which it was spoken: we do not know when "yesterday" was, who "my neighbor" or "that woman" was, or where the house was. We have to know minimally when and where the speaker spoke to make any real sense of his utterance. Such pragmatic utterances can in fact be quite creative. Imagine the difference between "Yes, father, I have sinned" and "Yeah, you old bastard, I sinned," said by the same person in the same place to the same person. The honorifics "father" and "you old bastard" change the context of the two utterances dramatically. It is this pragmatically creative function of language that can be an embarrassment to the strict literalist who ideally wants words (or the Word, at any rate) to be as context-independent as possible. They tend toward positivism and model their understanding of language on the (scientific) proposition. Still, in their sermons and prayers, in their reconstructions of biblical stories, in their legal arguments, their re-creations of the scene of the crime, they exploit, inevitably, the pragmatic dimension of language. We tend to identify it with the rhetorical.

Related to the pragmatic function of language is its performative function. As the Oxford philosopher J. L. Austin pointed out, we do many things with words beside designating things or making propositions.[22] We promise, vow, give notice, authorize, advise, condole, bet, declare war, marry, and christen. These performative expressions are measured not in terms of their truth value, as are propositions, but in terms of their sincerity, their efficacy. I can determine the truth value of the proposition: "There are four houses with red doors on Mulberry Street": there are either four houses with red doors on that street or there are not. But it makes no sense to talk about the truth value of such performatives as "I promise to give you the money tomorrow" or "I christen you the *Queen Mary*," or "I hereby declare war on Boetia": either the speaker is being sincere and has the appropriate qualifications to promise the money, christen a ship, or declare war or he does not. If he does — if, as Austin says, the conditions in which the performative utterance is made are felicitous — then the words accomplish something directly: the promise is given, the ship named, war is declared. And we act in accordance with these acts. Words can have, in other words, performative, or illocutionary, force.

I bring up performatives here because they figure importantly in establishing the status of the texts the literalists treat. This is particularly evident in the Constitution, whose words, once they were ratified, constituted a new government — and, by implication, however circular, constituted the people, the citizens, of that government. It also established a set of rights and values, the specificity of which has been the subject of legal argument ever since. The literalists, as we might expect, insist on the particularity of rights and values and refuse wherever possible to extend them. There is a sense in which the whole Bible can be read as a constitutive text, establishing the cosmos, the social world, its customs, its laws. Insofar as the Fundamentalists read it as a set of commandments, Scripture functions this way. Of course, there is a discrepancy between the way the world is biblically constituted and the way it really is. It is here that the Fundamentalists require explanation, and they find it in man's fallen condition. They are motivated, as we shall see, to make their own lives as biblical as possible—to obliterate the gap between the ideal, literally described and commanded by Scripture, and the real. The conservative lawyers need no such theological justification for the discrepancy between the ideals postulated by the Constitution and derivative laws and the world as they find it. Indeed, their profession rests on this gap.

We live under an interpretive regime, or interpretive regimes, which for the most part we take for granted. We do not usually realize how determining—I am tempted to say "tyrannical"—they can be. Seemingly removed from the moral and political dimensions of social life, they may in fact have enormous moral and political consequence. Their effectiveness may even be enhanced by the fact that we do not ordinarily see interpretation in moral and political terms. The literalism proclaimed by the Fundamentalists and advocated by originalists is a mode of governance—of therapeutic import. It is thought to be a way to eliminate potentially dangerous plays with language and meaning encouraged by language's figurative, symbolic, allegorical, and rhetorical potentials. For the Fundamentalists, these are associated with man's fallen condition, with promiscuous flights of imagination, and with his propensity to manipulate meaning for his own depraved purpose. For the literalist lawyers and judges, it is a way of controlling meaning, stabilizing the law, and promoting social order and continuity.

In his *Introduction to the Critical Study and Knowledge of the Scriptures*, the Fundamentalist theologian Horne writes that in "common life, no prudent and *conscientious* person, who either commits his sentiments to writing or utters anything, intends that a diversity of meanings should be attached to what he writes or says; and, consequently, neither his readers, nor those who hear him, affix to it any other than the true and obvious sense."[23] Horne's description of speech and writing is moralistic—so moralistic that it bears little relationship to the way people either intend to speak and write or actually do speak and write. He is judgmental: he speaks of "prudent" and "conscientious" speakers. They become ordinary speakers, who seem to have full command of their language and intentions. Horne does not seem to recognize ambivalence and the ambiguities it generates. He ignores speech genres and the usages they promote and interdict, wordplay and the pleasures it may give, and, of course, figures of speech that not only render speech more complicated but call attention to its artifice. He adds, now with reference to Scripture, that the literal sense "is that which the words signify, or require, in their natural and proper acceptation, without any trope, metaphor, or figure, and abstracted from mystic meaning." He naturalizes the literal meaning and declares thereby any other meaning unnatural—suspect and perverted. He associates such meaning with mysticism!

One might be tempted to distinguish between a naive and an instrumental literalism. The naive literalist would see literalism not only as the only satisfactory mode of understanding, the only path to truth, but as one to which he or she has to be fully committed. The instrumentalist would view literalism on pragmatic grounds, as, for example, the best way to understand a text, win an argument, maintain the social order, or accomplish a particular mission—outlaw abortion, for example. The naive literalist would probably view instrumentalism as morally suspect, exploitative, and hypocritical. We might be tempted to identify the one with Fundamentalism and the other with conservative legal textualism, but that would be to oversimplify. There is an instrumental dimension to all literalism and a naive one as well. After all, the Fundamentalist uses his literalist interpretation of the Bible to convince us of the truth of his religion or how best to respond to a particular life crisis or moral dilemma. There are of course the proverbial—and real—Elmer Gantries who preach the literal word of God for their own material ends. And there are instrumental literalists, like Antonin Scalia, who are sometimes so caught in a naive commitment to a literalist understanding that they are forced to conclusions that contradict their stated position.

Though the literalist is generally opposed to figurative interpretations—except, of course, when the text indicates that a figurative interpretation is in order, as in a parable or poem, or when no other interpretation is possible, as in the assertion that Queen Victoria was made of steel—the instrumental, or rhetorical, use of literalism renders literalism itself a figure or alibi. The literalist's antifigurative stance comes to function figuratively. We see this most dramatically when literalism is carried too far, as in the famous case of a Massachusetts abortionist who argued that he was protected by the Statute of Frauds, which stated that no one should be held for the debt, default, or "miscarriage of another" unless evidenced by a memorandum in writing."[24] We may laugh at the argument, but we are also outraged by it, if only because it recalls less egregious ones, like the Scottish case I just mentioned, or Bill Clinton's claim that he did not have sex with Monica Lewinsky because there had been no mutual genital contact. Literalism can fuel moral outrage; it can also field moral allegory. Indeed, its study inevitably reflects—at a remove—this allegory and is not immune to its effect.

Fundamentalists and most originalists have little patience with arguments that suggest that meaning is socially constructed, a product of interpersonal engagement, or the result of plays of power and desire; that interpretations are never fixed, result from the coincidence of "passing theories" of understanding, or are the consequence of dialogical encounters with whatever is to be interpreted; and that "objectivity" is itself a cultural category, conventional, and socially determined.[25] Indeed, the Fundamentalists themselves argue that these modernist and postmodernist arguments are symptoms of the confusion that results from a failure to regard Scripture as foundational—as God-given and, therefore, absolutely authoritative. They resist then the flexibility, the play, the openness that more liberal interpreters extol (but do not always practice, as the Fundamentalist is quick to point out in the liberal's treatment of Fundamentalism) and see as a necessary and admirable correlate of democracy in a heterogeneous society.

Whatever merit the Fundamentalist's critique has, it does rely on questionable assumptions about textual meaning, interpretation, and objectivity. It assumes, for one, that there is a single correct interpretation of Scripture. I have found that many Fundamentalists extend this mode of reading to other texts—to life generally. Their critique also assumes, and in a corollary fashion, that meaning (as distinguished from personal significance) is timeless.

To the liberal mind, the Fundamentalist's commitment to the Bible, to literal understanding, and to the single, unambiguous, inerrant meaning of Scripture is simplistic, confining, and devoid of creativity. Fundamentalists appears to be judgmental, intolerant of any ambiguity, any ambivalence, and therefore authoritarian and bigoted. They lack sympathy for other points of view, and their insistence on their—God's—truth often produces in their unregenerate interlocutors (as it sometimes did in me) a sort of cognitive-emotional claustrophobia and, not to polish the point, desire to flee. The literary critic Harold Bloom, who sounds off against the Fundamentalists, at least the recent Baptist wing—the "Know Nothings," he calls them—without any attempt to move beyond received clichés, writes, for example, of their "devaluation of all language and thought."

> Even as the Fundamentalists insist upon the inerrancy of the Bible, they give up all actual reading of the Bible, since in fact its language is too remote and difficult for them to begin to understand. What is left is the Bible as physical object, limp and leather, a final icon or magical talisman.[26]

Even more sympathetic critics than Bloom mistrust the born-again Christian's claim to objective understanding. They understand the biblical edifice the Fundamentalist has constructed as an enormous rationalization, providing an authoritative repertoire of moral and spiritual "truths," which masks self-interest and desire, fear and small-mindedness. One elderly Episcopalian priest, whose church had lost many of its members to the conservative evangelicals, put it this way:

"Sometimes I think that I've spent the better part of my life here fighting them and their Bible. It has, you know, nothing to do with Christ's teachings. But they are determined, and I suppose that determination has its appeal. It's all so simple, so uncaring, except for their own of course, and socially irresponsible. They hide behind the word—with such self-righteousness."

Despite born-again Christians' claim to total submission to God, they remain—for liberal Christians—arrogant and self-involved, as individualistic and avaricious as any other American. Indeed, their conviction that they have been saved and that those who have not been are doomed to eternal damnation is thought to reflect—is perhaps the source of—this arrogance. It is seen as a particularly virulent arrogance because it is articulated in transcendent, fated terms. Without love and generosity of spirit, it is found to be un-Christian. To the foreign observer, it is an extreme expression of American moralism, its sure-footed claim to truth, its innocent self-righteousness, its sense of privilege and destined exception.

One might argue that Fundamentalists and originalists are simply traditionalists, but that would be an oversimplification. In one of my first interviews, a journalist who covers religion and politics for one of the California papers warned me not to think of Fundamentalism as premodern. He was right, but only up to a point. Both religious and legal fundamentalists make use of the latest communicative technology and science, at least where it does not counter their basic worldview. But technology aside—it's easily accepted in as pragmatically realist a society as America—the temporal orientation of fundamentalist thought, the weight it gives to the past, its allegiance to an original text, an originary moment, its projection forward of the "eternal" truths of that text, that moment, into a future that, like a wayward child, requires disciplining and ordering in terms of these truths (as if there were no others) runs counter to modernist and even postmodernist figurations of time. These figurations are looser, less past-embedded, less text-determined, less origin-privileging. Claims to the eternal are treated with skepticism, and the future is seen as pure, promiscuous possibility contained, if at all, by an unsubstantiated faith in progress — an attitude of it-will-all-work-out-in-the-end despite (or even because of) our doomsday fantasies. Of course, neither temporality is pure. Despite their premillennialism, which stresses decay, corruption, and entropy, most Fundamentalists I talked to shared mainstream American attitudes about progress — even if it involved only the "progress" of their own salvation. The most literalist of lawyers recognized, however reluctantly, the need from time to time to adjust the law to changes in American values — so long as they didn't stray too far (there's the problem) from those constitutional values that for them defined the American polity. They often sidestepped the issue of change from within the law by demanding change — by amendment, for example — through political process, as though law and politics could be nicely separated. Certainly, those of us who are not literalists have yet to recognize in our outlook a stabilizing respect for literal meaning and a longing for past certainties. We are, after all, not immune to the sentimentalizing nostalgias manufactured by politicians and the media of both the Left and Right.

It is has often been noted that a psychological idiom has replaced the moral idiom that was prevalent in America into the twentieth century and is still prevalent in some sectors, including the Fundamentalists'. Indeed, it can be argued that the moral idiom is beginning to replace the psychological. This is evidenced in the spread of biblical counseling and the new philosophical therapies; in politics, most dramatically in Clinton's impeachment; and, I suspect, in legal argument. The prosecutor in the popular television program *Law and Order* remarks cynically that it's no longer Freud but the Bible that persuades a jury. What is often ignored in these arguments is that the moral idiom itself is very American, by no means universal. As my Brazilian colleagues remind me, we have no political idiom: we talk a lot about politics, but talk of politics is not the same as articulating our experience of the world and our position in it in political terms. Our psychological and moral idioms share a focus on the individual, his or her agency, rather than on the political, social, and economic structures by which, some would argue, individuality, sense of self, and agency, are determined.

The moral idiom (whether or not it's translated into the psychological) penetrates deeply into many facets of life that we do not immediately associate with it, including, as I have been insisting, language. It is, of course, possible to speak of linguistic conventions, etiquettes of usage and the like, but insofar as we ignore their moralization, we also ignore the effects of moralizing on our commitment to language, discourse, and texts and their truths—on the way we use words and how we classify and evaluate genres, figurative locutions, and rhetorical ploys. Haunting all communication is the fear that one's interlocutor is not or might not be committed to its conventions. We fear manipulation, verbal chicanery, and casuistry. It was for this that Plato attacked the sophists. Lawyers are often criticized for manipulating meaning to their own ends. Many of us find it offensive when a Scalia or a Bork, or other conservative plays rhetorically on the moral dimension of language or their commitment to the word, its literal meaning. Such play is rooted in a deep semantic nihilism, for not only are words to be manipulated for our own purposes, ultimately without regard to meaning, but so is our basic—moral—commitment to meaning.

Given the heterogeneous nature of American society—exacerbated by a new global intimacy—and given the collapse of a single predominate discourse, we will probably never again agree on the terms, let alone the content, of any single set of moral and spiritual values. We may continue to sacralize texts like the Constitution, to promote nostalgias for an earlier time—the time of the Framers, for example, when a sense of statesmanship was supposed to have prevailed—and to advocate a return to the values of those times, but if history and anthropology have taught us anything, it is that nativistic movements always fail in the end. We can no more restore the values of the past than we can its understanding, if only because such restorations are precisely that: re-storations, attempts to annul history, to stop time. This doesn't mean that the putative past, its values and meanings, are not without rhetorical force. We have learned—at least *I* have learned—that for rhetorical force to be effective its rhetorical quality—its rhetoricity, if you will—must be denied. It is the real, what-in-fact-occurred, that is declared. Literalism facilitates this translation of the rhetorical into the substantive. Uncritical, lacking irony, it can perpetuate potentially dangerous illusions—dangerous less, I suspect, for their content, which can always be argued, than for the fact that in the place of aspiration they promote a restoration of something that can neither be sufficiently known nor regained in its original fullness. We are left with empty imitations, no more vital, and certainly less entertaining, than our theme-park recreations of the past.

One of the consequences of this restorative turn is that the open and creative discussion of aspirations is replaced by a stale hermeneutics, which argues repetitively the niceties of methodology, promotes fixed meanings, fetishizes texts, and idealizes the original. Texts and interpretations always inhabit the betwixt and between of past and present as they mediate the conversations in which they occur. Whatever weight and fixity they may in fact have, they are subject to the push and pull of interlocution. They cannot be divorced from the micropolitics of such encounters. To argue otherwise is to surrender to a politically determined version without recognizing that determination. However well masked, interpretive practice is always implicated in plays of power, be they of ordinary conversation or in legal argument. The Fundamentalists' commitment to literalism supports not only their particular understanding of the Bible but the certainty of their theology. Theirs is an assertive discourse: one does not debate them. Their proselytizing numbs you with "truth." The historian Margaret Bendroth sees the rise of Fundamentalism as a male reaction to the dominant role women were playing in evangelical Christianity in the late nineteenth century.[27] Indeed, there is something masculine about Fundamentalism. It is very much a male discourse. Women take only a secondary place within its understanding and practice. Though most of the Fundamentalist women I met seemed content with their secondary role, their subservience to their husbands and preachers, their "job" as mom back home, I personally felt that they were so restricted, so dominated, that they had little ocassion for self-expression, let alone for self-assertion. Their lives appeared emotionally flattened, seamlessly removed from all worldly complexities, so politely God-filled that they seemed at times to disappear. They were deprived, I often felt, of even the possibility of resignation.

I have often thought, though I don't know how to substantiate this, that the emphasis on the literal is a male preoccupation—a sign, if you will, of the pragmatic, tough-minded realism that Americans attach to the male persona. It is a way of cutting through the clutter associated here with ambiguity and figuration. Poetic language, indecision, and confused thinking are, of course, associated in American culture stereotypically with women. Is it possible to see the emphasis on literalism as a form of male protest against the powers (shall I say figurative powers?) of women? I am not much given to this sort of argument, but I have to admit that it would account for the correlation we find between literalism and the denigration of women. Women are—they have to be—held in place, the way meaning, literal meaning, has to be.

Lurking behind our concern for correct interpretation is the fear of a total loss of meaning. We are never fully oblivious to the fragile bonds of social and communicative exchange. Breakdowns in the moral order of a society—in Corcyra, as Thucydides describes it in *The Pelopponesian War*, or during revolutions and other periods of rapid social change, or in the anomic conditions that prevail in so much of the world today—produce a sense of meaninglessness that has been described as a loss of connection between word and thing, or meaning. T. S. Eliot describes it well in *Burnt Norton*.

> Words strain,
> Crack and sometimes break, under the burden,
> Under the tension, slip, slide, perish,
> Decay with imprecision, will not stay in place
> Will not stay still.[28]

Yeats also describes it in *The Second Coming*: "Things fall apart, the center cannot hold; Mere anarchy is loosed upon the world."[29]

Part One

THE PULPIT

1—Election

This is Ralph Barnes, a master's student at one of the most conservative evangelical Bible seminaries in Southern California:

"The Bible is a divine book, an inerrant one, without error. It's God-breathed. It's also a human book. And it says, Peter wrote, that Scripture was not given from one source but when men of God were moved by the Holy Spirit. In the same way that you would pick up a pen and write a letter, it is the pen that actually did the enscripturating. God used men. Through His Spirit, He used the full capacity of men to write the words that He wanted. So that the words themselves were the words of God. . . .

"But here's the thing. The Bible was written in ordinary language. God can speak truthfully without having to speak exhaustively. We can know truth, and we can know truth truthfully, and we can know it, though we may not know it exhaustively. So when you look at Scripture, you're looking at a book in which God has—God is able to communicate to man, though we are not able to comprehend the fullness of God because we are finite and He is infinite. Nevertheless, God is able to communicate to men, and He is able to communicate in a language which represents reality. It represents reality truthfully. . . .

"God had spoken to Adam and Eve in clear propositional truth. But the created being, the serpent, who was indwelled by Satan himself at that point, came and spoke and caused Eve to question the word of the Creator, the revelation of the Creator. She subjected herself to the Serpent and listened to him instead of to the revelation of the Creator. We can't know anything truthfully unless God reveals it to us. God had revealed truth. He hadn't revealed exhaustive truth. We have far more truth though than Adam had—through Scripture. However, God had given him adequate truth, everything he needed to know. But, you see, the problem is that Eve—1 Timothy 2—was deceived by Satan. He came and deceived her by saying, 'God didn't really say that. You won't die. Go ahead and eat it.' He caused her not to trust the word of God but rather to rely on her own experience. 'Look, Eve, is this a nice apple?' She trusted her experience instead of the word of God. Adam—the Bible tells us—was not deceived. What he did, he did in full knowledge of his rebellion against God. In each case, you had a human being who refused to listen to the word of God.

"Now they were created in perfection. They had minds which had not been tainted from the curse and fall. *And yet* they were subject to corruption and they were subject to error, because they did not listen to God. How much more are we? You see, we need to understand that the Bible is a unique book—there is none other like it in the world—and that what God speaks in and through it, He speaks authoritatively and accurately, and truthfully."

The commitment and the fervor with which Ralph Barnes speaks of the Bible, his insistence on its truth, its divine inspiration, its "God-breathedness," his dedication—his surrender—to its every word is not limited to strict Christian Fundamentalists. According to polls, between 34 and 40 percent of Americans say they believe that the Bible is the "actual word of God and is to be taken literally."[1] In 1983, 44 percent were found to believe that "God created man pretty much in his present form at one time during the last 10,000 years." In 1995, nearly two thirds (65 percent) affirmed their belief in the devil, 73 percent believed in Hell (up from 67 percent in 1981 and 66 percent in 1968), 90 percent believed in Heaven, 79 percent believed in miracles, and 72 percent believed in angels.[2] While one must treat figures like these with caution, they do point to a dramatic increase in Bible-believing, or evangelical, Christians.[3] Associated with right-wing politics, the so-called Christian right, these evangelical Christians are often identified with Fundamentalists. However, such a label is inaccurate and usually derogatory. It oversimplifies evangelical Christianity.

For most lay people Fundamentalism simply refers to Protestants who take the Bible literally. They are confused with Pentecostalists. They are stereotyped. One thinks of a fanatic, hell-and-damnation Fundamentalist preacher from the Bible Belt, entertaining his congregation with tales of fornication and depravity that would have embarrassed Paul's Corinthians; or of a Bible-thumping revivalist—Jimmy Swaggart or Jim and Tammy Bakker—conning his flock into spiritual rectitude and self-denial as he himself wallows in sin and the guilt that ensues. And one thinks of Oral Roberts, who once had to stop a sermon to raise a dead person,[4] calling the infirm up to their television sets—their personal altars—to give themselves to Jesus; or of Benny Hinn, slaying whole audiences in the Spirit (that is, causing them to fall in ecstasy as they receive God's fiery baptism) with a wave of his hand; or of Billy Graham, or Jerry Falwell, or Pat Robertson and his Ralph Reed calling Americans to self-righteous, God-given, biblically inspired politics. And we must not forget Bill and Hilary Clinton's one-time favorite, Robert Schuller of Crystal Cathedral fame, whose weekly "Hour of Power" advertises that for a pledge of six hundred dollars a year you can become a member of the Eagle Club and receive a fine porcelain eagle that, evoking America, symbolizes membership in Schuller's exclusive Christian community—and the power to survive in the constant threat of extinction by the forces of evil.

While these images, like all stereotypes, are not without their truth, they do not do justice to the belief, the longing for belief, the pain, despair, confusion, fear, disappointment, and loneliness as well as the hope, certainty, love, contentment, and ecstasy of the Bible-believing Christian. You can hear these feelings through all the glib preaching and *prêt-à-porter* testimonies on radio and television and in the media-inspired services of the megachurches spawned by "church growth" consultants like C. Peter Wagner, who apply the latest marketing techniques to increase church membership. (Wagner himself, I've been told, has the whole church exorcised before he begins his work.) You can hear them in ordinary churches and in the pleadings for advice that are the stuff of call-in church radio and twenty-four-hour church counseling services. You can hear them in the conversion tales, miracle stories, and confessions told at prayer meetings and in Bible study groups and recorded on countless audio and video cassettes. And you can read them on thousands of web sites and in countless tracts, evangelical novels, and biblically inspired self-help books.

Miracle tales, conversion stories, and other testimonies attest to God's love and care—his intervention—in the lives, usually the stricken lives, of ordinary people. The stories are, for the most part, conventional, but that conventionality is usually concealed by their intensely personal quality. To give one example: a missionary, who returned to his home church from Thailand, gave a sermon in which he talked about the meaninglessness in his life, the despair and desperation, the whirl toward extinction that had led him, when he was nineteen, to put a loaded shotgun in his mouth. As he was about to fire it, he caught sight of a Bible. He wasn't a Bible reader. He had no faith in God. Once only, as a child, had he prayed for his dying grandmother, and she had died anyway. Yet, somehow, he was moved to pull the gun out of his mouth and to pick up the Bible. He opened it at random, without much conviction, without understanding why, and read the first verse of Psalm 116: "I love the Lord, because he hears my voice *and* my supplications." He did not understand the significance of this verse until he read the psalm's third verse: "The sorrows of death compassed me, and the pains of hell got hold upon me: I found trouble and sorrow." He was so stunned by the relevance of these words that he called upon the Lord for deliverance.

Stories like the missionary's tell of terrible disappointment and despair as they promote hope. Not only do they reveal the most intimate details of the storyteller's life but they attest to a special relationship with Jesus. Jesus is cast as a caring friend, who has, of course, the powers, of grace, forgiveness, and redemption, that no human being could ever possess. He sacrificed himself—in evangelical terms, He died a substitionary death—on behalf of sinners. Under most circumstances these stories simply could not be told. They would be too personal, too private, too revealing of the storyteller's vulnerabilities. But insofar as they attest to God's power, concern, and love, they can be told in public, even on television. They tell how sinfulness and depravity and the despair that comes with them were overcome by the grace of God. The storyteller is so removed from his sinful past that he can treat that past with a detachment that promotes, paradoxically, the wonder inspired by God's love and grace. Depraved, that past becomes a figure for moral and spiritual rectitude. It serves self-understanding and brings faith to others.

The stories reflect an ambiguity inherent in evangelical Christianity. Who is the hero of these stories? Ultimately, it is God, but He is no ordinary hero, for He commands the storyline. Man's position is more complicated. His fate is already determined—he is either one of the elect or he is not—so how can he be a hero in the stories he tells? And yet he is. He has overcome his sinful way of life; he has resisted the temptation to sin; he has remained true to God despite great adversity. He has given himself to God and accepted His word. It is in this way that the storyteller becomes the hero of his tale—but his heroism is not that of an Achilles or an Odysseus. Those are heroes in and despite the throes of fate. The evangelical hero is one whose heroism attests to the glory and mercy of God. He submits to his predetermined fate, his salvation, the way the Greek hero cannot, for the Greek hero has neither the promise—the certainty—of salvation nor the loving, personal, and personalized concern of a Jesus. He has only his own glory and honor, which are of course submerged if not condemned and foreclosed in the evangelical's heroism. The evangelical's stories are success stories in miniature—the American dream cast in spiritual terms (that are not altogether resistant to material claims). They proclaim humility as they announce election.[5]

Election, which is an essential feature of the Reformed churches, Presbyterianism, and most Baptist belief, runs counter to the American emphasis on the individual and his freedom. I have found that most of the Fundamentalists I talked to, even the strict Calvinists, sidestepped election even as they emphasized being chosen. One elderly Baptist pastor in upper New York State—a man who was clearly going through a period of intense self-reflection—preached the mystery of election. "No, not even I can understand election," he said, implying at once his own election and his—any one's—incomprehension, and he went on to define election as "being special to God." He stressed God's absolute sovereignty and yet argued that we also have responsibility for our election. "Both are important," he said. "It is only when we have examined our lives and seen change, real change, that we know we are of the book of the Lamb." For him, from the vantage point of his age, the change in oneself, more perhaps than the experience of being reborn, gives evidence of one's chosen status. I detected a certain pride in his election. For many evangelicals, those younger than he, those given to greater faith in personal experience, particularly for the Pentecostals, certainty comes with conversion—with going up to the altar.

The attribution of belief is always problematic. We have to recognize changes in understanding, emphasis, intensity, and commitment not only over a person's lifetime but in much shorter periods of time—during a conversation, for example, a testimony, a church service, or a moment of tribulation or elation. We also have to recognize a certain consistency in belief, a sense of permanence, of orientation and reference, of that which transcends the immediacy of experience and the contingencies of circumstance. We cannot dismiss attestations of belief as mere rhetoric, or performance, unless we include in our understanding of that rhetoric, that performance. Reference to the transcendent at once denies the power of rhetoric as it affirms it; for rhetoric—and performance—requires that stability, that gravitational point, that center, from which to depart in its constitution of the here and now. A text may incarnate that center, as Scripture does for the Fundamentalist.

It is in this context that the Fundamentalists' literalism has to be understood. Despite the differences among them, Fundamentalists believe what the Bible tells them in plain, ordinary words, and they try to live their lives in accordance with what they have been told. They are committed to the inerrancy of Scripture and they resist, often passionately, any theology that departs in their eyes from the teachings of Scripture. For the most part, they are committed to "pretribulational premillennialism"—the belief that Christ will return to "rapture" true Christians before the time of tribulations and the reign of the antichrist that will precede Satan's defeat at Armageddon and the millennium. This lends itself to a prophetic reading of the Bible and to a sense of imminent apocalypse. Most are militantly hostile to liberal theology and modern biblical criticism. George Marsden, one of the leading authorities on Fundamentalism, argues that what distinguishes the Fundamentalists from other evangelicals is their militant and uncompromising combat against modernist theology and its secularizing trends.[6] They tend to be hard-line, pragmatic empiricists and yet to contain the intellect in what they consider to be biblically permissible.[7] They are certain that anyone who does not share their faith is not a true Christian and will not be saved. In Calvinist fashion, they insist that salvation is by the grace of God alone—and never by works.[8] As premillennialists, they look to the second coming of Christ as the only cure for the world's social and political ills. Given their dismissal of anyone who does not share their beliefs, they tend to polarize the world and resist any contact, certainly any real dialogue, with those who might challenge their views. Though separatism is still strong among the strictest Fundamentalists—like those at Bob Jones University in Greenville, South Carolina, who refuse contact with even those Fundamentalists who do not share their views—others engage, with caution, in efforts to make the United States a "Christian" nation. Their typical church is independent.

Fundamentalism falls within the conservative wing of evangelical Protestantism, which is itself conservative and difficult to define both institutionally and theologically. Mark Noll, an evangelical historian, notes that evangelical Christianity "has always been made up of shifting movements, temporary alliances, and the lengthened shadows of individuals."[9] It is essentially a Bible-centered religion that believes salvation to be possible only through a regeneration, or spiritual rebirth, that comes with personal trust in Christ and his atoning work. The spiritual transformation that results from being reborn is characterized by a life of devotion—Bible reading and prayer—morally explicit conduct founded on biblical precept, and evangelical and missionary zeal.[10] Evangelicals tend to view the church as a voluntary association of believers who are bound by biblical authority. They have been traditionally anti-Catholic, though in the last few years, mainly for political reasons, many of them have underplayed their differences with Catholicism and have even attempted to work hand in hand with Catholics on common concerns. Generally, evangelists have not been as committed to the inerrancy of Scripture as the Fundamentalists have; instead, they speak of the Bible's "infallibility" or of its being "authoritative" and "reliable."

Unlike the Fundamentalists, evangelicals are not wedded to premillennialism.[11] In fact, nineteenth-century evangelicals were taken with a postmillennial vision of moral and spiritual progress toward an age in which the gospel would be triumphant throughout the world, after which Christ would return. They believed that the prophecies in the Book of Revelation concerning the defeat of the antichrist (often understood as the pope) were actually taking place, opening the way for the thousand-year golden age before Christ's return and the end of history. Persuaded that the defeat of Satan was imminent, they saw America as playing a leading role in the cultural advancements—learning, science, technology—that would ensue. The great nineteenth-century revivalist Charles Finney (1792–1875) wrote that the Christian church (by which he meant the Protestant church) was designed "to lift up her voice and put forth her energies against iniquities in high and low places—to reform individuals, communities, and government."[12] Distinctly patriotic, this vision reflected the optimism of the age—faith in scientific and material progress. As a whole, evangelicals have been, and continue to be, more at ease than Fundamentalists with the mainstream American ethos of individualism, freedom, and progress. They have been committed to social reform and have played an important role in the abolition of slavery, in temperance movements, in prison reform, and in private charities. Today, as we know, many are involved in conservative political reform, in anti-abortion, "family values," and antipornography movements, and in the condemnation of drugs, violence in the media, homosexuality, and other "sinful" sexual practices.

Until after the Civil War and then, less forcefully, into the first decades of the twentieth century, evangelical Protestantism was America's religion of reference and provided the rhetoric for self-depiction, social understanding, and political policy. American higher education was in fact distinctly "evangelical" in orientation, at least until the 1870s, when the model of the German university began to take root in the United States. This model stressed specialized—secular and scientific—knowledge over the building of moral and spiritual character, which had been a primary goal of American higher education. In 1839, fifty-one of the fifty-four presidents of America's largest colleges were clergymen, mainly Presbyterian or Congregational.[13] Evangelical publications were immensely popular. Between 1790 and 1830, evangelicals founded over six hundred magazines. By 1830, two of them, the Methodist *Christian Advocate and Journal and Zion's Herald* and the interdenominational *American National Preacher* each claimed circulations of 25,000, giving them the largest circulation of any journal of any kind in the world.[14] The drive to spread the gospel intensified with the "businessmen's awakening" in the years preceding the Civil War. Noonday prayer services, stressing inner peace in the midst of external turmoil, were especially appealing to urban merchants who had suffered during the financial panic of 1857. During the Civil War, the Young Men's Christian Association and the United States Christian Commission were able to mobilize more than five thousand volunteers who brought evangelical Christianity to the Union soldiers.

Among these volunteers was Dwight L. Moody (1837–1899), who was to become one of the most important progenitors of Fundamentalism. He started out as a shoe salesman, first in Boston and then in Chicago, but after experiencing the inflow of the Holy Spirit, he devoted most of his time to spreading God's word. In 1873, he moved to England where he became a well-known revivalist and was soon able to parlay his reputation there into a series of enormously successful revivals in the United States. He stressed conversion, insisted on the infallibility of Scripture, and tended to avoid any theological elaboration, particularly if it was controversial. His message was simple and sentimental, told through anecdotes, and cast in slogans, such as the "Three R's"—Ruin by sin, Redemption by Christ, and Regeneration by the Holy Ghost. Unlike Finney, but like many of his own generation, he gave far greater importance to saving souls than to social reform. He argued, as do Fundamentalists today, that the spiritual and moral uplift that comes with conversion would lead inevitably to a social improvement far superior to that brought about by social activism on the part of the churches. Yet he worked with the newly founded YMCA, started a Sunday school for the poor, a Bible training center in Chicago for lay workers, which later became the Moody Bible Institute, summer missionary conferences, and the evangelical Student Volunteer Movement. Toward the end of his life, he founded the Mount Hermon Northfield Academy in his home town in Massachusetts. Moody was a practical man: he looked and spoke like a businessman. He appealed to the middle-class individualism and pragmatism of his age, and, as one of his admiring biographers put it, was "a benefactor of men." He stood "boldly, manfully, and squarely" against their retreat from religion.[15]

As the century progressed, however, the evangelicals' commitment to cultural and scientific progress began to undermine their religious outlook. The supernatural dimensions of their postmillennial faith were brought into question. Their world was becoming naturalized—subject to the laws of nature that science revealed. Change—geological, biological, social, and cultural—was at the heart of this new scientific view. History could no longer be understood simply as a cosmic battle between God and Satan whose outcome was preordained. Historical processes had to be understood in their own right, their laws discovered. Darwinism was devastating to the biblical faith. Religion came to be understood less in absolute terms, as revealed by God, than as reflecting developing conceptions about God and morality. The Higher Criticism, which developed in Germany in the nineteenth century and sought to determine the authenticity, authorship, and chronological construction of Scripture, regarded the Bible as simply a record of ancient Hebrew religious experience.

In reaction to these changes, evangelicals like Moody began to stress personal holiness and commitment to Christ over active social reform. They moved from an optimistic postmillennial view of the future to a more pessimistic, certainly more conservative, premillennial one. Marsden refers to this move as a "profound alteration" in the "basic epistemological categories" of evangelical thought. He argues that despite their disagreement on the time of Christ's return, the premillennialists shared until after the Civil War the postmillennialists' vision of history and their conviction that at least some biblical prophecies could be taken literally, that they were in fact being fulfilled in the present age.[16] However important this move may have been theologically, it does not constitute a profound epistemological alteration, for there was no change in the categories of historical understanding themselves. Indeed, as we shall see in Chapter Three, these persist today. The historical account of the first chapters of Genesis—Creation, the Fall, the Flood, the collapse of the Tower of Babel, and the genealogy of nations—had not been questioned by postmillennialists any more than it was by the premillennialists. Nor had its historical and anthropological presuppositions. Both shared, in the words of the historian of Victorian anthropology George Stocking, the same "anthropological paradigm"

> whose temporal framework was both finite and confined, whose psychological and epistemological assumptions were innatist and a priori, whose principle of social order was patriarchal, whose principle of human diversification was genealogical, whose principle of temporal change was degenerationist, and whose privileged reconstructive data were those of linguistic relationship. . . .[17]

Unlike their antebellum predecessors, the new premillennialists were dispensationalists. They offered a systemic view of history in which biblical prophecies were thought to refer to real historical events. History itself was divided into distinct eras, or dispensations, usually seven in number (for example, the Dispensation of Innocence in Eden or the Dispensation of the Law from Moses to Christ), during which God exercised his stewardship over man in different ways. Thus were the dispensationalists able to account for inconsistencies in Scripture, which were especially salient given their commitment to the Bible's total and inerrant harmony. Of particular importance were the discrepancies between Christ's teachings and Paul's theology—a point dramatically made in George Moore's novel, *The Brook Kerith*, in 1916. They regarded the present era—the Church age—as a sort of parentheses and insisted, contra the liberals and postmillennialists, that Christ's kingdom was wholly in the future, supernatural in origin, and discontinuous with the history of the present.[18]

It is out of nineteenth-century premillennialism that Fundamentalism grew.[19] (The term was coined in 1920 by Curtis Lee Laws, the editor of the Baptist *Watchman-Examiner.*) Fundamentalism is usually associated with the publication between 1910 and 1915 of *The Fundamentals: A Testimony to the Truth*, a series of twelve religious pamphlets, that defended Scripture, offered a surprisingly restrained critique of modernism, and avoided any social and political causes.[20] Promoted by California oil millionaire Lyman Stewart and his brother Milton,[21] these "testimonies of the truth" were distributed free to more than three million pastors, missionaries, theologians, YMCA and YWCA secretaries, college professors, and Sunday school superintendents throughout the English-speaking world. Although the *Fundamentals* did not have the impact Stewart had hoped for, it did help define the "Fundamentalist" position. By 1919, some six thousand delegates met in Philadelphia to found the World's Christian Fundamentals Association (WCFA), the first of a series of Fundamentalist organizations that were to spring up over the century. Among the delegates was the former White Sox second baseman, Billy Sunday, America's most popular revivalist, who drew enormous crowds preaching what the sociologist William Martin has recently called "a kind of muscular perfectionism," that is, the conquering of vices like smut, illicit sex, a taste for pool halls and the theater, and drink, which Sunday saw as the principal cause of war and crime.[22] Determined to wrest evangelical Christianity from what he saw as its feminine trappings, Sunday directed his appeal to men. "Jesus is no ascetic," he proclaimed, but a "robust,

red-blooded man." H. L. Mencken was struck by the preponder-
ance of men at what he called Sunday's "bull-ring devoted to the
saved."[23] Sunday's theology was slim: his basic message; according
to William Martin, was that being a good Christian was "adhering
to dominant political and economic orthodoxies and upholding the
moral standards of the Anglo-Saxon Protestant middle class."[24] He
always said there could be no religion without patriotism, and during World War I taught children to hiss at the German flag. At the
request of President Wilson he helped sell one hundred million dollars in Liberty Bonds. Though most strict premillennialists would
have been troubled by his social and political commitments, they
probably shared the values he preached.

Within the conservative evangelical fold, and often confused with
Fundamentalism, is Pentecostalism, which grew out of Methodism,
the Holiness movements and the revivalism of nineteenth-century
America.[25] It also has roots in African-American religion, which are
reflected in its music, it style of worship, its enthusiasm, and its millennial expectations.[26] Its name derives from the account of the day
of Pentecost in the first two chapters of the Book of Acts.

> And when the day of Pentecost had come, they [the apostles?] were
> altogether in one place.
> And suddenly there came from heaven a noise like a violent,
> rushing wind, and it filled the whole house where they were sitting.
> And there appeared to them tongues as of fire distributing them-
> selves, and they rested on each one of them.
> And they were all filled with the Holy Spirit and began to speak
> with other tongues, as the Spirit was giving them utterance.[27]

To the dismay of many Fundamentalists, Pentecostalists find in
these lines reason to give greater credence to experience than to
doctrine and the careful reading of Scripture. Though they focus on
the so-called gifts of the spirit, especially speaking in tongues, or
glossolalia, faith healing, and casting out demons, they also stress
salvation and the Second Coming of Christ. Their theology is based

less on Paul than on Luke and Acts—that is, on narrative texts that are notoriously difficult to interpret.[28] The majority of Pentecostalist preachers have no seminary education;[29] they tend to bombard parishioners with Bible verse after Bible verse with little concern for theological subtlety and system. They make continual reference to the passage from Acts just quoted and to one from Mark, whose authenticity has been questioned by many biblical scholars:

> And these signs will accompany those who have believed: in My name they will cast out demons; they shall speak with new tongues; they will pick up serpents; and if they drink any deadly *poison*, it shall not hurt them; they will lay hands on the sick, and they will recover.[30]

They understand these gifts as signs of salvation. Indeed, the historian Robert M. Anderson claims that in its early years all that distinguished Pentecostalism from the Holiness movements was speaking in tongues.[31] It was—and is—their assumption that the gifts are a sign of salvation that offends the Fundamentalists and most other Christians.

Appealing largely to the poor and marginalized, Pentecostalism is said to be the fastest growing religion in the world today. Some claim there are as many as twenty million new converts a year and a total membership of more than four hundred million.[32] Even in the United States there are enormous differences in the style of Pentecostal worship. Of course, the most extreme are the snake-handling services in Appalachia, in which believers demonstrate their "gifts" by taking up rattlesnakes, but there are other churches whose enthusiasm can be quite wild. The assembled enter a sort of ecstasy dancing, jumping around, praying, shouting, prophesying, speaking in tongues—it sounds a bit like a soft, eerie gurgle—and falling to the ground in a seizure. Many Pentecostalists take the words they speak in tongues to be those of some ancient, holy language they do not know. In some churches, they seem to heave sounds out of their belly. They cough and grunt and even laugh as did revivalists in the great Kentucky revival of the last century. Most Pentecostal services, particularly in the larger churches, are more sedate, and their members seem to have mastered the "decorum" of the gift. A few parishioners will speak in tongues during the service, but most do so at the altar after the main service. If they are slain in the spirit and fall to the ground, they are ministered with an awe-inspired gentleness by others who may also be in ecstasy. There may be some laying on of hands on these occasions, but usually faith-healing takes place in smaller groups. And still other evangelical churches, the most discreet, ask their Pentecostalists to pray in tongues in separate rooms or at separate services.

Pentecostalism is conventionally said to have begun in 1906 at a revival in an abandoned Methodist church on Azusa Street in a poor, industrial section of Los Angeles.[33] Led by a mild-mannered but fervent black Holiness preacher, William J. Seymour, the Azusa congregation was taken up by the "Holy Spirit." People shouted wildly, sang praises to the Lord, leaped, ran and jumped about, kissed and hugged one another, and spoke in strange languages unknown to them. The *Los Angeles Daily Times* described a "weird babel of tongues" among "a new sect of fanatics."[34] Frank Bartleman, an itinerant Holiness preacher, who attended services at Azusa, wrote that the "meetings were controlled by the Spirit, from the throne."

> Someone might be speaking. Suddenly the Spirit would fall on the congregation. God himself would give the altar call. Men would fall all over the house like the slain in battle, or rush for the altar en masse, to seek God. The scene often resembled a forest of fallen trees.[35]

People soon flooded the church. They "would fly to pieces on the street," Bartleman wrote.[36] Within two or three blocks of the Mission, "they were seized with conviction." Meetings lasted from ten in the morning until midnight or later; sermons were short and "spontaneous" and always declared tongues a gift of the Holy Spirit and a sign of salvation. They were soon attended by people from all over the country and, within two years, Pentecostalism had spread to fifty countries.[37]

John MacArthur, a strict Fundamentalist pastor in Los Angeles, and one of the harshest critics of Pentecostalism and other charismatic religions, argues that the Pentecostalists give "undue emphasis" to the baptism of the Holy Spirit.[38] "Those who have not experienced the baptism and its accompanying phenomena are not considered Spirit-filled; that is, they are immature, carnal, disobedient, or otherwise incomplete Christians." Such thinking, MacArthur argues, "opens the floodgates for believing that vital Christianity is one sensational experience after another" and leads to "a contest to see who can have the most vivid or spectacular experience."[39]

> And, of course, those with the most awesome testimonies are held in the highest esteem spiritually. Incredible claims are made, and they almost always go unchallenged.

MacArthur's *Charismatic Chaos* is filled with "incredible claims." They range from that of a medical missionary who had spent five and a half days in heaven to that of a preacher who was carried away, in the middle of a sermon, to watch from the back seat of a car the woman he was involved with have sex with a married man. By giving priority to personal experience rather than to Scripture, the Pentecostalist has, according to MacArthur, no standards for the critical evaluation of his experiences and those of others. Experiences can be false, MacArthur insists, but God's word is truth.[40]

As a force within Protestant thought Fundamentalism reached its zenith in the mid-twenties. Historians such as Marsden attribute its militancy to a pervasive fear that evangelical Christianity had lost is biblical moorings and that Americans had lost their "Christian" values. They speak of the sense of cultural crisis that gripped the United States during World War I, the loss of Victorian values, the rise of jazz-age morals, the influence of Roman Catholicism that came with the massive immigration during the previous fifty years, an increase in anti-Semitism as Jews established themselves in America, and, recalling the "Red Scare" of 1919 and 1920, the fear of bolshevism. The war itself was thought to be a sign that Kingdom of God was now upon us, thus confirming the Fundamentalists' premillennial position. Whatever the reasons for the rise of militant Fundamentalists, they led a major offensive against the "modernists" in many Protestant denominations, most notably among the Northern Baptists and Presbyterians, and managed to create schisms in several denominations. These battles were mostly fought in the North and not in the backwater South. The most dramatic Fundamentalist cleansing action took place at the Princeton Theological Seminary, one of the oldest Presbyterian seminaries in the country. The conservative contingent of the faculty under the leadership of J. Gresham Machen left and founded the Westminster Theological Seminary in Philadelphia in 1929. It was to become one of the most distinguished conservative evangelical seminaries in America.

Central to the Fundamentalists' attack on liberal trends in American culture was biological evolution, which they saw as an assault on the account of creation in Genesis and on biblical truth more generally. Former Secretary of State and three-time presidential candidate William Jennings Bryan (1860–1925) was at the vanguard of the anti-evolutionist movement. He declared, "All the ills from which America suffers can be traced back to the teaching of evolution. It would be better to destroy every other book ever written and save just the first three verses of Genesis."[41] Bryan's campaign culminated with the Scopes trial in Dayton, Tennessee in 1925, in which John T. Scopes, a biology teacher, challenged a Tennessee law that declared it illegal "for any teacher in any of the universities (or public schools) of the state to teach any theory that denies the story of the divine creation of man as taught in the Bible and to teach instead that man has descended from the lower order of animals."[42] Although Scopes lost and was fined one hundred dollars, Bryan, who led the defense, was ridiculed roundly by his opponent Clarence Darrow and in the press, most notably by H. L. Mencken. He died within a week of the trial. Scopes received a scholarship to the University of Chicago and became a successful geologist.

During the decades following the Scopes trial, many Fundamentalists, embittered by public defeat and humiliation, retreated from the public eye. Still, aided no doubt by their millenarian outlook, which allowed them to incorporate their failures and to accept the inevitability of their marginalization—their time would come—most Fundamentalists remained dogged in their belief and firm in their evangelical mission. Though their fortress mentality offered them some protection, it was not satisfying, according to the historian Joel Carpenter, for they could not give up their vision of a Christian America and their role in its formation.[43] They continued to consolidate, to define and redefine themselves against a modernity they found ever-more corrupt, and to pursue a revival that gained them converts as it restored their wounded spirituality, their vision and confidence. Ultimately, they became, as Carpenter sees it, "the most broadly influential American evangelical movement in the second third of the twentieth century."[44]

The conservative envangelical churches of the interwar years were preacher-centered. "Heroes of the faith," to use William Martin's expression, like Carl McIntire in Philadelphia, "Fighting Bob" Shuller in Los Angeles, and the "Texas Cyclone" J. Frank Norris, were famous in evangelical circles though less well known than Moody and Sunday had been in mainstream America. Norris (1877–1952), a friend of presidents, a bigot, and a master of conspiracy theory—Reds and Catholics were lurking everywhere—was one of the most notorious of them. He was accused of murder and burning down one of his churches. With enormous churches in Fort Worth and Detroit, he had more followers than any other preacher of his time and is credited with having brought Fundamentalism to the South.[45] Movements like Youth for Christ with chapters across the country and weekly rallies spread rapidly during the war years.[46] Radio ministries, which were already important in the twenties, reached their pinnacle with Charles E. Fuller's "Old Fashion Revival Hour" whose audience, the largest of any program in the United States, numbered between fifteen and twenty million in 1939.[47] The number of Bible colleges and institutes increased from 49 in 1930 to 144 in 1950.[48] Two new Fundamentalist associations were founded in the early Forties: the militant, separatist American Council of Christian Churches (ACCC), whose first president Carl McIntire had fled Princeton with Machen, and the National Association of Evangelicals, which was created in opposition to the reactionary ACCC.

In fact, there were numerous, bitter controversies within Fundamentalist ranks, and they often led to the splitting-up of churches and church groupings. In 1936, for example, Machen and McIntire were expelled from their Presbyterian denomination; they went on to found the Presbyterian Church in America, later named the Orthodox Presbyterian Church.[49] A year later, finding Machen and Westminster insufficiently pure, McIntire founded the Bible Presbyterian Church and Faith Theological Seminary. (He was to found in 1948 the International Council of Christian Churches, whose principal aim was to oppose the liberal World Council of Churches.) This fissioning of Fundamentalist churches, seminaries, and associations has not abated. Indeed, it seems to be a structural feature of the independent church, which submits to no organizational hierarchy, and which depends for its definition on its particular pastor.[50]

At the end of the war, a younger generation of conservative evangelicals, including Harold John Ockenga, Carl F. H. Henry, and Edward J. Carnell, organized a "neo-evangelical" movement that attempted to broaden Fundamentalism's scope. They started *Christianity Today*; which is still the most popular evangelical magazine in the country with a circulation of between 150,000 and 170,000. With Fuller they organized the Fuller Theological Seminary in Pasadena in 1947, which like so many Fundamentalist seminaries, including BIOLA (the Bible Institute of Los Angeles) and Westminister in Philadelphia, has become more liberal over the years. Indeed, its liberal tendencies are excoriated by conservatives like MacArthur and Bob Jones. The very conservative Grace Brethren Church put one pastor—I shall call him Ted Winter—on probation for attending the Fuller Seminary.

Billy Graham, perhaps the most important revivalist in the second half of the twentieth century, gave the neo-evangelicals an enormous boost. That ended with his New York crusade in 1957, in which he cooperated with prominent liberal church leaders. Sepa-

ratists such as Bob Jones, Sr. (1883–1968), John R. Rice (1895–
1980, the founder of the *Sword of the Lord*, an influential Fundamentalist magazine), and McIntire anathematized Graham and the
neo-evangelicals. Despite his ostracism, Graham's influence grew
throughout the world as did a more moderate evangelicalism. By
the seventies there were between forty and fifty million evangelicals
in the United States, and that number has increased dramatically
since then. Some of the evangelicals I talked to claimed—on what
grounds I do not know—that today they number seventy million.
As Joel Carpenter, always a partisan, observed, Fundamentalist
leaders have "turned failure into vindication, marginality into cho-
senness, survival into opportunity for expansion, and a religious de-
pression into a prelude for revival.

> The contemporary fruit of their dynamism is all around us today, to
> be seen in burgeoning independent megachurches, thriving and
> ever-diversifying parachurch ministries, an astonishing popular ap-
> petite for spine-chilling interpretations of biblical prophecy, and a
> major upsurge of religiously inspired conservative cultural
> politics—all of which have been driven by a finely honed instinct for
> popular appeal and well-practiced skills in communication and
> marketing.[51]

By the seventies the media "discovered" evangelicalism and being "born again" became a political asset. It has tended to attribute
to the evangelicals a more monolithic shape and organizational co-
hesiveness than evangelicals in fact have or, in my view, can ever
have. Aside from the differences between the strict Fundamentalists
and the more moderate evangelicals that we have discussed, there
are important differences between the conservative and relatively
conservative evangelicals and African-American Protestantism, the
Southern Baptist Convention, the largest evangelical group in the
United States (which is struggling today with the conservative factions in its ranks), the holiness denominations and evangelical
Methodists, the Peace churches, and the Pentecostalists. The Missouri Synod Lutheran and the Christian Reformed churches are

sympathetic with evangelicalism but have preserved their own doctrinal traditions.

As in the past, contemporary Fundamentalist and evangelical churches tend to be organized around a single preacher, though the Baptist Bible Fellowship, which was founded by Norris, has several million members. Within the last two or three decades, there has in fact been a rapid increase in enormous churches, the so-called megachurches, many of which claim weekly attendance of over ten thousand.[52] Among these are Jack Hyles's First Baptist Church of Hammond, Indiana, Lee Robertson's Highland Park Baptist Church in Chattanooga, and, most famous of all, Jerry Falwell's Thomas Road Baptist Church in Lynchburg, Virginia. Many of these churches are little empires with branch chapels, schools and colleges, mission stations around the world, their own publications, radio and television networks, and adherents who are connected to them primarily through the net. As such their voice is far greater than their actual membership.

Many megachurch preachers like Falwell (as well as a good number of preachers in small churches) are involved in politics despite their separatist position. The Harvard theologian Harvey Cox argues that in recent years postmillennialism has been making a comeback in conservative evangelical circles.[53] In fact, Fundamentalism, along with evangelical Christianity, gained considerable political purchase with the formation of the Moral Majority in 1979 and, more recently, the Christian Coalition. (In many of the smaller Fundamentalist churches I attended, I found Christian Coalition literature mixed in with religious pamphlets.) Their activism—particularly when it involves cooperation with liberals, Catholics, Jews, and "atheists"—is condemned by conservative separatists. I met many Fundamentalists who, though sympathetic with the values of the Christian Coalition, condemned it for its political interventions.

The seminarians with whom I worked were particularly critical of extremist movements like Dominion-Theology, or Christian Reconstruction, as it is sometimes called, which they attacked on theological rather than moral and social grounds, as postmillennial and based on the misreading of Scripture. (They were not surprised by Pat Robertson's flirtation with it. After all, they said, he was a Pentecostalist.) Rousas John Rushdoony is the founder of the movement, whose headquarters, the Chalcedon Foundation, is in a small town in northern California. Though of Armenian parentage, he is a strict Calvinist and an admirer of the theocratic city-state that Calvin tried to create in Geneva. (Rushdoony claims membership in a royal lineage of priests extending back to 315 A.D.) On the basis of Genesis 1:28 ("Be fruitful and multiply, and fill the earth, and subdue it; and rule over the fish of the sea and over the birds of sky, and over every living thing that moves on the earth"), Rushdoony and his followers insist that Christians—that is, born-again Christians, and in some accounts, Jews—are biblically mandated to rule the earth until Christ's return.[54] They argue that everything that has been touched by sin—the individual, the family, the church, society, and the state—must be "reconstructed" according to the Bible. Though they are not opposed to the separation of Church and State, as some of their critics claim, they insist that both are subject to God's law. Greg Bahnsen, one of their proponents, puts it this way:

> Whereas the Reformers sought to sanctify their culture by bringing the inscripturated law of God to bear upon both the individual and the civil magistrate, the church of today has either joined hands with the Enlightenment in insisting that the individual and state be free from scriptural direction or has declared that the law of God is no longer valid at least in its socio-political details (e.g. its penal sanction).[55]

Unlike the premillennialists, the reconstructionists promote what their critics regard as an "Old Testament theocracy." Andrew Sandlin, one of their spokesmen, argues that "the Bible is the civil magistrate's ultimate legal code" and that the state may not "enforce what the Bible does not require."[56] In his view, "the only valid role of legislatures in a state circumscribed by Biblical limits is to establish laws extrapolated from Biblical revelation"—and not even "to establish laws merely on the grounds that they are not at variance with Biblical revelation." Since the Bible posits few criminal acts, the magistrate is not empowered to punish most sins. Where stipulated by Scripture, for adultery, homosexuality, and blasphemy, for example, the death penalty is in order. "Economic inequalities may tear at our hearts and elicit charitable responses," Sandlin writes,

> but the state may not attempt to enforce those responses. The ignorance of vast sectors of a nation or society may seem to clamor for the institution of schools, but the state may not be the agent of that institution. Citizens may unwisely neglect to invest their wealth for their retirement or older years, but the state may not seize (or require employers to seize) wealth from citizens' income to invest for their retirement.

Although the reconstructionists argue that real social and political change occurs through the reordering that comes with regeneration in Christ, they play an active role in right-wing American politics. They have close connections with the Christian Coalition and the Rutherford Institute, which offers legal counsel to Christians who fight for Christian education in their schools and were active in the legal pursuit of President Clinton.

Although Fundamentalists are known stereotypically for forbidding drinking, smoking, dancing, card-playing, premarital sex, theater, and even movies—television presents a problem for some of them—and for having strict dress codes (no slacks or short skirts for women, no beards, long hair, or flared pants for men), most Fundamentalists today are not so strict, particularly with regard to dress codes, movies, and television. Men attend church without ties; many have beards and mustaches. Women frequently wear slacks, and some church singers dress as modest versions of some of America's pop singers. Churches like the Moody Church in Chicago even include theatricals in some of their services.

It is important to note the persistent discrepancy between the general public's stereotyped view of Fundamentalism and the complex reality of Fundamentalism in the United States today. Certainly, in my own encounters with Fundamentalists, I frequently observed the way in which one or another of these stereotypes was evoked and used rhetorically in discussion or in an attempt to intimidate me—often as a prelude to witnessing, that is, evangelizing me. I was rarely ever asked directly about my views on abortion, homosexuality, or evolution. The people I worked with *assumed* I shared their views. Their assumption was their challenge to me: I could accept it or not. When I did, they would argue with me, never budging from their position—it was God-given. When our discussions heated, when they felt vulnerable (if they ever did), when they felt that my own position was weakening, they would quote Scripture—to bolster their position, to snare me (so I often thought), to flip me into their reality.

Fundamentalist militancy is not impermeable. It is, like so much Christian theology, apologetic at heart. Although Fundamentalists may reject any engagement with their opponent, preferring simply to assert their truths—including their vision of their opponent—they are nevertheless orienting their thought toward that opponent, who then takes on a kind of articulatory power. It is the opponent, at least as perceived by the Fundamentalists, who determines their defensive posture—how truths are framed, and expressed, what is selected and what is neglected, the way to read and interpret. Insofar as that opponent is kept at bay, insofar as his or her position goes unacknowledged and remains opaque, the opponent takes on mythic proportions that reveal perhaps more about the Fundamentalist's doubts, desires, and convictions than about the opponent him- or herself. The historian Ernest Sandeen argues that the Fundamentalists have a "symbiotic," even "parasitic," relationship with their adversaries.

> The very breath of life seems to be provided for the Fundamentalist by those whom he opposes, each of his positions and opinions being conceived through opposition to a liberal stance or utterance. In their annoyance over this behavior, the critics of Fundamentalism have failed to notice that they are themselves benefiting from the vitality of the movement.[57]

The Fundamentalist's interlocutor is always at some level an opponent until he has been converted. As Frances FitzGerald has noted, the pastors at Jerry Falwell's church were "always preparing their flock to deal with negative reaction."[58] The "Christian" way of relating to such an interlocutor, as I was continually reminded of in my conversations with Fundamentalists, is evangelistic.

Although nearly all Fundamentalists with whom I spoke were open, cooperative, and even interested in my research, I had the feeling, often confirmed as my interviews progressed, that they saw my interest in their religion as God-given. With the faculty and most of the students at the Bible seminaries with whom I spoke, I adopted a collegial relationship, as did they. We were teachers and scholars and sometimes talked about teaching, the number of courses we had, salaries, the price of books, and even postmodernism. I recall a conversation on Wittgenstein I had with Robert Bromley, an older, distinguished professor of New Testament theology. I do not remember how we ended up talking about the philosopher. Dr. Bromley had not read him but had heard that he was an atheist and had an especially destructive theory of meaning. (I was always shocked by how dependent faculty and students at the Bible Institutes were on hearsay and secondary and tertiary sources for their knowledge of the non-Fundamentalist world. They would never have found such standards acceptable in their own Bible studies.) Dr. Bromley did not have much patience with Wittgenstein's philosophy, at least as I tried to explain it to him. But when I told him about the philosopher's spiritual longing, he was at first incredulous and then fascinated as he began to relate that longing to what he took to be the subjectivism and instability inherent in Wittgenstein's notion of meaning as use. Most of the professors and students were, however, less open than Dr. Bromley and talked with an authority I rarely find among my own university colleagues and students. Several of them took a more confrontational—anti-intellectual—stance, arguing that I could not possibly understand their faith without being reborn.

Occasionally, someone I was interviewing tried to convert me. This was often triggered by a reference to my own life. My interlocutor would then quote a passage from Scripture he found relevant to my situation and from there proceed to biblical passages, mostly from Paul, that had to do with man's sinful condition and his salvation. If I could not get the interview "back on track," he would ask me to pray for my salvation. I was embarrassed by this and soon learned to avoid references to my own life. As the people I interviewed often talked about theirs, I found myself breaking one of the common American communicative conventions: if your interlocutor talks about his or her personal life, then you respond by talking about yours. On several occasions, when the person I was interviewing revealed more of himself than he had wanted to (that is, as I saw it), he would then try, as a defensive gesture (again as I saw it), to witness me. I had had similar experiences among white Pentecostalists in South Africa.

The Bible, its physical presence, was always there, the centerpiece, as it were, of Fundamentalist evangelizing. In fact, I do not recall a single interview with a Fundamentalist in which the Bible was not present. They pointed to it, read from it, occasionally raised it for emphasis. They showed respect for it, took pleasure in a fine edition, and were proud of its worn condition. Its presence, the evidence of its having been read over and over again, marked their total commitment to it and the truths, the stability, the guidance, and the discipline it gave them. The strictest of them would have been troubled, I am sure, by a special advertising section (a sort of infomercial) in *Christianity Today*, called "Befriending the Bible" in which the Bible is referred to as a friend and efforts to make it "friendlier" and "more enjoyable" are uncritically lauded.[59] These include new study guides, illustrated handbooks, "approachable" translations, and targeted editions like the *True Love Waits Bible* for "youth who have begun to explore issues related to sexuality." This edition, with extensive commentary, encourages young people to save sex for marriage. It comes with a "Fingertip Counselor" that "provides insight—along with detailed Bible references—on topics from abortion to virginity." Christ is called in the infomercial "the best-known Bible personality" and "the world's best friend."

It is, of course, not the concrete Bible, the book as such, that the Fundamentalist venerates. It is Scripture—the biblical text, God's word, His revelation, His truth—that articulates his religion. It is "a sort of correlate of Christ" and plays a complementary role to Him," James Barr observes.[60] No friend of the Fundamentalists, Barr insists that in some ways the Bible is more important to them than is Christ. "It is the Bible, because it is the accessible and articulate reality, available empirically for checking and verification, that provides the lines that run through the religion and determine its shape and character." It is the Fundamentalist's "supreme religious symbol." "If you possess a Bible, you have the earthly essence of the Church," Barr argues exaggeratedly. Certainly, no Fundamentalist I met would have agreed with him. However important the Bible is, it is Jesus who is at the center of their belief. A particular Bible, a family Bible, for example, the Bible one was given at baptism, can take on symbolic significance—through commemoration, through use, through the guidance, the comfort, it has offered, through the truth it reveals—and become even a "friend." But that symbolic value has to be kept separate, the Fundamentalist would argue, from the value of God's word as revealed by Scripture. It is, perhaps, too earthly a concern.

The symbolic value of a specific, concrete Bible reflects an ambiguity in the notion of text, indeed of the word itself, that occurs in even our most philosophical understandings of "word" and "text." They are at once abstract and concrete: they materialize meaning—through their phonic, their graphic, indeed their electronic, expression. The role, the significance, of this materialization will vary with our understanding of language and communication. It will also vary with different speech and literary genres. We tend, for example, to give greater weight to the contours of sound and graphic shape in poetry than in ordinary prose. Many of us, who are indifferent to the quality of print, paper, and design in the prose we read, are sensitive to them in poetry. The linguist Roman Jakobson refers to the quality of language that calls attention to its medium as the poetic.[61] We have to recognize in any sacred text the importance of this poetic quality: as we quote poetry, so we quote Scripture. Not only do we take pleasure in the sensuous surface of its words—we speak of the "beauty" of Scripture—but believers identify those words, their materialization, with the specificity of meaning, with the truth revealed. They feel something is lost if they cannot give an exact quotation.

The Fundamentalist's literalism, his moral commitment to the tight identification—the coalescence—of signifier (the "acoustic image" in Saussure's terms) with the signified (the "concept") exploits, rhetorically at least, the materiality of the sign. This is evident less, perhaps, in the expository sermons of the strict Fundamentalists than in the exhortatory preaching in Pentecostalist and African-American churches; but it can be discerned in the Fundamentalist's sermons as well. I am suggesting, in other words, that the tendency to give symbolic value to a particular Bible—the Bible as book—is facilitated by the implicit stress on the materiality of the word in Fundamentalist literalism. The Bible as book is to biblical truth as God's word in its materiality is to God's truth.

———

For the conservative Protestant, the Bible is the *sola fidei regula*, the only authoritative voice of God, and not just the *prima fidei regula*, the primary authority among others (for example, the ancient creeds and the rulings of the church councils), as it is in the Roman Catholic and Eastern Orthodox churches. Indeed, the one point on which all Protestant denominations agree is the supremacy and sufficiency of Scripture. The Word, inerrant and infallible, Calvin wrote, "has flowed from [God's] very mouth." "We can only seek God in his Word, nor think of Him otherwise than according to the Word."[62] It is the sole foundation of faith and the one fountain of wisdom. The human spirit left to itself, can "do nothing but lose itself in infinite error, embroil itself in difficulties and grope in opaque darkness." Reason alone is an insufficient guide. For Calvin, of course, man's salvation depends wholly on the unfathomable grace of God.

The Fundamentalists I worked with, mostly of a Reformed orientation, were committed to the sufficiency of Scripture; they acknowledged the insufficiency of human reason for leading to the knowledge of God and believed that man's salvation rested entirely on God's grace. The Statement of Faith of John MacArthur's Master's Seminary offers a succinct and accurate summary of strict Fundamentalist belief. They teach, and I quote without the biblical citations, that:

1.) the Bible is God's written revelation to man, and thus the sixty-six books of the Bible given to us by the Holy Spirit constitute the plenary (inspired equally in all parts) Word of God.

2.) the Word of God is an objective revelation, verbally inspired in every word, absolutely inerrant in the original documents, infallible, and God-breathed. We teach the literal grammatical-historical interpretation of Scripture which affirms the belief that the opening chapters of Genesis present creation in six literal days.

3.) the Bible constitutes the only infallible rule of faith and practice.

4.) God spoke in His written Word by a process of dual authorship. The Holy Spirit so superintended the human authors that, through the individual personalities and different styles of writing, they composed and recorded God's Word to man without error in the whole and in the part.

5.) whereas there may be several applications of any given passage of Scripture, there is but one true interpretation. The meaning of Scripture is to be found as one diligently applies the literal grammatical-historical method of interpretation under the enlightenment of the Holy Spirit. It is the responsibility of believers to ascertain carefully the true intent and meaning of Scripture, recognizing that proper application is binding on all generations. Yet the truth of Scripture stands in judgment of men; never do men stand in judgment of it.

The Statement's authority is in fact entirely justified by Scripture. With the exception of the teachings on creation, which refer to Genesis and Exodus, the section quoted above (as so much evangelical doctrine) relies primarily on Paul's letters, though it also cites the Gospels of Matthew and John and the letters of Peter and John.

I have quoted this section of the Master's Statement of Faith at length not only because it is a carefully worded statement of Fundamentalist belief of a generally Reformed orientation but also because it plays an important role in the lives of the seminarians. Most of the faculty and students I interviewed at Master's answered my questions in terms of this Statement. Sometimes they said "we believe," referring to those of us at Master's; sometimes they said "John believes," referring to John MacArthur for whom they had enormous respect and with whom they often identified; and sometimes they said "I believe" as though they had worked out the answers to my questions themselves. What I found noteworthy was the unquestioned authority the Statement had for both faculty and students and their ventriloquial assumption of its authority. Before reading the statement, I had interviewed several students; I was surprised when, upon reading it, how closely they had been quoting it without ever citing it. They were not plagiarizing—they had simply internalized it.

Many of the students I interviewed had spent hours pondering statements like this from the seminaries they were considering before deciding which one to apply to or attend. (Others simply accepted the advice of their pastor or some other adviser they respected and trusted.) It was a serious matter—they did not want to be corrupted by false doctrine. They did not feel they were spiritually mature enough to be able to discern error or resist false belief. One of them, Ron Saywell, a man in his late twenties, who was finishing up his master's degree, told me that even if he were given a full fellowship to Harvard Divinity School, he would not attend at this point in his life because he did not yet have enough confidence in his own judgment, in his ability to see and fight error.[63]

Students like Ron were able to spot differences of emphasis which I had missed in the statements of faith, and these differences were what determined their choices. (I do not know how much of the school's reputation they read into the statements.) Several of them pointed out that the section on the Bible in BIOLA University's Doctrinal Statement had appeared to them more liberal than one at Master's, and they made their decision accordingly. The BIOLA Doctrinal Statement reads in part:

The Bible, consisting of all the books of the Old and New Testament, is the Word of God, a supernaturally given revelation from God Himself concerning Himself, His being, nature, character, will and purposes; and concerning man, his nature, need and duty and destiny. The Scriptures of the Old and New Testaments are without error or misstatement in their moral and spiritual teaching and record of historical facts. They are without error or defect of any kind.

Was it the absence of the word "inerrancy" that lead them to this reading? Was it that the section on Scripture was not as extensive as the one from Master's? Or was it other sections that led to it, as, for example, the one on creation? Unlike the Master's Statement, which is explicit in its commitment to creation in six days, the BIOLA statement leaves more room for interpretation.

The existence of the Creation is not explainable apart from the roles of God as the sovereign creator and sustainer of the entire natural realm. Concepts such as theistic or threshold evolution do not adequately explain creation.

The Master's Statement begins with a preamble that at once acknowledges its human fallibility in trying "to summarize and systematize the riches of an infallible divine revelation" and its importance not only as a framework for teaching but as "an anchor to protect the institution against theological drift." Members of the board of directors, administration, and faculty are required to sign each year an affirmation of their agreement with it. The paradox created by the acknowledgment of human fallibility and the insistence on the importance, the authority, of the Statement is in part circumvented, as we shall see, by its many references to Scripture. The inerrant, God-given status of Scripture is itself contained in the Statement. This circularity recalls another, more important one — the Bible's internal affirmation of its own authority.

Each of the teachings of the Statement is in fact justified by the citations from Scripture. They constitute the basic hermeneutic assumptions of Fundamentalism — assumptions that do not divorce the ethical and the spiritual from the cognitive and intellectual.

They affirm the status of Scripture as a God-breathed, verbally inspired in all parts, absolutely and totally inerrant, infallible, objective, propositional revelation that "constitutes the only infallible rule of faith and practice." Indeed, Barr considers inerrancy (rather than literalism) to be the hallmark of Fundamentalism.[64] "What fundamentalists insist is not that the Bible must be taken literally, but that it must be so interpreted as to avoid any admission that it contains any kind of *error*." Certainly, all the Fundamentalists with whom I spoke insisted on the absence of any error in Scripture. Many of them, even at Master's, were unwilling to qualify their belief by "in the original documents" as does the Master's Statement. ("Original documents" refers to the autographed originals, which of course are no longer extant.) They—the most extreme—argued that God would never have permitted error to creep into later versions or translations. Many other Fundamentalists, though none of the students at Master's, have used this argument to justify the exegesis of translated texts without reference to the original tongues.) They resisted, indeed they attacked, any biblical criticism that acknowledged the possibility of error in the transmission of Scripture.

Despite their embrace of inerrancy, Fundamentalists do recognize differences in genre and authorial style in the Bible. They are (in their own terms) good readers and (in any one's terms) careful ones. They are well aware of the difference between Paul's more philosophical style and Peter's simpler, down-to-earth one. In his influential *Moody's Handbook of Theology*, Paul Enns of the Dallas Theological Seminary argues that inerrancy allows for a variety of styles.[65] He attributes differences in the gospel accounts to their being translations of Jesus's words from the Aramaic and to this author's different viewpoints. He argues, further, that inerrancy does not demand the verbatim reporting of events (for, among other reasons, "it would have been impossible to unroll the lengthy scrolls each time to produce a verbatim quote"); it acknowledges departures from standard grammatical forms; and it recognizes problem passages.

Differences in style are attributed to the personalities of the human authors through whom "God spoke in His written Word." Although some Protestant theologians of the sixteenth and seventeenth centuries—and even later—argued that God dictated his words to the biblical authors, Fundamentalists insist that the authors were not simply scribes who took down God's words[66]—they were inspired by God. His words were in-breathed into them so that they were able to give expression to His message in a manner that accorded with their own personalities, styles, and cultural horizons. They do not claim to understand, yet are filled with wonder by, this process of in-breathing.

Dual authorship does present the more scholastic of the evangelicals with problems.[67] They ask whether or not the human authors of Scripture could have appreciated the full, divine meaning of God's words. Did they share God's intention? Does dual authorship imply multiple intentions? Multiple meanings? Are there both literal and spiritual meanings? Does meaning remain the same over time? The more conservative evangelicals who think about these possibilities are threatened by them. They fear that their questions will open the floodgate of multiple interpretations and release the imagination from unambiguous biblical discipline. Most of the Fundamentalists I talked to, however, were not bothered by them. There was simply one meaning, God's meaning—the plain, ordinary meaning, and one intention, God's intention, that was manifested through the divinely inspired authors of Scripture.

Fundamentalists adhere to what is popularly called a "domino approach" to the Bible. For them to admit even one error in Scripture would be to destroy their faith in the whole. "If you decide that even one single word is in error, then what's to stop you from deciding that any other word is in error. Soon you'll be saying the whole Bible's wrong." "How would you decide what's true and what's false? You'd be playing God. You'd become the judge of His Word." "It's the easy way out. You just declare what you don't like an error, and then you don't have to reckon with it." These responses illustrate two important characteristics of Fundamentalism: its all-or-nothing quality—either you give yourself to Christ or you don't, either you're saved or you're not, either you accept the inerrancy of Scripture or you don't—and the belief that, without external control (ideally through Scripture), human desire, imagination, and reason will inevitably lead further into error and sin. If inerrancy is abandoned, "reason becomes the source of authority and reason sits in judgment upon the text of Scripture."[68]

If one accepts the inerrancy of the Bible and its plenary inspiration, one is confronted with a series of apparent contradictions in Scripture that must somehow be reconciled. One cannot, as more liberal theologies do, argue that certain passages are figurative, corrupt, or the product of human intervention. "There are no degrees of inspiration," a professor told me, "but some passages are more significant than others. If I were left on a desert island, I would rather have John than Ecclesiastes." Others I talked to were reluctant to admit to degrees of significance, so tight was their commitment to the whole, the value of each and every word. They did not deny that they themselves favored certain passages, certain books, but they cautioned against equating what they favored with value. Indeed, there might even be a danger in preferring certain passages to others. I took their caution to be an indication of their fear that personal predilection might lead to a failure to appreciate the meaning and significance of other passages. "The temptation to say more than Scripture says is always a hazard, for we mortals are a most curious lot."[69]

Still, even those who warned against favoring particular texts, recognized the importance of certain key passages—"chair passages," they called them, from the Latin *sedes doctrinae*—which provide the most extended basis for doctrine. Among these are Genesis 1–2 on Creation, Isaiah 53 on atonement, 1 Corinthian 15 on the Resurrection, and Philippians 2:1–11 on incarnation. As one authority put it, these chair passages "represent a self-policing function of Scripture, one particularly important to Protestants, who have typically rejected external limitations (e.g. by the church or tradition) on their interpretations of the Bible."[70] They are "boundary setters" for interpreters of other topically related texts in that they limit misreading and application.

It is our failure of understanding, Fundamentalists argue, that leads us to see contradictions in Scripture. It results from our sinful nature. If sin is the chief obstacle to our relationship to God, and to one another, so their argument goes, then sin is going to hinder any interpretation. As the story of the Tower of Babel attests, man's ability to communicate is weakened by sin; his ability to interpret is never without error.[71] In fact, Fundamentalists spend considerable effort in trying to reconcile contradictory passages. Their solutions often appear sophistic to the outsider. One example, often cited by critics, is the cleansing of the Temple by Jesus. In the synoptic gospels (Matthew, Mark, and Luke), this occurs at the end of Jesus's ministry, at the beginning of passion week;[72] but in John, it occurs at the beginning of Jesus's ministry.[73] Many Fundamentalists "resolve" these discrepant accounts by suggesting that there were in fact two cleansings.[74]

Although many of the seminarians I talked to were willing enough to discuss the harmonizing of seemingly contradictory passages, they tended to ignore them just as they tended to ignore the questions of authorship. For them, Deuteronomy was written by Moses, Titus by Paul. They certainly did not bring these questions up in their sermons or their Bible study classes, as they interfered with the work of understanding Scripture. Although they were careful in the classes I attended to give an overview of the particular book of the Bible they were teaching, they tended not to relate it to the overall structure of the Bible. To be sure, they read it as God's "special revelation" of Himself and His relationship to His creation, especially to man, and they understood this relationship in redemptive-historical terms. That is, God's special relationship to man concerns His rescuing and redeeming His people from sin, and He reveals this relationship through history—the history recounted in the Bible that "reverberates" prophetically with the passage of subsequent events. (My phrasing here does not do justice, as we shall see in Chapter Three, to the Fundamentalists' historical understanding.) They found justification for their position in Luke 24:44–47:

> Now he said to them. "These are My words which I spoke to you
> while I was still with you, that all things which are written about Me
> in the Law of Moses and the Prophets and the Psalms must be ful-
> filled."
> Then He opened their minds to understand the Scriptures and
> He said to them, "Thus it is written, that the Christ should suffer
> and rise again from the dead the third day; and that repentance for
> forgiveness of sins should be proclaimed in His name to all the na-
> tions, beginning from Jerusalem."

I found that the seminarians focused on particular passages, and
their interpretation of these passages was oriented around the spiritual and ethical guidance they gave. Indeed, they shunned the
larger philosophical-theological dimensions of Scripture, though
they always pointed out the specific theological implication of whatever passage they were reading. "Philosophy" had negative connotations for many of them: it was too "heady," too removed from
reality, from the ordinary meaning of words and life. (When my
questions became too abstract, too speculative, they would refer me
in frustration to a friend or colleague whom they said was interested
in philosophy.) They seemed to read—or want to read—Scripture
in the imperative mood, as a series of commands that required narrowly construed obedience. They did not advocate imitating
Christ; indeed, several expressed horror at the thought of it. That
would have been too Catholic; an attempt to play God—one of the
most heinous sins. Rather, one reads the Gospels for guidance, either through Christ's words or by abstracting from his behavior te-
nets of faith and rules of conduct.

They describe their approach to interpreting Scripture as literal,
grammatical, and historical. By "literal," conservatives refer to the
"plain," "ordinary," "obvious," "proper," "natural," "normal,"
"common-sensical," meaning of a word. It is not that they do not
recognize figurative usage—they do— but rather, they insist that, in
order to understand the figurative meaning of a word, one must first
know the word's literal meaning. "Whenever we read a book, an essay, or a poem we presume the literal sense in the document until
the nature of the literature *may force us* to another level,"[75] Bernard

Ramm, the author of a standard conservative textbook on biblical interpretation, wrote. Indeed, the literal meaning serves to control irresponsible figuration, which the conservatives often associate with Roman Catholic allegorizing. The "literal" opposes the "allegorical," Ramm observed.[76] The Fundamentalists like to give this example to illustrate their approach to metaphor:[77] "When Christ says in John 10:9 'I am the door' he does not literally mean he's a door. But to understand what he means, that he's the door, the way, into salvation, you have to know what an ordinary door is." I believe it is particularly popular because it is itself part of Christ's attempt to explain an earlier "figure of speech" he addressed to the Pharisees in which the door metaphor occurs several times. "Truly, truly, I say to you, he who does not enter by the door into the fold of the sheep. . . ."[78]

Even in the interpretation of a work as symbolically rich and as filled with allegorical possibilities as Book of Revelation, the Fundamentalists resist symbolic and allegorical interpretation. Robert L. Thomas, who teaches at the Master's Seminary and has recently completed a two-volume exegesis of Revelations, insists, for example, that the book is basically prophetic and, as such, should be read as literally as possible. He argues that though God chose to communicate his message through symbols and visions, "they do not furnish grounds for interpreting the text in a non-literal fashion."[79] One should assume a literal interpretation unless there is some indication in the text to do otherwise. There is no reason, for example, to look for hidden meaning in the number of bond-servants (one hundred forty-four thousand) who were "sealed" — protected from harm, saved — by angels.[80] But, according to Thomas, "Sodom" and "Egypt" in Revelations 11:8 should not to be taken literally:[81] "And their dead bodies *will lie* in the street of the great city which mystically is called Sodom and Egypt, where also their Lord was crucified." It is the "mystically" (*pneumatikos*) that justifies a figurative reading here.

The grammatical and historical or grammatico-historical or

historico-grammatical or philological approach—evangelical theologians delight in such classifications—refers to a method of exegesis that focuses on the original language or languages of the text and its historical situation. It serves, ideally, to eliminate the prejudices with which the reader comes to a text and which hinder his understanding of its original meaning. Fundamentalist hermeneutics is intentionalist; that is, meaning is what the authors, ultimately *the* author, of Scripture intended.[82] What they do not recognize is that their literalism is itself a prejudice. What they want to avoid, above all, is reading into the text, which they call "eisogesis" and oppose to exegesis. Ramm quotes Luther: "The best teacher is the one who does not bring his meaning into the Scripture but gets his meaning from the Scripture."[83]

There was a time, which has become proverbial in both Fundamentalist circles and in those of their critics, when some Fundamentalists believed that the King James version was so inspired by God as to be sufficient for biblical study. Fundamentalists no longer assume they can understand the Bible without reference to the original languages in which it was written. Doctoral candidates are required to learn Greek, Hebrew, and Aramaic as well as French and German. Many of the larger churches now offer courses in Greek and Hebrew to their parishioners. I have rarely been to a service, never to a Bible class, where reference to the Greek (less often the Hebrew, rarely the Aramaic) was not made. Indeed, manuals on expository preaching advise the preacher to make occasional reference to Greek and Hebrew words that lie behind the English translation.[84] I have met parishioners who do not know Greek but can discuss the differences between *eros*, *agape*, and *philos* at length. Or they can list and cite the occurrence of the words for "hell" in Hebrew and Greek—*sheol*, *hades*, *gehenna*, *tartaros*, or *abussos*—as rapidly as they quote Scripture.

The focus here is on the word. "They are the bricks of our conceptual formulation," Ramm wrote.[85] For Dan McCartney and C. Clayton, the authors of another standard treatise on conservative evangelical hermeneutics, whose understanding of language is more sophisticated, "The basic unit of meaning is not the word but the sentence."[86] In either case, meaning is understood in terms of referential or propositional content. Rhetorical and figurative locutions are reduced whenever possible to their simplest, least ambiguous meaning. To quote from the Master's Statement of Faith again: "There is but one true interpretation." The performative features of language, its ability to evoke contexts, to frame its subject matter, are generally ignored. Rarely did I hear preachers or teachers in Bible class refer to the syntax of Hebrew or Greek in their expositions. Once, Ron Saywell, who was teaching a Bible class at his church, talked about the middle voice in Greek but lost his students so quickly that he gave up. Ron's reference to the middle voice was text-specific; he certainly did not want to suggest that grammar determines the worldview of the Greek speaker. Indeed, with the exception of the occasional missionary, who has worked in foreign languages, most Fundamentalists (if they think about it at all) are opposed to any kind of linguistic determination of worldview. They are adamantly opposed to the linguistic derivation of theological truths. They criticize those scholars in the first decades of this century who argued that as the Hebrew *dabar* can mean "thing," "event," or "word," the writers of the Old Testament thought of word and thing as the same thing.[87]

It is my impression that, for Fundamentalists, the "original languages"—or examples from them—often substitute for the original, autographed manuscripts of Scripture. The fact that we do not have these manuscripts threatens the Fundamentalist's scriptural edifice. It is as though they have a foundational text without the founding text. Fundamentalists argue, as do more liberal theologians, that because the earliest versions of Scripture we have are so similar, we must assume their accuracy. More important, they argue that God would never have let His Word be falsified or perverted by inaccurate versions. Yet, there are different versions; there are other texts—the Apocrypha, for example—that purport to be God's word and are accepted by some Christians as such. There are better and worse Bible translations. All of these, in a certain sense, pervert God's word. Or, to shift the argument, if God would never permit His Word to be falsified or perverted in Scripture, then translations ought to be as true as those in the original languages. Weren't those early Fundamentalists who argued that the King James version was the true—inspired—word of God, right?

My point is that once you insist that every word in the Bible is true then you run into difficulties like these, which would be less devastating to a more liberal approach to the Bible. When these problems arise, in class discussion for example, Fundamentalists tend to invoke the original languages as though they were the symbolic equivalent of the original autographed manuscripts. In many of the Bible classes I attended, when students asked about differences in their translations—some of them were quite dramatic—the teacher would immediately refer, quite properly, to the original language. He would treat it with an awe, a rhetorical awe, that suggested its special, symbolic, status. Generally, though, Fundamentalists argue that different translations can be an aid to understanding, for they respond to different connotations of the Hebrew or Greek that cannot be entirely caught by a single English word or turn of phrase. Many of them have more than one Bible or make use of parallel Bibles, concordances, and interlingual Bible dictionaries.

Fundamentalists are highly critical of theologians who see Scripture as "a book of its times" and are opposed to attempts to understand the Bible historically rather than as divine revelation. They are infuriated by Rudolph Bultmann and his followers, who argue that it is necessary to take account of the mythological accretions in Scripture in order to grasp its true, existential meaning.[88] What right have we, depraved as we are, to question and select the Word of God? For the Fundamentalist, "historical" refers to those events, customs, and facts in biblical times, often enough derived— circularly, of course—from the Bible itself, which enrich the understanding of a particular word or passage. Thus, Ron Saywell referred to the fact that Peter was written at the time Nero was emperor of Rome. This "historical fact" gives added force to Peter's command to submit "to every human institution."

Many of the sermons and Bible classes are centered around the retelling, anachronistically, of a Bible story. In one instance, when Jesus dined with the Pharisees and did not wash his hands, a preacher noted that washing one's hands was a matter of ritual cleanliness and obedience to the law and not a matter of hygiene.[89] In another, when a Bible instructor discussed the passage in Kings in which, after the Arameans' defeat at Aphek, Ben-hadad's servants put sackcloth around their waists before pleading for mercy from the conquering Israelite army, he explained that sackcloth, made of goat or camel hair, was worn during mourning or as a sign of submission.[90] "It would be like wearing burlap sack." he said. "Just imagine how itchy it would be. How humiliating." Such recountings "clarify" the story, making it relevant and applicable. In effect, they destroy the gap, the puzzlement, the disquiet the stories creates, rendering their message—the messages the Fundamentalists see in them—clear, present, and eternal. For the Fundamentalists, the historical detail serves more than merely illuminating a word or story, marks a gap in time, a difference in culture—even as it jumps the gap, declares difference sameness, and translates a particular incident or reference into one of common understanding.

Historical and cultural detail are not incorporated into an organized and coherent picture of biblical culture and society. They are not meant to evoke the possibility of a totally different cultural outlook.[91] To do so might so relativize society and culture and thereby undermine the literalist understanding of Scripture. It might call into question the universalist dimension of the anthropology upon which that understanding is based.

The local color, which these bits of information provide, masks narrative strategies that present a deeply ethnocentric vision of the past and thereby obliterate history, making what happened "in biblical times" stunningly relevant to the present. Among the most important of these strategies is the attribution of contemporary psychological motivation and values to the people of the Bible. Sometimes there appears to be a recognition of psychological difference as, for example, when a pastor says that where the Bible speaks of demonic possession, we speak of hysteria, multiple personality, or dissociative disorders. Usually, however, particularly among the most conservative, this observation is offered as a critique of our secular, psychiatric categories. More liberal evangelicals will say that hysteria, schizophrenia, multiple personality, and dissociative disorders are not necessarily caused by demons, though demons are sometimes responsible for them. A pastor in New York City observed when a medical student, who had asked him how to reconcile the psychiatric and the "Christian" view of mental illness, that insofar as Christians recognize demons, they are in fact more sensitive to all the possible causes of mental illness than the secular psychiatrists who ignore the demonic. "Every psychiatrist has come across cases he cannot explain in terms of modern medicine. Whereas he has to throw up his hands in ignorance, the Christian will recognize Satan's role."

I remember in particular a sermon in a small Fundamentalist church in Whatcom County in northwestern Washington. The church had lost its preacher, and the man who was delivering the sermon was being considered as a replacement. Although he was known to the congregation, he began nervously—and without much eloquence—to preach about forgiveness; his text was the parable of the Unforgiving Servant.[92] In it, Peter asks Jesus how many times he should forgive a church member who has sinned against him. Jesus answers seventy-seven times or, in another version, seventy times seven times:

> for this reason the kingdom of heaven may be compared to a certain king who wished to settle accounts with his slaves. When he began to settle *them*, there was brought to him one who owed him ten thousand talents. But since he did not have *the means* to repay, his lord commanded him to be sold, along with his wife and children and all that he had, and repayment to be made. The slave therefore falling down, prostrated himself before him, saying. "Have patience with me, and I will repay you everything." And the lord of that slave felt compassion and released him and forgave him the debt. But that slave went out and found one of his fellow slaves who owed him a

hundred denarii; and he seized him and *began* to choke *him*, saying "Pay back what you owe." So his fellow slave fell down and *began* to entreat him, saying, "Have patience with me, and I will repay you." He was unwilling, however, but went and threw him in prison until he should pay back what was owed. So when his fellow slaves saw what had happened, they were deeply grieved and came and reported to their lord all that had happened. Then summoning him, his lord said to him, "You wicked slave! I forgave you all that debt because you entreated me. Should you not have had mercy on your fellow slave, even as I had mercy on you?" And his lord, moved with anger, handed him over to the torturers until he should repay all that was owed him. So shall My heavenly Father also do to you, if each of you does not forgive his brother from your heart.

The preacher read the text and then began his explication by retelling it. He started by speculating why Peter might have asked how many times he should forgive someone who sinned against him. "Suppose someone right here in this church borrowed money from you and didn't pay you back, would you forgive him? And suppose he did it again? You probably wouldn't even want to lend him anymore? But let's say you did. I've done it, and I'm sure some of you have." There was ripple of laughter.

"And we've all wanted to regulate our affairs. That's what the king was doing. He was trying to get his house in order. It's hard to forgive — to really forgive, from the heart, and not just in words. Words are hard enough for most of us. Sometimes they just don't come out even when we want them to. You know, you feel superior and powerful and judgmental, holding them back, but of course you're not. You yourself are sick and sinful if you don't forgive. Sin's contagious. Remember Paul's word in Colossians 3:13: 'Bearing with one another, and forgiving each other, whoever has a complaint against anyone: just as the Lord forgave you, so also should you.'

"Well, now, the king wanted to put his house in order. So, he called in his debtors. And there was this slave who owed him ten thousand talents. That was an enormous amount of money. Maybe a million dollars. Maybe more. A lot of money. More than you'd earn in fifteen years. That's what the commentaries say. Imagine if you were owed a million dollars, and the person couldn't pay you back. Of course you'd want to cut your losses. And that's exactly what the king tried to do. He was going to sell his slave and his slave's wife and all they possessed. Of course he wasn't going to get all that much for them. Slaves were cheap in those days. Nothing like a million dollars. But he'd get something all the same. And then, just imagine, the slave kneels down before him and asks him to have patience. Well, the king took pity on him. He knew the slave would never be able to pay him back even if he worked for the rest of his life and his children worked for rest of their lives. And so he forgives him. A million dollars! Just imagine. And the slave, what does he do. He goes out and meets another slave who owes him a hundred dinarii. That's nothing. Just a few cents. Maybe a dollar or so. It's what a man earned in a day, and in those days they didn't earn much. But even if it was forty or fifty dollars, it wasn't much compared to ten thousand talents. And the slave who'd just been forgiven ten thousand talents, a million dollars, asks for his money. And when his debtors says he can't pay and asks him to be patient, he refuses to forgive him and sends him to prison."

The preacher went on to compare the second slave to the hearers and not doers in James 1:22–24 who look at themselves in the mirror and on going away immediately forget what they looked like. "That first slave forgot what it was like to be a miserable debtor and what it was like to be forgiven. He just couldn't forgive. He didn't learn from the king. And so when the king finds out, he throws him in prison. And the Lord, Jesus says, is just like that King."

The preacher did not discuss the slave's torture. He did not ask how the slave came to owe so much money. He did not consider anger and torture in terms of the contagion of sin. He did go on to describe his visit to Coventry Cathedral in England and how impressed he had been by the Coventry parishioners' decision to collect money for rebuilding churches in Germany before rebuilding their own cathedral—which the Germans had bombed. By this time, he had achieved an eloquence so moving that many of those who were listening to him were in tears. Quoting Paul, "But whom you forgive anything, I *forgive* also; for indeed what I have forgiven, if I have forgiven anything, *I did it* for your sakes in the presence of Christ." He asked his congregants to pray.[93] And they did, many of them deeply touched, many couples looking at each other, pressing each other's hands, in what I could only understand, however sentimental I found it, as a transcending moment of forgiveness that knew no historical boundaries.

The lines between interpretation and exposition and between exposition and application are never clear. Understanding comes with time, with the reading and rereading of the texts we want to understand and our applying them to our lives. The Fundamentalists—particularly the seminarians, but others too—refer to the *work* of interpreting. In the strictest churches, such as John MacArthur's, the sermons last about an hour and half and are far more scholarly than the Whatcom County preacher's. (MacArthur delivers three each Sunday; two cover the same material. He works his way systematically through the Bible in two cycles.) The first fifteen minutes are devoted to prayer, the reading of a brief passage from Scripture, hymn-singing (the chorus is dressed in brown robes), a brief musical interlude, often by a guitarist, announcements, and the collection. The remaining hour and a quarter is devoted to a detailed exposition of rarely more than two or three verses of Scripture, which always reminded me of a French *explication de texte*. The meaning of each verse is determined by situating it within its biblical context; by comparing words and phrases to other biblical passages; by comparing translations and referring to the Greek or Hebrew original; by relating it, cautiously to be sure, to doctrine; and, finally, by considering its significance for the present. Unlike many other pastors, MacArthur spends less time on application than on exegesis. He is not given to high oratory or rattling off biblical verses. He is a careful man. He rarely raises his voice, dutifully cracks a joke once or twice, and demands of his parishioners the strictest of attention. Though they were clearly moved by his preaching, their response was, I believe, primarily intellectual. I never saw them moved as a group to tears, as I saw in Whatcom County, though sometimes I did see a single parishioner or couple so moved. Parishioners are in fact advised to take notes and, as in many Fundamentalist churches I attended, the church weekly distributed at the beginning of a service has a section for notes in it.

MacArthur's exposition is reminiscent of the way Victorian classes were supposed to have been conducted. (Frances FitzGerald notes that for the Thomas Road people, education "is simply the process of learning, or teaching, the right answers."[94]) There is little room for debate—and of course there is no debate during the sermon. The meaning of the text is given priority, and "personal relevance" is downplayed. MacArthur insists that before the significance of a text can be determined, its objective meaning must be uncovered, for otherwise texts can be used to justify almost anything. He is highly critical of those preachers who misuse Scripture, especially by indulging their audience to their most worldly wishes and fantasies. One New York pastor, a conservative Presbyterian, called MacArthur hypercritical and an ideologue. What is striking is how attentive his parishioners are to him. They number between two and three thousand at each service and come from all over Los Angeles and as far as San Diego, I am told. The majority are white, though there are Asians (especially Koreans) and some blacks. Their Southern California "cool," their bright, informal clothes, their sense of body, the women's make-up, and the men's long hair contrast dramatically with MacArthur's style.

Aside from the sermons, many if not most of the parishioners participate in Bible study groups or take courses at the church during the week. They are caught up in learning, and, though many of them express anti-intellectual ideas, they recognize that it is only through continual Bible study that they can enrich their understanding and, thereby, enrich their own lives and perhaps even—as heretical as it may be to the Reformist—facilitate their path to salvation. "It is the responsibility of believers," the Master's Statement of

Faith says, "to ascertain carefully the true intent and meaning of Scripture."

———————

Fundamentalists justify their faith in the authority of Scripture on the basis of Scripture itself. They refer to 2 Timothy 3:15–16, which not only asserts the authority of Scripture but its divine inspiration (*theopneustos*).[95]

> [A]nd that from childhood you have known the sacred writings which are able to give you the wisdom that leads to salvation through faith which is in Christ Jesus.
>
> All Scripture is inspired by God and profitable for teaching, for reproof, for correction, and for training in righteousness.

They reject those critics who argue that Paul did not in fact write the Epistles to Timothy, and that they are marginal books.[96] For them, there are no marginal books. They are generally not bothered by the fact that they find within the Scripture the source of its own authority.

We have to ask, however, how one can take a text's self-characterization and attestation of its own authority as evidence for that authority. If I assert that Napoleon is the reincarnation of Caesar, and that my assertion was inspired by God and must therefore be true, are we then to believe that Napoleon is in fact Caesar reincarnated? Obviously not. How then can the conservative evangelical accept Paul's assertion that the Bible is inspired by God? The question is by no means new—it is one of the principal concerns of Christian apologetics. It extends beyond Scripture and other sacred texts to founding documents, such as the Declaration of Independence and the U.S. Constitution—indeed, to all texts, for every text, at some level, either directly or indirectly, through style, for example, proclaims its authority.

A proclamation of textual authority is a performative claim: through the very act of proclamation, the proclamation is accomplished. Its author must, of course, have the authority to effect the proclamation. Does Paul have this authority?[97] Like all authors,

Paul makes use of all sorts of rhetorical devices to advance his own authority and that of his declarations. Among these are self-descriptions, such as the one with which he begins 2 Timothy, "an apostle of Christ Jesus by the will of God, according to the promise of life in Jesus Christ"; casting his interlocutor in a particular fashion, as, again in 2 Timothy—as "my beloved son"; by referring to his relationship to a figure of authority—God, Christ, or the Holy Spirit—as when he speaks of the Holy Spirit dwelling in him and his "son"; and by implicit and explicit reference to other, authoritative texts. (We should note the circularity here, for Paul refers back to other texts in Scripture, texts that by his own declaration are inspired by God, in order to establish his own authority to declare, among other things, the inspiration of Scripture.) Indeed, a very considerable part of 2 Timothy is devoted to the establishment of Paul's authority.

For the Fundamentalist and those other evangelicals who believe in the God-breathed origin of the Bible, including Paul's letters, there can be no question of Paul's authority. It is through him, under the superintendency of the Holy Spirit, that God revealed His message. Such is the power of dual authorship. The Master's Statement, in a way that exemplifies conservative evangelical beliefs, quotes 2 Peter 1:20–21 as well as 2 Timothy 3:16.[98] Peter reads, "But know this first of all, that no prophecy of Scripture is *a matter* of one's own interpretation, for no prophecy was ever made by an act of the human will, but men moved by the Holy Spirit spoke from God." Leaving aside the question of whether Peter is referring to all of Scripture or just to prophecy, the point is that Paul is speaking through and for God. God's words are fully performative.[99] Remember the role of his words in the creation of the universe in Genesis. Remember the opening of the Gospel according to John: "In the beginning was the Word, and the Word was with God, and the Word was God." God's Word is, so to speak, unhampered by the context of His utterance, for He creates as He creates the conditions of His creation. Therefore, as God's spokesman, Paul speaks with His authority and his/His words are to be taken as truth, with full illocutionary force.

It is not my aim here to enter into philosophical or theological debate over the nature of God's Word or Paul's words. I merely want to point out the logical paradoxes produced by the evangelicals' total commitment to Scripture as sufficient unto itself, and the ways they exploit the grammatical and structural complexity of Scripture in their attempt to resolve these paradoxes. Multiple authorship permits, for example, the sort of commentary that Paul makes in 2 Timothy 3:16 and Peter in 2 Peter 1:20–21. Such commentaries are at once text-internal and text-external. They are internal insofar as they are part of Scripture, and they obtain their authority from that position; they are external insofar as they occur in different books by different authors. They gain thereby a certain "objective" distance from the biblical texts to which they refer.

We find this sort of structural exploitation in many of the conservative evangelical treatises concerned with the divine origin of the Bible. They tend to cite single verses or short passages without contextualization to support their position. The conjoining of these passages creates a "space" in which the different authorial and narrative perspectives of the cited texts are implicitly exploited to produce the illusion of an external objectivity. Enns notes, for example, that there is considerable evidence for the entirely unique character of the Bible: "The unique claims within the Bible itself bear witness to its unusual character."[100] Among these are the fact that the Bible says 3800 times "God said" or "Thus says the Lord" as well as Paul's declaration in Corinthians "that the things which I write to you are the Lord's commandment" and were recognized as such by the Thessalonians.[101] He also cites the verses in Peter's Second Epistle that we have discussed and John's assertion: "We are from God; he who knows God listens to us; he who is not from God does not listen to us. By this we know the spirit of truth and the spirit of error."[102] Enns goes on to argue that "the writers who made those claims for the Scripture were trustworthy men who defended the integrity of the Scripture at great personal sacrifice." He refers to Jeremiah, whose life was threatened and who was rejected by his family because he defended Scripture;[103] citing the same book, he notes that false prophets were recognized.[104] Finally, he warns his readers not to understand the Bible's claims "as arguing in a circle or by circular reasoning" and concludes: "The testimony of reliable witnesses—particularly of Jesus, but also of others such as Moses, Joshua, David, Daniel, and Nehemiah in the Old Testament, and John and Paul in the New Testament—affirmed the authority and verbal inspiration of the Holy Scriptures." He does not seem to be troubled by the fact that Moses, Joshua, David, Daniel, Nehemiah, John, Paul, and Jesus are known only, or primarily, through Scripture and cannot as characters in Scripture be trusted to evaluate the texts in which they figure. Having distinguished them in his argument, Enns then exploits the continuity of their thought, but again stressing their number—forty authors—their frequent ignorance of one another's writings, their diverse professions (Moses, a political leader; Joshua, a military one; David, a shepherd; Matthew, a tax collector; Paul, a rabbi; Peter, a fisherman), and the different places, circumstances, and times in which they wrote and preached.[105] Yet Scripture is "a marvelous, unified whole," he writes.

> There are no contradictions or inconsistencies within its pages. The Holy Spirit is the unifier of the sixty-six books, determining its harmonious consistency. In unity these books treat the trinity of God, the deity of Jesus Christ, the personality of the Holy Spirit, the fall and depravity of man, as well as salvation by grace. It quickly becomes apparent that no human being(s) could have orchestrated the harmony of the teachings of the Scripture. The divine authorship of the Bible is the only answer.[106]

When I asked Fundamentalists how they could accept Scripture as inspired by God, given that the only evidence they had for it was from Scripture itself, many of them seemed both not to understand my question and yet to find it familiar. (To explain what I meant, I used examples like the one about Napoleon as the reincarnation of Caesar.) They advanced arguments like Enns's in a less systemic way. Robert Bromley, the theologian I mentioned earlier in this chapter, stressed the "supernatural marks" in the Bible which vouched for its divine inspiration. He said that much of it defies human understanding; the triune nature of God is far too complicated for man to have invented. Perceiving my skepticism, Dr. Bromley went on to discuss the Bible's realism—its realistic picture of man. "Look at the Bible," he said. "It was written by forty people over a period of sixteen hundred years. It kind of coheres. How could so many men over so many years produce so coherent a text?" When I asked him about the contradictions in the Bible, he said they only appear as contradictions because we cannot understand God's words fully. He then turned to the prophetic nature of Scripture. The prophecies confirm its divine inspiration. What was prophesied in the earlier books of the Bible, he noted, came to pass in the later ones and even after biblical times. He referred with less passion to all the archeological and historical evidence that supports the Bible's veracity.

"History shows us that Jesus lived. So we have to listen to what Jesus said about Scriptures. The Bible is a kind of supernatural book. Jesus was more than just a man like me. I stake my eternal destiny on what he taught. We should accept what Jesus said about Scriptures. The faith we have in Scriptures reveals its supernatural marks, its responsiveness to the unique needs of man. If one stakes one's life on the doctrine of salvation, then why not accept Christ's teachings on what Scripture is?"

Finally I asked him how we knew the Bible was inspired by God and not by Satan. He smiled, relieved by my question, for he had an easy answer. "If Satan were responsible for the Bible, then Satan would be God-like. He would be doing good. He would be uplifting human beings. That would be a contradiction."

Ultimately, Dr. Bromley's position rested upon faith and could not be justified fully on intellectual grounds as I was demanding of him. And yet I detected in him a reluctance to let his case rest on experience—that would be too subjective, too risky. It is the text, the Bible, that affords protection from the errors that come from subjective understanding and evaluation, from depending upon personal experience. I could not help thinking that what Dr. Bromley and other Fundamentalists with whom I spoke lacked was a category of experience, of consciousness, the certainty of which transcended the subjective—an apodeictic consciousness, like that of a mathematical proof. Some just talked about knowing: "When you knew, you knew," one said, referring to his conversion. "There was never any question after that. My world had changed completely." Perhaps that change of consciousness, that certainty, the rearticulation of one's worldview is what Dr. Bromley meant by faith. He had been raised as a Bible-believing Christian and had never experienced a dramatic conversion. His faith rested on his "staking his eternal destiny on what [Jesus] taught."

———————

When I pressed seminarians on the validity of the Bible's self-characterization, many of them mentioned hard-line Reformed apologist Cornelius van Til's theory of presuppositionalism. They found his argument "philosophical and difficult to follow." (It was, I suspect, their last-ditch defense against my questioning.) As they put it, since all systems of knowledge have presuppositions, why not just accept "Christian" presuppositions, for once you do, then you will become certain of their validity. These words certainly do not do justice to van Til's position. Van Til argued that "if Christ is to be presented to men as a challenge to their thinking and living then he must be offered without compromise."[107] He was particularly critical of the Roman Catholics and Protestants who merely ask natural man—the non-Christian—"to *add* the wisdom and work of Christ to that which man has in and of himself" instead of challenging him "to make his every thought captive to the obedience of Christ." The apologist's argument cannot rest on a theory of man, according to van Til, because there is an unbridgeable gap between natural man's and the Reformed Christian's presuppositions.[108] For the Protestant, "man's consciousness of self and of objects presupposes for their intelligibility the self-consciousness of God." For natural man, man is himself the final reference point for knowledge. (This self-referentiality is the result of man's first sin.) The point of contact must be through natural man's inescapable sense of deity.[109]

Van Til sidesteps the question of Scripture's self-characterization by simply asserting its validity.[110] It is, and attests to, the Reformed Christian's, the proper Protestant's understanding of man. Either one accepts God's revelation or, as Paul wrote, one suppresses it. An apologist must "blast" through natural man's presuppositions, his presumptuous self-referentiality, to the knowledge that he is a "creature of God and responsible to God."[111] Only then will he recognize what he has always known but suppressed: the derivative nature of his mind, the truth of the self-contained God. He will appreciate that the laws and facts of nature he has uncovered can only be "facts" and "laws" when there is no recognition and acceptance of the basic epistemological and metaphysical presuppositions revealed in and through Scripture.

Although van Til insists that the Christian apologist has to place himself in his opponent's position—for argument's sake, to be sure—and ask of his opponent to place himself in his own position, his approach is not dialogical. Rather, Van Til's stance is openly combative: "If there is no head-on collision with the systems of the natural man there will be no point of contact with the sense of deity in the natural man."[112] *The Defense of the Faith* is filled with military images. Van Til refers to the "all-out war between the Christian and the natural man" and to the need to apply "atomic power and flame-throwers" to non-Christian presuppositions.[113] He sees no contradiction between these martial images and Christian love. "He who loves men most will tell them the truth about themselves in their own interest."[114] (FitzGerald notes the practice of "aggressive evangelism" at Thomas Road Church. Falwell and his pastors also use military and sporting metaphors: "The war is not between fundamentalists and liberals but between those who love Jesus Christ and those who hate Him."[115])

Rather than arguing himself out of a circle, van Til accepts the inevitability of circular reasoning.[116] Starting points, methods, and conclusions are mutually implicated. One must simply accept the revelations of Scripture as true and unquestionable and proceed to convince one's interlocutor. Van Til shifts here from an argument by reason to a demonstration through method—strategic and violent. You force your interlocutor (or opponent) to recognize the truth of your position. Is this shift facilitated by van Til's refusal to separate intellectual knowledge and ethical responsibility from each other? He insists that man's self-referentiality, his failure to recognize the revelations that surround him, and his suppression of his inborn knowledge of God are the product of sin.[117] Adam originally had both the capacity for and the possession of truth. With sin he lost possession of it but (if I understand van Til correctly) not the full capacity for it. The regenerated, who have regained that truth within the limits of their sinful nature, are illuminated by it: their world becomes intelligible in a way it could never have been, had they not been able to uncover the suppressed truth of God's revelation and their absolute dependency on Him.

The dramatic change of consciousness that this regeneration entails can no longer—I am extrapolating here from van Til—separate the intellectual from the ethical, reason from method or, as we are more likely to say, practice. At a certain point in argument, indeed in interpretation, reason just falters. You can only assert the truth of revelation. Such assertions are not simply propositions whose truth or falsehood can be intellectually determined (as natural man would attempt to do) but they have enormous performative force, provided the conditions of assertion are felicitous. When one tries to convince or convert a nonbeliever, the conditions are not felicitous because there is no common understanding of the situation. You do not have sufficient (institutional) authority to frame the situation. You depend on the force of your (propositional) truths to determine the situation—the presuppositions which are entailed by and entail these truths.

It would of course be naive to assume that the propositional truths are in themselves so forceful as to bring about this determination. We are not dealing with as systemic a domain as mathematics. We have to recognize the role of the way—the rhetorical and dramatic way—in which the truths are presented. When van Til switches from reasoned argument to method, his language becomes more figurative, and he makes greater use of examples.[118] The conviction he aims to produce rests less on reason than on the recognition that come with the ripping away of the defenses that support suppression. Natural man "is the man with an iron mask," van Til writes. "A true method of apologetics must seek to tear off that iron mask."[119]

Several Fundamentalists tried to convert me with such military tactics. One was Bob Murray, a full-time evangelist in downtown Los Angeles. He had been a gang leader in one of the Los Angeles slums before "becoming a Christian." Listening to him, I began to see a parallel between the violence of his past and that of his present militancy. Finally I just fled. I had been interviewing him when he suddenly and quite rudely interrupted me. "Let me just ask you one question," he said. "Have you received the baptism of the Holy Spirit?" That was the beginning. Systematically, relentlessly (mercilessly, I kept thinking to myself), he proceeded as best he could — and his best was good — to expose the errors in my thinking, to declare my view of the world an enormous, Godless defense, and to chip away at it, punctuating his attacks with biblical quotation, prayer, and the demand that we pray together. He tried to shame me into accepting any one of a number of his presuppositions, for then we would share a common ground that would lead, God willing, to my conversion. He caught me off guard and offered me no escape for more than four hours.

In certain respects, van Til's aim is not dissimilar to that of psychoanalysis insofar as it depends upon uncovering the suppressed (read: "repressed") that was brought about through sin (read: "guilt") and coming to recognize the truths one has always known (read: "insight"). However, psychoanalysis depends, in van Til's terms, on the very self-referentiality that was produced by sin for uncovering truth — the patient with the aid of the analyst comes to discover what he has repressed; the apologist, on the other hand, comes with the truth and forces recognition on the unbeliever. The apologist would find the patient's insight, insofar as it depends upon self-reference, to be delusional, the product of Satan.

2—Sanctification

Ralph Barnes, the Fundamentalist student with whom I began the last chapter, had been a Christian for ten or twelve years. Of all the students I talked to, Ralph was the most argumentative and least trusting of my interest in Fundamentalism. He flirted with what must have seemed to him to be my fear of being converted. Ralph had come from a secular family, studied business finance at college, and worked as an accountant in Las Vegas, where he led a completely secular life before being reborn. This is what he says about the Bible and salvation:

"Over the past eleven years I've learned that God has given us a book that is authoritative, without error, and fully adequate. I've learned experientially—through the study of Scripture—that any resistance to its authority is the result of my own will, which doesn't want to submit to God's authority and obey him in every respect. Jesus said, 'If you love me, you will keep my commandments' . . . Now, when I come to the Bible, I don't have to philosophically question its value, because it has shown itself to be an extremely reliable document. It has been open to falsification and has withstood the attacks of its opponents. It's a truly incredible book. . . ."

"Did the meaning of Scripture change for you when you became a Christian?" I asked him.

"Well, before I was a Christian, I really didn't have any exposure to Scripture. But, you see, the Gospel is the power of God to salvation for everyone who believes. When I heard the truth of Jesus Christ, of my fallenness, of my need for a savior, I believed."

"And you accepted the authority of Scripture. But for someone who has not been saved . . . ?"

"Well, your question is answered in 1 Corinthians 1 and 2," Ralph interrupted. "Paul says there that a natural man, an unsaved man, does not accept the things of the Spirit, for they are foolishness to him. He cannot understand them for these things are spiritually discerned."

"But to get to that position, something has to happen to you, which is outside Scripture."

"The miracle of regeneration. It's not necessarily extra-Scriptural. Scripture is the medium. It brings the message of truth which the Holy Spirit uses to bring regeneration within the soul of the believer. . . . Now, that doesn't mean an unsaved person can't read about Jesus being crucified and can't understand intellectually that two thousand years ago a man was crucified on a cross. But he cannot embrace what Paul meant when he said natural man cannot accept the things of the Spirit for they are spiritually discerned. That would be impossible. . . . You see, we are not saved by our own choosing and our own will. Salvation is a gift from God. . . ."

Ralph wanted to discuss predestination:

"God calls men to salvation. He draws them to Himself. He saves them. He justifies them. There's a process. What you see at the moment of justification, that is, God says, 'I declare you just and righteous,' is something that has an eternal decree behind it. What you see is the temporal outworking of it. I cannot look at my life and say, 'This is when it happened.' Many people can. But the issue is not about subjective experience. It's about objective reality. You're transferred. There's a spiritual transformation in which a dead soul is made alive by the Spirit of God because the individual has believed the message of truth. It's faith. It's by faith that you receive Christ. It's a gift. It's by grace. It's God's gift, but it's through the agency of faith. It's not because of anything we did. . . .

"True salvation is only known to God in an ultimate sense — when it occurs. The Gospels indicate that its fruit is evidenced in life style. Spiritual fruit in the sense of a reception of divine truth and a transformation in life that results from the abiding presence of God's Spirit."

When I asked what makes the experience dramatic, Ralph answered:

"We have to look at the objective reality of God's relation to us versus experience. Do we permit experience to be the judge of divine truth? No, we cannot. We cannot allow our experience to become the judge of truth. Some people would say, 'I did this and I did that' and even 'I performed a miracle.' That's no proof of salvation, because Jesus said that many will say on the day of judgment, 'Lord, didn't we cast out demons in your name and perform miracles.' And Jesus will say, 'Depart from me. I never knew you.' So human experience cannot be the test of truth. It's a heart, a repentant heart, that willfully embraces the Gospel of Christ and in repentance believes in Him for salvation."

"But," I asked, "when you became a Christian, something happened that you experienced. One moment you were one way and the next you were another way."

"Spiritually, in a moment of time, I became a new person in Christ, and everything else that was old passed away in a moment in time. But I can't point to anything in my outward life that would say, 'Here's when it was.' "

"Was it a sense of clarity?"

"Nothing at all, in a moment in time."

I had the feeling Ralph was putting me on. He was trying to create a mystery, a puzzle, that would affect me. It was a preliminary to witnessing me. He never did but was always on the verge of doing so.

"Was it an emptiness?"

"I can point to nothing in my life in a point in time when 'Ah.' " Ralph snapped his fingers. "But the change, that spiritual transformation, began to quickly make itself evident in my life—through a process we call 'sanctification' in which we grow in holiness. Justification is forensic. God proclaims we stand justified before Him. Sanctification is a process and continues until death—until Christ's return, when He brings the process to a culmination in which Christians will be brought into perfect conformity with the moral character of God."

"What happens to your past at the beginning of sanctification?"

"What happens to your past? Well, forensically, legally, it's all washed under the blood of Christ, so you're no longer seen as a

wicked rebel by God. God looks upon you based on the righteousness of His son. The past has been totally covered by the blood of
Jesus Christ, and for that matter every future sin will also be covered
under the blood of Jesus Christ. Sin in the believer's life—Christian sin—can of course create a break in his harmonious relationship with Christ. But in terms of the past and future sins, there is no
condemnation, as Paul insisted in Romans 8."

"With regeneration, was your sense of the future changed?"

"Immediately," Ralph said, with some excitement.

"It varies with the individual. Some people may [he snaps his fin-
gers] in a moment in time. They dump everything they knew was
wrong and immediately. . . . For others, it's a gradual process of
transformation. For me the change began slowly but surely. There
was no total turnabout in my worldview in a moment in time. You
see, becoming a new creature in Christ—2 Corinthians 5:17—does
not remove the indwelling sin that is part of our fallen human condition. That is part of our mortal being—sinful and corrupted. In
redemption, God proclaims us righteous, objectively based on the
finished work of Christ. We can't add to it. It's a completed process
based upon what Christ did. Really, in a sense, it continues a process that began in eternity past when God called, when God fore-
ordained that person's salvation. How that divine predestination
connects with the human element of faith is only known to God."

Ralph never told me directly that I could not really understand
Scripture because I was not saved, but he certainly implied it. Like
the other students I interviewed, he was much too polite for that. It
was only Bob Murray, the downtown Los Angeles evangelist, who
dismissed me, saying that since I was not a "Christian" I was wasting my time—and his—trying to make intellectual sense of what
could only be understood through the Spirit. Just as it was the Holy
Spirit who authored Scripture (Bob cited 2 Peter 1:21), it was the
Spirit who ensured understanding. "You remember Jesus's words
in John 14:25-26?" he asked me. "'These things I have spoken to
you, while abiding with you. But the Helper, the Holy Spirit, whom
the Father will send in My name, He will teach you all things, and

bring to your remembrance all that I said to you.'"[1] (I was not alto-gether certain that Bob was not referring to himself when he quoted Jesus's "I.")

All the Fundamentalists I talked to insisted that regeneration was a prerequisite for the correct understanding of Scripture. "The first spiritual qualification of the interpreter is *that he be born again*," Ramm insists, noting that Christ's first recorded words assured the Pharisee Nicodemus that "unless one is born again, he cannot see the kingdom of God."[2] Arthur Pink—a Baptist theologian writing in the first half of this century, whom even John MacArthur finds acid in his criticism of "easy believism"—wrote, "There never was a more foolish notion or pernicious idea entertained than that the holy mysteries of the Gospel so lie within the province of human reason that they may be known profitably and practically without the effectual aid of the blessed Spirit of Truth."[3] Pink is an equally harsh critic both of "natural men" (who may approach Scripture with enthusiasm but whose joy of discovery can lead only to a sense of self-importance) and of unregenerate Christians (who have only a "notional" sense of truth):

> Ten of thousands of graceless professors possess an intellectual knowledge of spiritual things which is considerable, sound, and clear; yet they are not Divinely taught. . . . In like manner, there are a great number of preachers who abhor the errors of Modernism and contend earnestly for the Faith. They were taught in Bible insti-tutes or trained in theological seminaries, yet it is greatly to be feared that they are total strangers to a supernatural work of grace in their souls. . . . [4]

Pink argues for "holy caution" and a sense of humility when reading the Word of God. "Since the imagination of man, like all the other faculties of his moral being, is permeated and vitiated by sin, the ideas it suggests, even when pondering the Divine oracles, are prone to be mistaken and corrupt," he writes in strong Calvinist language.[5] He insists that the veils of ill will, ignorance, prejudice, and pride cover the hearts of man. "So long as he remains in this evil world and the corrupt principle of the flesh continues in him, the

believer needs to be led and taught by the Spirit." He quotes Paul:
"'If any man think that he knoweth anything, he knoweth nothing
yet as he ought to know.'"[6] Although Pink's language—his insistence on the corruption of the flesh and the evil of the world—rings
of another age, it can still harrow the hearts of millions of conservative and not so conservative evangelicals, and of others too. It may
be given less expression in the sermons of the megachurch preachers who, having constantly to think of church growth and debt, are
reluctant to cross, frighten, or even distress their congregations; but
it does sound through (or is made to sound through) the pleas for
help, confessions, and recriminations that are spoken on evangelical
call-in radio programs, on dial-a-prayer calls, and in biblical counseling. Resonant idioms are not easily lost; they go underground.

Pink lists five spiritual qualifications for the interpreter.[7] The first
is *a mind illumined by the Holy Spirit*. Pink plays on biblical images
of light and unveiling within the context of "overcoming our native
anticipation for and hostility to Divine things." The Bible is God's
law, he insists. "It contains not so much good advice, which we are
free to accept at our pleasure, but imperious edicts which we reject
at our peril." Our hostility, "our love of sin and hatred of holiness,"
can be subdued only by the Spirit. Pink's second qualification is *an
impartial spirit*. He observes that nothing clouds judgment more
than prejudice: we must approach Scripture with an honest heart,
not to prove a point. Pink's plea is not for the openness demanded
by science and secular hermeneutics. It is an openness to Scripture
which, paradoxically, requires submission to God's Word. Pink's
third qualification, *a humble mind*, follows directly from his second. The interpreter's mind and will must renounce all trust and
confidence in themselves: "The knowledge of the proud man is the
throne of Satan in his mind." The interpreter must also have *a praying heart*: "We must first get down on our knees and cry unto God
for light." And lastly he must *recognize holy design* and question his
own reasons for acquiring scriptural knowledge.

The inspiring motive should be *honestly examined*. Do I search the
Scriptures in order to become better acquainted with their Author

and His will for me? Is the dominating purpose which actuates me that I may grow in grace and in the knowledge of the Lord? Is it that I may ascertain more clearly and fully how I should order the details of my life, so that it will be more pleasing and honoring to Him? Is it that I may be brought into a closer walking with God and the enjoyment of more unbroken communion with Him? Nothing less is a worthy aim that I may be conformed to and transformed by its holy teaching.

As the great German sociologist of religion, Ernest Troeltsch, points out, "the predominant idea in the Calvinistic conception of God is not love, but majesty, holiness, sovereign power, and grace."[8] The force of Pink's stress on the individual is exceptional—as is his arrogant self-certainty—but it reflects the decentered egocentricity of the American Fundamentalists', indeed the evangelicals', vision of man. Salvation is at once an individual affair and something that requires total submission of individuality to God and His Word.

The Fundamentalist (and here I am extrapolating from Fundamentalist hermeneutics) sees the secular critics' attempts to disengage themselves—their personality, desires, spiritual allegiance, and moral character—from understanding and interpretation to be, at best, naive and foolish and, at worst, arrogant and sinful. The Fundamentalist insists on interpretive objectivity but, unlike the secular interpreter, believes that that objectivity comes by way of the Holy Spirit. To be dependent, to acknowledge one's dependency on the Holy Spirit, involves a radical reorientation of the self, which is stressed by all Fundamentalists. In submitting to the authority of Scripture, their relation to the world, indeed to themselves, is constantly mediated—measured is perhaps more accurate—by the Word. With the help of the Spirit and the tools of their literal, historico-grammatical hermeneutics, they aspire to as objective and understanding of Scripture as is humanly possibly and thus to as godly a relationship to their world and to themselves as possible. Ideally, they are able to view Scripture, and by extension their world, with an "impartial spirit" and a "humble mind." The unregenerate interpreter remains, as van Til often observed, his own reference point and suffers all the confusion that comes with that position.[9] He can never really compensate for his personal interests and desires. He may struggle to set them aside by elaborating complex methodologies for achieving objectivity, but, in the Fundamentalist's eyes, that objectivity will always be false. It is for this, among other reasons, that the Fundamentalist is suspicious of secular scholarship and education which ignore the moral and spiritual condition of students and faculty.

The Fundamentalists, at least as I understand them, do point to a contradiction in secular America's approach to interpretation. In our attempt to disengage knowledge from individual interests and desires, we often fail to consider, at least formally, the effects of those interests and desires. The sciences have elaborated methodologies to facilitate disengagement and consequent "objectivity," though, as feminist critics such as Evelyn Fox Keller have argued, we have not been as successful in bracketing off our (male) interests and desires as we have assumed.[10] In the social sciences, particularly the interpretive ones, the humanities, and of course in everyday life, our claims to objectivity are even less secure. Even psychoanalysis, which offers one of the most systematic (though questionable) procedures we have for achieving insight and self-mastery—in consequence, one could argue, objectivity—is limited on its own admission. Can we ever be sure that an interpretation by someone who has evaluated it in terms of his psychoanalytically generated insights is not a projection?

Central to the Fundamentalists' anthropology is the belief in man's total depravity, the origin of which is understood historically in terms of Adam's "original" sin. They insist, citing Paul, that sin is not only an act but a principle indwelling in man.[11] They note, however, to quote influential Fundamentalist theologian Charles Ryrie, that total depravity does not mean "that everyone is as thoroughly depraved in his actions as he could possibly be, nor that everyone will indulge in every form of sin, nor that a person cannot appreciate and even do acts of goodness; but it does mean that the corruption of sin extends to all men and to all parts of all men so that there is nothing within the natural man that can give him merit in God's sight."[12] Man cannot even desire God on his own. John MacArthur quotes Paul:

> There is none who understands, there is none who seeks for God; all have turned aside, together they have become useless; there is none who does good, there is not even one. Their throat is an open grave, with their tongues they keep deceiving, the poison of asps is under their lips.[13]

Natural man's condition is likened to death. MacArthur writes severely:

> Unregenerate sinners have no life by which they can respond to spiritual stimuli. No amount of love, beseeching, or spiritual truth can summon a response. People apart from God are the ungrateful dead, spiritual zombies, death-walkers, unable even to understand the gravity of their situation, They are lifeless. They may go through the motions of life, but they do not possess it. They are dead even while they live.[14]

The world of "death-walkers" and "spiritual zombies" provides the rhetorical background for the promise of salvation. Reformed Fundamentalists insist that man cannot seek, let alone achieve, salvation on his own. It is only through God's grace—in MacArthur's words—"the free and benevolent influence of a holy God operating sovereignly in the lives of undeserving sinners" that man can arise from his deathly condition.[15] Fundamentalists, like other Protestants, speak of common and saving grace. Common grace is bestowed on mankind in general. It imposes moral constraints, promotes order in human affairs, enforces a sense of right and wrong through conscience and civil government, facilitates the appreciation of beauty and goodness, and blesses people in all kinds of ways.[16] It is not, however, redemptive; it can neither pardon sin nor purify sinners. Saving grace is "the irresistible work of God that frees men and women from the penalty and power of sin, renewing the inner person and sanctifying the sinner through the operation of the Holy Spirit." It is redemptive and fully efficacious. For the Reformed, it is granted only to those whom God elected in eternity past; for others of an Arminian bent, like the Methodists and some Pentecostalists, its application is more general. That it is fully efficacious does not thereby mean that man is freed of all sin during his earthly existence. Nor does it mean that man is fully passive. "Grace is not coercion," MacArthur asserts. "But by transforming the heart, grace makes the believer wholly willing to trust and obey."[17]

The Fundamentalists I interviewed rarely talked about desire, and when they did (within a theological context) they tended to identify it, negatively, with the desires of the flesh.[18] More often they talked about will, which, as I understood them, seemed to straddle two not altogether compatible positions. On the one hand, they stressed the need to submit one's will to God, to make it one (insofar as that is possible) with His will. They quoted Colossians, in which Paul prayed that "the saints and faithful brethren in Christ" in Colossae "be filled with the knowledge of His will in all spiritual wisdom and understanding" so that they may "walk in a manner worthy of God."[19] They also quoted Psalm 40:8–9: "I delight to do Thy will, O my God; Thy Law is within my heart." On the other hand, they spoke of the will in its ordinary sense in which one has, or ought to have, control over one's will—one's self—so as to resist temptation, so as to do God's will. Philosophically, we would have to postulate two orders of will to render these two senses compatible. We would have to declare a primary will that wills to be willed by God's will and then a secondary one that is the result of this primary will: a will that has submitted to and becomes identical with God's will and thereby ideal. The Fundamentalists would find this argument all wrong, for it leaves man, unabetted, responsible for submitting to God's will. It ignores the role of God, His grace, His granting those He has chosen with the ability—the will—to submit to, to identify with, His will. Self-control, we should remember, was for Paul one of the fruits of the Spirit.[20]

This incompatibility, though unmarked, manifests itself in Fundamentalist preaching and writing. In answer to the question of how one can learn self-control, Henry Morris, one of the most vociferous exponents of creationism, and Martin Clark note in their popular *The Bible Has the Answer* that even after salvation, self-control does not come easily. They write revealingly, "Yet the Christian who genuinely *desires* to please God will *bridle* his intellect, emotions, and will, '*taking* every thought captive to the obedience of Christ' (II Corinthians 10:5)" (emphasis added).[21] Note the primary agency of the Christian—he desires, bridles, takes—despite his obedience to Christ. Is this attribution of agency simply an effect of our grammar? Morris and Clark emphasize the individual's responsibility: "Learning self-control usually involves a process of dogged determination, the education of the will through the experience of repeated trials." And yet, following Peter, they argue that "ability to exercise self-control comes as a gift of God's grace."[22] It is "appropriated through faith" and "nurtured by a knowledge of God," which is increased through reading and obeying God's Word, praying, and trusting in Him. They conclude:

> The discipline of self-control illustrates the intimate connection between God's sovereign grace and man's responsibility. . . . To learn self-control, the Christian must humbly submit to Christ's Lordship, confidently rely on His power, and actively concentrate his energies on doing all things for the glory of his Lord.

For the evangelical Christian the question of agency, understood in terms of will or, as here, self-control, is articulated in terms of "God's sovereign grace" and "man's responsibility." As in many other religions, there is no logical resolution of responsibility, only an experiential resolution (though theologically ultimate responsibility always lies with God). The experiential resolution can be understood in psychological or, as the religious would prefer, spiritual terms. Its significance is, however, always ethical, whether cast in human terms as a moral issue or in divine terms, as an accounting for the presence of evil in a world created by a wholly benevolent deity. Who finally is responsible for an act? God or man? The question reverberates through Fundamentalist thinking, as indeed it does through all Christian theology. The psychological or spiritual understanding of the experiential resolution of the incompatibility between the two sources of responsibility for an act can figure, dangerously, in the imputation of final responsibility.

Despite their attribution of ultimate responsibility to God, the Fundamentalists do not hesitate to attribute responsibility to man. Indeed, their judgments are often harsh. Though they argue that no individual ought to judge another's heart, they are, for the most part, as ready as anyone else to judge others. I have observed great restraint in the way they talk about members of their church. Although the individual should never be judgmental, the church body as a whole has, in MacArthur's words "a responsibility to maintain purity by exposing and excommunicating those who live in continual sin or defection from the faith."[23] Expelling someone from a church is always a serious matter and weighed heavily before it is done. Ideally, church elders will approach the sinner individually, asking him to repent. If he refuses, then they will go to him in a small group and, as a final resort, as a church. Their model is of course Christ's.

> And if your brother sins, go and reprove him in private; if he listens to you, you have won your brother.
>
> But if he does not listen to you, take one or two more with you, so that by the mouth of two or three witnesses every fact may be confirmed.
>
> And if he refuses to listen to them, tell it to the church; and if he refuses to listen even to the church, let him be to you as a Gentile and a tax-gatherer.[24]

Ron Saywell told me about a conflict in his church that arose when one member was "disciplined out" because he had publicly attacked the integrity of a deacon without evidence and had refused to apologize. The man's accusations did not seem all that serious to me — they had to do with confusion in the church finances — but they were taken very seriously by the church. Several members thought of leaving the church if he were not expelled. Others, his friends, were tempted to leave if he were expelled. Ron himself was very upset; he mentioned it several times over a weekend we spent together. It was he who had rebuked the man in church. He had had no choice because the man had acted in public. There was apparently no way that he and the other church members could have visited the man privately or in a small group. In the church's eyes, not only had the man falsely accused the deacon but he had also carried his accusation to the public, to the church as a whole, before confronting the deacon privately. His act had been divisive; he had forced people like Ron into acting in a less than ideal biblical way.

"It's OK to say you have a problem with your temper," Ron said in one of his many reflections on the expulsion that weekend. "But you have to ask how many people you have destroyed along the way because you haven't learned to control your temper. We wanted to let him know that losing his temper was only part of the problem. We wanted him to know we were going to take it seriously enough. 'If you don't make this right, then we don't want you here. And not because we don't care about you but because we love you.'" After a long pause, he continued. "Yeah, it was the most loving thing not only for him—'because we love you too much to let you get away with this'—but for everyone else in the church. 'If we sacrifice them to keep you happy. . . .'" Ron stopped, lost in his imagined conversation with the man. I had never heard him speak this way.

"Now, if he were to write a letter of apology at this point," I started to ask.

"And sign a statement," Ron interrupted—he was himself again. "Then he would be able to reapply for membership. But I, for one, have several questions I would want to ask him to determine whether his repentance was genuine."

The line between individual judgment and the judgment of the church is easily crossed.

———

Incompatibilities or near-incompatibilities like those in a Fundamentalist understanding of the will and self-control are found throughout Fundamentalist thought. We find it in the notion of a freedom that comes through obedience to God. We have found it in a theory of knowledge in which man must submit to God's Word in order to gain true knowledge. We have touched upon it in our discussion of the Fundamentalist's evaluation of experience, and we shall consider it in greater detail when we discuss the role of experience in sanctification and biblical counseling. We should note that these incompatibilities are not unique to Fundamentalism but are characteristic of evangelical—indeed, Christian—theology generally. Given its rigidity, the incompatibilities are perhaps more salient in Fundamentalist theology. (Of course, for the Fundamentalists, as well as other Christians, what we see as incompatible is not seen as incompatible and the fact that we see it as incompatible is—for them—a symptom of our "natural" condition. We are, in Paul's words, "conformed to this world" and not "transformed" by a "renewing" of the mind.[25])

For Fundamentalists, as for other evangelicals, salvation is the single most important event in their lives. It completely transforms their experience of the world. As Ralph Barnes insisted, it is not so much a change in the way the world is experienced subjectively, but in the world itself, as it comes to be known, as it presents itself objectively. With respect to responsibility for salvation, we find the same tension between God's and man's role that we found in our discussion of the will and self-control; but here—particularly among evangelicals, who believe in divine election—there is no doubt whatsoever of God's full responsibility. No phase of the process can be thwarted by human failure nor pressed by human merit or effort.[26] The saved have been chosen by God the Father. They have been released from the bondage of sin by Christ's substitionary atonement (that is, His having died not as an example or a martyr, but as a substitute for them—as sinners). They have been regenerated—indwelled—by the Holy Spirit. They have a security so total that they are genuinely puzzled by how those who do not have it can lead their lives. Yet man is not without responsibility. Though he cannot seek, work for, or in any way merit salvation on his own, he must believe in the gospel. And he must have saving faith, which requires knowledge and an inner conviction of the truths that are fundamental to man's salvation: man's sinfulness, Christ's atoning sacrifice, and His bodily resurrection. He must have trust, which MacArthur defines as "a personal commitment to and appropriation of Christ as the only hope for eternal salvation."[27] Enns, less rigorous than MacArthur, stresses the will: "a decision must be made as an act of the will."[28]

To the outsider, the Fundamentalist's theory of salvation appears to be circular. The tension between God's and man's respective role in salvation seems to be displaced onto another plain, that of faith, which then rests on notions of human "commitment," "appropriation," and "will." These moves parallel those of mythic thought, as least as it is understood by the French anthropologist Claude Lévi-Strauss, the father of structuralism, and they are not dissimilar to those which occur in any rationalizing argument.[29] For Lévi-Strauss, myths serve, among other purposes, to mediate contradictions inherent in the cultural system in which they occur. They do so subtly, by changing the terms of the contradictions from those which are incontestably contrary, say life and death, to those which are less apparently so, say, living and killing, until a mediational term is found which can absorb the contradiction (say, hunting — one kills to live). Mythic thought is inherently unstable since it rests, if Lévi-Strauss is correct, on an illusory resolution of contradictions that are for the most part irresolvable. Indeed, I would argue that most of the time no mediating term can be found which offers even an illusion of resolution. In either case, myths can only repeat themselves endlessly in different registers. Unlike myths, in which cultural contradictions are expressed in concrete symbols, in terms of real and fantasized animal and plant life, and cast as stories, rationalizations are usually expressed in abstract language (though they may make use of concrete symbols) and depend less on story than on logical argument. They tend, as such, to be more compelling, though, as I hope I have shown with respect to human and divine agency in Reformed evangelical thought, they also tend to rephrase and shift registers when no "logical" resolution can be found in any single register.

Fundamentalists would not, I believe, completely disagree with what I have said. They would find my argument, and no doubt my description of mythic and rationalizing thought, to be a symptom of the ego-centered thought of one who has neither faith nor the security of salvation. You cannot possibly understand the transformation that comes about with salvation, they would say. They may be right. But what I find puzzling is their resistance to mystery. Yes, like the Baptist preacher I mentioned in the last chapter, many of them recognize the mysteries of election. They acknowledge their inability to understand God fully. He remains a mystery to them, though I have rarely heard them speak about God in terms of "mystery." Unlike Catholic mystics, Fundamentalists are not given to stressing the inadequacy of their words just as they are not willing to consider the possible inadequacy of biblical language. They are affronted by such a suggestion. The failure to understand lies with man.

Of course, some Fundamentalists are troubled by Fundamentalist theology. Many are anti-intellectuals, who condemn any systematic thought that smacks of "philosophy." Others are more reflectively critical; many of these come from the strictest churches. Ted Winter, the Grace Brethren pastor I mentioned in the last chapter, is one. He was the most reflective, and perhaps even the most radical, of the people I interviewed. (I sometimes wondered whether his radicalism came from the Anabaptist tradition out of which the Brethren grew.) He talked to me with ease and seemed to enjoy our conversations. He discussed William James and C. S. Lewis in the same breath that he talked about Jonathan Edwards, and was not loath to quote Charles Dickens or discuss the film *The Missionary*. He was able to assume a critical, if never truly ironic, attitude toward his beliefs. He is an impassioned man, who impressed me as being trapped in his commitment if not his faith. He did admit that he continually wrestles with doubt. It is God's way of strengthening his faith, he says. Ted argued that MacArthur was too rigid and had "a deficient theology of the Spirit." "It is the Spirit who promises to teach us all things and guide us into the true. If I do not have an active spirit, but a passive, compartmentalized, or even handicapped spirit, then I would fear that any attack would weaken my position instead of giving me strength."

Ted went on to say, to my surprise, that the Fundamentalist belief that words have only one meaning is poor linguistics. "We don't even assume single meaning in common speech nor, should we, in theology." I found, however, the example he gave to be the product of the very literalism which he was questioning. "So the 'Kingdom of God' and the 'Kingdom of Heaven' would have to be two very different things because 'Heaven' and 'God' are two different words." Ted implied that a lot of theology was based on this kind of distinction. "My conviction is that with Calvinism, Arminianism, dispensationalism, liberalism, whatever -ism you want, you give up the Bible in some sense or another." Though he always referred to himself as a Fundamentalist, Ted seemed more open to the plays of language than any other Fundamentalist I met. He concluded the interview I have been describing with the suggestion that words, those in Scripture, had a meaning that "comes through and across" and need not be quoted directly but can be paraphrased. One of the weaknesses of Fundamentalism, he said, is that it rejects paraphrase. "Their understanding of words is magical. They get angry if you say that, but it is magical rather than dynamic."

This mistrust of systematic theology is found among the systematists themselves. Many of them recognize, if not the artifice of their project, then its human—and therefore potentially faulty—construction. "Man will never be able totally to comprehend God," Enns reminds his reader.[30] "He must be satisfied with limited knowledge." For the Fundamentalist, Scripture always has priority over systematic theology and, that theology, any theology, must be corrected by it. Charles Hodge, one of the most important of the conservative theologians of the last century, insists that all of the facts of divine revelation out of which theology should be constructed are in the Bible.[31] Others recognize other sources, including nature.[32] With considerable hedging, Enns even includes tradition as a source, of understanding. Systematic theology is frequently justified on apologetic grounds, enabling "Christians" better to defend themselves against their opponents. "This is perhaps even more important today," Enns remarks, "with the emergence of humanism, Communism, cults, and Eastern religions."[33]

To dismiss this mistrust of systematic theology on anti-intellectual grounds is to fail to appreciate the Fundamentalists' position. I believe that their commitment to the divine inspiration and inerrancy of the Bible undermines through contrast their confidence in the language of their theologies. Mistrust results not simply from their theologies' human authorship, nor from the sense of distortion and even betrayal that accompanies the systematization of any work as loosely assembled as the Bible; rather, their understanding of God's Word makes any reference to it suspect other than direct quotation (and perhaps even then, if only because it is taken out of context). An analogous experience might be when you say what a poem is about rather than quote it. It may be this kind of experience that accounts for the Fundamentalists' constant quotation of Scripture and the priority they give to the Word over experience in their formulations of "experience."

Evangelical theologians have worked out the logical order of salvation—an *ordo salutis*—which must not be taken chronologically since it is, in a sense, contained in a timeless moment that extends from eternity past to eternity future. In Reformed theology, it would include election, calling, regeneration, conversion, repentance, faith, justification, sanctification, perseverance, and glorification. Each of these "experiences" is described by MacArthur (he is no exception in this respect) in biblical terms—not in the terms used by those who have been saved.[34] God "foreknows and foreordains the elect (Rom. 8:29), calls the sinner to Himself (Rom. 8:30), draws the soul to Christ (John 6:44), accomplishes the new birth (John 1:13; James 1:18), grants repentance (Acts 11: 18) and faith (Rom. 12:3; Acts 18:27), justifies the believer (Rom. 3:24; 8:30), makes the redeemed holy (Eph. 2:10), and finally glorifies them (Rom. 8:30)." Perhaps the closest MacArthur comes to describing the experience itself is still through quotation and commentary, on Ephesians 2:1–10, which reads:

And you were dead in your trespasses and sins, in which you formerly walked according to the course of this world, according to the
prince of the power of the air, of the spirit that is now working in the
sons of disobedience.

Among them we too all formerly lived in the lusts of our flesh,
indulging the desires of the flesh and of the mind, and were by nature children of wrath, even as the rest.

But God, being rich in mercy, because of His great love with
which He loved us even when we were dead in our transgressions,
made us alive together with Christ (by grace you have been saved),
and raised us up with Him, and seated us with Him in the heavenly
places, in Christ Jesus, in order that in the ages to come He might
show the surpassing riches of His grace in kindness toward us in
Christ Jesus.

For by grace you have been saved through faith; and that not of
yourself, *it is* the gift of God; not as a result of works, that no one
should boast.

For we are His workmanship, created in Christ Jesus for good
works, which God prepared beforehand, that we should walk in
them.

The experiential references in this passage are, of course, purely
rhetorical, and in many respects that rhetoric is mirrored in conservative evangelical preaching. However, we should remember that
our articulation of experience is derived largely from nineteenth-
century assumptions.[35] This rhetoric therefore derives its force
from the evocation of experiences understood in psychological
terms that were no doubt alien to Paul's world.

The intertwining of biblical quotation, formulation, and understanding with experience is characteristic of evangelical conversion
stories. They are rarely, if ever, simply objective accounts of the experience of being saved. They are a revivification, a continuing re-
enactment, of the initial conversion experience. As the
anthropologist Peter Stromberg argues, they may formulate in a canonical language aspects of experience—unacknowledged conflicts, problems of identity, and illicit desires—which cannot be

given direct expression in ordinary language.[36] They always have an evangelizing dimension. They affirm God's greatness, His grace, His power. They are intended to convict—to impress with guilt—those who have not been saved and those who have begun to renew their faith. Ted Winter brought up his own conversion, delicately, as an example, in the course of a rather free-ranging discussion on separatism, evangelizing, and salvation, without trying to convert me. Unlike many Fundamentalists, Ted was not adverse to engaging in what he at least took to be a dialogue with people with different beliefs. He often made reference to his own experiences at Fuller, for which, as I mentioned, he was roundly criticized by his church. "I went to the wrong schools deliberately because the schools I was supposed to go to were indoctrinational schools."

Ted went on to quote verses 16–21 of Galatians 5:

> But I say, walk by the Spirit, and you will not carry out the desire of the flesh.
>
> For the flesh sets its desire against the Spirit, and the Spirit against the flesh; for these are in opposition to one another, so that you may not do the things that you please.
>
> But if you are led by the Spirit, you are not under the Law.
>
> Now the deeds of the flesh are evident, which are: immorality, impurity, sensuality,
>
> Idolatry, sorcery, enmities, strife, jealousy, outbursts of anger, disputes, dissensions, factions,
>
> Envying, drunkenness, carousing, and things like these, of which I forewarn you just as I have forewarned you that those who practice such things shall not inherit the kingdom of God.

Like other Fundamentalists, Ted took a delight in reciting the "deeds of the flesh." Later in our conversation, he explained that he—his Christianity, as he put it—was saved by Galatians 5.

"I'm already perfect in Christ, but I'm not yet experiencing it. My daily struggle should be to experience more of it. 'Become what I am' is a phrase I use a lot. There is a dynamic to faith, to living. It's not static. You can't beat anyone into it. You can't prove it. You can demonstrate it. You can give reasons, but you can't compel. I believe we have certainty, but I can't pretend I'm always certain. There's a living tension in faith, and apparently this tension, the uncertainty, is ultimately good for us, because it is this faith that pleases God. Not arrogance, not intelligence, not voluminous reading. It is faith that pleases God, and we are not naturally creatures of faith. . . ."

Ted had fallen for a moment into a preaching mode.

"Well, we're promised in this passage that even in Christians the flesh and the Spirit are going to war. In fact it is only in Christians that they war because the Spirit's not in the unsaved. . . .

"How will I know the true religion? By producing true fruits. I preach this. It was this distinction that set me free to be a Fundamentalist Christian. I mean to believe in the Bible, to identify with the group."

Later in the interview, I mentioned that I had observed a big difference between those Fundamentalists who had converted and those who had grown up, like Ted, in a Fundamentalist church. The latter did not have as intensely emotional a centering experience as the former.

"All I can do is answer for myself," he said. "I want to invite, or induce, people to a conversion experience, and let that be in the broadest sense, without manipulating them or focusing unduly on experience. If it is true that the Spirit comes in and gives new life, a born-again life — use whatever term you want — to those of us who are dead in trespasses and sins and blinded to truth, then something should happen. I believe that's it: something should happen. We're not told what will happen.

"So what is the experience? I often say, 'I've received Jesus at least three times before I was born again.' I began to be fearful of Hell. I knew I wanted something. I was eleven going on twelve — that's a critical age psychologically in the development of children:

probably passing from innocence to maturity. I was in the hearing of the Word. I'd hold my hand up in Sunday school and pray with the teacher. I walked the aisle—I grew up in an aisle-walking church—and prayed with the pastor. I don't know what I prayed. I must have satisfied him. It might have been, 'God is great. God is good. Let us thank Him for our food.' I went into a room with him and another woman, and we both prayed together. But it was when I was all alone in my bedroom one night when something happened. At that time we lived in a big old farmhouse. I went to bed alone. My parents probably said something like 'Say your prayers.' But it was like, the lights came on in my experience at that point. As far as I remember, I wasn't even thinking about God or being saved or anything like that at the time. I was just going to bed. It was like, 'Oh, that's what it is.' I believe it was at that point that I was converted and then dwelt with the Holy Spirit. There were no tears. I was baptized after that more because I walked an aisle than because of that experience. So I say that I received Jesus several times before I was born again.

"Unfortunately we have identified conversion with an event. I do not have altar calls for that reason. Not that altar calls are wrong. Historically we've acted as if God lives in the flowers at the front of the church. If you walk up there, you can meet him. Or the pastor's hand. You can shake it, and it's all settled. Or some formula. Pray this prayer: 'Dear God, I'm a sinner.' You know—the sinner's prayer. These are all tools that can serve a purpose, but they are not conversion. The emotions of conversion and the events of conversion are almost beyond our control. But good conservatives, which almost all Fundamentalists are, like to control things. We struggle for some kind of control, some kind of a seal. We're handicapped in a variety of ways."

Ted's reflective style, concern, and humility contrast sharply with Paul Conway, a master's student at one of the conservative seminaries in California. Paul had immense charm: he was passionate, outgoing, and energetic, but also arrogant and self-involved. Though a Fundamentalist, his emphasis on experience was more "Pentecostalist" in style than "Fundamentalist." His stress on change and personal growth remind me of New Age power and growth stories. He used his story to witness me. He had come from a secular family, studied applied physics, and planned a career as a navy officer. While in the navy, he became a Christian. Like many of the conversion stories I heard, his had an autonomous quality—God-driven, one might say—in which improbable characters suddenly appeared in his life, calling attention to his sinful condition and offering him the possibility of salvation. As Paul described the sins of his past, he began to relive them, taking a sensual pleasure I could not help but observe, in the life he was recounting, feeling perhaps a tinge of regret for having surrendered that life to the chaste and disciplined one he was now determined to lead.

"Personally, personally. . . I know. There is an ability to know if you're saved by the works you do, by the fruits of the Spirit." I had asked Paul how you knew you were saved. He was not as advanced a student as the others I had interviewed. He could not quote Scripture with their facility, and his theology was still awkward. He explained that by loving God and obeying His commandments, one is saved.

"And so I have assurance of my own salvation based on the fact that when I open the Word of God, it convicts me. I say I am wrong, and I grieve of the fact I offended One I love. I am able—slowly, it seems very slowly—to act in accordance with the Bible. Even my feelings are slowly beginning to change, to match what the Bible says. So if I do something wrong, I grieve over it. . . . It doesn't feel right. . . . I just mourn and feel guilty."

Paul went on to discuss justification, the "legal act wherein God pronounces that the believing sinner has been credited with all the virtues of Jesus Christ":[37]

"God's character is perfect, and he defines what's perfect. Because of Adam's sin, because it came down to us, our character is different from God's. God says that anyone who is different from Him cannot be in His presence. So I do not deserve to be in His presence. I deserve to die. So someone has to pay the penalty for my sins. And that's what Jesus did. He paid my penalties. I have to accept that. I have to say, 'Yes, I trust that Christ—' I don't know how this works exactly. But I trust that Christ paid the penalties for my sin. That's when I'm justified."

Paul apologized for using "all these big words" like "justification." "I'm not trying to impress you with my knowledge." He laughed. "The words are nice. They pack in a lot of meaning. But unless you know the meaning, then they just flump around."

After a long digression, during which Paul asked me to explain my research in more detail, he began to describe his own conversion.

"I—when I was a senior in college I was, you know, grabbing for different things. I had a beautiful girlfriend, and my grades were doing wonderfully, and everyone loved me. My fraternity loved me. But I was drinking heavily and into marijuana and also—with my girlfriend. And it was getting to the point, you know, when holding hands is nice but boring. You've got to go to the next level and then the next. It was getting to the point of perversion. 'I'm like, this is just incredible. What's going on? I'm just having no peace, no tranquillity in my heart at all. I need something to stuff in there to cover over, to fill my heart, to feel full.' But actually what I wanted was to cover over all my guilt. I don't remember this too often. I went with Joel, a friend who was a born-again, to his chapel. It was this little teeny chapel. I sat there and studied the Bible, studied it inside out, probably more than I do now.

"I mean I was just very adamant about studying it. And I looked at all those people there studying it, and I studied them. But the whole time I was removed. It was my physics mind, my scientific mind. I wanted objective facts. It wasn't until later that I looked at the Bible afresh, like 'OK, I understand that my way of living has gotten me no place, gotten me to hopelessness. I am looking for something I can trust in.' I was no longer looking into the Bible, saying, 'Is this trustworthy? And let me prove how it's not.' I had begun to look into it, saying, 'I need something to trust. How can I start trusting this? OK, if this is true, what it says here, let's say it's true, then what should I do?' I remember doing that when I was being converted. I started to *read* the Bible. But then in that little chapel I was reading it with the intention of disproving it, so I could get on to more exciting things. But it was too confusing. I wasn't smart enough to disprove it. So I said, 'Well—I don't know why I did this. What if it's true? What should I do right now if it's true?' I started praying. And then, 'OK, enough of that.'"

He laughed nervously. I was fascinated less by what Paul was saying than by how he was saying it. He was so removed, except when he laughed. He did not find it necessary to put his story in context. Like many evangelicals I talked to in California, Paul often expressed his past thoughts in direct quotation and seemed even to enter into conversation with them.

"You know, one second, one minute of that. 'Yecch, something's going on, and I don't know what.' I mean, I tried to pray. I was like, 'Who am I praying to? What's going on here?'

"It was very strange. What drew me into this was the person who was witnessing me. It was a year after college. At that time I was into Buddhism and Zen. I wasn't really into it. I wasn't trusting it. I was objectively studying it and trying to get out of it what I could. A friend, Joel—he wasn't a friend at the time—came up to me. Here I was studying nuclear power and all this high scientific stuff—I thought I was the cream of the crop—and this guy comes up (he's very meek, mild, a wimpy guy) and says, 'I heard you're into Buddhism?' I said, 'Yeah.' And he goes on, 'Can I explain to you what I believe, you know, from the Bible?' I said, 'Sure.' He started to explain. And I said, 'Wait a second. You believe in Noah? You believe that a bunch of animals went on this raft and floated around on the earth?' He says, 'Yes, I believe it.' And I said, 'You believe that

Jonah went inside the whale's mouth, and that the whale spit him out?' I was just amazed. I could not believe that someone would actually—I mean, here we are studying nuclear power, and he believes in this boat and the whale. So I just let loose on him. I just ripped him up and cut him down and got angry at him. I said, 'How can someone like *you* believe in such a stupid thing and still be here studying this engineering stuff?' He meekly and mildly and apologetically backed off and said, 'I'm sorry. I didn't mean to offend you.' And he went back to his desk. I had no satisfaction from that at all. I was trying to punch him, and he was just, you know—it was like punching a pillow.

"I really wanted him to get defensive with me so I could scrap it up. What really nailed me was when I realized he was the strongest person in the class. Everyone else in the class would have got defensive if I challenged their beliefs. But he didn't. He didn't defend himself. He said, 'This is how I believe. I'm sorry that you're angry at me. I'll move away.' So I was like, 'What makes this guy tick?' I even went to church with him. I couldn't get enough of—I just wanted to open his mind and look in there and say, 'This doesn't make sense. How could a person be doing this?' I just watched and watched."

After finishing his nuclear power training, Paul was sent to a nuclear power plant in the desert in Idaho.

"There was this guy, Ezra, and he was a nut. He was just a total freak. I remember walking out of the plant one time, and he goes, 'Paul! Look at that star! Look at that star! Do you know who made that star?' I said, 'Ezra, I don't know who made that star.' And he goes, 'I do. I talked to the guy this morning. I talked to the guy who made the star. You can do that too. You want to talk to him now? Let's talk to him.' And I'm like, 'Ezra, get away from me, man. You are weird and weird.' He just had an incredible, fanatical faith. I just wanted to get away from him and not be associated with him at all. Every time I'd sit down with him on the bus out to the plant or back—it took about an hour and a half—he'd go into his Bible and say, 'You know, Paul, what you're doing is sin.' I wasn't really dating at the time, just sleeping with women. 'It offends God,' he'd say, 'and you deserve death because of it. It's not just your actions but even your thoughts. You know, in Matthew 5, it says if you look at a woman for the purpose of lusting that's adultery and is deserving of death.' I just couldn't tell Ezra anything I did because he'd call it sin. He'd just nail me, nail me, nail me, nail me. I'd say, 'Enough, Ezra, enough. I'm not talking to you anymore. I'm leaving.' I'd get up and sit somewhere else on the bus. The next day I'd get on the bus and see Ezra sitting there, waving at me. I'd sit down next to him. I'd say, 'OK, Ezra, tell me again what's going on.' That showed me God's sovereignty, God's drawing me. Even though someone's telling me I'm a sinner, and I'm offending God, and I felt horrible about it, I still wanted to know more."

"So, there was a longing there," I said. Paul had run out of steam.

"I had a desire to understand the Bible—to read more, to try to understand this Person I was going to have a relationship with."

"When did a change come about?"

"I was going with Ezra to this church, and the pastor would be preaching. I'd lean over to Ezra and say, 'Ezra, why did you tell him about me?' And he goes, 'I didn't tell him anything.' He was just preaching the Word of God, and I thought I was the only person in the whole place. I thought he was just pointing to me. That's the conviction of the Holy Spirit. The Holy Spirit was using the Word of God and revealing it to my heart and showing me that I was wrong. I finally came to the point when I said, 'OK, Ezra, I'm convinced. It's time for me to make a decision.' Ezra said, 'OK, let's go back and talk with one of the deacons.' I said, 'I'm ready. I'm ready to make a commitment. I don't know what all this includes—smoke and bubbles and all that—but I'm ready to make a commitment.' They said OK and explained it to me. And I said, 'OK, I'm ready to pray.' We bowed down, and I prayed. 'God, I'm convinced that you're out there. I'm convinced from what I see in Ezra, from the feelings I get when I'm with him, when I am listening to someone preaching to me. I can't really get that feeling when I'm reading by myself. I know you're out there. I know something's out there. So I commit myself now, Lord, to pursue You and to understand You. Lord, please help me to understand You. Amen.'

"I looked up. Ezra looks at me and goes, 'That's not the way you're supposed to do it. That's wrong. You don't do it that way. You think you can go toward God and kind of meet halfway. But you've got to realize that there's nothing you can do to earn anything with God—not even saying, God meet me halfway. God has to do it all. God has to totally save you and bring you back from the pit.' It didn't nail me until then, Vincent. I'm not sure why I was— how I got that far—because certainly Ezra had told me that before.

"Basically, I was taking a boat hook and reaching out for God and saying, 'God, be there somewhere, would ya? Because I want to tag onto ya.' When Ezra said that, all the Scripture that I had read came before me. I realized this boat hook was useless. I threw it away. I said, 'God, just save me. God, I have offended You. I don't deserve to be saved. I do not deserve to be in your presence. I ought to be separated from You, Lord. You are righteous, and I am not. If You choose to have me in Your presence, that would be just. That would be, that's the way it should be. Yet I ask You to save me somehow—mercy.'"

Paul had lost command of his words, dropping the negative in "If you choose *not* to have me in Your presence that would be just."

"Did you pray again at that point?" I asked.

"Yeah, yeah." Paul was still elsewhere.

"Did the deacon say anything to you?"

"I don't remember him at all. I just remember Ezra."

"How did you feel then?"

"I felt weird. I felt as if I didn't know what had happened. I didn't have a clue. I just kind of felt, 'OK, what happened? I don't know. What happened?' So I drove around by myself on my motorcycle. I went to this park and talked to these kids and asked them if they knew anything about God. [laughs]

"I wanted to explain to them what I did. They weren't too interested, and so I said, 'OK, forget it.' That was the same day, the same day I got saved. Then, a week later—I just felt out of control. I guess that's the best way to explain it. I didn't feel like I knew what was going on. I didn't have control over my spirit. It was shifting around. It was starting to be weird. I wanted to grab control of my spirit—for me to be in charge again. And so, a week later, we had time off, I hopped on my motorcycle and drove to Sun Valley, which was three, four, maybe five hours away. I drove on my motorcycle through the snow. The sun had broken just a little bit. That was enough, and I was out. I had a Suzuki 1000 at the time, this little junker. I just went hauling across the desert to this woman who I had been sleeping with. I finally got there. I don't think she—yeah, I had called her and told her I was coming. It took me a while to just warm up because I was so cold. Then, I forced her to sleep with me, basically, and right after—I apologize for being graphic—right after the event, my eyes were opened. I realized what I was doing. I realized that here is this person that I don't even know and I'm trying to force, trying to get happiness out of her, trying to get contentment out of her, trying to get something out of her, and it doesn't exist in her. I was just devastated. I just could not believe what I was doing. All these emotions—I felt like puking. I really wanted to vomit. I didn't want to vomit but I felt like I was going to. I was rubbing my head and trying to figure out what was going on. You know, a month ago I had slept with her and felt great. And yeah, a little bit guilty. I was able to push that off. Now I was totally consumed by guilt and disgust at myself. 'What's going on? What's changed?' Then I remembered that I had gone forward and had talked to Ezra and prayed. I'm like, 'Maybe something actually happened there. Maybe it was something real. Maybe I'm changing.' That in fact was the case. God had started to change me. I no longer enjoyed doing the things that God's Word said was wrong. I now wanted to see Him. I wanted to be with Him. I wanted to have a relationship with Him. I wanted to talk to Him. I wanted to sit on His lap. I wanted to know and understand Him. I would do anything for that. And His words—and the Bible—started to make sense. I could read something, and it would have the same effect as if Ezra or a preacher was talking to me. I could get that for myself out of the Bible. That's called the illumination of the Holy Spirit. It quickens the Word into our hearts. The Holy Spirit chooses to use His Word to reveal the character of God. It's just like you wrote me a letter. I can read the letter and study the letter. But it's another thing to understand the person who wrote the letter."

"What happened to her? Did you talk to her about what was going on?"

"Yeah."

"She must have been confused."

"She went through this whole thing about how she wasn't going to have another abortion. This time she was going to have the kid and blah, blah, blah, blah. I just left the next morning. I talked to her later. I determined that the right thing to do was to support her if that was the case. So I continued to write to her. I wanted to cut it off. I wanted to just say, 'All right, God, can I start fresh now?' But again I felt horrible about that. I knew I had to pay for what I'd done. I had to reap what I had sown. So I explained to her what had happened to me. Like, 'Look, I'm just as amazed about all this stuff as you are. I don't want to be a Bible freak. I don't want to be a Fundamentalist. I don't want to be any of this. But this is what happened to me. What do you think?' She said, 'Well, in fact I am God,' and all this other strange stuff, because she was into meditation and metaphysics. She was out there. But she wasn't pregnant so eventually our relationship dissipated. I went back to her twice to share my experience. At that time, I'm like, 'Who wouldn't want to be saved? What knucklehead wouldn't want to be saved?' So I'm running up to her and saying, 'Look at this! Maybe someone hasn't told you about this. Maybe you just kind of went through life and never knew about it. We can be forgiven for our sins. We can have a relationship with God. Oh, it's wonderful! I can talk to God. I have peace with God. I know that he's not angry with me. I know that he's excited by what I do. Isn't that exciting?' And she says, 'Get away from that stuff.' You know she was just rebellious against it because it was challenging her autonomy—the autonomy of her mind."

"How had she reacted when you felt sick after making love to her?"

"I think she was just consumed by her own thing. . . ." It was clear that Paul had not thought about her reaction.

I asked him how he reconciled his science with a literal interpretation of the Bible.

"Good question. The two are extreme opposites and conflict. When I got saved in 1988, I decided to just open myself up totally to the Bible. When it came to the stuff about Noah, I'd turn off my scientific mind. I remembered reading the New Testament and finding how sweet its words were, how delicious, how soothing, how comforting, how they just told me about God, how close they brought me to His person, to a relationship with God. Then I turned to Genesis and said, 'Well, this stuff can't be true,' but the sweetness started coming from it also. 'This is the same book. I accept it all as the same.' I just didn't feel that you could say that the message is there but it is not true historically.

"I was placing the condition of my soul and my eternity on what these words said. I was trusting. How minuscule and foolish it seemed to ask whether or not these words were true. To ask whether this guy actually existed. I mean a big boat with a bunch of animals on it is a very small thing compared to the fact that He saved me and was changing my heart. I now have new desires that I never had before. I am now changing from inside out. Now I am chewing on things that I used to love, and I spit them out and say they taste horrible. And I chew on other stuff that I used to hate, and now it tastes wonderful. It's the Word of God that did that. So if it had the power to change my life, then why can't I trust it to be historically true?"

I asked Paul why he decided to leave the navy to become a preacher.

"I could very easily be a Christian, loving and serving God, and in the navy, working on nuclear power, working on a submarine. That could be pleasing to God, and God would want me there. When I had gone into the navy, however, I had told them that I had never smoked marijuana. Then, five years later, in a periodic review, they asked me again if I had smoked marijuana. I had been saved in the meantime. I had to decide. Do I tell the truth or do I lie? Now, there were two little boxes on the form. If I checked one on the right, no one would know. I'd do fine, and everyone would be happy because the navy doesn't really care whether I'd smoked drugs. They just don't want to know about it. But if I checked the box on the left, then they might court-martial me, take away my security clearance, throw me out. 'Where am I going to go? What am I going to do?' I'd spent basically ten years in the navy. 'So why throw all this away for one little check mark?' I thought and prayed about it. I asked, what is the question 'Have you ever smoked drugs?'? And the answer: 'Yes.' That's all I need to know.

"They ousted me. My captain took me aside and chewed me out. He said, 'Let me be frank with you. There are a number of people who have smoked marijuana who are in the navy and that's fine. Do you realize you are throwing your career away? In fact you're hurting the navy.' I said, 'Sir, they asked me a question, and I had a decision to make. My decision was not to find out what was best for the navy. My decision was to find out what was best for me. My decision was to lie or to tell the truth. It was a choice to obey God or not to obey God. I am not as smart as God. He has the big picture. I just see a little peep-hole. I'm going to defer to Him. He tells me very clearly what I am to do. So I'll do it and hold to it and see what happens.'

"It did turn out to be the best. I left the navy. I actually received an honorable discharge. They took away my clearance and my dolphins. So there is a black mark on my face if I ever want to get another security clearance. . . .

"I wasn't sure, and I'm still not positive now, that I'm called to the ministry. While I was in the navy, I continued to live a double life. The Lord was working on me—that's for sure—but I was not living in accordance with His commands. I just had a hunger, a deep desire to study the Bible. But I didn't have the discipline to open it when I needed to and spend time with God. I would go back to my old ways and chase after soap bubbles and try to get satisfaction from them. 'How can words on a page give me satisfaction? How can they relieve my loneliness? How can I have fellowship with a person I can't see?' It made no sense to me—'So forget it.' But then I'd be drawn back to the Bible. You know, when I sit down and pray, I want to know who it is I'm talking to. I want to know who is in charge of my life. There were things that were happening in my life that I didn't understand, that were painful. I figured they were happening for my good. I wanted to figure out how. I thought of James 1, where he says, 'Consider in all joy, my brethren, when you encounter various trials.' 'Why should I consider all these trials that I went through with joy? Because knowing that the testing of my faith produces endurance. And let endurance have its perfect result, that you may be perfect and complete, lacking in nothing.' So I discovered in these words that I could have joy in the midst of difficulty. I know He's working on me and making me able to continue to do what He says even when it looks like it's not going to work out right. It's like sitting in a 3-D movie. You see all these things coming at you and you know you have God sitting next to you saying, 'Don't worry. The rock's not going to hit you in the head.' But we still have the 3-D glasses on that make things distorted. So I look into the Word. I am able to take those glasses off and say, 'This is just a stupid movie. I can trust God. I don't need to do what I feel is right.' "

I have quoted Paul at length because, of the many conversion stories I heard, his best describes the transformative role God's Word plays in salvation. Like Saint Augustine's story, like the story of the missionary to Thailand, it tells of coming to know the Word. It can be read as an allegory of reading: how he learned to read—at once to trust the Word and to know God. Fundamentalism precludes the separation of these three processes, to read, to trust, to know God and His Word. It is for this reason that so much evangelical thought makes little or no sense to the non-evangelical.

Paul's approach to the Word is far more sensuous than that of the other Fundamentalists I know. It convicts him. He is overwhelmed by his depravity. The preacher "was just preaching the Word of

God. . . . I thought he was just pointing to me." But, as he tells us several times, when he first began to read the Bible, "adamant" as he was, he was "removed" from it. He blames this on his "physics," his "scientific" mind; it is only later with the help of the Holy Spirit ("The Holy Spirit was using the Word of God and revealing it in my heart") that he is able to read the Bible with illumination. (Enns defines illumination as "the ministry of the Holy Spirit whereby he enlightens those who are in the right relationship with Him to comprehend the written Word of God."[38])

Although illuminated reading depends completely on God, it requires, as Ezra admonished Paul, complete surrender. Paul cannot approach God "halfway"—he must have limitless trust in God, no matter how incomprehensible He may be. Paul has to abandon his "scientific mind": his critical spirit, his sense that he is the measure of all knowledge. Paul struggles with this surrender; he casts his surrender in terms of the desire to understand—the Bible, God, what was going on in Joel's head ("I just wanted to open his mind and look in there"), in Ezra's head, and, presumably, in his own. He looks with wonder at the changes that are taking place in him. He is drawn to Joel and Ezra, the two men who witness him, despite the fact that he "rips up" one of them and finds the other a "freak." His contradictory relationship with them and the autonomous style in which he describes it—their unexplained appearance—attests to the inscrutable ways in which God calls those He has elected. He prays and is terrified by the effect of his prayers. Even after his rebirth, he has to bracket off his critical stance toward the Bible— toward the story of Noah. He comes to experience the words of Genesis as he had experienced those of the New Testament, as "sweet," "delicious," "soothing," "comforting." He realizes that as he has staked his soul on them, he cannot very well deny their historical truth. Although he is unable to describe what happened to him when he was saved other than to say that he felt weird, didn't have a clue, and lost control of his spirit, "all the Scripture that [he] had read came before [him]." He is able to read the Bible with the same effect he had when Ezra or a preacher was talking to him. By looking into the Word, he is able to take off his "3-D glasses" and see what a "stupid movie" he had been seeing and living.

I found Paul's last observation—"I don't need to do what *I* feel is right"—terrifying. It seemed to me that by subordinating his own desires to those of God—in fact, those he *took* to be God's—Paul risked abrogating responsibility for his own acts. Less sophisticated theologically, less adept at quoting the Bible, more involved in his own experience than other seminarians I knew, Paul sharpened my awareness of the ethical dimension of Fundamentalist interpretation and application. How could one be sure that one was not projecting one's own desires onto God and His Word? Arthur Pink warns against the perversions of the imagination: "God's Word requires to be handled with reverential fear, and with much prayer for discernment and guidance, lest we tread on holy ground with the shoes of carnal wisdom."[39] It is only the careful exegesis and interpretation of Scripture, guided by the Holy Spirit, that protects us, the Fundamentalist holds, from the guiles of human ingenuity and Satan's counterfeiting readings. Once uncovered, it is our commitment to the meaning of God's words and the principles we derive from them that saves us from a second play of the imagination when we seek the significance of Scripture for our own lives.

Unlike the liberal theologians who question it, the Fundamentalists insist upon the traditional distinction between meaning and significance—interpretation and application.[40] They quote the conservative literary theorist E. D. Hirsch, who has insisted on the permanence of textual meaning. For Hirsch, meaning is "that which the text is taken to represent."[41] Significance is "meaning-as-related-to-something-else." Meaning is a principle of stability in this account while significance embraces change. The Fundamentalists like to say that while God's words have only a single meaning, they have multiple significance. Sometimes they speak of relevance instead of significance.[42] Application is then communicating the present-day significance or relevance of a text and demonstrating how it can lead to appropriate action. This is one of the principal dimensions of expository preaching and lies at the heart of biblical counseling.

Just as there is always a gap between the biblical text and the life situation to which it is to be applied, there is always a danger that application will be faulty. It requires careful monitoring. One must subject any biblical text deemed to be relevant to a particular life situation to careful, independent interpretation before it is applied to that situation. Fundamentalists insist on the separation of interpretation and application—otherwise, they argue, there would be no control over application. It would come to resemble allegory, a reading of unintended meaning into a text, which they roundly condemn. They cite Deuteronomy: "You shall not add to the word which I commanding you, nor take away from it."[43] Arthur Pink sees such allegorical interpretations as twisting "the plainest and simplest texts into the most grotesques shapes or meanings."[44] Jewish Kabbalists, the early Christian theologian Origen, and the eighteenth-century religious mystic Swedenborg are the subject of his venomous attacks. Although a case can always be made for non-figurative readings of Scripture, it is impossible to make such a case for application since it always depends upon a metaphorical link between text and (present-day) context.

Henry A. Virkler, who teaches at Jerry Falwell's Liberty University in Lynchburg, Virginia, attempts to sidestep the problem of metaphorical or figurative linkage through what he calls "principalizing," that is, uncovering through exegesis and interpretation the spiritual, moral, or theological principles behind the biblical text that have relevance today.[45] It should add nothing to the text that is not there. According to Virkler, the temptation of Eve in Genesis 3:1–6 can be read as an outline of one of the ways Satan tempts people today.[46] "The author of Genesis," he writes,

> intended to give us a narrative account of the first temptation—not a psychological analysis of the temptation process. In order for our application of the text (through principalizing) to be valid, it must be firmly grounded in, and thoroughly consistent with, the author's intention. Thus, if the author's intention in a narrative passage was

to describe an event of temptation, it is valid to analyze that passage deductively in order to understand the sequence and process of that particular temptation and see how it might apply to our lives. . . .[47]

Virkler's "principalizing" reading seems allegorical to me. It is certainly open to all the criticisms of allegory the Fundamentalists make; it also reflects their propensity to read Scripture as a series of commands and propositions about reality. Does the performative force of the commands and propositions serve to eliminate, or give the illusion of eliminating, the gap in interpretation and application between Word and experience, text and life, which would otherwise have to be bridged metaphorically?

All the Fundamentalists I talked to emphasized the changes that followed conversion. Paul Conway said, "I am able to—slowly, it seems, very slowly—to act in accordance with Scripture." Ted Winter referred to the "already" and the "not yet": "I'm perfect in Christ, but I'm not yet experiencing it." Ralph Barnes explained the change in theological terms. "But the change, that spiritual transformation, began to quickly make itself evident in my life—though a process we call sanctification, in which we grow in holiness." Others spoke of the love of God they came to know and count on, of a feeling of purpose or worth they had never before experienced, or of a sense of connection with life, with reality, that they began to feel. Still others, less educated for the most part, spoke more concretely in terms of miraculous cures they experienced, of a new confidence that improved their relations at home or at work, of the ability to take control of themselves and their children, of a sense of belonging, of developing meaningful relationships they had never had before, or of containing their tempers, their sexual promiscuity, or even their weight. All of them, either directly or indirectly, referred to the significance the Bible now had for them—the security it gave them.

The sanctification to which Ralph Barnes refers is a spiritual maturing, a becoming holy, a discipline, under the guidance of the Holy Spirit, and requires continual Bible study, prayer, and the vigilant application of biblical precept to one's life. The saved must make their lives as biblical as possible. They must "put on the new self, which in the *likeness of* God has been created in righteousness and holiness in truth."[48] Sanctification, as a discipline or process, is given greater importance in some conservative denominations than in others.[49] It is often ignored or minimized by those preachers, many of them Pentecostalists, who identify sanctification with the baptism in the Spirit and are, in many Fundamentalists' eyes, more interested in counting the souls they have "saved" than in the spiritual welfare of those they claim to have "saved." A South African Fundamentalist once told me that evangelists like Billy Graham or Oral Roberts were like midwives who delivered a baby and then abandoned it. Most of the Fundamentalists I talked to shared the South African's view of revivalists—they found them irresponsible—though they were less graphic in their criticism. Becoming a Christian, the Fundamentalists say, includes membership in a church in which one is ministered to and in which one ministers. It is a way of life, total and consuming, precluding in the stricter churches fellowship with "non-Christians." It is not, however, otherworldly, or world-negating, as are some mystical sects. American Fundamentalists are as concerned about their material well-being as any other Americans.

Sanctification is usually paired with justification—a forensic, or legal, act. Justification "describes what God *declares* about the believer, not what He *does to change* the believer."[50] It brings about no actual change in the believer but guarantees that changes will follow. MacArthur likens it to the declaration of marriage or to a jury's verdict. In linguistic terms it would then be a performative.

> In biblical terms, justification is a divine verdict of "not guilty—fully righteous." It is the reversal of God's attitude toward the sinner. Whereas He formerly condemned, He now vindicates. Although the sinner once lived under God's wrath, as a believer he or she is now under God's blessing. Justification is more than simple pardon; pardon alone still leave [*sic*] the sinner without merit before God. So when God justifies, He imputes divine righteousness to the

sinner (Rom. 4:22–25). Christ's own infinite merit thus becomes the ground on which the believer stands before God (Rom. 5:19; 1 Cor. 1:30; Phil. 3:9). So justification elevates the believer to a realm of full acceptance and divine privilege in Jesus Christ.[51]

Justification is an event; it brings about a change of status the instant it is declared. Sanctification is a process; it changes the believer's inner condition. It makes them holy by conforming their character, affections, and behavior to the image of Christ. "At justification we surrender the *principle* of sin and self-rule, in sanctification we relinquish the *practice* of specific sins as we mature in Christ."[52] Sanctification is effected over time through the offices of the Spirit and the concomitant effort of the believers who, reborn, have ceased in Paul's words to be "slaves of sin" and have become "slaves of righteousness."[53] It is important to stress that, for Reformed Christians, the human effort involved in sanctification gives the believer no merit in God's eyes. Good works simply follow from justification.

MacArthur and other theologians insist that sanctification cannot be separated from justification. They argue that it has an immediate aspect, sometimes called "positional sanctification," which is simultaneous with justification but which continues throughout the believer's life and beyond. Others, such as Charles Ryrie and Zane Hodges, argue for the separation of justification and sanctification.[54] They distinguish between conversion and consecration— the receiving of and surrendering to Christ. In their understanding, justification does not provide the basis for growth in Christ. A second experience is necessary, a decision to become Christ's disciple. The distinction may seem slight to the outsider, but it has been the source of vituperative argument among Fundamentalists. MacArthur and other critics of the second position argue that it can lead to antinomianism, that is, to the belief that behavior is unrelated to faith and thus to the conviction that the "Christian" is not bound by moral law. MacArthur's argument rests on his reading Paul's Letter to the Romans and Calvin's *Institutes of the Christian Religion*.[55] As we might have suspected, it does not rely on personal testimony.

Indeed, MacArthur insists that statements like "I received Christ as my Savior at age seven, and didn't make Him Lord until I was in my thirties," so frequently heard in evangelical circles, "reflect people's misinterpretation of their own experiences."[56]

A phrase like "people's misinterpretation of their own experiences" demands careful consideration if we are to appreciate the role of the Word in the lives of conservative evangelicals. It is a question of priority: the Word has priority over experience, which, subject to the wiles of the flesh, is always untrustworthy. Scripture provides the grid through which experience is to be interpreted, evaluated, and acted upon. This does not seem at first to be that different from anyone's interpretation and evaluation of experience in terms of some set of guidelines—a book of etiquette, for example, a color chart, or a law book. Indeed, some Fundamentalists, at least some of the time, speak in these terms: they look to Scripture as an independent, external, and objective guide for understanding and acting on their experience. But most evangelical Christians mean more than this when they speak of the role of the Word in interpreting and evaluating experience; they insist that the act of interpreting their experiences through Scripture actually changes the way they experience and even perceive the world. Paul Conway said his feelings were "slowly beginning to change, to match what the Bible says." He spoke of how his heart was changing. "I now have new desires that I never had before. I am now changing from inside out." With this profound cognitive, emotional, and spiritual reorientation comes the transformative role of interpretation through Scripture of experience. In evangelical terms, the reborn have surrendered to the Word and are being sanctified. In philosophical terms, the interpretation of experience is immediately realized in the experience itself, at least in its articulation.

The first time I heard Ted Winter speak was in a class he gave on the descriptions of Hell in the Bible. After a long discussion of the various words in Hebrew and Greek that had been translated as hell, he went on to point out a contradiction between two descriptions of Hell, one, *tartaros*, as "pits of darkness" and the other as "a lake of fire which burns of brimstone."[57] He said that he had not been able to resolve this contradiction between these two descriptions, both of which referred to a place of punishment—for angels in Peter, for the beast in Revelations. One elderly woman in the class volunteered that a fireman had told her that the darkest place he had ever been in was the center of a house fire. Ted thanked her patiently. A young man then said that people who had near-death experiences often reported seeing light at the end of a dark tunnel. Ted had no patience with this. "Those are hallucinations and perceptions, and they have to be corrected by Scripture," he thundered.

When I met Ted a few days later, I asked him what he had meant by "corrected by Scripture." He said he had probably overstated his case; that he had in fact meant that all experience has to be evaluated in terms of Scripture; that Scripture said nothing, to the best of his knowledge, about near-death experiences; and that he had really wanted to warn the class about the dangers of the mysticisms that are so popular among New Agers in Los Angeles. Not satisfied with his answer, I raised the question in different ways during our meetings.

"When we met last, " I said in our third interview, "I think I misunderstood you when you spoke of testing perception against Scripture. Is the perception real—"

"It's a real sensory perception, a real experience," Ted interrupted.

"Then it is the interpretation that has to be corrected?"

"Yes, because experiences can come from all kinds of places. A classic line is Ebenezer Scrooge's in *A Christmas Carol*, when he meets the first spirit. He thinks it may come from an undercooked potato. He's trying to find in indigestion the cause for his having experienced something uncomfortable. It could have been indigestion or enthusiasm or demonic spirits or the Holy Spirit. There's a lot of impetus in the world.

"When I came to California, I was a blatant materialist. I didn't realize then, but my religious training was basically scientific materialism. Early in my ministry I'd try to tell people they hadn't experienced the things they had. It took the school of hard knocks to make me realize that that was both a faulty and futile effort. The experience was real. Now they're only real in the neurons of the brain, but they're still real. We have to test them. You don't question the experience. You find some authoritative grid to compare it with. That's the word I didn't use last time. It is key for me and my church. Without an agreed-upon or recognized authority, we are going to be divided. We are going to be hypocrites. The fundamental issue in virtually all religions is where is your authority. For the Brethren it is in inerrant Scripture. For the Catholics it's in Scripture and tradition. The Pentecostals say it's Scripture, prophecy, and the revelations of God. The New Agers have a direct hotline to their other."

Ted laughed. He had referred to himself in earlier interviews as a materialist—and though he talked about having had to change his views, he usually ended up coming back to the position that, however real perceptions are at the neuronal level, they can and must be corrected or tested by Scripture. Through the acceptance of God's Word, the continual study of Scripture, and the careful application of biblical precept to one's own life, with the aid of the Holy Spirit (he was always careful to add) one can actually change the way one perceives the world. He called this process of change "correction." Where he stumbled, in my view, was on the question of time. Sometimes he referred to the change as gradual, as the result of discipline and training; at other times, like many evangelicals, he regarded the change as instantaneous. One woman put it this way: "It's like, well, you have, you almost have, this experience but before you have it, something happens and you see things differently, biblically." I think Ted would have agreed with her.

Ted, no philosopher, did not differentiate between experience and the articulation of experience. He did not ask whether or how the articulation of experience was realized in the experience itself. He was, in my view, a constructionist *manqué*—one who had the authoritative model for his construction. Given that Scripture is inerrant and can only be interpreted in one way, I asked him, is it true that the only way to make one's life biblical is by changing oneself, one's experience, and one's perception of reality. He agreed. But he resisted my argument that the application of Scripture to life is always metaphorical. I think Ted found my argument too intellectual, too motivated by human concerns, too spiritually insensitive. Put in Paul's words, I—my argument—was conformed to the world rather than "to the image of His Son."[58]

Sanctification mediates, I believe, a paradox in Protestant theology, which Martin Luther recognized and described as *simul justus et peccator*, "at once just and sinful."[59] Through Christ's substitutionary atonement, which all Fundamentalists believe in, the "Christian" is freed of his sins. And yet, the reborn are not immune to sin. They are still of the flesh, still human, and therefore subject to temptation. "For that which I am doing I do not understand; for I am not practicing what I *would* like to do, but I am doing the very thing I hate," Paul wrote; Fundamentalists like to quote this when they describe themselves. It is this struggle which is encompassed in sanctification and from which the "Christian" will finally be delivered.

Although sanctification is an individual affair, it has an important (though restricted) communal dimension. Christian mystics typically engage in all sorts of private spiritual exercises, including prayer, meditation, fasting, and self-mortification; Fundamentalists, who have no patience with such practices—read, study, and memorize Scripture both alone and in groups, with family members, in Bible study groups, at Sunday schools, and in church. Though some Fundamentalists are given to introspection and self-scrutiny, it is my impression that, unlike the Puritans—who, to paraphrase the historian Perry Miller, assiduously probed every recess of their being, "leaving no place unexplored in which sin might hide"— today's Fundamentalists tend more to externalize their self-understanding, judging their acts and thoughts as directly as possible in terms of biblical precept. They stress study, testimony, prayer, and fellowship, which is often intensified by hymn-singing, which in turn intensify the experience—the presence—of the Word.

Fundamentalist families usually hold daily Bible-reading sessions, in which, after praying for God's help, they read a passage from the Bible, discuss its meaning, and relate it to their current life. Sometimes they sing hymns or play or listen to religious music. These sessions are usually led by the father of the family. When a difficult decision has to be made or a crisis resolved, the family will pray together. Several people told me that after praying they had opened the Bible at random and found the answer they were seeking in the first verse they read; still others claim to have actually heard God's Word. The last two practices are, of course, condemned by strict Fundamentalists. What is clear is that Scripture mediates family and community relations in complex ways. It allows them to be both personally involved and yet "objectively" removed.

Aside from family Bible-readings, many Fundamentalists go to Bible study groups during the week. The informal Bible study groups usually take place at a church member's home over coffee and cookies. After an opening prayer, the study group leader reads and comments on the passage he—or, more likely, the group—has elected to study. Often the group has a project: working their way through the gospels, for example, or through Paul's letters. In some of the more sophisticated groups, members not only read Scripture but also well-known commentaries. Usually, more formal academic study, including Greek and even Hebrew, takes place at Sunday school or other church classes. (Some of the megachurches give a dozen or more classes each night of the week.) Home study groups are more personal and for the most part are concerned with the practical application of Scripture. A particular passage might inspire someone in the group to discuss a personal problem. Some groups have a theme, such as the role of women in the church, teaching adolescents a biblical approach to life, or being a "Christian" in the workplace. Guidance is sought everywhere in Scripture and through prayer. Rarely does a group maintain its focus on the passage under study. Indeed, some study groups are reminiscent of consciousness-raising sessions or group therapy, though there is probably less probing of the participants' pasts or inner lives.

Bible study not only deepens one's understanding of the Word but also serves a defensive role. It can protect the believer from temptation not only through the wisdom it provides but by displacing the world one lives in—the temptations it offers—with constant, even compulsive reading. Scripture becomes a barrage of words. One loses oneself in it without having to reflect. I remember one preacher referring to the sin of reading, by which he meant getting so lost in what you were reading that you ignored yourself, your responsibilities, family, and church. He was referring to his habit of reading science fiction, but he implied, with caution, that you could also lose yourself in the Bible. He stressed the need to relate what one reads to one's life. He argued that interpretation without application was academic and dead.

When Ron Saywell, who had been converted by his aunt when he was eight years old, was in high school, his parents sent him to Mexico on an exchange program. He was alone, scared, homesick, and suffering sexual temptation. He had never been away from home for more than a few days and he missed his church immensely.

"It was during this period that the Lord was so gracious to me because all external constraints were removed. There was no church keeping watch on me. My aunt was now further than two hours away. My best friend and his family were three thousand miles away. So basically in that period in my life—I would say that it was a turning point—it was just me and God. Everything was internal. I didn't have to keep on being for God. I didn't have to keep on studying Scripture. I didn't have to have a life I knew was the right kind of life. The Mexicans were all Catholic. There was no church for me there. I had to have an absolute dependence on God to keep me from doing something that would have complications for the rest of my life. I was afraid of getting sexually involved with someone. I didn't know what would happen. I didn't know what I'd be getting into. All this made me very conscious of the importance of reading Scripture. I think that during that year I spent probably between six and eight hours a day just in Bible study. Not out of self-righteousness. Part of it was out of an internal desire to learn. And part of it was that I was scared to death I was going to do something that would dishonor God. And I wanted to find out what His words said to keep me from doing that."

Ron ended his story by telling me how, several months after his arrival in Mexico, he finally discovered an American Baptist church which turned out to be only a few blocks from where he was living. He said this with irony, but I could not help feeling that the discovery of the church was a vindication of his biblical discipline.

Ron was able to find protection in Scripture from the temptations that Mexico offered him. But often the saved "fall victim to the flesh" and require counseling in order to continue the work of sanctification. As I have said, Fundamentalists are generally opposed to psychotherapy, psychoanalysis, and psychiatry. Comments like the following are common:

> Except where there is organic difficulty, the root of all conflicts in the home is not mental, but spiritual. Psychology and psychiatry are usually totally irrelevant. A spiritual problem always has a spiritual cause and requires a spiritual solution. . . . Many spiritually discerning persons are quite convinced that psychiatry is Satan's substitute for the biblical remedy for disturbed relations.[62]

Popular accounts of psychiatry and psychoanalysis read like double-demonic tales: the psychologist or psychiatrist who is cast as a demon demonizes his patient's world. Wayne Mack, who teaches biblical counseling at the Master's College and Seminary, summarized a case he had read about somewhere.

"A woman and a man were having some marriage problems. They went to a Christian psychologist. He began to fiddle around with how she got along with her parents. She said, 'Fine. I respect my daddy. He's a great man.' And this psychologist began to subtly introduce lots of suggestions that her father wasn't that great a person. He didn't do that directly but he planted the seeds in her mind: that she was her father's victim, that he had abused her, that in their church they had Satan worship and offered sacrifices. She really bought it. She became resentful and bitter—of her husband too. Her husband went along with all this at first, but finally the stories became so weird that he began to show her that the things she was talking about weren't logical or rational. As she had described having Satan worship and offering sacrifices in the basement of the church, he took her to the church and showed her there was no basement. He wanted to show her reality so she'd know she was having fantasies. Eventually she got over it."

Professor Mack added that this abuse of therapy occurs among Christian as well as secular psychologists. He himself tells his students that you never reproduce the past, you always reconstruct it and therefore cannot—contrary to the claims of secular psychotherapists—trust your reconstructions.

Bruce Narramore, an evangelical psychoanalyst who has promoted the integration of psychology and theology, finds this rejection—indeed, this demonization—of psychology to be characteristic of the Fundamentalists' black-and-white picture of reality. Narramore relates this "cognitive style" to what the English psychoanalyst Melanie Klein called the "paranoid-schizoid position of mental functioning." (He likes to tell people that the most negative thing Ernest Jones, the English psychoanalyst and Freud biographer, could say about Klein was that her work was "basically a maternal vision of original sin.") For Fundamentalists in the paranoid-schizoid position, Narramore explains,

"everything is divided into good or bad. There's a lot of projection here. Cognitive processes are stuck at a very concrete level: 'OK, we've got to have twenty-four-literal-hour days,' or 'Look, if these guys are pro-choice, they're bad by definition.' They can't admit, 'Hey, there are real issues here that need to be looked into.'"

Narramore is quick to add that many psychoanalysts and psychologists are extremists too. They show no understanding or interest in conservative Protestantism. When I met Narramore at his office at BIOLA for the first time, he proudly pointed out that he kept Freud's complete works next to Calvin's.

"They are the two major commentators on the depth of human nature. No one has dealt with sin the way Calvin has. Certainly not behaviorism. Only analysis says there is something in the individual apart from the environment. You may grow up in a 'perfect environment' and still have problems. There's something endemic in the human personality."

Fundamentalists are particularly critical of the marriage of psychological and theological counseling. John MacArthur is of course one of the most vocal critics.[63] He condemns the proliferation of self-help books published by evangelical presses which urge readers to look inside themselves in order to discover the answers to their problems. "Nowhere does Scripture advise people to seek answers by looking within," he writes. "In fact, Scripture explicitly teaches us that we are sinners and should distrust our hearts." He is referring to Jeremiah 17:9-10: "The heart is more deceitful than all else and is desperately sick; who can understand it?" Those who seek within will only get lies, he continues, and therefore psychology cannot help. We have to look to Scripture for answers. We must not sacrifice the sanctification by the Holy Spirit for "psychological sanctification." "Can the earthly therapist achieve more than a heavenly Comforter?"[64] MacArthur asks.

It was in the mid-sixties—when Americans were freeing themselves from the constraints of traditional sexual morality, family values, and social arrangements; when they were experimenting with mind-enlarging drugs, Eastern religions, and exotic rituals and therapies—that the Fundamentalists claim to have "rediscovered" biblical counseling. Jay E. Adams is their hero.[65] He was born in Baltimore in 1929, converted in high school, received a Bachelor of Divinity from the Reformed Episcopal Seminary in Philadelphia before obtaining a B.A. in classics from Johns Hopkins. He later received a master's in Sacred Theology from Temple and a Ph.D. in speech from the University of Missouri. He was ordained in 1952. He has written over sixty books that describe his highly directive, confrontational system of biblical counseling, which he calls "nouthetic," from the Greek *noutheteo*, literally "to place in mind" — to admonish, warn, teach. Like many evangelical pastors, Adams is a man of immense energy. Aside from writing, teaching (at Westminister from 1963 to 1976), lecturing, research, and counseling, he founded a counseling center in Hatboro, Pennsylvania (with affiliates elsewhere in Pennsylvania, New Jersey, and California), a professional organization called the National Society of Nouthetic Counselors, and the *Journal of Pastoral Practice*, which he edited for fifteen years.

Adams's influence on Fundamentalist counseling has been enormous, though, I should note, many Fundamentalist pastors make use of evangelical counseling techniques that Adams would frown upon. I have chosen to focus on Adams's approach to counseling because, like MacArthur's and van Til's work, it reveals, in it extremity, underlying patterns of Fundamentalist thought which may be masked in even slightly more liberal thinking. Adams is the dominant influence on counseling at many Fundamentalist churches and seminaries. More liberal evangelicals have criticized him for rigidity, harshness, oversimplification, insensitivity to intimate relationships, and a behavioral focus on sins rather than sin.[66] Narramore describes Adams's approach to counseling as "Let's get the problem out here on the table; let's analyze it; let's pray about it; let's get Scripture applied to it; and let's get on with life." He questions the competence to counsel that Adams attributes to the ordinary conservative evangelical minister.

As Adams tells it, he discovered how little he had learned about counseling in seminary when, in his first pastorate, he found himself helpless before a parishioner who, unable to speak, had burst into tears.[67] When the parishioner died a month later, Adams became convinced that he had wanted counsel about dying. Adams began reading whatever he could find on counseling and was soon disenchanted. He could not "re-translate what seemed to be sin, as 'sick-ness,'" as many counselors did. As far as he was concerned, calling the effects of sin, sin itself, a sickness was to indulge the sinner and to encourage him to blame others for what he himself had done. He thought it "ludicrous to nod and grunt acceptingly in detachment without offering biblical directives." He found that many patients who had been referred to psychiatrists returned worse off. He be-gan in a hit-or-miss fashion—but, he claims, with success—to use Scriptural exhortation in his counseling.

At Westminister, Adams began to "exegete" every passage in Scripture he felt had a bearing on counseling. His task was mam-moth, he said, because the Bible had so much to say about counsel-ing. Psalms 31, 38, and 51 were concerned with the "psychosomatic effects" of guilt. James 5:14-16 (part of which reads, "Therefore, confess your sins to one another, and pray for one another, so that you may be healed") affirmed the importance of confession. He be-gan to read O. Hobart Mowrer, the learning-theory psychologist whose *Crisis in Psychiatry and Religion* challenged psychiatry and condemned psychoanalysis. Mowrer argued that their medical model released the "ill" from the moral responsibility they had in-curred. He advocated a directive, confessional therapy in which "patients" are made to take responsibility for their actions and, whenever possible, offer restitution to those they have offended. Al-though Adams never became Mowrer's disciple (Mowrer's system gave no place to God and Scripture), he did work with him one summer. "We conducted group therapy with Mowrer for seven hours a day. Along with five others, I flew with him, drove with him, ate with him, counseled together with him, and argued with him five days a week." From his work that summer, Adams con-cluded that patients were suffering simply "because of their unfor-given and unaltered sinful behavior." Their problems were of their own making. "Some had written bad checks, some had become en-tangled in the consequences of immorality, others had cheated on income tax, and so on." It was with this insight, Adams claims in-genuously, that he began to develop his nouthetic counseling. Its understanding of human behavior is so biblically derived that there is little room for human experience and relationship.

Sin is central to Adams's approach to counseling, and, like other Fundamentalists, he seemed to take pleasure in describing it in our interview:

"Sin has cosmic dimensions. The entire universe has been brought into a state of misery. The whole of creation groans like a woman in labor. Man is included as part of that groaning creation, and his misery, which is due to the very existence of sin, is part of the problem of counseling. Counselors must take note of this underlying dimension of guilt, for man is born guilty (culpable) before God. He sinned in Adam. . . . Man is not only guilty in the sense that he has sinned in Adam as his federal or representative head, but man is also corrupt by his relationship to Adam. Man's corruption leads to actual transgressions [and they] bring further misery to his soul. Thus there is a double layer of misery and guilt in men before they are forgiven in Christ."[68]

The theology is pure Calvin. It is Adams's language that is revealing—to the psychoanalyst, to the feminist, indeed, to the gay critic—but they are the enemy, the presumptuous.

Adams's point is that the counselor must begin by acknowledging, and having his client acknowledge, man's sinful nature. Depravity is the ground of what we mistakenly call "mental illness." In my terms, it is an existential—for the Reformed, it is *the* existential condition of man. This, I believe, is what Adams means when he says "man sinned in Adam." Of course, man can do nothing on his own to change his condition; only Christ can. Man can strive, however, always with the help of the Holy Spirit, never alone, to resist temptation. This is what sanctification is all about. As sanctification demands "personality change," so, Adams observes, does nouthetic counseling. "Naturally enough, the problem in counseling is that, contrary to God's mandate, clients have allowed the environment to control them."[69] Man must have dominion over himself (within the limits of his depravity). "The client who whines "I can't; I'm helpless" is simply submitting to the rule of sin in a warped universe set against him." In words that evoke his confrontational method, Adams goes on:

> No Christian has a right to act that way. The Christian's task is to "subdue". . . . By God's grace he can. In this way he may once again reflect the image of God. . . . The picture of man crippled by and in subjection to his environment, cowering before it, crying out that he is helpless . . . is a pitiful distortion of the picture of God's all-powerful rule. . . . Christians, whose basic orientation has been reversed so that they now seek to glorify God, must learn to take the initiative, subdue, and rule. . . . To fail to bring biblical solutions to bear upon problems is to allow sinful conditions to continue. . . . The concept of adaptation to sin is non-biblical.[70]

Cast in biblical language, Adams's message is simple if not altogether simplistic: "You can't say 'can't.'" He notes that in nouthetic counseling certain words are forbidden "because words are not only indicative of but also influence thinking, attitudes, and behavior."[71] No doubt, particularly if one attributes as much importance to words as the Fundamentalists do. The examples that Adams gives confirm his oversimplification. He cites the case of John, who is troubled by masturbation and impure thoughts.

> John was compounding the problem largely by his attendance at pornographic movies. When John presented his problem, he said, "I just feel compelled to go into these movies; I can't resist the impulse. I don't understand it: I walk by and it's as if a magnet were drawing me in." The counselor asked John, "Do you have to walk by the movies in order to get to work?" "No," he replied. "To go home?" "No." "Well why, John, are you down there on the street where those so-called 'art films' are shown?" John had no reply. The simple answer was that John walked down that street in order to be drawn in."[72]

Adams goes on to compare John's contorted state of mind to Paul's, as Paul describes it in Romans 7:15–25. "For that which I am doing, I do not understand; for I am not practicing what I *would* like to *do*, but I am doing the very thing I hate. . . ."

The old desires conflict with the new. Clearly in John's case the problem was exactly that. On the one hand, he wanted to get rid of the habit which was enflaming masturbation and causing a great sense of guilt, but on the other hand, because he enjoyed his sin his actions were counterproductive. To keep from falling over the edge of the precipice, one should move as far back from the edge as possible. This was John's problem. As a starter, he needed to stop frequenting the street where the movies were.

I have quoted John's case at length because it is typical of the cases that Adams, his followers, and other biblical counselors present: thumbnail sketches, abstracted and decontextualized, peppered with manufactured dialogue, sometimes titillating, more often embarrassingly banal. They remind one of the personal examples evangelical preachers give in their sermons. Adams's *The Christian Counselor's Casebook* gives more than a hundred.[73] They have titles—"The Pistol at My Head," "I've Got a Secret," "It Was a Bad Week," "God Is Picking on Me"—and read like mini-treatments for a soap opera. They describe marriage problems, infidelity, threatened divorce, homosexuality, child abuse, shyness, loneliness, drug abuse, alcoholism, rebellious teenagers, fear of death, and resistance to counseling. Each is accompanied by a work sheet, in which the reader is asked to describe the problem and to suggest appropriate "homework" for the client to do before the next meeting.

Here are two examples. Adams calls the first "The Dispirited Minister."

> "What's the use of going on? I work hard all of the time, but no one appreciates it! I visit constantly, but get criticized because I don't visit more. I sacrifice my family for the Lord's work, I preach my heart out, but who cares? I rarely see any change in the members of the congregation. My salary is so low that I can hardly survive, but when my wife took a part-time job the women in the church complained and she had to give it up. Everyone else in the congregation has two automobiles, many of them go to Florida for a couple of weeks each winter, and eat well. We are doing well when we are eating hot dogs. I've had it! Tell me I'm right in thinking of leaving the

ministry and getting a job outside. Couldn't I serve the Lord just as well (or perhaps better) there?"[74]

The questions the students are supposed to answer include: "How would you advise the man?" "Is he contributing to his own problem?" "What are likely to be some of the central failures in his ministry?" "Would you want to see his wife at future sessions?" Students are expected to answer these questions with reference to biblical examples and precepts.

The second example, which I've cut slightly, is called "My Husband's a Peeping Tom."

> "He is, he's a peeping Tom!" Shirley shouted through her tears.
> "It's not true," Les responded. "She once saw me noticing a woman disrobing at an open window two years ago—How could I help it. . . ?"
> "But he goes out at night. . . . He won't tell me why."
> "Pastor, I told her until I got blue in the face why I went out, and she never believed me; so I just don't tell her anything anymore. . . ."
> "Well, tell him about last Tuesday, then!"
> "I've told you a dozen times; it wasn't the way you took it."
> "Oh, wasn't it. Then why did you buy those binoculars. . . ?"

The workbook questions are: "Where do you go from here?" "Is Les a peeping Tom? How will you discover the truth?" "What must you tell Shirley?"

No attention is given to how the student is to construct and to elaborate these minimum scenarios in order to answer the questions. They are like projective tests: one sees in them what one wants. In elaborating the case and in answering the questions, the student is forced to make unreflected and often stereotypic assumptions about motivation and behavior, which are questioned, if at all, by contrast with what are thought to be relevant biblical passages. But, as we have seen, because the same "psychological" assumptions are made in the interpretation of the Bible, they are rarely challenged. Scripture, read as the Fundamentalists read it, does *not* then offer a way to evaluate critically the associations the scenarios evoke. Its control is morally and spiritually preceptual but without recognition of the fact that all moralities, including the biblical, are grounded in a series of culturally and historically determined psychological presuppositions that require critical elucidation. Nouthetic counselors like Morris and Clark suppose a power of the will, abetted or not by the Holy Spirit, that I find altogether unrealistic.[75] Their understanding of sex is often mechanical. John's counselor assumed that if he kept away from pornographic movies, he would stop masturbating. A counselor I know ordered a married airline stewardess who had a man wherever she landed to stop letting the men know she was in town. "Call your husband instead," he recommended.

Nouthetic counseling stresses the "what" rather than the "why," Adams observes, because the "why"—man's sinful nature—is already known before counseling begins.[76] Al Carpenter, a counselor from New Mexico at a gigantic church in Orange County told me, "We don't wait around for weeks or months or even years for the counselee to come up with what's bothering him. We have God on our side. We work in the presence of God—primarily with the born-again. They know Christ died for their sins. We always begin with a prayer. If the counselee starts hedging, I tell him we can't waste time. God will listen to no bull."

Once the problem is discovered, the counselor confronts his client with its sinful nature. "We warn him; we admonish him; we teach him," Al said, parroting Adams's words. "We get him to acknowledge his guilt. That's always a big step forward." Adams warns counselors not to be softhearted, for then they are "most unmerciful" to their clients.[77] They must insist on their clients' responsibility and direct them to rectify their situation. As an example of nouthetic confrontation, Adams likes to quote Nathan's reproof of David for having Uriah, Bathsheba's husband, killed.[78] "You call a spade a spade," Al said. "You don't futz around with a lot of past history. Christ has taken care of that. You don't want to create dependency relations. I rarely see counselees more than four or five times."

Biblical counseling is short term, but usually not so abrupt and unloving as Al's comments suggest. (*Noutheteo*, Powlison tells us, "is associated with intense love: for example, Paul's 'admonishing with tears' in Acts 20:31 and his 'as my beloved sons I admonish you' in 1 Corinthians 4:14."[79]) It often lasts for six or more months. Rarely is there more than one meeting a week, though some counselors are quite flexible and may even ask their clients to call them at home. Usually, counseling sessions involve couples or whole families. Adams prefers to have two counselors present at every session. Many male counselors insist on having a female colleague present when they work with women. Counseling and teaching are among the few "church professions" open to women.

Like some family therapists, biblical counselors give their clients homework assignments. These range from confessing and apologizing to those one has wronged, to preparing budgets (for the spendthrifty) and schedules (for the disorganized), which they then have to show to their counselor. Assignments, particularly difficult ones involving other people, are often role-played during counseling. Carpenter advised a client who had been unfaithful to list the things she liked about her husband. He had them pray together silently each night. "You have to teach through the heart," he explained. "They weren't ready yet for more open communication. They'd have just sat around cursing each other out." Most assignments require the reading and memorizing of Bible verses that are thought relevant to the client's troubles. Adams makes considerable use of proverbs. For the quick to anger, he might suggest Proverbs 14:29: "He who is slow to anger has great understanding. But he who is quick-tempered exalts folly." For those who worry, a counselor might assign Philippians 4:6–7: "Be anxious for nothing, but in everything by prayer and supplication with thanksgiving let your requests be made known to God. And the peace of God, which surpasses all comprehension shall guard your hearts and your minds in Christ Jesus." Clients are told to think about these verses whenever they anger or worry and to keep them in mind as they pray. Adams points out that the Bible offers the counselor not grand theories but specific, practical guidance.[80]

One of the most popular techniques used by nouthetic counselors is the conference table. Families are instructed to sit down each evening to discuss their problems at a table which, Adams suggests, should have no other use.[81] It marks a special occasion, one in which "Christian communication" is reestablished. "Tables tend to draw people together," Adams says; they "soon become a symbol of hope, a place where previous problem have been solved successfully." Conference table rules reflect the Fundamentalists' idealized family organization and values. The father "as head of the home" calls the conference; the mother acts as secretary. Adams notes that "as one of the most prevalent problems in marriage is a reversal of the role of husband and wife," counselors should take every opportunity, including the organization of the conference table meeting, "to structure the proper relationship." The conference begins and ends with prayer. Each family member sets out his own failures "thereby preempting possible accusations by others around the table." By talking about him- or herself—failures, fears, and sins— the family member is said to open up communication and help.

It is, of course, delicate to ask people what happens at the conference table. Some families seem to have found it very helpful. Several other families I talked to said it had helped them but stopped when their problems were solved. Tim, a man in his twenties who had left his church when he went to college, said he and his sister dreaded the table; his father insisted on it each evening.

"He didn't care if we had homework or a date or were missing a game. He'd just make us sit there and listen to him and Mom rattle off their sins. Then he'd ask us to 'talk about our daily wrongs.' That's how he put: 'our daily wrongs.' We had nothing to say. I'd have nothing to say. Annie—that's my sister—was better at it than me. She always managed to say something and get us off the hook."

It does not seem to matter to Adams whether clients have been unfaithful, abused children, overspent, stolen, raged out of control, had an abortion, or become depressed, dissociated, or homosexual. All of these practices are sinful or caused by sin, and the treatment is basically the same. What varies is the content. Remember Adams's focus on the *what* and not the *why*. In practice, no doubt, different techniques are used for different problems, but there is very little reflection on the relationship between technique and problem. It is a matter of the counselor's intuition, constrained, however, by Scripture. How often have I heard counselors say, "As X was describing his problem, it occurred to me . . ." or "I was reminded of a passage in . . ." or "I suddenly thought of . . ." Sometimes, particularly among conservative evangelicals of a more charismatic bent, these "intuitions" are attributed to the Holy Spirit. Teaching counseling proceeds through example rather than theory and thus coordinates with Adams's insistence that the Bible focuses on concrete instances rather than generalities.

Adams insists that the pastor, who has knowledge of Scripture, goodness, and wisdom—by which he means the ability to apply what he knows to concrete situations in a biblically acceptable fashion—is as competent, indeed more competent, to counsel than the psychologist or psychiatrist.[82] He justifies his position, not on empirical grounds but on Scriptural ones, by referring to Romans 15:14: "And concerning you, my brethren, I myself also am convinced that you yourselves are full of goodness, filled with all knowledge, and able also to admonish one another." He translates the last phrase, "nouthetically confronting one another." He argues, again on the basis of Romans, that since a counselor must be familiar with Scripture, a seminary education is better preparation for counseling than graduate study in clinical psychology or medicine.[83]

Nouthetic training is practical, concrete, specific, on-the-job. It does not acknowledge the need to develop insight and a self-critical perspective in the counselor; it does not rationalize training on any theoretical grounds that might offer such a perspective. Students learn primarily by discussing cases, like those I quoted from Adams, with little regard to overarching theories of personality and its aberrations. The counselor is not required to go through any form of self-analysis. He is not given any systematic guidelines for even choosing relevant passages from the Bible. Indeed, the importance given to Scripture seems to deflect the significance of experience—to preclude, or at least limit, nuanced understanding of both client and counselor and their relationship. Insofar as he works as truly as possible with Scripture, the counselor is in a sense — I exaggerate perhaps — free from responsibility for failure. His authoritarian position in counseling mirrors the patriarchal role of the father among Fundamentalists. I have found that women counselors defer to the authority of their male colleagues or their preachers, at least when they discuss what takes place during counseling. (I cannot of course speak of what actually happens during therapy.)

The evangelical Christian would, of course, counter my critique of Adams by noting first that he is talking about counselors who have been saved and are being sanctified. The discipline of sanctification, they would argue, is certainly as rigorous as any analysis the secular psychotherapist might undergo, and unlike such analyses, it is backed by God's Word and the Holy Spirit rather than by human theoretical speculation. It is the Word that offers a critical perspective, the only true critical perspective. It must have priority over experience for the saved, as they strive to conform to it. The evangelical Christian might add that seminary study is entirely different from study at medical schools, secular universities, or psychoanalytic institutes because it takes place in a prayerful setting under the guidance of the Holy Spirit and does not divorce theoretical study from practical application. As for the choice of Scripture, a Fundamentalist would argue that aside from the practical knowledge of Scripture taught at seminary and the guidance of the Holy Spirit, Scripture, as the Word of God, is always helpful.

Many Fundamentalist pastors — by no means all or, I suspect, even the majority — are more flexible than Adams and have the wisdom to recognize the limits of their competence. They are perhaps more sensitive than Adams to styles of personality, depth of hurt, the fragility of the self, and the fear and turmoil that can beset even the evangelical Christian. I think many would be reluctant to accept Adams's observation that "it is a serious question whether a Christian whose conscience judges him according to the explicit standards of Scripture can ever become seriously depressed over the guilt of sin committed without that sin being 'ever before him.'"[84] Pastors often consult with one another over difficult cases, send those they cannot handle to more qualified counselors and even to psychiatrists if they suspect a "medical" problem. More than one counselor I talked to stressed, with what I took to be relief, the organic basis of many psychoses. They were not opposed to use of mood-altering drugs such as Prozac if there were sufficient "medical" reasons for doing so and if its use did not encourage a flight from responsibility.

Of the counselors I talked to, Wayne Mack was the most insistent on the need to cultivate a compassionate, respectful, though never indulgent, relationship with his clients.[85] I asked him how he treated psychotics. After warning me to be careful with what he was about to say, because it could be misunderstood and misused, Professor Mack quoted Ecclesiastes 9:3: "Furthermore, the hearts of the sons of men are full of evil, and insanity is in their hearts throughout their lives." He explained:

"Insanity is then in all our hearts. It is not a difference in kind but a matter of degree. From our perspective the only sane thing to do is to view life the way God sees it. Only He knows reality as it really is. If I am going to understand reality, either I have to be God or to receive information from Him. Now, to the degree that I move away from God's description of reality—and that is revealed in Scripture—to that degree, as I am using the word, I become insane. A sound mind is a mind that is totally conformed to God's perspective. Every thought is brought captive and made obedient to Jesus Christ, as Paul says it. So as people move farther and farther away from God's perspective on reality, the more bizarre, the weirder they become. (Of course I'm assuming that they don't have something organically wrong with them, like a tumor on their pituitary gland.)

"Well, I worked with a guy in Louisiana, when I was there for time. He was a spindly little kid, not very athletic, always picked on. He began to view the world as a very frightening place. People were out to get him. He began to generalize his experience: 'Everybody's out to get me.' Imagine living like that. He started doing some pretty bizarre things. He picked up on voodooism. He got out his school yearbook and passed a fire over photographs of the people who picked on him. Bitterness and resentment had grown up in his heart. If you view everybody as out to get you, you don't have confidence in the sovereignty of God—a God you can trust to take care of you—even if something pleasant happens to you.

"Now what do you do with somebody who is out of touch with reality? In some instances, and there are illustrations in the Bible, like David feigning madness, people behave in strange ways as a diversionary tactic—to evade responsibility, for example.[86] So if we observed this in a counselee, we'd call him to account and say, 'Cut out the nonsense.' But, if in his heart, he really believes these things—and that's always possible—then over a period of time, we'd try to establish some kind of relationship with him, some kind of involvement, that we could build on.

"With the guy from Louisiana, you try to bring him to the place where David was when he came against Goliath. Goliath was huge, and David was small. But David didn't compare himself to Goliath. He compared Goliath to God. Had he compared himself to Goliath, he would have said, 'I can't handle Goliath. I'm smaller.' But, by comparing Goliath to a God—a God David trusted—he trusted God to give him the strength to deal with Goliath. With hope, we'd try to accomplish this."

I asked Professor Mack how he treated homosexuality. He noted that there is no proof of any physiological or genetic cause for it and went on to criticize a conservative evangelical church he had heard about in the San Francisco area. The church had argued that, as there is a "gene" for homosexuality, God must have willed it, and that therefore homosexual practices can be "Christian."

"The way I see it, a person may have a predisposition to homosexuality the way I have a predisposition to get angry or whatever. The point is that a predisposition does not mean I have to—or ought to—act on it. People call us homophobic. Actually, we're not. We love regardless of that. I would be just as opposed to somebody who was an adulterer. Am I then adulterophobic? I'm opposed to murder. Am I murderophobic? Since my values and standards come from God, I love them and want to help them change. I've worked with many homosexuals and people who commit incest.

"The Bible is clear about homosexuality. In 1 Corinthians 6:9–11, Paul says: 'Do not be deceived; neither fornicators, nor idolaters, nor adulterers, nor effeminate'—'effeminate' here refers to men who take the female role in homosexual relations—'nor homosexuals, nor thieves, nor the covetous, nor drunkards, nor revilers, nor swindlers, shall inherit the kingdom of God.' Now, God never says you can't be part of his kingdom because of your genetic makeup. If they are excluded from the Kingdom of God, it is because of their lifestyle. We're not just talking here about episodes but lifestyle. The next verse says, 'And such were some of you.' Paul is saying, 'This is what you were, but you are no longer that. You've changed.' He says, 'But you were washed, but you were sanctified, but you were justified in the name of the Lord Jesus Christ, and in the Spirit of God.' Back at that time, Corinth was a cesspool. 'To Corinthianize' was about the worst thing you could say about a person. So Paul went there and preached the Gospel, and the people who were doing all these things changed. Because of our commitment to Scripture, we say it can't be genetic. The most we can say is that there may be a predisposition, which is not irresistible. And the fact of a predisposition isn't even proven. From the way Scripture presents it, it is learned behavior. Apart from that, we really don't know a lot about it. I mean there are a lot of different theories, and they don't agree. But as believers, however strong our sex desires may be, by the Grace of God and the Holy Spirit, we can control its expression."

Professor Mack has given a lot of thought to the role of hope in counseling and sanctification.[87] He is careful to distinguish between true and false hope. False hope is based on what is pleasurable and desirable in human terms, often on a denial of reality, on mystical or magical thinking, on an unbiblical view of prayer, and on the improper interpretation of Scripture. True hope comes, according to Mack, with salvation and requires daily renewal. It is a

realistic choice—we can choose to be hopeful or without hope—
that is based on the study of God's Word. The author of Psalm 130,
Mack notes, cries from out of the depths, "I wait for the Lord, my
soul does wait, and in His word do I hope." It is not a speculative
hope but a "believing" one secured by the promises of an all-
powerful God, which, as Mack understands it, what happens to
others, rather than to oneself.

As I read Professor Mack's description of true and false hope, I
was struck by the tension between the particularity of true and false
hope on the one hand, and the sweeping vision of redemptive history evoked by "God's plan for the universe" and deemed essential
for true hope on the other. In all that I had read about biblical counseling and in almost all my interviews, particularly when we were
talking about the application of Scripture, but also about its meaning, little reference was made to this vision. Fundamentalists
seemed bogged down in concrete detail. They mistrust formal
prayer. They strive for a personal relationship with Jesus, one that I
often found embarrassingly intimate and simple. When I was being
witnessed, I was corrected when I spoke too abstractly and addressed the topic of God in an impersonal manner. Professor Mack
stresses the need to develop a client's personal rather than historical
relationship with Jesus.[88] By "historical" he means something more
akin to autobiography than history in the ordinary sense, as when
someone answers the question, "Are you a Christian?" with "Yes, I
accepted Jesus as my Savior when I was four."

———————

Despite contextualization, Fundamentalists tend to read Scripture
as though it were an instruction manual, verse by verse, passage by
passage, story by story, always in a very narrow manner, with little
regard for context. They seem fearful not just of ambiguity, not just
of figurative language, but of the power of narrative itself—the interpretive possibilities it offers. Testimonies, confessions, conversion stories, case histories, the incidents pastors use to make a point
in their sermons are taken at face value. Little attention is given to
rhetoric and the implications, though recognized, of literary genre

on their understanding of Scripture. I once shocked a Fundamentalist friend by referring to the genre of testimony. There seems to be little room for depth in their vision, no desire to explore it. ("Depth" is of course a metaphor, historically and culturally constituted and evaluated, romantic perhaps, a precipitate of a particular interpretive style, a style of reading. It should be distinguished from profundity, as in the profundity of the doctrine of original sin, which cannot be denied to the Fundamentalists.) There is, I find, a bravado in the Fundamentalists' stress on surface: they are pragmatists, very much in the American grain, with no patience for what they see as intellectual obfuscation and cultural chicanery. Their discussions and monographs on systematic theology are prefaced by apologies and rely on biblical citation rather than theoretical elaboration. Adams, always critical of generalization, notes that one of the "amazing facts" about the Bible "is the concreteness with which even the most profound doctrine is given."[89]

The Word taken in its "true" (that is, literal) sense gives—and this is most difficult for the outsider to comprehend—the Fundamentalist's historical existence a timeless dimension, one that denies history even as it affirms it in its redemptive sense. Adams has suggested that the "seed" of every major problem encountered in counseling today is to be found in the Garden of Eden, at the time of the Fall, when "history" and "time" as we know them began.[90] (I shall treat this paradox in the next chapter.) At a more mundane level, we should note that in biblical counseling, more generally in the process of sanctification, and, indeed, in Bible study and application, submitting to the Word does give the Fundamentalists transcending occasion. Adams, among others, frequently cites 1 Corinthians 10:13: "No temptation has overtaken you but such as is common to man; and God is faithful who will not allow you to be tempted beyond what you are able, but with the temptation will provide the way of escape also, that you may be able to endure it."[91] Not only does this verse promise the capacity to endure temptation but, according to Adams, it offers hope to both counselors and clients; for they know that others have endured and overcome the problems before them.

Like other conservative evangelicals, Adams makes no attempt to articulate this identification in terms of the sweep of redemptive history that Christianity proposes and the Bible describes. Does the Fundamentalists' literalism, their focus on the specific and the concrete, preclude such an articulation? Does their stance toward the Word, however central it may be theologically, relegate it to mere background? For me, the Fundamentalists' approach to Word and meaning loses them in the detail, at times selfishly, at times with generosity. It impedes, if it does not preclude, the power of transcendence that the divine narrative might offer if granted its full figurative possibility. That, of course, is my presumption. Belief, the experience of belief, always defies description and evaluation, particularly when it is attributed to others. Indeed, the personal attestation of belief—"I believe in," "I believe that"—obtains much of its force from its resistance to description and in consequence our reluctance to evaluate it. Yet I cannot say that the progress of sanctification and the efficacy of biblical counseling, for which its practitioners make enormous claims, is negatively affected by its failure to carefully articulate and forcefully place the "Christian" in redemptive history. It has been said that the failure of psychoanalysis and other secular therapies—the Fundamentalists would call them humanist therapies—is the failure to offer their patients a transcending position in a resonantly transcendent story. Freud may have found the Oedipus complex to be universal, but the attestation of universality can never have the power of sacred narrative.

The fact that the Fundamentalists I spoke to and read did not speak about themselves and their world in terms of redemptive history does not mean that they were not affected by it. They are, I believe, profoundly affected by it, but at a remove: it provides them with a resonant matrix for understanding and situating themselves in the world. It manifests itself in the security they feel in their *own* salvation (rather more their own, I suspect, than Professor Mack would like) and in their hope. They believe themselves to be truly favored—God's elect—and they understand, at least some of the time (they are human, after all), that as they have been so favored they have a responsibility to live by the Word for the glorification of

God. That they accrue benefits from this, they do not doubt. Of course the theologically knowledgeable acknowledge that they receive no merits, no guarantee of entry into Heaven, from it. By and large, they are practical people. The benefits are in this world though oriented toward the future. They receive—I am certainly not doing justice to all that they receive—security, "believing hope," moral and spiritual guidance, structure, and understanding (even if that understanding posits an inability to understand). It is a confidence, I suppose, that allows them to acknowledge their sin and, in Professor Mack's words, to find in that acknowledgment "truly good news, because then there is plenty of hope," for Christ has delivered them from the power of sin and will eventually free them from its very possibility.[92] Through His intercession, through the Word and the power of the Holy Spirit, sanctification affords them the possibility of true communication. "Truth which is held in common, shared, and believed by all the parties who communicate," Adams writes, "is the foundation for all significant communication."[93]

As the gap between God and man is closed, so is the gap between man and man, producing thereby, as one awaits the Second Coming, a sense of loving fellowship. This fellowship, however, separates the Fundamentalists from others who may be as sincere in their belief or disbelief.

3—History

I asked Ralph Barnes if history is a relevant concept for understanding the Bible.

"What exactly do you mean by history?" Ralph asked.

"That's the question. Can we talk about the Bible as 'history' the way we can talk about a book that describes what happened in the nineteenth century in America as 'history'?"

"I'm hesitating, because I'm still not sure what you mean by 'history.' Here's how I would approach it. Genesis 1:1: 'In the beginning God created the heavens and the earth.' There came a point in time where, in the plan and purpose of God, He brought Creation into being—the entire physical realm of Creation. So in terms of a created order, history began, according to Genesis 1:1, at that moment. What you have seen since then is an unfolding of events that God has predetermined from all eternity past. And in His sovereign will, He has chosen to permit the corruptibility of His creation for reasons known to himself. Satan was created as an angel with no sin.

"We look at the Bible, Genesis through Revelation, and, because we live in this vacuum, we see it in relation to ourselves. But if you look at it from a divine perspective, there is much more. In other words, we are not the end of all things. Man is not the purpose of all existence. God is the purpose of all existence. In His plan, He had a purpose for bringing forth creation—ultimately, to bring glory and honor to Himself. Man was created to honor and glorify God. Now sin caused the purpose of God not to be fulfilled as He would have desired, but in His eternal plan, He made provision for the abolishment of sin and the redemption of His creation. Paul tells us this in Romans 8.

"I am saying all this for a reason. You see an unfolding of events that began in Genesis 1:1, with Creation, and you know that has led up to you and me sitting here right now. And that's going to continue on its present course in various stages—dispensations. We are now living in the Church Age which began at Pentecost and will continue until rapture. There will be seven years of tribulation during which God will bring judgment to this earth, and they will be followed by the return of His son, Jesus Christ, who will establish a literal thousand year rule upon this earth, at the end of which the mass of fallen humanity will rebel against Christ. He will thwart that rebellion, and God will once and for all bring an end to sin and death. It says in Revelation 20 that death and Hades are cast into the lake of fire. It also says in Revelation 20 that the heavens and the earth fled away. What you see is a picture that also receives light from 2 Peter 3: the material-created realm goes out of existence. And in Revelations 21, God recreates it, so that you have totally new created realm.'

"Now it's at the end of the millennium—the New Heaven, New Earth will remain in a perfect state for all eternity. As God has revealed, there will be no change. God will have an interaction with His created beings: an eternal relationship with them. They will not be subject to corruption. The fascinating thing is that the Second Person of the Trinity, Jesus Christ, will be for all eternity the God-Man. He has a body—a human body. Now it's glorified and immortal, resurrected, and yet God has taken on the form of His Son—human flesh. Now, that's heavy."

"But anyway, all that's to say that history—" Ralph was quite confused by this time and interrupted himself. "Yeah, there is a literal people: Israel. I went there last summer. I saw the places where they lived. I drank water from the well that Jacob dug three thousand eight hundred years ago. So there is literal history. It happened."

"But the events described in the Bible, excluding Revelations, stop at a certain point," I said. "The Bible does not literally describe the Reformation, for example."

"Well, even in the four Gospels you have roughly three and a half years of Jesus's ministry contained in four short books. So Scripture is not exhaustive."

Ralph was apologetic.

"Right, but if you draw a chronology from the beginning of creation until now, part of that is covered specifically, literally, in the Bible, and part is obviously not in Scripture."

"You could take the book of Acts up to roughly 62 A.D." Ralph said.

"Right," I said. "Now there is a difference between what is recounted in the Bible and what follows, say, 62 A.D. Is the notion, the sense of history in the Bible, as you read it, different from the notion of history that treats later events? That's not in the Bible?"

"Well, here's the difference. History is personal experience. When Satan came to Eve, that was personal experience. What Eve chose to do was to rely on her own personal experience and her evaluation of that experience. She deemed herself to be competent to become the judge of truth rather than trusting the revelation of God.

"Of course, the Bible records the errors of men. It records the error of Peter when he tried to dissuade Jesus Christ from going to the cross and said, in Matthew 16, 'No Lord, this shall never happen to You.' Jesus rebuked him. So the Bible recorded Peter's error. It records the sin of David. Now these are untruths that are stated in the Bible, by men, but they are not given as propositional truth. In other words, when Satan said, 'You shall not die,' that was a lie. Within the context, we can see that it was a lie. . . .

"Now, if we were to try to determine the principles of life from the French Revolution, that would be like letting experience be the judge of truth. It would be saying, 'This is what I believe is the right thing to do.' Or it would be like a man, for example, who said, 'Oh, my daughter has become pregnant and cannot really bear the financial responsibility, therefore, in light of the situation, I've changed my opinion about abortion.' And so on. This man changes his position because it was based on personal experience. Whether you look at experience today or two hundred years ago or even within the Bible, the errors of man cannot become the judge of truth. . . .

"Scripture will often give the interpretation of actions. When Peter rebuked Jesus and said, 'This shall never happen to You,' Jesus rebuked Peter. He told him that his thinking was influenced by

Satan. He said, 'Get behind Me, Satan, for you are not putting your mind on God's thoughts but on men's.' So you see we can learn directly from the context of Matthew 16 that even though Peter thought he was doing a good thing by trying to keep his friend from being crucified, Jesus informed him that his thinking was in error. He corrected him by saying in effect, 'You're thinking on a human plane. If I'm not crucified, there can be no redemption.'"

Ralph went on to discuss the "reliability" of the Bible, arguing that where the Bible does not speak on specific issues, it still gives adequate truth from which principles can be derived for responding to these issues.

I questioned Ralph about history after several equally confused conversations with other Fundamentalists about history. We clearly did not have the same thing in mind when we talked about history. These conversations went something like this: I would ask, "Well, in that case, how do you look upon nonbiblical history?" or "Is there anything to be learned from history that is not in the Bible?" or, as with Ralph, "Do you approach events that have occurred after those in the Bible the same way you do those that are recounted in the Bible?" The occasion was of little importance. My interlocutors were puzzled by my questions. I soon realized that "nonbiblical history" made no sense to them because biblical history was all-comprehensive, extending from eternity past to eternity future. Given the eschatological books in the Bible, such as Revelation and Daniel, nothing could exceed its scope. I tried, as I did with Ralph, to rephrase my questions about "postbiblical history" by eliminating these endtime texts. To no avail. Either the person did not understand what I was talking about or, like Ralph, took refuge in Genesis or some other biblical passage deemed relevant.

My interlocutors simply could not exclude any book or even verse of the Bible from consideration. Scripture was too solidly cohesive. What then was the nature of this cohesion? Clearly, it involved more than the thematic unity of God's revelation, for that unity, at least in detail, poses interpretive problems for even the strictest Fundamentalists, who have had to find support for it in a reconciling dispensational theology. Nor could one attribute cohesion to the references in later biblical texts to earlier ones, nor to a sense of organic linkage between ideas and their later development.[1] They did not seem to me—at any rate—to be sufficient to the Fundamentalists' understanding. It was equally clear that canonical authority could not explain biblical cohesion.

As I struggled to make sense of the Fundamentalists' notion of history, I became less and less satisfied with my understanding of their sense of biblical cohesion. I was paying too much attention to what they said about it, to their theories of interpretation, and not enough on their practice of reading. Fundamentalists could and often did talk about single books (not to mention chapters and verses) of the Bible. True, their explication of these books, chapters, and verses invariably made use of others. I had looked at this extension in terms of their desire to clarify the text they were considering by comparing the meaning of words and phrases in it—or, more broadly, its message—with those in other passages. I had also understood their continual (and, in my view, often promiscuous) citation of verses throughout the Bible—as a way to demonstrate their authority, their knowledge of Scripture, or (especially among Pentecostalists) of virtually drumming away contradictions, troubling ambiguities, and counterrealities.

All of us who were required to read Francis Bacon's "Of Studies" in school know that the way people evaluate a text affects the way they (ought to) read it. "Some books are to be tasted," Bacon wrote, "others to be swallowed, and some few to be chewed and digested."[2] Students of anthropology and literature will read an ethnography in very different ways. Anthropologists read for information and theory, whereas students of literature look, for example, to the way an ethnography is constructed, the way "facts" and "theory" serve rhetorically to support that construction. These differences relate not only to their different goals but also to how they were taught to read in their respective disciplines. I was struck many years ago by the way my Moroccan field assistant, Yousef Hazmaoui, read *Uncle Tom's Cabin*, which I had given him. Yousef could read French and Arabic but, with the exception of a few pages from Victor Hugo's *Les Misérables* in a French textbook, he had never read a novel. A few days after he had begun reading *Uncle Tom's Cabin*, I noticed three different bookmarks in it. He explained that he liked the book so much that he had begun rereading it before he had finished it for the first time, and had even begun rereading the part he had already read twice. By the time he had finished the novel (if one can speak of his ever having finished it) he cycled so many readings into each other that he had produced what seemed to me to be an arabesque comprehension—a megareading—of it. Yousef was, in fact, a good reader; he had simply not learned our conventions of reading literature.

Our everyday notion of literacy, and often the tests by which we measure it, reduce highly complex processes of encoding and decoding information to simple, mechanical procedures. They tend to ignore the understanding and evaluation of reading and writing and the effect of this understanding and evaluation on the practices themselves. We know that there have been dramatic changes in the way people read since Roman times. As scholars such as Walter Ong have pointed out, there has been a move from the aural, characteristic of oral societies, to the visual, which can be associated with literate and especially print cultures—a move from reading aloud through silent vocalization to the nonvocalization of speed-reading.[3] Saint Augustine found worthy of comment the fact that Saint Ambroise, the bishop of Milan, read silently: "When he read, his eyes scanned the page and his heart explored the meaning, but his voice was silent and his tongue was still."[4] He surmised that Ambroise read silently because he did not want to be bothered by visitors who might want to ask him about some difficult point they heard him read or simply to save his voice for his sermons. What Augustine did not mention, though it no doubt affected his surprise, was that Ambroise thought hearing to be more reliable than sight. In his *Commentary on Luke*, Ambroise wrote, "Sight is often deceived, hearing serves as a guaranty."[5]

As I thought about the relationship between reading and cohesion, I realized that I had been ignoring an important dimension of Fundamentalist interpretation, a dimension that had been brought up in almost all my interviews—namely, the prophetic. I had assumed naively that when Fundamentalists talk about prophecy they are talking about either the Old Testament prophets or the way the Bible can be used to predict future historical events. Sometimes they do speak this way. They are far from immune to best-sellers like Hal Lindsey's *The Late Great Planet Earth*, which understands contemporary events in biblical terms and makes predictions on the basis of this understanding. The Russians (Lindsey's book was published in 1970) are understood in terms of Ezekiel 38 as Gog who will attack Israel and be completely crushed in the last great world war.[6] The professors and students with whom I talked were very critical of these works, arguing that it was one thing to recognize this prophetic dimension and quite another to make specific historical predictions from Scripture, and that to do so was to misread the Bible and encourage cults and occultism.

Yet such prophecies, or at least the biblical analogies upon which they are based, occasionally crept into what they and other theologians who shared their views had to say. Ted Winter, who is in principle opposed to such prophecies, admitted that he could not resist books like Lindsey's. In his explication of the prophetic meaning of "north," as it occurs in the Bible, Walter Kaiser, who is usually careful to restrict allusions to the north to biblical ones, such as Assyria, Babylon, or the Syrian monarchs, suddenly refers to the former Soviet Union when he discusses Gog in Ezekiel.[7] Most seminarians were particularly distressed by doomsday predictions and those announcing the date of the millennium. They were embarrassed and outraged by the easy prophecies of many popular preachers, who, they said, gave their Christianity a bad name. They themselves were in fact more concerned with intrabiblical prophecy or what we, in a more secular spirit, might call its proleptic or prefigurative dimension.

Evangelicals who are interested in prophecy often emphasize its importance in Scripture in quantitative terms.[8] They like to note that of 31,124 verses of the Bible, 8,352, (roughly 27 percent) are concerned with predictions of the future. Only Ruth, the Song of Solomon, Philemon, and 3 John, they say, have no prophetic passages. They have even numbered the prophetic topics: 737. The conservatives, certainly the Fundamentalists, do not read the prophetic texts in terms of their revolutionary potential. They tend here, as elsewhere, to read anachronistically, projecting their sense of time and history back onto ancient Israel. They ignore the tension, for example, between an earlier cultic sense of time in which primordial, or "saving," events were (as the Heidelberg theologian Gerhard von Rad sees it) made immediately present during sacred festivals and a later, linear sense, in which unrepeatable events were understood to follow on one another chronologically.[9] They recognize that the prophets introduced an eschatological sense of time, one oriented toward the future rather than toward a reactualization of the past, as in these early festivals. However, they ignore the historical consequences of this temporal reorientation and how it relates to their own expectant sense of time. Even more significantly, they stress the predictive over the social-critical dimension of prophecy. They do not take the prophets' social criticism to be imperatives for social change. They look askance, for example, at Walter Brueggemann, a member of the United Church of Christ, whose well-known book on the prophetic imagination advocates a "prophetic ministry" that is critical of the dominant culture in order to energize the faithful by offering them, as Moses did, an alternate to that culture. (Brueggemann is less interested, I should note, in addressing specific public issues than in challenging, as Isaiah and Jeremiah did, the ways in which a dominant culture co-opts and domesticates any alternate.[10])

Fundamentalists are, in my experience, less troubled by prophetic activism than by the language of prophecy, which tends to be figurative and resists specification. Bernard Ramm notes that there is no "royal road" to the study of prophecy because prophetic Scriptures are so extensive and their language so ambiguous.[11] He quotes favorably Robert Girdlestone's *The Grammar of Prophecy*, which was written almost a century ago.

> That which makes the language of prophecy so vivid and yet so difficult is that it is always more or less figurative. It is poetry rather than prose. It abounds in peculiar words and expressions which are not usually to be found in prose writings of the same date. It is rich with allusions to contemporary life and to past history, some of which are decidedly obscure. The actions recorded in it are sometimes symbolical, sometimes typical. The present, the past, and the future, the declaratory and the predictive, are all combined and fused into one. The course of individuals, the rise and fall of nations, the prospects of the world at large, are all rapidly portrayed in realistic language.[12]

The prophetic texts appear to present the Fundamentalists with a limiting case for their literalism. Even Ramm advocates a middle road between literalist and "spiritualizing" (that is, symbolic) approaches to them.[13] He notes that a strict, literalist approach would require David, and not Christ, to sit on the millennial throne! Still, Ramm insists that prophetic reading must be founded on literalist exegesis in order to temper the excesses of the prophetic imagination. The only controls we have over the interpretation of symbols, McCartney and Clayton note, are to discover what they meant to their author and audience and how they are used throughout the Bible.[14]

McCartney and Clayton suggest that the "notoriety" of prophecy has in fact less to do with symbolic language than with a misconception of the kind of information it conveys.[15] The repetitions of God's promises, which often accompanied the Old Testament prophets' condemnations of wickedness, threats of punishment, and exhortations to repent, "encourage us with regard to the future," they say, "as we look forward to God's ultimate deliverance and the destruction of all his and our enemies." It has nothing to do with receiving "news headlines in advance." In other words, prophecies point toward salvation, the end of history, and the eternal glorification of God.

Conservative evangelicals acknowledge that prophecies are never precise historical accounts ahead of time.[16] They occur in symbolic settings which preclude our being able to tell which details will be literally fulfilled. If Psalm 22, a lamentation, can be read prophetically, then its lines 16–18 ("For the dogs have surrounded me; a band of evildoers has encompassed me; they pierced my hands and my feet. . . . They divide my garments among them, and for my clothing they cast lots.") predict the piercing of Jesus's hands and feet and the casting of lots for his garments, mentioned in John 19:24. McCartney and Clayton add with true literalist concern: "But the piercing was not done by literal dogs (v. 16) and there is no record of any bulls (v. 12), lions (v. 21), or swords (v. 20) at the crucifixion."[17]

Prophecies must also be understood, Ramm (among others) argues, in terms of the historical circumstances in which they were made.[18] To understand Jeremiah and Ezekiel, one must know of the captivities. Without considering its historical situation, Ramm remarks, one would be tempted to interpret Habakkuk 1:5ff. as predicting the dispersion of the Jews rather than as an announcement of God's punishment of the wicked in Israel by outsiders, the Chaldeans. ("For behold, I am raising up the Chaldeans, That fierce and impetuous people who march throughout the earth to seize dwelling places which are not theirs.") Ramm suggests, if I understand him correctly, that the Chaldeans, as outsiders used by God to punish the wicked Jews, parallel the gentiles, who, when God saves them, will bewilder Israel. Is Ramm suggesting here that an historical event, albeit recounted in the Bible, can itself be a prefiguration of later "historical" events, like the salvation of the gentiles? Or does that first historical event have itself to be valorized by prophecy in order to function as a prefiguration of future events? It would seem that "historical contextualization" is at once "objectively" independent of the event being contextualized and fully implicated in and through it.[19]

Christ's discourse on Mount Olivet, Fundamentalists and other biblical scholars argue, relates at one level to the destruction of the Jerusalem in 70 A.D. (which occurred probably before Matthew and perhaps Mark and Luke wrote). At another level, it is said to refer to the end of time when the Son of Man will appear in the heavens and angels will gather the elect. ("And then the signs of the Son of Man will appear in the sky, and then all the tribes of the earth . . . will see the Son of Man coming on the clouds of the sky . . . His angels . . . will gather together His elect. . . ."[20]) Some interpreters have understood these events, announced by Christ, to have been fulfilled in their entirety in 70 A.D. Others argue that they will only take place at the end of time. McCartney and Clayton, from whom I have taken this example, suggest that it might be simpler "to take the whole as immediately but partially fulfilled" in 70 A.D. and—most interesting from our perspective—"to recognize that the events of A.D. 68–70 themselves point forward to the ultimate denouement of God's power and the Son of Man's sovereignty at the end of history."[21]

Again, we have to ask whether in Fundamentalist understanding an historical event can be prophetic, a prefiguration of future events. If so, what would make an event prophetic? Is it that Scripture has already marked it as such by having predicted the prefiguring event? In Habakkuk, the historical event had taken place and served as the context for prophecy. In the Olivet discourse, the destruction of Jerusalem had not taken place when Christ uttered it; but the event was known to the writers of the synoptic gospels. It served as their context but not Christ's. In both cases the event was integrated through prophecy into redemptive history. McCartney and Clayton are quite explicit about the relationship between what they call a preliminary, or shadow, prophecy and the complete, or real, one.[22] They argue that preliminary fulfillment is itself prophetic of the complete fulfillment. Although some evangelicals do not accept the possibility of multiple fulfillments of prophecy, it would seem, at least for those who do, that prophecy integrates the prophesied event into what can be conceived as a progressively prophetic history—a history that points continually to its end.

If this is so, then any historical event that is biblically prefigured can become prophetic of future events, including the apocalypse.

Fundamentalists—at least those who believe in multiple fulfillment—are not troubled by this possibility. However, they *are* concerned with the correct interpretation and attribution of the
"prophetic" text. How can one know that a particular passage from
the Bible is in fact prophetic? How do we know that, unless its historical referent is specified, it in fact predicts *the* future event? In
other words, how do we control the prophetic imagination? The
Fundamentalist is confronted here, yet again, with the "dangers" of
figuration, for the link between the biblical prophecy, its shadow
fulfillment(s), and it complete fulfillment is always metaphorical, always subject to the play of desire. As we noted, the Fundamentalist
tries to control his prophetic readings, his prophetic imagination,
by surrendering to the authority of God's Word as it is correctly interpreted through his grammatico-historical hermeneutics.[23] It is
for this reason that Ralph Barnes seemed relieved when he was finally able to lead our discussion of history to that of Scriptural authority. "History is personal experience," he said with relief. He
might simply have said, "Scripture is truth."

In talking to Fundamentalists about history, it became clear to
me that they distinguished what I awkwardly called "biblical" and
"postbiblical" history in terms of truth and authority rather than in
terms of chronology. I am not saying they have no sense of chronology; they certainly do. Rather, their understanding of history, *all*
history, is subsumed to Scripture. The Bible describes with unquestioned authority the course and truth of history. It provides not
just a model for understanding the chain of events that we come to
call history, but it actually modulates the perception of the events
and their concatenations. For the Fundamentalist, Scripture is to
history as Scripture is to experience: its truth, its authority, the formulations it provides, override "empirical reality" as it is perceived
by those who have not submitted to God's Word. It was this understanding that led Ralph Barnes to say, "Now, if we were to try to
determine the principles of life from the French Revolution, that
would be like letting experience be the judge of truth." Truth as it is
revealed through Scripture must prevail.

Susan Harding, an anthropologist who has been studying Jerry Falwell's Thomas Road Baptist Church and his Liberty University, has looked at the way in which Falwell and other Fundamentalist preachers use the Bible in the articulation of their own experience, their social and historical understanding, and their evangelizing and fund-raising. Harding says that Baptist Fundamentalists do not distinguish between story and event.[24] "The story is not a system of clues to extranarrative realities (prestoried emotions, experiences, events, or post hoc psychological processes), but a generative moment in which the event, characters and narrator, feelings, motives, and moral and theological meanings are brought into existence through language." In this sense, they are always true. "Their stories do not represent history," Harding says, "they are history."[25] By "splicing" God's Word to their own, the storied events call forth a web of prefiguring allusions, or types, that give them broader historical and theological meaning."

> Fundamentalists are still writing the Bible, inscribing it in their lives endlessly generating a third Testament in their speech and action. Their Bible is alive, its narrative shape enacts reality, infills it with form and meaning. It is, we might say, miraculous, this discourse which effects the world it speaks by constituting subjects who bring it about.[26]

Although the Fundamentalists I talked to would appreciate Harding's desire to describe how they experience, articulate, and live their lives in biblical terms, they would object to her way of understanding their reality. They would argue that she has given too much credit to the formal features of Scripture and insufficient credit to the Holy Spirit. They would be offended by her metaphor "still writing the Bible," though they would probably not be particularly troubled by her depicting their attempt to live as biblically as possible as "inscribing" the Bible "in their lives." They would find "endlessly generating a third Testament in their speech and action" too human-centered. Remember Ralph Barnes's comment:

"We look at the Bible, Genesis through Revelation, and, because we live in a vacuum, we see it in relation to ourselves."

Harding describes the way in which biblically condoned story-events were used by a Baptist preacher, Milton Cantrell, who tried to convert her, and by Jerry Falwell in his fund-raising for Liberty University. In both cases, Harding shows how the preachers wove biblical imagery into their appeals—for accepting Christ, for giving money—and thereby created a complex verbal tissue of allusion to Bible stories which "generated" the storied events they recounted. Falwell likened his fund-raising to the story of Joshua and Jericho: "He asked his local and television 'prayer warriors' to go into battle and circle the walls of impossibility, praying for a miracle."[27] During the last week of his campaign, which proved to be more successful than any one had expected, Falwell drove around Liberty Mountain, the site of his university, six times for six days and seven times on the seventh day, as Joshua had circled the walls of Jericho. Harding observes that just as the fall of Jericho is taken by Fundamentalists to be a prefigurement of Christ's victory, so is it, as Falwell preached it, a prefigurement of his successful fund-raising.[28] Falwell and his prayer meeting were "infilled" by other Joshuas, other prophets, other mountains, other Jerichoes.

> God spoke to Jerry through the story of Jericho as plainly as he (the unseen Captain) had spoken to Joshua that night thousands of years before. He gave them each a plan of victory and God's plans never fail, because their outcomes are, from God's vantage point, already "an accomplished fact." God always "looks back," he always speaks from the point of view of the end of history, when everything has indeed already happened. Jerry's encompassing was not magical, it did not induce God to act on his ministry's behalf. His circling was submissive, an act of obedience and sacrifice. It was Jerry enacting God's plan for him. . . .[29]

Harding calls attention here to the paradox between activism and submission to God noted in the last chapter, but she places it within a historical dimension I did not consider there. Jerry Falwell, the actor, enacts what God has already ordained in eternity past.

Unlike our vantage point, God's perspective is from the end of history. By identifying (though that term is perhaps too active) with Joshua—and, by extension, with Christ insofar as he is prefigured in Joshua—Falwell places his fund-raising in a chain of prefigurements, which, however he and his audience understand it, gives his appeal great rhetorical force.

In Milton Cantrell's evangelizing, Harding finds similar prefigurements, though (*pace* Harding, *pace* Falwell) they are not as blatantly manipulated as Falwell's.[30] The denouement of his witnessing Susan was the dramatic announcement that he had accidentally killed one of his sons. As his son was dying in his arms, Milton looked at God, uttering his un-understanding. "'And I've given you my heart, my life, my soul, given you everything about me. And now I can't understand this, why you've taken my son.' God spoke to Milton's heart. 'Milton, you know maybe you don't understand what I've done at this particular time, but can you accept it?' And I said, 'Yes sir, I can accept it.'" With that acceptance, Milton was given "peace in his soul." Cantrell concluded his witnessing by offering his story—his storied event—to Susan. "Of all that I could give you or think of ever giving over to you," he said, "I hope that what we've talked about here today will help you make the decision, to let Him come into your heart. . . ." Harding notes that Cantrell had offered her "access to the pattern of history"; she had only to accept it. (Susan was convicted that day but not converted.) Harding further notes that Cantrell's story of his son's death resonates with the stories of Job, Abraham and Issac, and Christ, all of which revolve around sacrifice and acceptance and were "prefigured" in what Cantrell had been telling her before he told her about his son's death.[31] Cantrell "set up a powerful, deeply compelling, figural sequence of sacrifice stories, from Abraham and Isaac, to Christ's passion, to his own terrible tale, a sequence that 'looked forward with hope' to the next story, my own self-sacrifice of faith."[32] "Reverend Cantrell sacrificed his son, narratively speaking, for me," Harding concludes. "Through the cumulative pattern of his Bible-based storytelling that afternoon, Cantrell created a space for me to take responsibility, for determining the meaning of his son's death."[33]

There are no doubt many other interpretations one could give to the conversation that afternoon. Harding focuses on the way Cantrell tried to save her. He "uses" his son's death, now associated with all the biblical sacrifices it evokes, to that effect. He puts her in a debt relationship. (The power of sacrifice always lies in the debt it produces). Susan owes Milton her rebirth. Though convicted, she refuses to convert, and, as in every incomplete exchange, she attempts—perhaps through writing her story and offering an explanation—to pass her debt on to us, her readers. Cantrell's telling her about his son's death can be taken as a validation of that death, for otherwise it would simply be a confession and its manipulation obscene. God has offered him no reason for that death. He can only find through analogy, with Job, for example, explanatory solace and guidance, the test of his faith, the model for uncomprehending acceptance. He must, I believe, depend upon Susan for making it meaningful. The Reverend Cantrell will no doubt accept his failure to convert Susan as he has accepted his son's death. It will become a prefigurement, to be passed on.

It is the separation of story and event—which Harding denies the Fundamentalists—that inspires Cantrell's story of his son's death and the use he makes of it. Harding offers Cantrell, through an evangelizing act, essential to his sanctification, the opportunity of creating a "storied event"—of becoming one with the father he narrates and all the biblical figures, Abraham, Job, and Christ, with which that narrated father is associated. Unlike Harding, I believe that for the Fundamentalists, as for us, story and event are always separated from each other, however much they (and we) would like them not to be. Fundamentalists would find the origin of this separation in the Fall of Man and its perpetuation in their sinful nature. As they struggle in sanctification to overcome their sinful ways, so, I suggest, do they struggle (but, given their sinful nature, never fully manage) to render story and event one, in and through God's Word. When they are preaching, praying, witnessing, confessing, describing their religious experiences, and perhaps even fund-raising, Fundamentalists often give the impression that they do not separate story from event. They appear at such times to be carried away by their enthusiasm, their performance, the power of the Word. That they speak with such fervor has great rhetorical power over their audiences and, I suspect, over themselves. We might want to liken their condition at such times to Coleridges's notion of "that willing suspension of disbelief for the moment which constitutes poetic faith," but that would be the reverse of what I believe the Fundamentalists would say they experience. They would object to the negative phrasing; they might speak of the willing intensification of belief that constitutes religious faith.[34]

The seminarians I interviewed said that the study of prefigurements, or, as they called them, types, was one of their toughest subjects. Though typological readings of the Bible played an important role in eighteenth- and nineteenth-century Protestant theology, they have been more or less abandoned by liberal and many (though by no means all) conservative Protestants.[35] However, the historical presuppositions of typology are still held by Fundamentalists and, as Harding has shown, affect their preaching and evangelizing. Typology has been defined as "the interpretation of earlier events, persons, and institutions in biblical history which become proleptic entities, or 'types,' anticipating later events, persons, and institutions, which are their antitypes."[36] For Christians, it is primarily concerned with prefigurements in the Old Testament of the New, though earlier events and characters in the Old Testament may also be read as anticipations of later ones. The strong prophetic dimension of the Old Testament is said to establish a vital link with the New, showing that divine revelation is of a single piece. "The New is latent in the Old," typologists like to say, "the Old is patent in the New." Or, as Pink would have it, in the Old Testament we have promise and prediction, "the blade," and in the New performance and fulfillment, "the full corn in the ear."[37]

Fundamentalists justify typological readings on several grounds. The most important is what Christ said about the prophetic quality of the Old Testament. In Luke 24:27, He explained to His disciples "the things concerning Himself in all the Scriptures." He says that "all things which are written about Me in the Law of Moses and the Prophets and the Psalms must be fulfilled."[38] In John, He says that Scripture "bears witness of Me."[39] The author of Hebrews refers to the Law as "only a shadow of the good things to come *and* not the very form of things."[40] In Romans, Paul refers to Adam as a "type [*tupos*] of Him who was to come," and Peter likens baptism to the eight who were saved on Noah's ark.[41] Ramm, always word-centered, argues that words used in the New Testament of the Old establish the "typical character" of the Old.[42] Like other Fundamentalists, he is anxious to distinguish typological from allegorical interpretation.[43] Unlike the typological, he argues, the allegorical introduces the "foreign, peculiar, or hidden" into the meaning of a passage. He warns, and the seminarians repeated, that as typology involves two layers of meaning, it facilitates the intrusion of the imagination into interpretation and risks obscuring the Word of God.[44] They would be troubled by viewing as prefigurements the biblical analogues Falwell and Cantrell use to describe the present. They are, as I have said, quite suspicious of prophecy when applied to the "lived" present and future.

Many students of typology insist that it is a way of viewing history. Ramm, quoting the German evangelical theologian Frederick Torm, refers to it as a "kind of philosophy of history."[45] McCartney and Clayton note that it presupposes a history that is under God's control, proceeds according to His divine plan, and "intimates" from within where it is going.[46] They insist that this intimation is not a construct "after the fact" but the result of the anticipatory, revelatory nature of history. "What God had done in the past was an indication of the greater deeds of God in the future." Pink puts it this way: "The Christian dispensation excels the Mosaic in a fuller and clearer manifestation of God's perfections (1 John 2:8), in a more abundant effusion of the Spirit (John 7:39; Acts 2:3), in its wider extent (Matt. 28:19, 20), and in a larger measure of liberty (Rom. 8:15; Gal. 4:2–7)."[47] Pink, like other dispensationalists, suggests a progressive revelation, which accords with God's particular "dispensation," or stewardship, at any one time.

———————

Before looking at the "shape of history" presupposed by dispensationalist theology, I would like to return to the notion of reading and suggest that typology and prophecy are in fact ways of reading that encourage, at least complement, their practitioners' historical outlook. I am not claiming that a style of reading produces a philosophy of history any more than that a philosophy of history produces a style of reading; rather, I am simply calling attention to a striking coordination between the two. It first occurred to me when Eric Lanier, one of the seminarians I talked to about prophecy, said, "You are assuming that a prophet understands his prophecy fully. He doesn't—only partly. It's only when the prophesied event occurs that we begin to understand its full significance." What struck me at the time was Eric's shift from the prophet's understanding to our understanding. "Does that mean we have a better understanding of the prophecy than the prophet does?" I asked Eric. "Yes," he answered, not altogether comfortable with my comparison. "Of course we do because we know more of God's revelation." Still a bit uncomfortable, he added with relief, "Christ has come since then. We are living in the Church Age."

It was Eric's observations that led me to consider the possibility that Fundamentalists read and reread Scripture, and perhaps other texts, differently from the way more secular seminarians do.[48] Eric's premise is basic to the study of prophecy and types. McCartney and Clayton write, "Thus, typology implies that, just as an earlier revelation is only ultimately understood in the light of later, so the later revelation can only be understood in relation to the earlier."[49] Reading as such becomes a sort of adventurous retrogression that, always, paradoxically, points forward to what extends beyond the text but is already inherent in it. It is like the march of redemptive history: it is all laid out since eternity past, but we, the historical actors, though we know through Scripture that it has been ordained, have only intimations of that ordination. With time and experience, with historical reflection and biblical study, these intimations are enriched and become more and more certain. As Fundamentalists—particularly those who are less cautious about prophecy than the seminarians—discover deeper and deeper significance in the biblical terms through which they articulate and rearticulate their lives, so they discover deeper and deeper meaning and implication in the prefiguring and prefigured events they encounter again and again in their rereading of Scripture. Reading as such is no more repetitive than life. Though the movement cycles back on itself, it is not retrogressive: what is reencountered in the past, "earlier in the text," and now enriched by the knowledge of what has followed (from the reader's point of view, "later in the text") points forward again, illuminating those later events and promising to illuminate still later ones in the text—in life—which are yet to be encountered. Indeed, can there ever be a reencounter in the usual sense of the word?

No one who reads Tolstoy's *Anna Karenina* will be able to reread the following lines from the first chapter the way he did the first time. "Everything was upset in the Oblonskys' house. The wife had discovered an intrigue between the husband and their former French governess, and declared that she would not continue to live under the same roof with him. This state of things had now lasted for three days, and not only the husband and wife but the rest of the family and the whole household suffered from it. . . ."[50] The "re-reader" will understand these lines as an announcement of the book's theme, a prefigurement of Anna's adultery. He will contrast the "low" comedy of Tolstoy's depiction of the Oblonsky household with the "high" tragedy of Anna's and Vronsky's understanding of their fateful situation. He will compare the "upset" at the Oblonskys' with Karenina's demand for orderliness, propriety, and the preservation of form. He will understand the "three days" of suffering at the Oblonskys' in terms of the permanence of Anna's suicide. If he should note that Oblonsky's affair with a French governess is really no more banal than Anna's with a dashing military officer, he will appreciate the doubly ironic banality of Tolstoy's opening observation: "All happy families resemble one another, but each unhappy family is unhappy in its own way."[51]

But the difference between our rereading Tolstoy and the Fundamentalist's rereading the Bible is enormous. The anticipatory figures of a literary text are just that. They enrich the text, thicken it, intimate things to come, create suspense, enforce narrative structure, promote cohesion, and thereby define transgression, affirm characters and institutions, support judgments, sustain the reader's progressive understanding of the text, and confirm literary-conventional notions of motive and cause, time, and history. They may be planted, wittingly or unwittingly, by the author, who, in our contemporary understanding, is thought to have incomplete control over what he writes. Though they project forward, their projection—their predictive power—is always in-text. They may help relate the text to the extra-textual world, as in political satire or moral allegory, but they have no real prophetic value. For Bible-believing Christians the anticipatory figures of Scripture also enrich the text, create suspense, promote cohesion, and all the other things they do in the literary work—but they do more, too. They are planted not by an author whose control is incomplete but by a omniscient and omnipotent God. They point forward with the certainty of truth to real events: those that are described later in the Bible as having already occurred; those, like the French Revolution, which have occurred but are not described in Scripture, though, if one adopts a prophetic stance, are prophesied in it; and those which are yet to come, like the end of time. They call forth and confirm a particular historical outlook that, given the declared origin and inerrancy of the Bible, is unquestionable. So comprehensive, authoritative, and consummately true is the text in which these prefigurements occur that they always extend beyond the text itself, narrowly construed, to give shape, meaning, and significance to that which has and will occur.

For those of us who were taught (simplistically, I am now certain) that there are two great conceptions of history, the linear and the cyclical, this prophetic view of history suggests a complex coalescence of the two.[52] They are often associated by biblical scholars with, respectively, the ancient Hebrews and Greeks. For the Hebrews, as in the ancient Iranian theology and primitive Christianity, the symbol of time was the line; for the Greeks it was the circle— events were thought to keep recurring. Man was bound to time and experienced it as a form of enslavement, a curse, from which he sought escape in a Beyond. Redemption was to be freed from time. This understanding of redemption contrasts sharply with that of the Hebrews and primitive Christians in which redemption occurs squarely within time and history. Their linear notion of time is progressive, anticipatory, and messianic. Of course, for the Jews time is divided in two: the present age extending back to creation and a future age that will come with the messiah. For the Christians, time is more complex, ternary, one might say, for its mid-point, the appearance (*parousia*) of the messiah, of Christ, has already taken place and centers history. The mystery of communion, of the eucharistic feast, points in a timeless, ritual moment to both the past, as a commemoration, and to a redemptive future.[53]

In Fundamentalist understanding, history moves forward inexorably toward its pregiven end. Like a vector, it has direction: its thrust is linear but not endless. Speaking generally of the Jewish and Christian conception of history, the student of comparative religion Mircea Eliade notes that "the irreversibility of historical events and of time is compensated by the limitation of history to time."[54] The terror of history, its irreversibility, is tolerable, Eliade suggests, because it is known that history will cease one day, in a single regeneration that has been announced in the eschatological texts of the Bible. This end of history, the details of which are, as we shall see, the subject of very considerable debate and controversy among evangelicals, does in fact govern their preaching, their evangelizing, their notion of salvation, indeed, their anthropology, their sense of identity. One of the questions asked in Henry Morris and M. E. Clark's popular *The Bible Has the Answer* is "Is the end of the world near?"[55] Citing Psalm 104:5, "[He] laid the foundation of the earth that it should not be removed forever," they answer that the world will last forever but not without dramatic change.[56] They refer to 2 Peter 3:10, "The earth also and the works that are therein shall be burned up," and go on to summarize their position. "The earth and its atmospheric heavens will thus not be annihilated but will be completely purged by fire, cleansing it of all the age-long effects of sin, decay and death, and enabling God to erect on its foundations a renewed earth which will exist forever in divine perfection." The born-again will also be cleansed of their sins and death, they add, and will receive "glorified bodies in the great resurrection day and thus will be equipped for eternal life in the ages to come on the new earth and in the new heavens." These "great events" are awaiting Christ's return, the exact time of which, they say, we cannot know. "He could come in any moment, and Christians should be ready for Him whenever He comes." Yet, they argue, there are signs that His coming is approaching. For the Fundamentalists, the future then is in broad outline certain and knowable and in detail uncertain and unknowable, at least unpredictable. But there is always room for prophecy, which, given the anticipatory nature of Scripture, is not without foundation. Taking a moderate prophetic stance, Morris and Clark observe that for men who study, believe, and love the Word of God the "political, social, religious, scientific, and physical realms are all fulfilling the prophetic descriptions of the 'last days,' as recorded in Scripture."[57] Among these signs they list, always with Scriptural justification, the decline in faith and morality, the "prevalence of naturalistic, evolutionary philosophy in science"— their particular bête noire—youths' rebellious attitudes, conflicts between the rich and the poor, the rise of anti-Christian leaders and philosophers, the infiltration of false teachers in the Christian churches, world wars, fear and confusion concerning the future, the restoration of Israel as a nation, the return of Jerusalem to the Jews, and worldwide preaching of the Gospel.[58] Evangelicals, I should add, are pointing to these and other signs with greater frequency and passion as we approach the year two thousand.

History does not just end for the Fundamentalist; it begins. And that beginning, like its ending, is of great conceptual significance. Morris and Clark emphasize the uniqueness of the concept of "special, recent creation by an eternal, all-powerful, personal God."[59] The Fundamentalists frame the beginning and end of history by "two periods of eternity," which they call "eternity past" and "eternity future." By "eternity past" they mean the period before God created the world, before the events described in Genesis 1; by "eternity future" they refer to the New Heaven New Earth proclaimed in the Book of Revelation. The seminarians understood the inadequacy of this formulation. How can there be two periods of eternity? We humans in our ignorance are compelled to divide it by history, as recounted in Scripture, as lived by us. From God's perspective it would be different, that much they knew; but what that understanding might be they balked at saying. They did not treat it as a mystery in any mystical sense; rather, they saw it as a simple cognitive impossibility.[60] They recognized God's omniscience, his preordination of "history." In my experience, they did not stress preordination. Several California preachers told me they did not focus on questions of predetermination, not because they were not important, but because such questions confused—one said discouraged—their church members. Ted Winter observed ironically that preaching predetermination used to be in fashion but today freedom's in. No one raised the question of God's breaking eternity by performing historical acts such as Creation or election, which "God had already determined in eternity past."

It is noteworthy that the periods immediately after creation, with the appearance of Adam and Eve (that is, Paradise) and immediately before the New Heaven New Earth (that is, the millennium) approach timelessness if not eternity.[61] It is as though these two ends of the "historical period" mediate the transitions between eternity and history and then between history and eternity. Like the structuralist "mediators," I referred to in the previous chapter, they partake of the polarities they mediate. They are timeless like eternity and in time like history. The in-and-out-of-time of Paradise is also borne stylistically. God creates; Adam, at most, names. Adam is without character. It is with an unspecified "now"—it could have been days or eons—that human history begins: "Now the serpent was more crafty than any other wild animal. . . ." And with the serpent's seduction and Eve's disobedience, and Adam's too, always given greater significance by the Fundamentalists, not only is history born but plot and character. Indeed, from Adam and Eve's transgression to the Joseph stories by way of Abraham's sacrifice, Genesis can be read as a progressive elaboration of character and plot—of individuation and historical narrative. This stylistic development also serves to mediate between the temporality of God's creation and human history. A similar, though more complicated, case can probably be made for the eschatological texts, in which character and personality (of even Christ) are little developed and plot is pregiven and though in God's hands seemingly autonomous.

Of course, Fundamentalists do not read Genesis or eschatological texts this way. They focus on the temporality of Creation, and at least implicitly on the moral dimension of history. It is sin that brings about the Fall and, with that Fall, history. God tells Adam in Genesis 2:17 that if he were to eat of the tree of knowledge of good and evil, he would die. Death and the knowledge of good and evil, it would seem, are constitutive of history. Certainly, as the Fundamentalists see it, Christ's "death" offers them not only the possibility of immediate rebirth, once they accept Him, but eternal life. With the end of history comes the end of death, for their sense of history is, as I have suggested, constituted on death. Though their vision of the end of history, with the elect eternally glorifying God, was communitarian and collective, the Fundamentalists I talked to seemed to be primarily concerned with their individual salvation, their own spiritual and bodily resurrection at the end of history.[62] To be sure, they also cared about the salvation of those closest to them, though I must confess I was surprised by how seldom (except during sickness and at the time of death) they expressed this kind of concern for others. Salvation was in God's hands after all, not in their own. It seemed to me—and here I am no doubt being presumptuous—that despite the historical perspective their religion gave them, the Fundamentalists had reduced this historical perspective, its collective concern, to the autobiographical. This seemed true at least of those I talked to, at least in what they chose to confide to someone ungraced by God.

Nevertheless, as I have tried to show here, the Fundamentalist has a very articulate view of history, one which he often describes and even charts. Dispensationalist tracts of late nineteenth and early twentieth century are often illustrated with the pictures of time and history. I have one, a few years old, called *A Chart on the Course of Time from Eternity to Eternity*.[63] It lists six dispensations, through which "God works to recover man from the moral ruin in which man's fall has brought him." These are correlated with the six days of Creation, the seventh day, or sabbath, being equated with eternal rest. As in many of the other charts I have seen, the end of time is rich in detail and imagery — scrolls, trumpets, thrones — prophesied in Revelation, Ezekiel, and Daniel. Such charts are often filled with intricately related "historical" detail, the correlation of which reminds one of allegorical and even numerological readings of Scripture, anathema though they are to the Fundamentalist; they attest to an at once unified and disjunctive view of Scripture.

Dispensationalism is a philosophy of history, an approach to reading, that developed in the nineteenth century out of the typologically oriented theology of seventeenth- and eighteenth-century Protestantism.[64] Although liberal and many conservative Protestant churches find it theologically suspect, it is still the dominant position of most important Fundamentalist seminaries.[65] The founder of the Plymouth Brethren, John Nelson Darby (1800–1880), a prodigious writer of more than forty volumes of at least six hundred pages each, is generally credited for its first elaboration.[66] The American Cyrus I. Scofield (1843–1921), who, like Darby, was a lawyer turned theologian, was responsible for its rapid spread among conservative evangelicals through the publication of his Reference Bible in 1909, which sold more than two million copies in its first generation.[67] Its text is that of the King James Version, but its divisions and notes encourage a very definite dispensational reading.[68] Scofield divides the biblical narrative into seven distinct dispensations, in each of which God has a different method of treating and testing mankind. Professor Bromley likens dispensations to the

Greek *oikonomia*, a household, stewardship, or administration. John MacArthur also prefers an organizational to a historical understanding; he insists that salvation by grace through faith is the same in all dispensations. It is the way God administers His grace that changes. In one dispensation, for example, Israel is the focus of God's redemptive plan; in another, it is the church.

From a secular point of view, it is possible to view dispensationalism as a way of meeting the challenge of the Higher Criticism, by offering an explanation for contradictions in the Bible. Some contradictions—differences, say, in Paul's teaching—can be reconciled, at least rationalized, through interpretation. Others, like the varying pictures of Hell that Ted Winter discussed, may remain an irresolvable puzzle. They are recognized, and our failure to understand them is thought to arise from our human perspective and incapacity. In effect, they enhance our anthropology and theology. How can we presume to understand God's ways? That we understand as much as we do is a sign of God's benevolent grace. But there are other contradictions that are more difficult to resolve. How, for example, does one reconcile monogamy with the polygamy of the ancient Hebrews? How does one justify animal sacrifice? How does one understand Christ's attitude toward the Law? How does one harmonize the dietary laws of Leviticus with "Christian" practice? Many of these reflect social and cultural practices that, unlike those of, say, Sodom and Gomorrah, were not condemned by God at the time of their occurrence. It is social and cultural contradictions like these that can be explained away by dispensationalism.

All dispensationalists believe in at least one future dispensation—the millennium. They read prophetic texts literally not just to be consistent with their reading of other parts of the Bible but because they firmly believe that as the prophecies of Christ's first coming were literal so are those of His second. As pretribulational premillennialists, they believe that Christ will raise up and rapture the born-again Christians before the seven years of tribulation, or outpouring of God's wrath, that precedes Christ's Second Coming and the ensuing millennium.[69] They differ then from the amillennialists who believe we are already in the millennium and the postmillennialists who believe that Christ will appear at the end of the millennium. They also differ from those premillennialists, conservative evangelicals like George Eldon Ladd, who do not admit Christ's pretribulational rapture.[70]

To an outsider, the differences between these positions seem of little significance, but to their adherents they are enormously important. Fundamentalists argue about their positions passionately, often deprecating their opponents in language reminiscent of the hyperbolic rhetoric of the Reformation. Their concerns are not just with the niceties of doctrinal difference nor even with the meaning of history; they are about understanding the present and, above all, the future—their future. As one liberal theologian I know put it:

> You have to take their literalism seriously. They really believe in the "desolating sacrilege"—the earthly convulsions, the earthquakes, the rivers running with blood, the famine, the torments, the scorching, the "foul and painful sores." No wonder they worry about the rapture.

Pretribulational premillennialists believe that the demonic element in history is on the increase, and that the present age will end suddenly in catastrophe.[71] The evil will suffer great judgment, but the righteous will be rescued. Writing in the late fifties, John Walvoord, a former chancellor of the Dallas Theological Seminary, describes the present age in terms similar to those of the Fundamentalists of the first decades of the century but still resonant today.[72] The picture he paints is bleak indeed. The present age is increasingly wicked. The gospel is preached throughout the world, but relatively few people are saved. There is no prospect of a golden age before the second advent. Nor, for the strictest premillennialists, ought we (*pace* Falwell, the Christian Coalition, and other conservative activists) devote ourselves to the political, social, moral, or physical improvement of the unsaved world."[73] Paul, Walvoord notes, "made no effort to correct social abuses or to influence the political government for good." He was concerned with "saving souls out of the world rather than saving the world." "Central to that purpose of the present age," Walvoord goes on,

> is the formation of the church, the body of Christ, out of believers in the gospel. The body of believers is quite distinct from Israel in the Old Testament and is not a revamped Judaism. The truth regarding the church as the body of Christ is declared to be mystery, that is, a truth not revealed in the Old Testament. Composed of Jew and Gentile on an equal basis, and resting on New Testament promises of grace and salvation in Christ, the new entity is a new creation of God, formed by the baptism of the Holy Spirit, indwelt by the Spirit of God, united to Christ as the human body is united to its head.

Walvoord's distinction between Israel and the Church, which is fundamental to the pretribulational premillennialists, reflects their deep ambivalence about the status of the Jews.[74] MacArthur writes: *"Dispensationalism is a system of biblical interpretation that sees a distinction between God's program for Israel and his dealings with the church. It's really as simple as that."*[75] The pretribulationalist premillennialists adhere "on biblical grounds" to a revival of the Jewish nation and their repossession of their ancient land. (Some, as I have mentioned, believe that the founding of the state of Israel heralds the coming of the millennium.) Following, among other texts, Romans 11, they argue that the Jews, at least some of them, will be "engrafted" back onto "their own olive tree" once their "blindness" has been lifted and will accept Christ as the messiah. They hold, however, that the reborn Christians, the saints, will be raptured before the tribulation, while the Jews will have to suffer, along with the unsaved, its horrible punishments before some—those Jews who accept Christ, sometimes called the "Christian Jews" and said to number 144,000—will enter the Kingdom of God. Many Fundamentalists (though none of the seminarians I knew) insist on this figure of 144,000, from the Book of Revelation 7:4 with the same tenacity that they hold to six literal days of creation. Whether or not they were under the influence of Hal Lindsey, who speaks in *The Late Great Planet Earth* of 144,000 "physical, literal Jews"—the "Jewish Billy Grahams"—who will be let loose on the earth to evangelize as never before, it seemed clear that some of them were content with this small number.[76]

The Fundamentalist picture of history I have drawn is linear but not open-ended. It assumes progressive revelation: over time, God reveals more and more of Himself and His divine plan.[77] Walter Kaiser understands it in organic terms: "The progress of revelation has an organic aspect in which the identity of the germ contained in the earliest mention of a theme continues in the buildup of that theme as the seminal idea takes on more developed form in later revelation."[78] Fundamentalists do not dwell on the process of progressive revelation, though the dispensationalists among them criticize those theologies (for example, covenant theology) which do not allow, in their eyes, for changes in God's relationship to man. They have not founded a theology of progressive revelation but some such as Darryll Bock at Dallas Theological Seminary and Robert Saucy at Talbot are now speaking of progressive dispensations, which are more "holistically" unified than the traditional normative ones.[79] For the traditionalists, at least, history is punctuated by God-given dispensations. Insofar as these dispensations are understood as proceeding directly from God, and not progressing serially by means of some inner dynamic or motivation, they appear, like any framing category, to transcend history. They "contain" it, however.

Like other Christians, the Fundamentalists center their sense of history on Christ's birth, death, and resurrection—a divine intervention, a miracle, singular among others, anticipated and anticipating, integrated into the great sweep of redemptive history. Christ's first coming divides that history into a "before" and an "after" which are understood not just in temporal but in moral and spiritual terms. A miracle, it puts into question all of the ordinary categories of historical understanding and explanation. As Ladd puts it: the Resurrection "is a miracle, not in the sense that it is a violation of the laws of nature and human history, but in the sense that it is the appearance within history of a higher order that transcends the world of nature and history—the realm of eternal life which belongs to the world to come."[80] Note the stress on the eternal life to come. Though Christ's sacrifice is all-important historically and for the individual, its centering role in the Fundamentalists' articulation of history is, I believe, weakened by their overriding concern for Christ's Second Coming and the world to come.[81] Thus, the Fundamentalists' vision of history is linear, disjunctive (for it is punctuated by divine interventions), universal, and stolidly teleological. Though it is nonrepetitive, it is prophetic: it always points toward its announced end. It also points toward mediate events in the future, the objects of prophecy, which, prophesied, may themselves, once they occur, become, prophetic of still later events. Here, as in so much Fundamentalist thought, Scripture has priority over reality experienced by the individual in the raw. It is more than a template for experience, for it has prophetic force: it continually reaches beyond itself, toward later events that are contained within it, like Old Testament prophecies of the coming of Christ or those of the apocalypse in Revelation. But, for many, the prophetic outreach of the Bible extends to current and imminent events in "the real world." Aside from facilitating, however falsely, the extravagant prophecies of the Hal Lindseys who appear again and again in evangelical circles, the prophetic dimension of Scripture gives to its application in everyday life a powerful rhetorical, if not downright instantiating, force. It is richly formative, indeed transformative, but within the limits it sets itself. It promotes a closed-ended view of history, in which everything is already known, not to us but indubitably to God. The Bible gives us, however, more than an inkling of what will happen. We have God's announced end: for Fundamentalists, objectively the glorification of God, and subjectively their personal salvation. Despite their acknowledgment of "general revelation"—that is, the truths God has revealed through nature, providential control, and conscience— Scripture is the only reliable source for understanding God's program. It requires continual study and application, which, as I have argued, aims at obliterating the gap between text and experience. Experience must be subordinated, transformed by Scripture. The study of Scripture becomes a sort of closed-ended adventure. Given its prophetic nature, given the fact that prophecies are only fully understood when the prophesied events actually occur, and given the fact that many of the prophecies are realized in Scripture itself, the Bible student is always discovering new dimensions to the events recounted in the Old and New Testaments. Interpretation, reading, is always cyclical: it is at once progressive and retrogressive, though never repetitive in the usual sense of the word, for it is always uncovering new relationships, new pre- and postfigurements, new types and antitypes, which are thereby enriched and prompted for still further implication, enrichment, and significance. The interpretive process, the act of reading, as performed by the Fundamentalists, mirrors their view of history. It cycles in backward movement forward to its own end.

———

This paradigmatic picture of the Fundamentalists' conception of history contrasts markedly with various paradigmatic conceptions of time and history that other Americans hold, often in contradiction to one another, and to which the Fundamentalists are not immune. They live, as we say, in the real world. They are taught history and science in school. Whether they like it or not, they are exposed to the theory of evolution. They read novels, biographies, and autobiographies; they go to the movies and the theater and watch television. They converse with others who do not share their views, and insofar as these other views do not compromise their faith they may easily accept them.

The various senses of history common in America are linear, but they are less weighted to the past, more open-ended than the Fundamentalists' understanding, less prophetic, less encompassing. They assume infinite (though punctuated) continuance rather more than finality articulated in a static notion of eternity.[82] For most Americans, history is articulated temporally, chronologically, and not morally and spiritually, though there is usually an intimation of moral and spiritual progress. In recent years, as every college professor will tell you, history as a source of understanding and explanation, not to mention of perspective and solace, seems to have played a diminishing role in young people's lives. History is flattened: it becomes a sort of databank for developing and confirming one or another "scientific" hypotheses about social, political, or economic behavior that can be generalized over time and have, ideally, predictive value. Or it becomes a set of stories to be told or filmed for entertainment, producing icons of identity, nationalist pride, and community sentiments. The power of many of these stories rests on the exploitation of longing and nostalgia for what may never have been experienced. They fill, magically, the absences they express and constitute. As data or story, these "historical events" are mechanically filed away in empty chronologies or poorly articulated periods like the "war years" or "Roman times." They are not integrated into vital and meaningful trajectories like the redemptive.

In the common American senses of history, there is concern for beginnings (as in Big Bang cosmologies) and for endings—not of time but of the world. These endings, now so popular as we enter the third millennium are usually imagined by Hollywood and sensationalist writers as man-made catastrophes like nuclear wars, or cosmic catastrophes, like drought or comets.[83] Beginnings and endings are always speculative and edge on the mythological. "It is difficult for anyone who cannot believe in God," Otto Friedrich observed, "to imagine the end of the world, or even to imagine the world itself as a unitary whole."[84] And yet, as the journalist Luiza Chwialkowska (who helped me with some of the research for this book) remarked, it is always easier to imagine eternity future than eternity past. Historical events are commonly viewed as local, particular, contingent, and yet causally determined and, therefore, subject to the laws of probability. They are not usually understood as revelation or in terms of some pre-given divine program, though their "contingency" may suggest either the play of chance or destiny. The physical and social sciences, especially economics, like "practical experience," are thought to offer some protection from sheer contingency; but in the most secular understandings of history there are no powers that can save one from the terror of contingency and irreversibility. Though one may "learn" from history, it is not prophetic. Nor is it subordinate to an authoritative, sacred text that models it and demands adherence to that modeling at the expense of experience.[85]

My aim here is not to draw a complete picture (were it even possible) of the common American senses of history. There are, no doubt, many such pictures—held even by the same individual—whose expression and degree of elaboration are determined by circumstance. As the anthropologist Carol Greenhouse observes, "concepts of time are flexible, permeable, and capable of proliferation." They are not "inscribed as fixed geometric blueprints in a culture's mentalité, but are contested, negotiated, defended, and transformed in the juxtaposition of personal and institutional forms that comprise social life anywhere."[86] My point is contrastive. The Fundamentalists' picture of time differs radically from (most of) these other pictures because of its insistent claim to truth. It is rather more "geometric." It is derived either directly from a text believed to be God-given and inerrant or indirectly from various kinds of discourse—oral, written, behavioral—that have been subjected to a morally and spiritually sanctified discipline determined by that text. The Fundamentalist works at living in the confines of a biblically constituted history. In this way, he differs from other Americans who have no such moral and spiritual compulsion. The consequences of this difference are enormous, though they are rarely acknowledged by either the Fundamentalists or the non-Fundamentalists.

———

Perhaps the best-known clash of Fundamentalist and secular senses of history is that between the creationists and the evolutionists. Of course, neither side casts its argument explicitly in terms of conceptions of time and history. They argue about textual authority and "scientific" fact and interpretation. Underlying their argument—and precluding, in my opinion, any possible reconciliation between them—are their dramatically divergent ways of articulating time and history. Opposing the creationists' moralized understanding of time as created and essentially wedged in between two eternities and history as providential, millennial, and redemptive, the evolutionists' deny any moral dimension to time and history. Like the creationists, their notion of time is linear but it is opened-ended and purposeless. Theirs is a historicist conception of history, that is, one in which all events in historical and geological time can be explained by prior events in that time.[87] They deny any divine plan, aim, or intervention and, in the creationists' eyes, promote a terrifying, meaningless version of history that is subject only to chance and mechanical causality—a causality that serves but poorly (because humanly conceived) to assuage the terror inherent in their godless vision.

The creationists base their argument on the authority of Scripture, and many of them, the "creation scientists," support it by what they take to be scientific evidence. For them, evolution is not science but philosophy—a worldview whose hypothetical, indeed fantastical, nature is masked by a series of altogether questionable observations and deductions from these observations that are expressed as though they were scientific certainties. They do not, so they claim, question science; they question "bad science," like evolution. They argue that good science, like theirs, confirms the account of creation in Genesis. The evolutionists counter in a vein that is sometimes embarrassingly similar to the creationists': they accuse them of justifying their Scripturally supported creationism on pseudo-scientific grounds. According to the evolutionists, creationists simply collect bits of "data" they claim to be scientific and interpret and arrange them to give support to their biblically based, presuppositions. They have at best a naive sense of the scientific method, often arguing that only that which can be directly observed has scientific validity. The Federal judge William Overton, who ruled that the teaching of creation science in Arkansas was unconstitutional, based his ruling on the fact that creation science did not meet the accepted criteria of science such as falsifiability, testability, tentativeness, and naturalness. It was a religion, he argued, and violated the separation of Church and State mandated by the First Amendment.[88]

Of course, there are several schools of creationism; some more sophisticated than others, but all rely or at least relate to one reading or another of Genesis. Unlike today's creationists, who insist on the recent creation of the world, conservative evangelicals of the late nineteenth century were willing to acknowledge an ancient earth and pre-Edenic life. They were able to accommodate the findings of historical geology and paleontology in two principal ways. Either they interpreted the "days" of Genesis 1 as indeterminately long ages or they separated creation into two phases with a long gap between them: a creation "in the beginning" and a later Edenic creation, which took six literal days. Even William Jennings Bryan, the great advocate of creationism in the Scopes trial, thought of the "days" in Genesis as "ages" and was willing to contemplate the possibility of organic evolution so long as it did not deny the divine origin of Adam and Eve.[89] Most of the Fundamentalists with whom I spoke were unwilling to accept either the day-age or the gap theory: they insisted on a literal reading of Genesis in which they find no evidence for a gap between two moments of creation. For them, a day is a day: "If God wanted Moses to mean ages," one preacher asked, "why would he have him write 'days'?" Like creation scientists, they explain away the fossil evidence for evolution by attributing it to the Noachian flood. The plants and animals that left their imprint on stratified rocks, they asserted, lived together in antediluvian times.

Assertions of this sort, which are often expressed in and through scientific-sounding language and argument, are characteristic of creation science. The Museum of Creation and Earth History in Santee, California, which is attached to Henry Morris's Institute of Creation Research, a powerhouse of creationism, opens its exhibit with the observation that while the evolutionary view of the origin of the universe and life "can interpret the evidence with some success, the creationist interpretation is better. This is not surprising, for this is what the Bible says." Or, to give another example from the museum, concerning the existence of transitional types, such as "Lucy" (*Homo erectus*, or the Neanderthal man) upon which evolutionists base their theory, an exhibition panel simply denies the existence of such intermediary types. They are declared either human or nonhuman. Wayne Frair and Percival Davis, two creationist biologists, argue in the same vein in their book, *A Case for Creation*:

> Around the turn of the century a number of fossil hominids thought to be ancestral to humans were known to paleontology. Essentially those were what we today call Neanderthal man (now generally acknowledged to be a race of *Homo sapiens* and clearly human) and *Homo erectus*, an example of which is Java man. Those forms surely were not apes or anything like apes, so they cannot be considered transitional forms between people and apes, or between people and the apelike, hypothetical common ancestor of man and apes.[90]

Ignoring the fact that physical anthropologists and paleontologists consider *Homo erectus* and Neanderthal man to be "transitional forms," Frair and Davis go on to say that a missing link was needed—and invented—to overcome the embarrassment of its absence. Like so many creationists, they focus on the Piltdown Man hoax, in which skeletal remains found in 1908 in a bog in Sussex were thought to be an early ancestor of man but were later discovered to be of modern origin (the jaw was that of a chimpanzee). "Why then do we resurrect his ghost?" Frair and Davis ask. "Merely to show that it is not too hard to find evidence to support firmly held convictions."

To the outsider, the passion with which Bible-believing Christians take on the evolutionists seems extreme if not grotesque. Although many evolutionists are also passionate defenders of their position, they do not seem to be as emotionally invested in it as the Fundamentalists are in theirs. One cannot help remarking that the affective response of the evolutionists, as sober as it tends to be, suggests that they too have more at stake in the debate than simply proclaiming a scientific theory. Whatever the causes for their response—outrage, for example, at the creationists' insistence on the absolute, undebatable truth of their position or on its being taught in school—the evolutionists end up as frustrated as the creationists. There is no dialogue, no mediation, no compromise: each side holds stubbornly to its truth. Intermediate positions such as theistic evolution—which holds, roughly, that evolution is God's method of creation—are rejected by the extremists on both sides.

As we have noted, the creationists argue (not without some reason) that if one accepts their literalist understanding of science, then evolution cannot be considered science. It becomes a worldview, a philosophy, a godless religion that attempts to explain the origin of the universe, of life, and of speciation. They observe, to quote John Klotz, who directs graduate studies at Concordia Theological Seminary, that because "the genius of modern science, controlled experimentation, cannot be applied to a study of the past," and because we cannot "compress a great deal of time into our laboratory studies," it is impossible "to reproduce the conditions of the past to determine if they could indeed bring about the changes assigned to them."[91] Morris puts it this way in a book that attempts to lay out the principle of a biblical science: "Science deals with systems and processes we can observe now, whereas history deals with what earlier generations have observed in the past and recorded for posterity. Once we go beyond the earliest historical record, however, we are outside the scope of human observations and, therefore, outside the scope of real science."[92] Though such restricted views of science are not held by all creationists, they are generally accepted by Fundamentalists.

The creationists have an interest in stressing the "gaps" in the fossil evidence for evolution—for, in their terms, the gaps support their belief that God created the full range of life in several, literal days. Though few of the Fundamentalists I talked to accepted Bishop James Ussher's (1581–1656) calculation that the universe was created in 4004 B.C.—a date long used in some editions of the King James' Bible—they generally assumed that creation took place around 10,000 B.C. Ted Winter, who decided to accept the literal days of creation because he had no reason to suppose that God needed more time to create the world, said that the Ussher's calculation was probably on the low side, because he did not take into account both gaps in the relevant genealogies and the ambiguity of the word "father" which could also mean grandfather or ancestor. Morris reasons this way:

It should be obvious to even the most casual reader that when the Bible is taken naturally and literally, it teaches that the earth is only a few thousand years old. Abraham lived about 2000 B.C., a date which is confirmed archaeologically as well as Biblically, and the chronologies of Genesis 5 and 11 add up to about two thousand years from Adam to Abraham, with the universe created six days before Adam. Even if it could be demonstrated that gaps exist in the Genesis 5 and 11 chronologies, they could be stretched out for a reasonable number of generations, possibly allowing for a date for Adam of, say, around 10,000 B.C. at the most.[93]

This reasoning is extraordinary, particularly for someone who claims to be a scientist and is always ready to criticize the evolutionists' dating methods. Morris shows more care for numerical accuracy in the six pages he devotes to the calculation of the size, capacity, and stability of Noah's ark in his *Biblical Basis for Modern Science*. The ark, we learn, was so stable it could not capsize in heavy waves and violent winds; had the capacity of 522 standard railway stock cars; and, thus capable of housing 125,000 sheep, was amply large for the 18,000 species of living or extinct land animals known today. (These inferences, Morris tells us, were confirmed by testing a scale model of the ark for the Hollywood film, *In Search of Noah's Ark*.) He adds that God Himself steered the ark, keeping its occupants reasonably comfortable.

In essence, the historical presuppositions of the creation story in Genesis, are of temporal disjunction—through divine intervention.[94] Morris and other creationists argue that, because we were not there, we simply have no way of knowing for sure whether certain conditions might alter the decay rate of radioactive isotopes such as carbon-14, rubidium-87, or potassium-40 (which are used in dating objects), or if certain events that might have accelerated or otherwise modified the formation of geological strata (also used in dating). Anxious to find a way to reconcile science and biblical chronology, they nevertheless suggest that there have been catastrophic events that have or may well have sped up radioactive decay or disrupted the uniform development of geological strata.[95]

This critique of uniformitarianism is not entirely without merit.

Creation scientists note that the uniformitarians often include limited catastrophes, such as volcanic eruptions and meteoric impacts, in their understanding but typically refuse to include major ones.[96] The major catastrophes these critics refer to—Adam's sin and the Flood—are not, however, those which would suggest themselves to geologists, astronomers, or physicists. I first came across this argument when I was visiting Morris's Creation Museum. I dismissed it with a laugh, as I dismissed most of the creationist arguments I saw demonstrated there. They were decorated with the trappings of science, as I saw it, with improbable though scientific-looking calculations, decontextualized and recontextualized bits of scientific data, and posters from NASA. I found it difficult to imagine how any reasonable human being could fall for them. Is our level of critical understanding so low? How could parents submit their children to such propaganda? There were reasonable-looking adults at the museum on the days I was there, and busloads of school children too, accompanied by parents and teachers. It was only later, as I came to a better understanding of evangelical thought, that I realized that the creationists like Morris had a wholly different understanding of time and history and, therefore, of science. It was not just a question of a disjunctive history, one that recognized miracles, one whose end was known, one that was, in a sense, already written; it was a history so morally saturated that morality could not be separated from any other understanding, including the scientific.

When Morris refers to Adam's sin and the Flood—he could have referred to the Tower of Babel or any of the other divine punishments meted out to the ancient Jews—as catastrophes of such proportion that they could have changed rates of decay of radioactive isotopes, he relates sin to fundamental principles of established science. From Genesis 2:3 ("Then God blessed the seventh day and sanctified it, because in it He rested from all His work which God had created and made"), Morris argues that God is no longer creating but simply conserving His creation.[97] According to Morris, God's conservation is demonstrated empirically by the First Law of Thermodynamics, the law of the conservation of energy; Morris disingenously extends it beyond its scientific parameters, no doubt to lend support to his anti-evolutionary stance. Structure is conserved. "Energy is conserved, matter is conserved, the biological 'kinds' are conserved, and each human being in God's image is conserved." He argues further that with Adam's sin, with the imposition of God's curse on the world (!), the law of conservation was drastically changed:

> Thenceforth not only did death come in, with all living organisms destined eventually to disintegrate and go back to their basic elements, but so do all other structures tend to become unstructured. Instead of the law of conservation of structure, there now prevails a universal law of breakdown of structure (morpholysis). Not only is there no more creation of order, but the reverse is taking place, a universal decrease of order (or increase in entropy).[98]

In essence, sin introduced the Second Law of Thermodynamics, whose application Morris extends to sickness, death, and extinction, to the atrophy of "once-vigorous societies," and "to the tendency of faiths which were once strong and dynamic to become lethargic and apostate."[99] He uses the Second Law to argue insofar as evolution describes a process of increasing structural complexity, it contradicts the entropic processes described by the Second Law.[100] He uses the play between the two laws to support the creation of the universe by a transcendent God.[101] His argument runs something like this: Given the law of entropy, were the universe eternal, it would already be dead—hence time has a beginning. Given the law of conservation, the universe could not have created itself; hence, there must have been a transcendent creator. "Genesis 1:1 is the most profoundly scientific statement ever written," Morris declares, "with all the systems and processes of the cosmos uniting in asserting this truth."

Predictably, Morris relates the laws of thermodynamics, particularly the Second Law, to Christian eschatology.[102] He observes that if the two laws were to function into the eternal future, the cosmos would suffer thermodynamic death. "The universe will (according to the first law) never cease to exist, but it will *die*." In theological terms, there will be a period of great catastrophe and tribulation—

the end of the universe as we know it—followed by the creation of a New Heaven and New Earth. Referring to 2 Peter 3:10-12 ("But the day of the Lord will come like a thief, and then the heavens will pass away with a roar and the elements will be destroyed with intense heat"), Morris describes this period in *his* scientific idiom. "The cosmos is not to be annihilated, but it is possible that atomic disintegrations are involved, which will convert mass into heat, sound, and other forms of energy." Then, with the New Jerusalem,

> All the age-long effects of sin (e.g. the fossils in the earth's sedimentary crust) will have been purged from the very elements, and there will be "no more curse" (Rev. 22:3). There will be "the times of restitution [or, better, "restoration"] of all things" (Acts 3:21). The perfect conditions of pristine Eden will be restored and no doubt vastly enlarged and varied as well. The Second Law of Thermodynamics will be repealed, and "there shall be no more death" (Rev. 21:4) in all the universe throughout all the ages to come.[103]

Morris's scientific-allegorical reading of the Bible (for, what else can one call it?) is by no means accepted by all creationists, nor by strict Fundamentalists who are opposed to such readings, if only because Scripture needs no support. It is not, however, without influence in conservative evangelical circles. It is, in a sense, a double allegory, for it allegorizes a premillennial theology, which foresees only decay until the millennium and in turn can be read, as some wit once declared of all theology, not without some truth, as itself an allegorical reading of Scripture.[104]

A student in one of the Bible classes I attended in Los Angeles introduced himself before class one evening. He had heard I was in residence at the California Institute of Technology and wanted me to know that he also worked there, at the Jet Propulsion Laboratory. He was one of their ground engineers. I was surprised and asked him if there were many "Christians" at the Laboratory. He answered, "We're all Christians in my unit." After we had talked for a few minutes, I asked him if he was a creationist. He said he was: he believed that God had created the universe in six literal days, and that the universe was probably no more than ten thousand years old. "How do you reconcile that with the research being done at Cal Tech?" I asked. "Have you read the latest research on light years?" he answered. In the brief time we had before class began, he told me that, regardless of that research (whatever it was, he never specified), it was clear from Genesis 1:14–19 that God had created the sun, moon, and stars to be seen by Adam. "Whatever the speed of light, God created the stars, however far away they may be, so that they would be immediately visible on earth. He jumped time and set the whole light thing going." He gestured, as though he were pulling taffy, demonstrating how God had stretched beams of light from the stars to the earth.

The engineer's argument was, I suppose, as indefensible (in his terms) as the last-ditch arguments of other creationists' against evolutionists who take their position from fossil evidence: God created fossils. There is simply no argument possible. In both instances, though more dramatically in the case of light years, time is obliterated or, at least, reduced to an asymptotic moment. The German philosopher of history Reinhart Koselleck argues that with modernity the European (and American) historical consciousness changed radically.[105] History was temporalized. In 1529, the German painter Albrecht Altdorfer could collapse in his picture of the Battle of Issus (333 B.C.) Alexander the Great and the Persians under Darius with the Emperor Maximilian and the Turks, who had unsuccessfully laid siege to Vienna, as he was painting his picture. Three hundred years later the German critic Friedrich Schlegel, who marveled over Altdorfer's picture, carefully distinguished between the time of its execution and the time it represented. He also distinguished between the time he was writing and the time Altdorfer was painting.

The temporalization, or *Verzeitlichung*, of history, which Koselleck associates with modernity, produces a gap, or temporal disjunction, between the time an event is described or interpreted and the time it occurred, between the act of narrating, representing, or interpreting, and what is narrated, represented, or interpreted. It is this gap that the historically sensitive interpreter tries to bridge through careful contextualization. Where truths of texts, whether of the Bible or, as for many, the U. S. Constitution, are thought to be "self-evident," there develops a tension between the claims of those texts to timeless and universal self-evidence and the fact of their having been proclaimed in a specific historical period. We find a related tension in Fundamentalism—in Protestantism generally—between a sense that the words of Scripture are awesomely clear (perspicuous) and an equally certain sense that they require scholarly exegesis and interpretation. In legal circles, it is also expressed in semantic terms; its most powerful expression is, as we shall, see in terms of intention. Though we speak of texts, like Scripture and the Constitution, the tension exists (and may be rooted) in the word, whose meaning at once transcends its context and is determined by that context. The Fundamentalist—and, I will argue, certain conservative legal scholars—may long for what Koselleck would regard as a premodern sense of history, but they are as condemned to the wrenching temporality of modernity and its historical consciousness as we are. The Jet Propulsion Laboratory engineer had not only to respond to the challenge posed by the speed of light but to gesture God's stretching light beams as He obliterated, or gave the illusion of obliterating, the time of the space-time continuum He had created and introduced to us.

Part Two

THE BENCH

4—The Constitution

SENATOR HATCH How would you define judicial activism, because that seems to be one of the central core matters here.

JUDGE BORK I think I would define it as a judge reading into a statute or into the Constitution his personal policy preferences—and let me be clear about this.

No human being can sit down with words in a statute, with history and other evidence he uses, and not to some extent get his personal moral view into it, because each of us sees the world, understands facts, through a lens composed of our morality and our understanding.

But there is an enormous difference between that inevitable bias that gets in and a judge who self-consciously tries to keep his biases out and tries to be as impartial on the evidence as he can be. There's an enormous difference between that and a judge who incorporates his idea of wise policy into the Constitution or into a statute. . . .

SENATOR HATCH In other words, in simple terms, judicial activism is when judges make law rather than interpret the law?

JUDGE BORK That is a good shorthand description.

SENATOR HATCH The fact of the matter is that you, as a federal judge, weren't elected to that position; is that right?

JUDGE BORK That is correct. . . .

SENATOR HATCH [Judicial activism] may occur as well when judges make a general statement of law and stretch it to cover instances beyond that which the authors really intended; is that right?

JUDGE BORK That is correct.

SENATOR HATCH And that's what you mean by original intent?

JUDGE BORK That's correct.

SENATOR HATCH And it doesn't just mean original intent of the Founding Fathers or the original meaning of what they meant; it means the original intent of us Members of Congress who are elected representatives to make these laws to the people, is that right?

JUDGE BORK That is correct, Senator. . . .

SENATOR HATCH What is meant by judicial restraint?

JUDGE BORK . . . It is the morality of the jurist who self-consciously renounces power and tries to enforce the will of the lawmaker.

SENATOR HATCH When courts read into the Constitution or particular pieces of legislation policies and rights that are not there, what happens to the ability of the legislatures of the respective States or of the Congress itself to make laws according to the needs of the people?

JUDGE BORK The people and their representatives have suddenly been ousted from an area that was legitimately theirs and the courts begin to set a social agenda instead of the people setting their social agenda.[1]

This exchange between Senator Orrin Hatch, a Republican from Utah, and Robert H. Bork, a federal appeals judge for the District of Columbia, took place on September 15, 1987, the first day of the Senate Judiciary Committee's hearings on Bork's nomination to the Supreme Court. (Article II, Section 2 of the Constitution requires the Senate to give "advice and consent" on all Supreme Court nominations.) The hearings were the most controversial in the committee's history. President Reagan's nomination of Bork, more than two months earlier, had sent fear through the liberal and moderate establishment. Bork was a well-known, highly articulate spokesman for Reagan's "judicial restraint" position on the law.[2] As the journalist Ethan Bronner puts it, Bork had spent most of his professional life—as a lawyer, a Yale Law School professor, Nixon's Solicitor General, and a judge—"as a hell raiser, as a gadfly of the intellectual and judicial communities."[3] A supporter of Barry Goldwater and later of Richard Nixon, he was one of the only conservatives on the Yale law faculty. When Nixon named him Solicitor General in 1972, he was heard joking in the law school cafeteria that the student newspaper's headlines should read, "Nixon Appoints One-Fifth of the Law School Conservatives" to office.[4] Later, as Solicitor General (on Nixon's orders) he fired Archibold Cox, the special prosecutor in the Watergate investigations, after both Attorney General Elliot Richardson and the Deputy Attorney General William Ruckelhaus resigned rather than do so.

Though called an intellectual, indeed *the* intellectual, of the right, he was in fact an anti-intellectual—an ideologue. He was known for his dogged commitment to "original intent" as the only legitimate way to interpret the Constitution, and for his apparent willingness to overturn well-established precedent. As Renata Adler pointed out in a *New Yorker* article just before the hearings, Bork believed he had found "a theory, a simple axiom, or principle, or formula, that the Court can—in fact, must—apply in constitutional adjudication to all cases that come before it." (Adler reminded us that the "the constitutional command that the courts consider only specific 'cases' or 'controversies' has precluded them from proclaiming theory—either philosophical or 'advisory' or in advance of any set of facts." She went on to note, "The law is discovered in the cases, and not the other way around."[5]) Bork considered most of the progressive constitutional decisions of the postwar years to have "been wrought by a cabal of law professors and judges acting as social engineers."[6] He was always ready to attack the liberal political and legal establishment, to defend the executive over other branches of government, to limit free speech (to political speech, basically), to restrict "fundamental rights" to those enumerated in the Constitution, indeed, to sacrifice individual rights or "gratifications"—his preferred term—particularly those of minorities and women, for larger governmental and economic interests. At the same time that he advocated strict, and I would say, limited "construction" of the Constitution, he opted for a majoritarian view of the law, in which the courts are obliged to administer the "will" or "preferences" of the majority as that will or preference is expressed (through the legislature) in the law. Oblivious to the possible contradictions in these two positions—certainly obvious to the abuses that a simple majoritarian approach to the law encourages—Bork seemed at times to forget, or preferred to ignore, that the principal function of the court is (in Chief Justice John Marshall's words) "to say what the law is" and thereby guard against the tyranny of majoritarian pressure.[7]

Within less than an hour of Bork's nomination, Senator Edward Kennedy, one of Ronald Reagan's most ardent critics, was already warning the nation about Bork:

> Robert Bork's America is a land in which women would be forced into back alley abortions, rogue police could break down citizens' doors in midnight raids, schoolchildren could not be taught about evolution, writers and artists could be censored at the whim of government, and the doors of the federal courts would be shut on the fingers of millions of citizens for whom the judiciary is—and is often the only—protector of the individual rights that are the heart of our democracy.
>
> America is a better and freer nation than Robert Bork thinks. Yet in the current delicate balance of the Supreme Court, his rigid ideology will tip the scales of justice against the kind of country America is and ought to be.
>
> The damage that President Reagan will do through this nomination if it is not rejected by the Senate could live on far beyond the end of his presidential term. President Reagan is still our president. But he should not be able to reach out from the muck of Irangate, reach into the muck of Watergate, and impose his reactionary vision of the Constitution on the Supreme Court and on the next generation of Americans. No justice would be better than this injustice.[8]

Kennedy's speech—startling, fiery, exaggerated—set the tone of the campaign against Bork. It was to turn into the biggest media blitz against any Supreme Court nominee in history. Reagan complained afterward that Bork had been the victim of a "lynch mob." Bork said, not without reason, that he had been "tarred, feathered, and ridden out of town on a rail."[9]

In previous hearings on nominations to the Supreme Court, the Senate had focused on the nominee's legal credentials and integrity. Kennedy now put forward Bork's worldview and legal philosophy, which, as he clearly saw it, cloaked a conservative political agenda behind a supposedly apolitical adherence to the letter of an apolitical law. Suddenly, Americans had to consider the political and social implications of a particular style of legal interpretation. It was not unusual in those months to hear laymen talking about judicial restraint, original intent, the meaning of precedent, and the right to privacy, and citing cases like *Griswold v. Connecticut, Harper v. Virginia Board of Elections*, and *Shelley v. Kraemer.* I remember endless discussions of the strange case of *Franz v. United States*, in which a divorced father sought to see his children, who had "disappeared" after his wife, who had custody of the children, married a man who entered the government's witness protection program. (Bork argued against visitation rights.) I also remember the outrage over Bork's decision in favor of the American Cyanamid Company, which had excluded from one of its plants all women workers of childbearing age who could not show proof of surgical sterilization.[10] Four women had decided on sterilization rather than lose their jobs.

The Bork nomination, and all the politicking around it, triggered a national debate on what American political and legal culture was all about, what its ideals were, and what dangers were hidden in it. The Senate received more mail and telephone calls on Bork's nomination than on any other issue in its history. No doubt forgetting the Federalist debates, Senator Joseph Biden, who was the chairman of the Judiciary Committee at the time, referred to the campaign as "the most extensive civics lesson on the Constitution the American public has ever been exposed to." Nan Aron, president of the Alliance for Justice, noted, "Whether you agree or disagree with the outcome, the Bork hearings were really a reflection of the best of our democratic process, a majestic debate about ideas." The alliance was a coalition of liberal groups which were instrumental in Bork's defeat. Harvard Law School's Laurence Tribe, who had played an equally important role in the defeat, said that the debate "was almost a national referendum that helped crystallize a national consensus on certain constitutional principles." Given the wild divergence of opinion, the acrimony, the politicking and all the media attention, it is hard to see where and on what basis a consensus lay. Certainly, Bork's supporters saw him, in Hatch's words, as "the victim of a misinformation campaign waged by liberal extremists who sought to further their own agenda." "They turned him into an absolute gargoyle, into a beast," Senator Alan Simpson of Wyoming, another Bork defender, reminisced.[11]

Had Bork become a justice of the country's highest court, as Kennedy pointed out, the balance between its conservative and liberal members would have been weighted for the foreseeable future in favor of the conservatives. Reagan had vowed to cut back the expansive interpretations of individual and civil rights which had characterized the court since Eisenhower's appointment of Earl Warren in 1953. He had promised to ban abortion, to allow religion in public schools, and to return power to the states. Reagan cast his view in near-theological terms. The court had gone astray by sacrificing the original intention of the Founders (by which American democracy was founded) to the personal predilections of its justices. Despite the scandals that troubled his administration — Irangate, for example — he had managed to rally enormous support around these three issues. Through them, he had given his supporters the chance to express values and longings that had been interdicted or, at least, dismissed as retrograde or shameful, during the previous, more liberal decades.

By the time he nominated Bork for the Supreme Court, Reagan had planted judges of his persuasion in all the federal courts. These included two Supreme Court justices, Antonin Scalia and Sandra Day O'Connor. He had also managed to promote William H. Rehnquist, a Nixon appointee, to Chief Justice. These justices opposed the "judicial activism" that had characterized the Warren, Burger, and — by Bork's standards — even the Rehnquist courts. They espoused "judicial restraint" and a textualism that gave special weight to "original intent" and meaning. With a feigned ingenuousness, they claimed that adherence to the letter of the law would eliminate, as much as was humanly possible, political considerations from legal decisions. Of course, everyone knew that Reagan, like other presidents, had chosen his justices not for their law review jurisprudence but for their political orientation. These political considerations and agendas were largely bracketed off in the Senate hearings on their nomination or else were taken as evidence of their personal integrity and legal qualifications. Comparing the Scalia hearings in 1986 with Bork's, one is immediately struck by how often Scalia was allowed to evade the kind of questions about his legal, moral, and political philosophy which Bork was pushed to answer. Of course, Bork was far less reticent than Scalia: he had let his views be known in any number of previous publications and speeches. On April 17, 1989, several months before his nomination, he told a reporter from the *Legal Times* that "the United States today would be a better country if the Warren Court had never existed."[12] During the hearings, his supporters, most notably Strom Thurmond, had to remind him that he did not have to, indeed ought not, answer a particular question that might reveal how he would decide a case likely to arise during his justiceship.

Reagan had clearly nominated Bork on political grounds. Bork had actively sought the nomination and was not adverse, so it appeared, to change some of his strongly articulated views during the hearings to further his confirmation. These included his position on the applicability of the Equal Protection Clause to women, on dissident political speech (that is, speech which advocates the violation of law), and on First Amendment protection of artistic expression. He had denied the first, was highly critical of the second, which had been settled for years by the court's "clear and present danger" doctrine, and had argued that First Amendment protection covered only political speech.[13] The Judiciary Committee's final report to the Senate puts the matter of Bork's "confirmation conversion" delicately but firmly.[14] "The Committee has concluded that Judge Bork's newly announced positions are not likely fully to outweigh his deeply considered and long-held views." Judging from the two books, *The Tempting of America* and *Slouching Towards Gomorrah*, that Bork has published since his nomination was defeated, the committee judged correctly. These books make many of his previous views look tame.

I do not bring up Bork's confirmation conversion to point to any duplicity. The human capacity for self-delusion and rationalization, the wiles of desire, the lure of power, and the force of ambition are not the point here; but the fact that they exist and are very potent, indeed determinative of the social fabric, must be accounted for in any legal philosophy. They play an inevitable role in any adjudication, though they cannot be acknowledged at the time of judgment, if from within the law, the judgment is not to become suspect. It is ironic, though expectable, that a Bork, like Reagan, should plead for judicial restraint in order to avoid politicizing the law. Judicial activism has usually been identified with a liberal political stance. It can, however, equally well serve conservative causes.

Senator Orrin Hatch, clearly a Bork supporter, tried hard to elicit a catchy statement of judicial philosophy from Bork, one that would be clear and appealing to the millions of people watching the hearings. Despite Hatch's prompting, as well as the prompting Bork received from experts before the hearings, Bork appeared incapable of picking up on the cues his supporters gave him. One thinks of his long, professorial answer to Hatch's question: What is judicial activism? All Hatch wanted Bork to say—and in the end said it for him—was that it was when judges make law. Hatch later observed, "It was very frustrating when you serve up a question that he ought to hit a home run on and he wouldn't do it."[15] Hatch did manage to underscore Bork's criticism of judicial activism, which, defined as judge-made law, allowed Bork to declare it undemocratic. Judges, at least federal judges, are not elected by the people, so the argument goes, but rather appointed for life. Though nominated by an elected president and confirmed by an elected Senate, they do not have to answer to an electorate. They are free, within limits even Bork had to admit, to interpret the law according to their own predilections. They can be removed from office only by impeachment.

In the popular imagination, the judge is at once human, subject to the same foibles as everyone else, and somehow capable of transcending that ordinary humanity, capable of achieving an exceptional, ethically inspired objectivity and fairness—a sense of integrity and justice. There are, of course, many explanations for attributing to the judge a superior sense of justice, none of which are satisfactory. They range from his training, experience, and expertise, to the obligations of his profession, his role commitments, and the dramatic accouterments, the orchestrated respect, the authority, that surround his performance and his person. They include the symbolic as well as the real role a judge plays in the social order, and the projections that it facilitates. His decisions, however specific, always have consequences beyond themselves. Like the doctor who, in preserving life, treats inevitably of death, attaining a special wisdom and authority whose source in death is and has to be denied—so the judge seems to attain a similar wisdom and authority in adjudicating the violence humans do to one another.[16] Not only is he touched by that violence, but, as the late Yale law professor Robert Cover reminds us, he perpetuates it; his every decision, however justified, does violence to one party or the other in the dispute.[17] Of course, the judge's perpetuation of violence is masked by the remedial role we give him. He is one of society's curers. An earlier generation of anthropologists would have recognized, in the attribution of this special wisdom, vestiges of more primitive times in which the curer and judge, the priest-judge, was surrounded by a sacred aura denied to his equivalent in today's hyperrationalized society. And yet the judge, like the medieval cleric, is still robed. He is in fact the only robed government official.

The anthropologist Carol Greenhouse argues that judges, especially the justices of the Supreme Court, belong to what she calls the temporality of justice, which is totalizing, cumulative, and reversible.[18] "The time of politics is the time of interests and their fulfillment, linear time. The time of justice . . . may borrow a linear time idiom, but it symbolically transcends it by virtue of the judiciary's claims to represent *all* interests and none." Unlike presidents, who are elected every four years, campaign publicly for office, and become the center of popular cults in which their personal histories and nowadays their most intimate lives figure, federal judges are appointed for life, do not campaign for office (at least publicly), and are (until the Bork and Clarence Thomas hearings, Greenhouse argues) without personal history.[19] They submit to what I would call an asceticism of neutrality. Like the priest, they renounce any display of personal interest and desire but they do not assume the priest's otherworldliness. As Greenhouse insists, they must also be exemplary citizens. They are "accountable to the people," but their accountability arises out of a renunciation of private interests and desires that allows them "to embrace all public interests."

Judges give voice to society's conscience. They are its moral *porte-parole*. "When justices interpret the Constitution," Justice William Brennan observed, "they speak for their community, not for themselves."[20] Like the great eighteenth-century English jurist William Blackstone, who described the judge as an "oracle of the law," one might relate him to that depersonalized voice of society's deepest, if at times most hidden, values.[21] Though we deny this "irrational" dimension to the role of the judge, less so perhaps to that of the priest or preacher, we are not immune to its effect. Despite our Borks and Scalias, and other more sober spokesmen and spokeswomen of judicial constraint, we allow the judge to speak for us, for the values of *our* country (even though we know the United States to be too heterogeneous to have any but a fictive set of shared values). We allow the judge to say that "the American people believe, hold, think, will not tolerate, will tolerate. . . ." The judge becomes the voice of "we-the-people."

We may deny or try to extirpate the oracular dimension of judgeship on rational grounds, and yet still respond to its rhetoric. Critics of Brennan's depiction of a justice of the Supreme Court—the conservative Lino Graglia of the University of Texas is one of them—are outraged by what they regard as an usurpation of the legislature, indeed, of the power of the people. "Justice Brennan does not explain why he thinks the community needs or wants unelected judges to speak for it instead," Graglia observes, "or why the judges can be expected better to reflect or express the community's views."[22] The point is not why but whether or not the community thinks so. Graglia insists that "the community" is "fully capable of speaking for itself through the representatives it elects and maintains in office for that purpose." That too must be determined, and in terms not just of the community's capacity but also of the representative's capacity, his or her will, to represent. I would argue that Graglia is simply giving expression, for *his* political purposes, to one of the foundational clichés of democracy.[23]

In our quest to promote the judge's objectivity and neutrality, we focus less on these "irrational" qualities than we do on ways to prevent judges from taking advantage of their position by reading into the law their own vision of our society. Advocates of judicial restraint, such as Bork and Graglia, are concerned primarily with the self-conscious manipulation of the law. They tend to ignore or sidestep the effect of the "lens composed of our morality and understanding" through which we look at the facts—and read. As Bork observed, "there is an enormous difference between that inevitable bias that gets in and a judge who self-consciously tries to keep his biases out and tries to be as impartial on the evidence as he can be." No doubt, there *is* an enormous difference. The problem is one with which we are by now familiar. The Fundamentalists referred to it as "eisogesis," the reading into a text one's own view that is not there. How do you know when you are reading into a text? Can you ever know your bias? Can your reader know? How, then, do we read Bork? How did he understand himself? Were his answers to the senators who questioned him sincere? Or were they hypocritical, manipulative, political? Did he in fact suffer a real confirmation conversion? A transitory one? Or none at all? The line between conscious and less than conscious awareness of what one is doing is always difficult, if not impossible, to draw. The Fundamentalist, like other believing Christians, can always invoke Jesus's help. The lawyer and the judge cannot—not, at least, publicly or professionally. They must depend on their self-critical wit, on their capacity to know themselves.

The Constitution is my legal bible; its plan of our government is my plan and its destiny my destiny. I cherish every word of it, from the first to the last, and I personally deplore even the slightest deviation from its least important commands.

Hugo Black, 1969[24]

Some men look at constitutions with sanctimonious reverence, and deem them like the arc of the covenant, too sacred to be touched. They ascribe to men of the preceding age a wisdom more than human, and suppose what they did to be beyond amendment. I knew this age well; I belonged to it, and labored with it. It deserved well of its country. It was very like the present, but without the experience of the present; and forty years of experience in government is worth a century of book-reading; and this they would say themselves, were they to rise from the dead. I am certainly not an advocate for frequent and un-tried changes in the laws and constitutions. . . . But I know also, that laws and institutions must go hand in hand with the progress of the human mind. As that becomes more developed, more enlightened, as new discoveries are made, new truths disclosed, and manners and opinions change with the change of circumstances, institutions must advance also, and keep pace with the times. We might as well require a man to wear still the coat which fitted him when a boy, as civilized society to remain ever under the regimen of their barbarous ancestors. . . . Let us [not] weakly believe that one generation is not as capable as another of taking care of itself, and of ordering its own affairs. Let us, as our sister States have done, avail ourselves of our reason and experience, to correct the crude essays of our first and inexperienced, although wise, virtuous, and well-meaning councils. And lastly, let us provide in our constitution for its revision at stated periods.

Thomas Jefferson to Samuel Kercheval, July 12, 1816[25]

These two quotations, not in themselves as extreme as some I could have chosen, describe the frame within which the status of the United States Constitution has been argued and evaluated. The Harvard legal historian Morton Horwitz has observed that insofar as constitutional law embodies a conception of "legal fundamentality"—that is, a sense that the Constitution is more basic than ordinary law—it is particularly vulnerable to modernism's and (now postmodernism's) challenge to traditional notions of objectivity, history, and legitimacy.[26] The "self-evident truths" that Thomas Jefferson invoked with such confidence in the Declaration of Independence are no longer so evident.[27] Modernism's destabilizing influence on the law (as on religion) has produced a significant split between liberal and conservative approaches to the law. The liberals (I will call them "pragmatists") are less threatened by the modernist challenge, view the Constitution open-endedly, as a "living document," and try, within limits, to incorporate change into their understanding of it. The conservatives, or "originalists," cling to the letter of the law. Though they may speak of the spirit of the Constitution, they tend to oppose attempts to extract unstated principles from its form, substance, or organization as a whole: they focus on the plain, ordinary meaning of specific clauses. They tend to be more respectful of tradition than the pragmatists; for example, they usually argue in terms of original meaning and intent as though that "original meaning" or "original intent," was—and is—*the* meaning of the text they are considering. Some extremists, like Bork, are so loath to depart from original intention that they even mistrust precedent, arguing that it can lead to their anathema— "judge-made" law. Though they worry about activist courts destroying the separation of powers mandated by the Constitution, they themselves often favor one or another branch: Antonin Scalia, for example, the executive, and Bork, in his later writings, the legislature.[28]

Law professors, who like to make nice distinctions in interpretive perspective, speak of legal conservatives as originalists, interpretivists, literalists, strict-constructivists, intentionalists, or textualists. The originalists hold that "judges deciding constitutional issues should confine themselves to enforcing norms that are stated or clearly implicit in the Constitution *as it was understood by those who ratified it.*"[29] Some originalists refer back to the framers of the Constitution. Judge Richard Posner dismisses this as "framer idolatry."[30] Non-originalists argue "that the task of interpretation authorizes courts to make particular judgments not foreseen by or even contrary to those of the Constitutional ratifiers."[31] Related to

this debate is the one between the interpretivists and noninterpretivists. Interpretivists hold that judges "must rely on value judgments 'within' the Constitution," while noninterpretivists (their
name notwithstanding) believe that judges should, or at least can,
look "outside" the Constitution and the decisions based on it. The
pragmatists have a looser view of the Constitution than the formalists. They speak in terms of its spirit, its aspiration, its unwritten
presuppositions, the thrust of the whole, its need to be in tune with
the times. They are willing to consider "creative" interpretations
that rely on exogenous theories of the law, society, and politics.
Their approach is future-oriented, more consequential, more
policy-oriented than that of the formalists. They tend to include social factors such as racism and gender discrimination, or economic
ones like cost-benefit analyses in their arguments and decisions.
Their approach is more figurative, more willing to extend what the
literalists would regard as the (original) meaning of the text.
Though the formalists are more text-bound than the pragmatists,
both believe that the (text of the) Constitution is binding. They differ in the weight they give to context at origin (that is, at the time the
Constitution or its amendments was written or ratified) and on application. The formalists mistrust figuration, metaphor, analogy:
they tend to ignore the ideological potential of words, the way
words and text precipitate, articulate, and frame their context. By
focusing on words and texts, they attempt to bracket off human and
social considerations.

In advancing or criticizing a conservative or a liberal position,
judges and lawyers tend to argue, narrowly, from within the law,
and to repeat in a different register arguments previously advanced.
To be sure some scholars do transgress and question the presuppositions and framing of legal argument. Robert Cover stressed the
violence inherent in judicial interpretation, indeed in any interpretation; Bruce Ackerman at Yale offers a dramatic revision of constitutional history and amendment; Roberto Unger, one of the
founders of Critical Legal Studies, understands legal interpretation
in terms of its role in the always self-deceptive attempt of political
theory to preserve the status quo; Martha Minow who, like other

feminist legal theorists who want to incorporate notions of difference in the law, argues for "embedding rights within relationships";
and the postmodernist Drusilla Cornell calls attention to the transformative, redemptive dimension of interpretive practice.[32] They
are the exception and are rarely conservative, although the politically conservative Posner does lay bare, often ruthlessly, the pretense of legal argument and adjudication.[33]

It is usually possible to correlate an interpretive stance with a political one, but in fact there is no necessary connection between the
two. Political conservatives often read the law loosely, to fit their
own agenda, and political liberals do not hesitate to make literalist
interpretations if it suits their purposes. Hugo Black is a case in
point. A Southern progressive, appointed to the Supreme Court by
Roosevelt in 1937, he defended the New Deal even as he insisted on
what he took to be a literal enforcement of constitutional guarantees. In his James Madison Lecture at New York University in 1960,
Black attacked those who tried to balance the Bill of Rights against
some expressly granted power of Congress. For him, there were ab-
solutes in the Bill of Rights, and they had to be respected as such;
otherwise the Constitution would offer no safeguards against legislative and executive encroachment. He insisted that phrases like
"Congress shall make no law" in the First Amendment are composed of "plain words, easily understood." "To my way of thinking, at least," he wrote, "the history and language of the Constitution and the Bill of Rights . . . make it plain that one of the primary purposes of the Constitution with its amendments was to
withdraw from the Government all power to act in certain areas—
whatever the scope of those areas may be."[34] Whatever balancing
was required had already been done by the Framers of the Constitution and its first ten amendments.[35] "Courts have neither the right
nor the power to review this original decision of the Framers and to
attempt to make a different evaluation of the importance of the
rights granted in the Constitution." However, given his belief that a
literalist reading of the Constitution is necessary to control judicial
power, Black was forced to dissent in *Griswold v. Connecticut*,[36] in
which the court argued that a state statute prohibiting the use of

contraceptives was an infringement of the constitutional right to marital privacy, for he could find no such guarantee in the Constitution. "I realize that many good and able men have eloquently spoken and written, sometimes in rhapsodical strains, about the duty of this Court to keep the Constitution in tune with the times," he wrote in Griswold. "For myself, I must with all deference reject this philosophy. The Constitution makers knew the need for change and provided for it."[37]

Black's approach to the Constitution partakes of what we might call a biblical temporality—one that suggests timeless wisdom and heroic foundation while demanding "sanctimonious reverence." In the same New York University lecture, he reads each of the amendments, as if their very enunciation evoked the absolute value he claims for them. He waxes poetic, patriotic, over the Constitution, insisting that it is "the best hope for the aspirations of freedom which men share everywhere."

> Since the earliest days philosophers have dreamed of a country where the mind and spirit of man would be free; where there would be no limits to inquiry; where men would be free to explore the unknown and to challenge the most deeply rooted beliefs and principles. Our First Amendment was a bold effort to adopt this principle—to establish a country with no legal restrictions of any kind upon the subjects people could investigate, discuss, and deny. The Framers knew, better perhaps than we do today, the risks they were taking. They knew that free speech might be the friend of change and revolution. But they also knew that it is always the deadliest enemy of tyranny.[38]

He cannot "agree with those who think of the Bill of Rights as an eighteenth-century straitjacket, unsuited for this age. It is old but not all old things are bad. The evils it guards against are not only old, they are with us now, they exist today."[39]

Black conflates the eternal truths he sees in the Constitution with the Constitution itself as a timeless text, denying, or at least ignoring, the extent to which interpretation, however literalistic, changes our understanding of the Constitution.[40] These changes in reading are of particular significance in American law, where, incorporated into opinion, they become binding precedents. To be sure, they may be overruled; but even when they are, they orient the argument of the overruling decision. This process of change is well illustrated in many areas of constitutional law, most notably and controversially in the court's understanding of due process, where, for example, the due process clauses of the Fifth and Fourteenth Amendments, understood in substantive terms, have served to extend many but not all of the specific guarantees of the Bill of Rights to the states.[41] I should further note that, with time, some decisions take on an authority that approximates that of the Constitution itself. The most dramatic example is Chief Justice John Marshall's decision in *Marbury v. Madison*, which inaugurated judicial review, by which the court had the power to declare acts of Congress unconstitutional.[42]

Unlike and long before Black, Thomas Jefferson worried about the consequences of static entrenchment in a "steady habit," of revering a text, and of subservience to the dictates of the dead.[43] The Jefferson letter quoted above was written in response to a pamphlet by Samuel Kercheval concerning equal representation in Virginia. (Though Kercheval later wrote *A History of the Valley of Virginia*, he is best known as the recipient of Jefferson's letter.[44]) To Kercheval's surprise, no doubt, Jefferson, who was in his late sixties at the time and had assumed a contemplative stance in his retirement at Monticello, wrote a lengthy response. Not only did he lay out his theory of multiple sites for representation, from ward to legislature, but he reiterated a concern for the continual renewal of a constitution, whether of the nation or state. He had already expressed this concern more than two decades earlier in a letter he wrote to James Madison from Paris, at the beginning of the French Revolution.[45] Jefferson argued his case for continual or periodic constitutional revision—"repairs," he wrote—in terms of the independence of passing generations from one another. Each generation has "a right to choose for itself the form of government it believes most promotive of its own happiness. . . ." The dead have no rights over the living, Jefferson argued. "This corporeal globe, and everything upon it, belong to the present corporeal inhabitants, during their generation."

Cast in terms of the people's right to choose for themselves the form of government they believe best, Jefferson's suggestion stresses the constraints imposed by the Constitution, which are or could be at variance with the will of the people at any given time. It presupposes changes in the popular will that could require if not continual at least periodic—generational—modification of the Constitution. It is, of course, an idealistic view, a utopian one, which Madison among others would find impractical and disorderly. It rests, I would argue, on a notion of the people and their will that is rather more animate than rhetorical—one that is dependent, metaphorically, on the psychological idiom (that of the faculties of the mind, current in the eighteenth century) in which *the people* is understood. It reflects Jefferson's strong, at times reckless, individualism. And it fails to look at the ways in which the government established by the Constitution is responsive to the people's "will" and subject to modification by amendment and authoritative interpretation.[46] But, it does call attention to the intransigence over time of the Constitution and the government it has constituted, and to the limitations of its—of any—system of representation.

One can view Jefferson's desire for continual constitutional reform as a response to the loss of the revolutionary *élan* that inevitably followed independence and the foundation of the American republic. It is, after all, a sequel to all revolutions, whether understood psychologically, in terms of an emptiness that follows a "revolutionary high," or sociologically, in terms of the disappointment and disillusion that appears with the first intimation of the routinization of newly founded institutions of government. But such psychological and sociological understandings, as revealing as they may be, deflect our attention from a paradox inherent in revolutionary aspiration and constitutional formation. As the political philosopher Hannah Arendt observed, "Nothing threatens the very achievement of revolution more dangerously and more acutely than the spirit which has brought it about."[47] That spirit arises out of building something new which aspires to permanence. It gives to the generation of founders a privilege of foundation, of a wholly creative freedom, if you will, that they cannot pass on to subsequent generations. Jefferson, like Thomas Paine, was outraged by this inevitable legacy of deprivation. To govern beyond the grave was, in Paine's always spirited words, "the most ridiculous and insolent of all tyrannies."[48]

Revolutionary fervor aside, there is another, structurally more significant paradox in any constitution, one that is reflected in the equivocal nature of the word itself.[49] "Constitution" refers both to the act of constituting a government, its rules and laws, and to the rules and laws once constituted. Paine focused on the one in his famous definition: "A constitution is not the act of government, but of a people constituting a government."[50] Of course, he was referring to the formation of the U. S. Constitution, which is in many ways quite exceptional. It did not grow, like the English Constitution, by accretion over centuries. It was not the result of governmental decree, as are the constitutions of many postcolonial and post-Soviet societies. It was very much the product of men who saw in their quest for independence the unique possibility of creating a new form of government. "How few of the human race have ever enjoyed an opportunity of making an election of government, more than of air, soil, or climate for themselves or their children," John Adams wrote.[51] Indeed, the work of the Continental Congress was hampered by the departure of many of its delegates, including Jefferson, who went home to write their own state constitutions. "Nothing—not the creation of this confederacy, not the Continental Congress, not the war, not the French alliance—in the years surrounding the Declaration of Independence engaged the interests of the Americans more than the framing of these separate governments," the historian Gordon Wood observes.[52] It is in this spirit, sobered to be sure by the failure of the Confederation, that the writing of the American Constitution must be taken.

The Constitutional Convention that met in Philadelphia in 1787, like the conventions and special congresses that were responsible for the various state constitutions, had an extralegal status, which, coupled with the idea of fundamental law, seemed to allay the mistrust of legislature most Americans had at the time.[53] However weak the Confederate Congress may have been, like the state legislature, it could not constitute its own foundational laws in a way that would guarantee their independence and immunity from legislative manipulation and alteration. It was, in fact, the Virginia Legislature—appointing commissioners in January 1786 to meet with commissioners from other states—that triggered the process by which the convention was finally called. Twelve commissioners from five states—New York, New Jersey, Pennsylvania, Delaware, and Virginia—met in Annapolis on September 11, 1786, and quickly recommended that a full delegation convene the following May in Philadelphia. On February 21, 1787, the Congress of the Confederation asked its member states to send delegates to the convention. All did except Rhodes Island, or, as the constitutionalists called it, "Rogues' Island."

It is well known that the members of the convention overstepped the mandate they were given by the Confederation—to meet in Philadelphia "for the sole and express purpose of revising the Articles of Confederation, and reporting to Congress and the several legislatures, such alterations and provisions therein as shall, when agreed to by Congress and confirmed by the States, render the Federal Constitution adequate to the exigencies of Government and the preservation of the union."[54] Instead of revising the Articles of Confederacy, as they were instructed to do, the members of the Philadelphia convention, under the guidance of Madison, wrote an entirely new constitution—one that would do away with the very government, the Confederation, that had promoted their meeting. The government that replaced the Confederation was a sort of compromise between those nationalists like Madison, who would have preferred a stronger central government, and those who, fearing the loss of state sovereignty, would have liked a weaker one. It was, as the political scientist John P. Roche never let us forget, very much a product of men who were preeminently politicians, practical, and exquisitely conscious of the need for a rapid and sure ratification in their respective constituencies.[55] The Philadelphia convention, Roche wrote, "was not a College of Cardinals or a council of Platonic guardians working within a manipulative predemocratic framework; it was a *nationalist* reform caucus which had to operate with great delicacy and skill in a political cosmos full of enemies to achieve the one definitive goal—approbation."[56] The promulgation of the new constitution framed the ensuing debate. Federalists and anti-Federalists argued over the principles of constitutional government, not over amendments to the Articles of Confederacy. It was, at least rhetorically, the people who would decide.

Given the weakness of the Confederation and its Congress, it is not clear who had the authority to authorize the convention and who had the authority to change the convention's mandate; that is, to write a constitution that did away with the Congress that authorized it. The Constitution, though, which can no more authorize itself than the Bible can declare itself inerrant, invokes the "people" as those who ordain and establish it. "We the People of the United States, in order to form a more perfect Union, establish Justice, insure domestic Tranquillity, provide for the common defense, promote the general Welfare, and secure the Blessings of Liberty to ourselves and our Posterity, do ordain and establish this Constitution for the United States of America." It does stipulate in Article Seven that the "Conventions of nine States shall be sufficient for the Establishment of this Constitution between the States so ratifying the Same." It does not, however, specify what these "conventions" are and how they are to be established.

In the case of constitutions that found new governments, as with all inaugural performatives, the question arises regarding who is authorized, and by what authority, to authorize the constitutive act. Arendt puts it this way: "Those who get together to constitute a new government are themselves unconstitutional, that is, they have no authority to do what they have set out to achieve."[57] I am not quibbling here, nor am I making an argument for the illegitimacy of the U. S. Constitution (though some have tried to); rather, I am calling attention to a paradox in any foundational act. It is, to speak extravagantly, always a violent act, which as it gives birth to a new order, illegitimately, illegally, some might say, does away with the old order that gave its founding what legitimacy it may have had.[58] The moment of transition, or rupture from the old order to the new is at one and the same time in and out of time. It is very much like that ever but never fully disappearing moment at the death of a king which is framed by the cries "The King is dead!" and "Long live the King!" The illegitimacy, or at least the lack of legitimacy, is of course unacceptable to the new order and is simply denied or masked by powerful images of rebirth, invocations of justice, higher truth, law, and authority, or manifestations of God's will or destiny.[59] As Jean-Jacques Rousseau put it: *il faudrait des dieux—* "one would need gods." One also needs *the people*.

Of course, the "people" have to be constituted and given voice, paradoxically by the same document that requires their voice for ratification. Their voice is, as it were, already presupposed in that originary moment in which they are constituted. The words of the Constitution, sounding forth from that moment, become if not the words of the "people" then what the words of the "people" ought to be. Deviations from these words, in fact and in representation—by judges for example—are prohibited. Through its constitutive act, the Constitution becomes the law that frames the "people" and determines (the idiom of) their representation. The move is from the people to the "people"—a move that of necessity is always obfuscated in the representations, at least the political representations, of the "people." There they must be taken not as "people" but as *the people*—the ordinary you and I who compose we-the-people. Of course, we do not normally acknowledge this dimension of peoplehood and the paradoxes upon which it has been founded. I suspect if we were to do so, we would be overwhelmed and even paralyzed by the pretense or artifice of our polity. Its fragile bonds, the tentativeness of its foundation in words alone—not even God-breathed, whatever appeal to God they make—would then give way.

It has become fashionable in academic circles to relate the Constitution to the Declaration of Independence.[60] It is said that the Preamble to the Declaration constituted "the people" who, their ties with England severed, became the population that could authorize—that is, ratify—the Constitution. It was to them that the Preamble to the Constitution appealed. As a constitutive act, the Declaration of Independence suffers from the same paradox as the Constitution. Pushed to the limit, one cannot find legitimacy in an ultimate antecedent, an origin, without invoking a god or his or her equivalent, since that antecedent or origin must itself have been created and constituted so as to authorize its authority to authorize, to legitimate. Like privileging genealogies whose origin, finally in an ordinary Adam, have always to be couched in myth or lost in the shadows of the past, the foundings of social order are cast in mythic terms, whether as divine marriages, social contracts, or simply declarations of God-givenness, or buried, like the English Constitution, in a now-lost history.[61]

Who had the authority to declare independence? And by what right?[62] The Preamble makes reference to the entitlements of the Laws of Nature and Nature's God. "When in the Course of human events, it becomes necessary for one people to dissolve the political bonds among the Powers of the earth, the separate and equal station to which the Laws of nature and Nature's God entitle them, a decent respect to the opinions of mankind requires that they should declare the causes which impel them to the separation." Written in the historical present and making reference to "the course of human events," the opening sentence of the Declaration suggests an inevitability, a destiny that impels. Nature, God, decency are all givens from which flow a course of events so inevitable that the inhabitants, the people, of a rebelling continent have no choice but to act in accordance with them. The next sentence confirms this inevitability cognitively—in terms of a self-evidence that has grounded Western thinking since Plato and Aristotle: a clarity so clear, so *apodeictic* as philosophers say, that it is timeless.[63] "We hold these truths to be self-evident, that all men are created equal, that they are endowed by their Creator with certain unalienable Rights, that among these are Life, Liberty, and the pursuit of Happiness." Already, in this second sentence, the people are, as if by magic, constituted. Unlike the historical impersonality of the first sentence, the second begins with "we" who become "we the people" who need only demonstrate, as the remainder of the Declaration does, the justice of their grievances and the failure of their attempts to seek redress from the Crown and their British brethren, in order to justify their declaration. "We, therefore, the Representatives of the united States of America, in General Congress, Assembled, appealing to the Supreme Judge of the world for the rectitude of our intentions do, in the Name and by the Authority of the good People of these Colonies, solemnly publish and declare, That these United Colonies are, and of Right ought to be Free and Independent States. . . ." We must note a slippage here from "we the people" to "we the representatives" who act in the name of a now "good" people. What or whom they represent remains of necessity at this founding moment ambiguous: "the united States of America"? "the good People of these Colonies"? "these United Colonies"?

Of course, the Declaration of Independence did not constitute the people in any but the most tentatively legal sense. The "people" figured mightily in the political rhetoric and philosophy of the period. They figured, for example, in the Declaration of Rights of 1765 and 1774 and in the Virginia Bill of Rights of 1776. Although the people, along with the nobility and the crown, were still understood in the eighteenth century as an estate, they had in effect become an oppositional category. The people, Gordon Wood writes, "were generally assumed to be a homogeneous entity, undeniably composed of an infinite number of gradations and ranks, but still an entity whose interests were considered to be connected and for the purposes of politics basically similar."[64] For the Whigs, the sole purpose of government was the promotion of the people's happiness. Their liberty was pitched at the extreme against absolute rule and tyranny. "What is good for the People," Thomas Gordon wrote in 1748, "is bad for their Governors; and what is good for the Governors, is pernicious to the People."[65]

During the revolution, both sides made reference to the people.[66] Their purity was a given. John Adams recalled in his autobiography that the notion that the people were the "Source of all Authority and Original of all Power" was not a new, strange, or terrible doctrine to the members of the Continental Congress. The

Tory Daniel Leonard called the rights of the people sacred and admitted that they had the right to change their government. What the Tories denied was that the rebels spoke for all the people. Despite their own allegiance to a homogeneous notion of the people, they were in effect calling attention to the factiousness of any society. The "people" was both a unifying figure of opposition and a cover for tendentiousness and diversity of interest. It was also preclusive, for it excluded women and slaves. It may well have evoked an ideal community of the virtuous-minded who were willing to sacrifice their own interests for the good of the whole, but it was also a way of referring to those inhabitants of the American continent whose divergent loyalties to their states and localities, to themselves and to their families, could not be acknowledged for political and military reasons in the struggle for independence and its immediate aftermath.

Within a few years of independence, it became clear that the vision of a government that assumed an organic unity of the people's interest was unrealistic. With the recognition that the people were, in Wood's words, "an agglomeration of hostile individuals coming together for their mutual benefit to construct a society," politics could no longer be thought of in terms of a simple opposition between the people and their rulers.[67] It had to take account of opposition among the people who strove for the control of a government that was divested of its former identity with society—with the people. Madison, who relates factions to the rights of property, wrote in *Federalist*:

> A zeal for different opinions concerning religion, concerning Government, and many other points, as well of speculation as of practice; an attachment to different leaders ambitiously contending for pre-eminence and power; or to persons of other descriptions whose fortunes have been interesting to the human passions, have in turn divided mankind into parties, inflamed them with mutual animosity, and rendered them much more disposed to vex and oppress each other, than to co-operate for their common good.[68]

(It is in this letter that Madison argues the power of a republican form of government to diminish factionalism.)

The recognition of division among the people, Wood argues, led to the "disembodiment of government from society," and thereby to "a conception of modern politics and the eventual justification of competing parties among the people."[69] In the conclusion to *The Creation of the American Republic*, he points out that the meaning and emphasis of words and concepts by which political reality was understood at the beginning of the American Revolution had changed by the time the Constitution was being written.[70] Tyranny was now used for the abuse of power by any branch of government and even by the people. The separation of the executive, legislature, and judiciary, rather than simply the participation of the people, became the best guarantor of liberty. Liberty, which had been understood by the Whigs as the right of the people to share in government, was now understood in terms of the protection of individual rights against all governmental encroachment. Though public virtue, which had played such an important role in the initial formulations of the republican ideal, was still rhetorically potent, it had ceased to be seen as necessary to the functioning of good government. Indeed, as Wood suggests, its function was being replaced by public opinion. "No government, Americans told themselves over and over, had ever before so completely set its roots in the sentiments and aims of its citizens."[71]

It was through public opinion and participation, through the government's rootedness in society—or so Americans of the period argued—that the new republic would be preserved from the decay and decadence that history suggested was inevitable. With Jefferson, they were concerned about the adjustment between a government frozen in time and the present-day needs of society and its citizens. "The confining of a people, who have arrived at a highly improved state of society, to the forms and principles of a government, which originated in a simple, if not barbarous state of men and manners," Nathaniel Chipman wrote in *Principles of Government* in 1833, was, like Chinese foot-binding, a "perversion of nature" which would lead inevitably to social upheaval.[72] But unlike the sclerotic old governments, men like Chipman argued, the American republic had built in its own "healing principle": the constitution incorporated its own plan of reformation. It could be amended and altered by the people.

Of course, it is one thing to call attention to the possibility of changing a constitution before it is ratified and another to change it once it *has been* ratified. In the first instance, signaling the possibility of change is rhetorical: it is done to assure those who fear constitutional constraint (especially if the constitution should prove faulty) that remediation is possible and in their hands. Or, it is to disquiet those who fear change, especially if it is out of *their* hands and in the hands of the people. In the second instance, once the constitution is ratified, once the new order has been constituted, change is always threatening to the constituted order and the constitutive force of the constitution. Change undermines its foundational status. It calls attention to its human origins—its artifice—which are but poorly masked by whatever sacred aura surrounds them. This is true even for those Americans who describe the Constitution as God-given, although it may not be true for those few—there are some—who believe it to be God's word.

Unlike the Bible, at least as the evangelists read it, the Constitution is for most Americans neither God-breathed, inerrant, nor above human alteration. Usually the threat of proposed change is understood pragmatically, in political terms. But such political understanding, however realistic, tends to ignore or at least to diminish the sacred dimension of the drama it describes. It certainly does not take into account the double temporality inaugurated by the constitution: the constitutive moment that is in and out of time, and the ensuing "historical" time that incorporates as it departs from (betrays, even) that founding moment in its understanding. Any alteration—the threat of any alteration—to the constitution so conceived produces an existential anxiety that affects the deepest structures of the world we live in: it gives a surprising urgency, or even a fearful sense of emergency, to political imperatives for change. Or, it may facilitate an almost iconoclastic, a risky display of self- and collective assertion.

Unlike John Locke and his chief legal interpreter, William Blackstone, who held that a people could replace a government only when those in power had disqualified themselves by endangering the happiness of the community to such an extent that civil society had reverted to a state of nature, Americans were quick to argue that because their constitution(s) rested on popular consent, they had the right to replace it with a new one.[73] Already in 1776, the New Jersey Constitution, the first new state constitution, had an implicit notion of amendment, and the Pennsylvania Constitution of the same year had an explicit amendment procedure, which depended on a special convention, the Council of Censors, rather than on the legislature. Taken from the ancient Roman republic, the council was to be elected every seven years to determine whether there was an "absolute necessity" to amend any article of the constitution that might be defective.[74] By 1780, the principle that the fundamental law could be modified by the people was so entrenched that nearly half the states had amending procedures in their constitution. Americans had invented, as the political scientist Donald Lutz notes, an amendment process that depended on "a public, formal, highly deliberate decision-making process that distinguished between constitutional matters and normal legislation."[75] It required the same level of popular sovereignty as the writing of the constitution itself. The process had neither to be too easy nor too difficult. "A process that is too easy does not provide enough distinction between constitutional matters and normal legislation," Lutz observes; but one that is too difficult impedes the rectification of mistakes.[76] That more than ten thousand amendments to the United States Constitution have been proposed since its ratification, and only twenty-seven of them have been adopted, either confirms the view held by many conservatives that the Constitution is nearly perfect or suggests that amendment procedures are in fact too difficult to bring about necessary changes.[77] (Of course, I am ignoring the possibility that many if not most of the proposals were unrealistic, rhetorical, politically threatening, or simply crackpot.) It certainly calls attention to the serious—I am tempted to say almost blasphemous—nature of amendment.

Article Five of the Constitution describes two ways in which amendments may be made. (It does *not* state that these are the *only* ways in which the Constitution may be amended.) The first and the only one used to date requires two thirds of both houses of Congress to propose the amendment, which must then be ratified "by the Legislatures of three fourths of the several States, or by Conventions in three fourths thereof, as the one or the other Mode of Ratification may be proposed by the Congress." The second requires two thirds of the legislatures of the several states to call a convention for proposing amendments, which must then be ratified, as in the case of amendments proposed by Congress. So ambiguous is the article that it appears to be the product of political anxiety and was certainly a compromise among different factions in the Philadelphia Convention.[78] The article does not specify, for example, how the ratifying conventions are to be chosen. It could be argued that, while Congress must propose specific amendments, the legislatures need not propose amendments for the convention. Rather, the convention—perhaps like the original Philadelphia Convention—is called to propose amendments. Although constitutional scholars have argued about the meaning of the article, it has never been necessary to test its meaning in the courts, since only the first, less cumbersome procedure, has been employed. Only once, in 1933, were state conventions called to ratify an amendment: the Twenty-first Amendment repealing Prohibition.[79] There have been no conventions called by state legislatures, although there have been more than four hundred attempts to do so.[80] Nor has there ever been any serious attempt to formally amend the Constitution by procedures other than those described in Article Five.

The failure to amend the Constitution by convention is often attributed to the fear that any such convention would, like the original Philadelphia Convention "run away." And it has been noted that there is no constitutional guarantee that a convention would have to adhere to its congressional mandate. It has been suggested, not unreasonably, that if a convention is called to propose, for example, a balanced budget amendment, it could slip in amendments to permit school prayer, outlaw abortion, or require the election of federal judges. Legal scholars like Paul Weber and Barbara Perry argue that there is little danger that such subterfuge would work, given—aside from political and media pressure—the safeguards built into the amendment process itself. Congress can establish convention procedures; the Supreme Court can rule on any challenges to such procedures; Congress can refuse to forward the proposals to the states for approval; and, of course, the proposals themselves have to be ratified by three fourths of the States.[81] In fact, attempts to call a constitutional convention have served mainly political ends—as scare tactics to force Congress's hand.[82] Recent calls for conventions to prohibit compulsory school assignment (busing), to permit school prayer, to outlaw abortion, to allow presidential line-item vetoing, and to require a balanced budget have, however, all failed to force Congress to propose such amendments—though they have had considerable political impact and have even effected legislation concerning the line-item veto and restrictions on abortion.

I suppose it is theoretically possible from a literalist point of view to so amend the Constitution that it would completely alter the structure of the U.S. government and the rights granted to its citizens. Democracies can, it is sometimes said, democratically do away with their democracy. In 1979, when one version of the now-familiar balanced-budget amendment was extremely popular, Richard Rovere wrote in *The New Yorker* that it is possible for a convention—though, the very thought of this, according to Rovere, was "chilling and subversive" to most lawyers and legislators—to

> reinstate segregation, and even slavery; throw out much or all of the Bill of Rights (free speech, free press, separation of church and state, the prohibition against unreasonable searches and seizures); eliminate the Fourteenth Amendment's due-process clause and reverse any Supreme Court decision the members didn't like, including the one-man-one-vote rule; and perhaps, for good measure, eliminate the Supreme Court itself.[83]

One might well add the possibility of amending away the amendment procedure itself, thereby fixing the Constitution forever.

Rovere's nightmare scenario, if theoretically possible, is extremely unlikely. It is true, however, that unlike the constitutions of many countries (most notably Germany's, where Article 79, section 2 of *Grundgesetz* prohibits the amendment of its first twenty articles, which treat basic rights) the U. S. Constitution does not limit the range and scope of possible amendments. In fact, there are two exceptions to this limitation. Article Five protects the importation of slaves for twenty years and guarantees that no state will be deprived of equal suffrage in the Senate without the state's consent. The first of these is irrelevant today, except as a possible source for some analogical argument, or somehow as evidence of the Framers' intentions. The second is as relevant today as it was when the Constitution was written. They were both political in nature: to pacify the slave-owning states and to allay the fear of the smaller states that they could be deprived of equal representation.

Aside from these two "entrenchment clauses," legal scholars have asked whether there are implicit restrictions to the range and scope of amendments. Those who favor such restrictions argue on two principal grounds. The first appeals to basic principles in the Constitution itself; the second evokes some higher, transcendent, or natural law. Thus, in 1893, Thomas Cooley, one of the most influential legal commentators of his day, argued for limitations on both grounds.[84] As the first fifteen amendments have all extended "the democratic principles which underlie our constitution," he wrote, amendments "must be in harmony with the thing amended." He continued, "If the makers of the constitution . . . stopped short of forbidding such changes as would be inharmonious, they did so because it was not in their thought that any such changes could for a moment be considered by congress or the states as admissible, since in the completed instrument no place could possibly be found for them. . . ."[85] Cooley also invokes by way of an extraordinary metaphor higher law: "The fruit grower does not forbid his servants engrafting the witch-hazel or the poisonous sumac on his apple tree; the process is forbidden by a law higher and more imperative than any he could declare, and to which no additional force could possibly be given by re-enactment under his orders."[86]

Cooley's arguments, which were not directed toward any particular amendment, were appropriated by conservatives who hoped they could be used to persuade the courts to invalidate the Fifteenth Amendment (the right to vote regardless of race, color, or a previous condition of servitude), the Eighteenth (outlawing the manufacture and transportation of intoxicating liquors), and the Nineteenth (the right to vote regardless of sex).[87] Similar arguments have been advanced by liberals. For example, Walter Murphy argues that some of the provisions in the Constitution are so fundamental, so essential to human dignity, which he holds to be a core constitutional value, that an amendment repealing them would be voided by the courts.[88]

Though the people's ability to amend the Constitution was hailed by some of the federalists, it was seen as a danger by others. (We must not forget that many of the Framers were skeptical about the rule of the people—the real people, not the rhetorical people.) Madison argued in *Federalist 49* against too frequent appeal to the people; he believed that by calling attention to defects in the government it "would, in great measure, deprive the government of that veneration which time bestows on everything, and without which perhaps the wisest and freest governments would not possess the requisite stability."[89] As is well known, he was opposed to calling a second constitutional convention, even before the first was ratified, something many anti-Federalists advocated, particularly those who wanted to incorporate a bill of rights into the Constitution. "The very attempt at a second Convention," he observed, "strikes at the confidence in the first, and the existence of a second by opposing influence to influence, would in a manner destroy an effectual confidence in either."[90]

5—Foundations

Virtually from the moment of its ratification, Americans have treated the United States Constitution not only as a legal instrument but also as a sacred symbol. Along with the flag, it is one of the totems of our tribe. We call it "the Constitution" and no one asks "which constitution?" We display the original document in public viewing much as religions display their sacred relics. The constitutions of the states never received such treatment, not even when state sovereignty was a more vital notion than today. Nor does any other nation treat its constitution in this way.

Thomas C. Grey, 1984[1]

By an odd twist of fate, it was not the government that became an object of veneration for the new nation but the Constitution itself. This is perhaps is not so odd upon reflection. The government is structurally stable but always the arena of politicking, negotiation, and compromise. The Constitution effected stability not only through the governmental (republican) structure it constituted but also symbolically by its very existence. We must not forget the aura of sanctity which still surrounds the original as it is displayed, below the reliquary containing the Declaration of Independence, in the rotunda of National Archives in Washington. Flanked on both sides by American flags, it is viewed, so the guards there told me, by more than five thousand visitors a day during the "summer season," by more than 1.2 million a year.[2] (Most of the visitors I observed seemed satisfied with their visit, despite the fact they could not have seen much of the Constitution through the scratched, yellow protective glass that covers it. One little girl expressed her disappointment. "It's just words," she told her father, expecting him to reveal some secret significance, and he did. "But, honey," he said, "it's the original—it's what made the American government." "Oh." She smiled.) Nor must we forget the enormous media hype that surrounded the bicentennial celebration of the Constitution—the fact of celebrating it. People were genuinely moved. The Texas law professor Sanford Levinson describes the reverential mood[3] of visitors to an exhibition in Philadelphia that was called the Miracle in Philadelphia. It was held in the Second Bank of the United States, which was modeled on the Greek Parthenon. A portrait of Benjamin Rush, one of the Founders, looked down on the visitor. Though Rush, a "New Light" Presbyterian, did not believe in the divine inspiration of the Constitution, he did declare himself "perfectly satisfied that the Union of the States, in its *form* and *adoption*, is as much the work of Divine Providence as any of the miracles recorded in the Old and New Testament were the effects of divine power."

So many Americans have, like Rush and Black, related the Constitution to Scripture, Divine Providence, and God's creation that it has been hailed the centerpiece of American civil religion. George Washington asked that "the Constitution be sacredly maintained"; Madison noted that so astonishing was the Founders' overcoming of seemingly insurmountable difficulties that it was "impossible for a man of pious reflection not to perceive in it a finger of the Almighty hand"; Lincoln pleaded that Americans adopt the principle of "reverence for the laws" as the "political religion of the nation." George Sutherland, who became a justice of the Supreme Court in 1922, believed the Constitution to be a "divinely inspired instrument." And in 1987 the conservative Irving Kristol declared the Constitution, along with the Declaration of Independence and the American flag, the holy trinity of American civil religion.[4] A Pentecostalist, an uneducated, politically conservative man, once told me that while he couldn't exactly say that the Constitution was God's word, he thought it was a lot like the Bible. He said that since God had spoken through Moses, he might well have spoken to the fathers of the Constitution. "It's God's country, isn't it?" he observed with no irony.

That the Constitution is often or widely understood in sacred terms should come as no surprise, for a sacred aura generally surrounds words constitutive of a social order. Moreover, American political and social understanding is continually articulated in and through religious, primarily Christian, symbols. That these symbols should be taken at face value, as indicative of heartfelt belief rather than rhetorically, as potentially moving conventions of oratory, is itself symptomatic of the literalism I am trying to delineate in this book. I am not, I confess, convinced that the Constitution is the centerpiece of American civil religion. Rather, I view these attributions of its centrality to what the French call *déformation professionnelle*—that is, the distortion of reality that comes with professional engagement. We must remember that it is people in politics and law, and students of the same, who are most given to these sacralizations. Indeed, I would question the very notion of American civil religion, which has always struck me as projecting a particular style of rhetoric onto "social reality" without acknowledging the plays of power and desire that lay behind that rhetoric and its projection. It is more evocative of an idealized, simplified, indeed evangelical, view of American society than descriptive of that society in its actual diversity and complexity. Civil religion has, in any event, become for many an emblem of American social identity and uniqueness and as such has so oriented our self-understanding, so entered our social ideology, that even the "restless analysts" among us cannot easily escape its persuasive grip.[5]

Sanford Levinson is one of the most articulate proponents of the central role the Constitution plays in American civil religion. His book, *Constitutional Faith* is an attempt to clarify the "wholehearted attachment" he claims that Americans have to the Constitution "as the center of their, ultimately their nation's, political life."[6] He himself is caught between a patriotic commitment to constitutional ideals and a wariness about celebrating his own country and its Constitution. He asks what "bonds us (or could bond us) into a coherent political community, especially after the triumph of a distinctly (post)modernist sense of the contingencies of our own culture and the fragility of any community membership."[7] Levinson's own faith in the Constitution, at least in its potential, not only motivates his book and the writings of many legal scholars, but would of course be regarded by postmodernists as a retrogressive and therefore impossible attempt to restore that which has been permanently lost.

I do not mean to say that we are living in the extreme world that many postmodernists claim we are. Rather, we are living in a world in which the challenge of whatever the postmodernists mean by "postmodernism" produces a frequently reactionary response— one that idealizes the past, fetishizes the original, and indulges in nostalgia for that which was never experienced and probably never existed. Levinson is less given over to these idealizations and indulgences than many others, but in the final chapter of his book, he acknowledges signing the Constitution at the Philadelphia exhibition (visitors could add their names to those of the original signatories). Recognizing faults in the Constitution, injustices such as the slavery promulgated by it, and the fact that it may have privileged him as "a white, male, well-paid law professor," Levinson still accepts the political ideals he finds inherent in it. "For me," he writes, "signing the Constitution—and agreeing therefore to profess at least a limited constitutional faith—commits me not to closure but only to a process of becoming and to taking responsibility for constructing the political vision toward which I strive, joined, I hope, with others."[8]

There is something charmingly naive, charmingly American, about Levinson's signing the Constitution—or so I can hear my European friends exclaim. They may be speaking of this innocence with a realism, a conventional cynicism, a facile condescension, or out of envy; but as outsiders they recognize at least at some level the unavoidable mystifications inherent in indigenous social understanding. I don't question the heartfeltness of Levinson's gesture, nor the courage of his admission, nor the sincerity of his probing intellect and conscience before signing, any more than I would question the feelings and commitment of the evangelicals I have met. Rather, I want to call attention to the peculiar, unquestioned qualities of belief that lie behind notions of civil religion and constitutional faith like Levinson's. These include personalism, confession, eventful commitment, a sense of renewal, positive aspiration coupled with a fear of constraint, and a promise of, working-toward, progress and perfection. Most important, for our purposes, is the consuming loyalty to a text, whether understood literally or aspirationally, and a marking of that loyalty, that commitment, by a real or symbolic signature.

As Levinson points out, the Constitution has often been compared to the Bible and other sacred texts and the Supreme Court to "an authoritative 'church' built on the 'rock' of the Constitution. The Court's pronouncements therefore become 'the keys to the kingdom' of the heavenly status of a country ruled 'by law' instead of the people."[9] Michael J. Perry, who teaches law at Wake Forest University, has made much of this comparison: he argues that the Constitution is more like a sacred text than a literary one.[10] Like the sacred text, it mandates the forms of life of the community and tradition to which it belongs and, as such, symbolizes that mandate. Perry, who has a markedly aspirational view of the Constitution, understands a sacred text like the Bible in a much more open-ended way than the Fundamentalists do. Indeed, like the Catholic theologian David Tracy, he holds that authoritarian theologies such as Fundamentalism are not theologies at all, for they do not interpret tradition;[11]instead, they look behind, simply repeating what they deem to be timeless truths. In its writtenness, in its permanence, the sacred text is, for Perry "irrepressible, disturbing, prophetic."[12] It looks forward as it recalls the aspirations it has constituted.[13] Like the sacred text, the Constitution is not peripheral to community and tradition. It is commemorative (as we have seen) and disturbing, for it calls attention to the gap between aspiration and present-day reality. "The polity must respond to the incessant prophetic call of the text, must recall and heed the aspirations symbolized by the text, and thus must create and give (always provisional and reformable) meaning to the text, as well as take meaning from it."[14] Symbolic of the aspirations of the political tradition it has founded, the Constitution is, for Perry, constraining—but not as constraining as it would be for the originalists who, loyal to the word as they conceive it, look "behind." Given its comprehensiveness and indeterminacy (Perry speaks of its excess of meaning), the Constitution is "a shared occasion for confronting and struggling with the not-to-be-forgotten aspirations of the tradition."[15] It always mediates past and present.

Perry's position has been criticized on a number of fronts. Stanford's Thomas Grey insists, for example, on the Constitution's profane status. It is quite different from the Bible, which, as Grey understands it, is "the necessarily indirect, evocative, even mythical expression of a fundamentally mysterious and literally inexpressible reality."[16] Grey notes that however complex and controversial Constitutional interpretation may be, its "complexity and uncertainty do not add up to ineffability." It is a legal instrument like, but more complex than, a contract or a will, and subject as such to interpretive conventions that "presumptively require *literal* interpretation—not in some impossible sense that excludes reference to context or purpose in interpretation, but rather in a sense that excludes taking the text as primarily figurative or symbolic.

> The existence of a legal document means that someone has taken the trouble to put the sense of some agreement or set of instructions in writing. The normal point of doing this—and here legal practice builds on presuppositions taken from ordinary life in a literate culture—is to make relatively definite and explicit what otherwise would be relatively indefinite and tacit. This presumption of literality is itself an essential part of the context of the drafting and the interpretation of every legal document.[17]

Perry himself would probably not deny Grey's observation, though he would certainly be less text-bound. He has noted that every part of the Constitution does not have the symbolic status of the whole. He never claimed that the Constitution was like a religious text in *every* way.

The point is that every text, religious, legal, or literary, has a certain symbolic value that, however forcefully announced by the text itself, is never fully produced by the text alone. Its announcement is essentially an appeal for the text to be taken in the terms announced. The reader, society, is—within limits—free to accept or deny that appeal. Once the appeal is accepted, in whatever fashion, it affects not only the status of the text but the way we interpret it and what we do with it. It has often been noted that the U.S. Constitution has far greater symbolic weight than the state constitutions. They are not granted the same constitutive status. They are far more easily amended;[18] in fact, there have been more than five thousand amendments to the various state constitutions and more than two hundred state constitutional conventions.[19] Even the highest state justices do not have the same priestly quality as the justices of the Supreme Court. We must be careful, however, to distinguish the symbolic quality, the sacred aura, of the Constitution from its "message," its laying-out of the structure of the American government. Perry tends to blur the distinction, and Grey, who is more careful, to dismiss the symbolic or the sacred value, which he feels justifies a more activist view of judicial review "by casting judges the priests of a civil religion whose central tenet is Constitution-worship."[20] He argues in a more conservative vein than Perry, but not in as conservative a vein as the strict literalists, that:

> When judges invoke the Constitution to decide cases, they should be guided by what it says in some fairly literal sense, with attention both to its context of enactment and its context of application. And when judges supplement the written Constitution with an unwritten one, as they do and should, we do better to describe the process in terms of the homely intuitive ethnography of the common law tradition than in terms of priestly mystery.[21]

That seems a supremely confident and courageous act—to create a nation through words: words that address no foreign prince or distant power, but the very entity called into being by the words themselves; words that address the government that they purport to constitute; words that speak to subsequent generations of citizens who will give life to that government in the years to come.

Laurence Tribe and Michael Dorf, 1991[22]

In *Marbury v. Madison*,[23] Chief Justice John Marshall referred several times to the written constitution. He observed that "all those who have framed written constitutions contemplate them as forming all fundamental and paramount law of the nation," and that the theory that "an act of the legislature repugnant to the constitution is void" is "essentially attached to a written constitution" and, therefore, one of the "fundamental principles of our society." To counter the doctrine that the Constitution is the paramount law "would subvert the very foundation of all written constitutions." It would reduce "to nothing what we have deemed the greatest improvement on political institutions, a written constitution, would of itself be sufficient, in America, where written constitutions have been viewed with so much reverence, for rejecting the construction [that the constitution is not superior to an ordinary act of the legislature]." Why does Marshall stress the written constitution? In part, it is in reaction to the "unwritten" British constitution, hardly in favor in Philadelphia in 1787, or in 1803 when Marshall was writing his opinion. The British constitution is implicit in the whole body of common and statutory law and the practices and traditions of government; the U.S. Constitution is bounded in textual form, and, as Marshall insisted, paramount. Unlike the British constitution, which is, at least in principle, more flexible than that of the United States, the latter cannot be modified by a simple act of Congress. It affords, so the argument goes, fundamental protection of civil and personal liberty and declares certain areas free from restrictive parliamentary legislation. As we have seen, it does not go as far as the postwar German constitution, which outlaws any amendment of certain of its articles.

––––––––––

Behind this historical account of Marshall's insistence on the written Constitution lies a series of assumptions about writing and texts. Such assumptions are of considerable critical concern today in literary circles and in law, philosophy, and theology. Here I want to call attention to certain salient features of writing that are implicated in legal argument.[24] As the written is inevitably detached from the context in which it was produced, it loses the immediacy of oral communication. Readers always, at some level, engage fantasmatically with a written text, its author, its real and implied readership:

they have to recreate the context of utterance, to imagine what was being referred to and for whom. The elaboration of these reconstructions depends on the transparency of the text, its genre and style, and the distance between its moment of production and the moment of interpretation. It also depends on the institutionally validated hermeneutics — on what is considered to be in and out of bounds. Just as literary critics learn to read in a certain way, so do lawyers. But insofar as the context of utterance is precipitated by a particular text, we are never as detached from that context as we might fear. We may read a text one way, say, with the conventional blinders of a legal reading in which the author's ambivalence, character, emotional tone, masked values, and hidden motivations, are out of bounds, and yet be affected in decisive ways by these factors.

Take, for example, the opening paragraph of Justice Scalia's dissent in *Romer v. Evans* in which the Supreme Court found unconstitutional an amendment to the Colorado constitution that repealed ordinances against discrimination on the basis of "homosexual, lesbian or bisexual orientation, conduct, practices, or relationships":[25]

> The Court has mistaken a Kulturkampf for a fit of spite. The constitutional amendment before us here is not the manifestation of a "bare . . . desire to harm" homosexuals . . . but is rather a modest attempt by seemingly tolerant Coloradians to preserve traditional sexual mores against the efforts of a politically powerful minority to revise those mores through use of the laws. That objective, and the means chosen to achieve it, are not only unimpeachable under any constitutional doctrine hitherto pronounced (hence the opinion's heavy reliance upon principles of righteousness rather than judicial holdings); they have been specifically approved by the Congress of the United States and by this Court.

These are hardly the words of sobriety one would expect from a justice of the Supreme Court, especially one who insists on the need — indeed, on his ability — to extirpate moral and political views from exercising legal judgment. In his confirmation hearings, Scalia said that he would "not feel comfortable imposing [his] moral views on the society."[26] However the circumstances of *Evans v. Romer* are described, however keen Scalia's legal argument may be, any reader of this paragraph is immediately aware of his stance toward homosexuality, his (feigned) scorn for his fellow justices (or at least their decision), his ingenuous characterization of the "seemingly tolerant Coloradians" and their "modest attempt . . . to preserve traditional sexual mores." But not even Scalia can quite bring himself to characterize the Coloradians as simply tolerant. There are quite enough clues in this passage for even a reader wholly ignorant of the "Kulturkampf" between gays and lesbians on the one hand, and straights, on the other, to divine something of that struggle, particularly its emotional tone. And enough clues to discern the more immediate situation, certainly its emotional tone—the "spite"—in which Scalia wrote his dissent. A legal reading would declare such contextualization out of bounds—though just as Scalia quoted "bare . . . desire to harm" for rhetorical reasons, so one might imagine another lawyer or judge quoting Scalia. (I should note that "bare . . . desire to harm" is itself quoted in the majority opinion of *U.S. Department of Agriculture v. Moreno*, in which the court was asked to decide whether a household including an individual unrelated to any other member of that household was eligible for food stamps.[27] As Justice William Brennan noted when he wrote the opinion, the legislative history of the act indicated an intention "to prevent so-called 'hippies' and 'hippie communes' from participating in the food stamp program." The full quotation reads: "For if the constitutional conception of 'equal protection of the laws' means anything, it must at very least mean that a bare congressional desire to harm a politically unpopular group cannot constitute a *legitimate* governmental interest.") Scalia's reference then to "bare . . . desire to harm" evokes not only the majority opinion but another controversial case involving a group threatening to and stigmatized by the politically conservative.

I have chosen an exceptional passage, indeed an exceptional case, one that has aroused very considerable passion, to make my point; but one does find such emotionally charged rhetoric in *many* cases, certainly in those in which the public has an intense interest.

For example, in *McCulloch v. Maryland*, which concerned the states' ability to impose taxes on the second Bank of the United States, to which they were opposed, Chief Justice Marshall wrote:

> That the power to tax involves the power to destroy; that the power to destroy may defeat and render useless the power to create; that there is a plain repugnance, in conferring on one government the power to control the constitutional measures of another, which other, with respect to those very measures, is declared to be supreme over that which exerts control, are propositions not to be denied. But all inconsistencies are to be reconciled by the magic of the word CONFIDENCE. Taxation, it is said, does not necessarily and unavoidably destroy. To carry it to the excess of destruction would be an abuse, to presume which, would banish that confidence, which is essential to all government.[28]

Consider the rhythm of the passage as well as the strength of the language and the emphasis on "confidence."

It is, of course, a cliché that lawyers are given to hyperbole. Judges are to show evidence of cool neutrality and sober judgment. They are not, however, immune to the effect of the rhetoric of the lawyers who argue before them. Nor are they insensitive to the language of appealed opinions and the precedents they invoke. Law, particularly the common law or the law of precedent, is in essence intertextual. Not only is continual reference made to texts other than those under immediate consideration, but their force is no doubt far more complicated than that conventionally attributed to them. Though one may argue narrowly in terms of precedent, the choice of precedent and the parts that are quoted, are often determined not just in terms of legal relevance but of strength of language.[29] This is also true of those sections of the texts—the contracts, wills, statutes, "propaganda," "pornography," or "slander"—under consideration or, in appeals, of the quoted court record.

In *Abrams v. United States*, for example, appeal was made by five self-proclaimed but unknown Russian socialists and anarchists who had been convicted of conspiracy for publishing leaflets that condemned the landing of marines in Vladivostock and Murmansk in the summer of 1918 as an "attempt to crush the Russian Revolution."[30] Both Justice John Clarke, who wrote the opinion affirming the lower court's decision, and Justice Oliver Wendell Holmes, who dissented, quoted extensively from the leaflets. Holmes wrote:

> The first of these leaflets says that the President's cowardly silence about the intervention in Russia reveals the hypocrisy of the plutocratic gang in Washington. It intimates that "German militarism combined with allied capitalism to crush the Russian revolution"— goes on that the tyrants of the world fight each other until they see a common enemy—working class enlightenment, when they combine to crush it; and that now militarism and capitalism combined, though not openly, to crush the Russian revolution. It says that there is only one enemy of the workers of the world and that is capitalism; that it is a crime for workers of America, &c., to fight the workers' republic of Russia, and ends "Awake! Awake, you Workers of the World! Revolutionists." A note adds "It is absurd to call us pro-German. We hate and despise German militarism more than do you hypocritical tyrants. We have more reasons for denouncing German militarism than has the coward of the White House."

Unlike Clarke, whose arguments were based on direct quotation, Holmes, who confounded direct, indirect, and paraphrased quotation, blurred the distinction between leaflet and opinion. From a strictly legal point of view, his quotations were in excess of what was necessary to support his dissent: he argued, among other reasons, that the conviction was invalid because the defendants did not have the intent by advocating a general strike "to cripple or hinder the United States in the prosecution of the war." They only wanted to help Russia, with whom the United States was not at war. How had Holmes's way of quoting the leaflets facilitated his argument? Though he observed that the relevant statute "must be taken to use its words in a strict and accurate sense," for otherwise it would "be absurd," he nevertheless made use of a distracting metaphor, embedded in a highly convoluted sentence, in his critique of the court's reading of the statute. "A patriot might think that we were wasting money on aeroplanes, or making more cannon of a certain kind than we needed, and might advocate curtailment with success, yet even if it turned out that the curtailment hindered and was thought by other minds to have been obviously likely to hinder the United States in the prosecution of the war, no one would hold such conduct a crime." Even Holmes had to admit that his "illustration does not answer all that might be said." Further along in his dissent, he made a more extravagant comparison: "In this case sentences of twenty years imprisonment have been imposed for the publishing of two leaflets that I believe the defendants had as much right to publish as the Government has to publish the Constitution of the United States now vainly invoked by them." Does the extravagance of these metaphors, exceptional even for Holmes, echo the hyperbole of the leaflets?[31]

There is a significant contradiction in the way in which legal opinions and even statutes are written and how they are generally read. No serious scholar of the law would deny that judicial opinion is a product of argument, and, though they might like ideally to deny the argumentative basis of statutes, they must acknowledge that they are, for the most part, the product of political debate and accommodation if not downright compromise. Once the opinions are written, once the statutes become law, their argumentative basis tends to be ignored in the way they are read, interpreted, and used in argument. In his now-classic *Introduction to Legal Reasoning*, Edward H. Levi attributed many of the ambiguities in statutes to their political origin—to the mixed intentions of their framers. He argued that "that once a decisive interpretation of legislative intent has been made, and in that sense a direction has been fixed within the gap of ambiguity, the court should take that direction as given."[32] The words the court uses in statutory interpretation "do more than decide cases. They give broad direction to the statute." But, despite the broad direction Levi insists on, the words—the court's decision, the now-interpreted statute—become for the most part solid—hardened, as Roland Barthes might have said. Even when their context of production, their history, is deemed relevant to their interpretation, that history continues to be read (at least for

242 - SERVING THE WORD

the sake of argument) in a solidifying manner. Insofar as they figure in new arguments, they cannot be taken any other way.

I am simplifying here. We must differentiate between opinions, statutes, and the Constitution itself. To those used to codified law, such as French law, American common law seems a strange bird. The judicial opinions that serve as precedent seem wordy, digressive, often contradictory, self-justificatory, revealing, at times to the point of confession (always an American obsession), of the debates, the anguish, the indecision that lie behind them, and thus the vulnerability. It is as though they undermine the law, or rather the Law, at the same time as they produce it. French decisions are terse, rarely more than a sentence, expressed in syllogistic form; the arguments that lie behind them and have been debated in camera, the *rapports* of the reporting judge and the *conclusion* of the advocate general, are not public.[33] They support a transcendent, universalizing picture of the law as a purely rational enterprise from which the Law garners its authority and independence. Of course, Anglo-American lawyers and judges do distinguish between holdings and dicta; that is, between the principles of law drawn from a decision and expressions in a decision of the judge's own views on law and even policy—his asides—which do not relate immediately to the case on hand. Holdings are binding; dicta are not, though they often have considerable weight in future arguments.

The Constitution is flexible. Period. Your point of view depends on whether you're winning: "My side won! I'm happy!" If you're against busing, you think an anti-busing amendment should be in the Constitution; if you're for busing, you complain that the Constitution is being wrecked. The Constitution isn't the real issue in this; it is how you want to run the country, and achieve national goals. The language of the Constitution is not at issue. It is what you can interpret it to mean in the light of modern needs. In talking about a "Constitutional crisis" we are not grappling with the real needs of running the country but are using the issues for the self-serving purpose of striking a new balance of power. Times are changing now. The Constitution is flexible. . . . Today, the whole Constitution is up for grabs.

> Donald Santarelli, Associate Deputy
> Attorney General under Richard Nixon,
> 1973[34]

[W]hen the Court gives the language of the Constitution an unforeseen application, it does so, whether explicitly or implicitly, in the name of some underlying purpose of the Framers. . . . [T]he federal judiciary . . . has no inherent general authority to establish norms for the rest of society . . . When the Court disregards the express intent and understanding of the Framers, it has invaded the realm of the political process to which the amending power was committed, and it has violated the constitutional structure which it is its highest duty to protect.

> Justice John Marshall Harlan, 1970[35]

Unlike the Fundamentalist, whose interpretations of Scripture should be as true to God's Word as possible—that is, as removed as possible from the always depraved and corrupting influences of any particular context of application—lawyers and judges, even those of a highly conservative bent, do not have this luxury. Their readings (except perhaps when they theorize) are always intimately bound to specific application.[36] They may resist, for example, considering the human dimensions of a case they are judging by adhering strictly to the letter of the law; but insofar as a decision concerning a specific conflict has to be made, they cannot altogether ignore its "real-life" circumstances without, in a sense, betraying themselves. One need only read the letters of judges who opposed slavery and yet upheld laws that condoned it to appreciate this dilemma. Joseph Story (1779–1845), one of the most important justices of the Supreme Court and the target of antislavery attacks for his decisions in two fugitive slave cases, wrote to a friend, "You know full well that I have ever been opposed to slavery. But I take my standard of duty as a judge from the Constitution."[37] Similar cries of conscience are found in other judges' opinions. In 1845, Judge Read of Ohio wrote in *State v. Hoppess*:

> Slavery is wrong, inflicted by force and supported alone by the municipal power of the state or territory wherein it exists. It is opposed to the principles of natural justice and right, and is the mere creature of positive law. Hence, it being my duty to declare the law, not to make it, the question is not, what conforms to the great principles of natural right and universal freedom—but what do the positive laws and institutions . . . command and direct.[38]

Indeed, it could be argued that many dicta are little more than a judge's rationalizations and justifications for deciding a case in terms of a law that is contrary to his or her moral sensibility.[39]

Legal readings are always designed to make a point—to win a case, make a decision. Citations from constitutions, treaties, statutes, and precedents, not to mention maxims, historical references, sociological and psychological generalities, economic principles, political observations, philosophical truths, and even poetic images, with which lawyers and judges alike spice their arguments are *at some level* always rhetorical. Here is the paradox: though they and the arguments in which they figure are rhetorical, they cannot be taken as such in argument. There they are logical truths derived from the law. There is—there can be—no irony in the law, at least when it is argued, even by cynics and opportunists like Santarelli, quoted in the epigraph to this section. Interpretive theories serve to cover the rhetorical dimension of the "truths" argued and, as such, are implicated in the argument's rhetoric. (I am not arguing against the truth of a theory, a legal interpretation, or a set of facts; I am simply observing that, cast in argument, their truth plays a rhetorical role that puts in question, even as it exploits, that truth.) Formalist arguments notwithstanding, the law is never pure: it is always engaged, always (in the ordinary sense) deconstructed or deconstructible. Despite conservatives' insistence on the letter of the law, on determinable meaning and original intent, they are as pragmatically implicated (to paraphrase the Fundamentalists) in the corrupting influences of context, in the figurative demands it makes. They may seek salvation in their literalism, their commitment to strict construction, to original meaning and intention, but that salvation is illusory. Such is the nature of application. What the formalists can and do argue, and not without some reason, as even their opponents must admit, is that their loyalty to the text serves as a control on the powers of the judiciary, on "judge-made law," on their constitutionally mandated oath to support the Constitution. Neither the literalists nor the aspirationalists — those less wedded to the letter of law than to its spirit — are immune to the effects of this oath (if only out of fear of impeachment). Despite their often vituperative and consequential differences, the literalists and the pragmatists share a commitment to the Constitution, to its word. It is at once the ultimate site of contestation and constitutive of that contestation, to its framing, its rules, indeed, its style(s) of argument.

Let me try to put this in another, perhaps simpler, way. Legal argument is, or can be conceived of, as a genre — in fact, as several highly ritualized genres of oral and written communication, the rules of which must be followed if the argument is to be effective. Like all such genres, while they are recognized (at least by as self-reflective a discipline as the law) their rules, certainly their presuppositions, their artifice, cannot normally be acknowledged by people communicating — arguing and interpreting — within them, for then their communications, arguments, and interpretations would fall away. The discussion of such presuppositions would have to be dismissed as "philosophical," beside the point, blasphemous, destructive, nihilistic. Even in modernist and postmodernist literature and art, not to mention criticism, which do not have the normative responsibility of the law, there is a limit to ironic self-reflection, something the postmodernist critic delights *ironically* in recognizing.

A Man's writing has but one true sense, which is that which the Author meant when he writ it.

John Selden, 1605[40]

To thrust aside the dead hand of the Framers is thrust aside the Constitution.

Raoul Berger, 1977[41]

In 1977, a Harvard law professor named Raoul Berger—a left-of-center Democrat, a former member of the Roosevelt and Truman administrations, and the author of books on impeachment and executive privilege which helped to bring down Richard Nixon—astonished his colleagues with the publication of *Government by Judiciary*. Berger argued that the historical records "all but incontrovertibly establish that the framers of the Fourteenth Amendment excluded both suffrage and segregation from its reach."[42] He claimed further that the Fourteenth Amendment confined its protection to "carefully enumerated rights against State discrimination, deliberately withholding federal power to supply those rights where they were not granted by the State to anybody, white or black." The due process and privileges or immunities clauses, he argued, were "terms of art" with precise meanings, not elastic ones, as judicial activists had assumed.[43] We must remember that the due process clause, which has been understood since the end of the last century to have both procedural and substantive scope, has been used more than any other clause to justify judicial activism. "Equal protection," Berger had to admit, was a new concept, which was understood to refer only to the right to contract, to own property, and to have access to the courts.[44] In effect, Berger questioned the constitutional validity of virtually every major judicial advance of the century: *Brown v. Board of Education*, which struck down segregation in public schools;[45] *Baker v. Carr*[46] and *Reynolds v. Sims*, which concerned reapportionment of state legislatures;[47] and, by extension, decisions like *Roe v. Wade* which made abortion legal.[48] Despite his own politics—which he claimed to bracket, noting simply that the Fourteenth Amendment, as he read it, was a "tragically limited response to the needs of blacks newly released from slavery"—Berger became an instant hero for conservatives.[49] The Fourteenth Amendment, as he put it, "reflected the hagridden racism that held both North and South in thrall; nonetheless, it was all the sovereign people were prepared to do in 1868." As such, it could not justify the use to which it had been put by activists, whom Berger was always ready to excoriate. "Where early claims to extraconstitutional power were made in the name of 'natural law,' the present fashion is to invoke the 'living Constitution' when it is sought to engraft or amputate a limb."[50] For Berger, deviant readings — that is, broadly construed readings, those invoking the "living Constitution" — were far more dangerous than limited, historically accurate ones. Were one to accept the validity and authority of such broad readings, one would risk destroying the delicate balance of power between the branches of government by giving the judiciary legislative power.

Government by Judiciary was immediately and vehemently attacked by liberals. Berger's history was called "fake antique"; he was charged with "the worst type of law-office history"; he was said to be "neither talented enough as an advocate nor knowledgeable enough as an historian to be taken seriously in either discipline."[51] To each serious review, Berger responded. He went on to write over forty article-length rebuttals, which were collected in 1989 in *The Fourteenth Amendment and the Bill of Rights*. In 1997, at the age of ninety-six, he published a second edition of *Government by Judiciary*, which included new supplements to most of the chapters. This is not the place to comment on the moral and political implications of Berger's study. One has always to balance truth as one sees it, if one claims to see it, against its timely revelation. But to suggest even the possibility of deferment, let alone compromise, would no doubt be offensive to Berger, who likes to quote Thomas Huxley: "The great tragedy of science is the slaying of a beautiful hypothesis by an ugly fact." Nor is this the place to comment on the details of Berger's history, and even if it were, I would not be qualified to do so. Rather, I want to examine several presuppositions and methodological tacks in Berger's "historical study," since they are characteristic of formalist, indeed literalist, approaches to the law.

Berger has certainly provided the reader with many ugly facts. He writes, for example:

The key to an understanding of the Fourteenth Amendment is that the North was shot through with Negrophobia, that the Republicans, except for a minority of extremists, were swayed by the racism that gripped their constituents rather than by the abolitionist ideology. At the inception of their crusade the abolitionist peered up at an almost unscalable cliff. Charles Sumner, destined to become a leading spokesman for extreme abolitionist views, wrote in 1834, upon his first sight of slaves, "My worst preconception of their appearance and their ignorance did not fall as low as their actual stupidity. . . . They appear to be nothing more than moving masses of flesh unendowed with anything of intelligence above the brutes. . . ."[52]

He quotes Alexis de Tocqueville:

We can scarcely acknowledge the common features of mankind in this child of debasement whom slavery has brought among us. His physiognomy to our eyes is hideous, his understanding weak, his tastes low; and we are almost inclined to look upon him as a being intermediate between man and brutes.[53]

And he quotes Abraham Lincoln, addressing a delegation of Negro leaders:

There is an unwillingness on the part of our people, harsh as it may be, for you free colored people to remain with us. . . . [E]ven when you cease to be slaves, you are far removed from being placed on an equality with the white man. . . . I cannot alter it if I would. It is a fact.[54]

Yes, the facts are ugly. They should be exposed and re-exposed, and they have been. They reveal the hypocrisy, the live and buried racism, that was behind even some of the noblest calls for abolition and for the granting of equal rights to former slaves. They reveal the facility with which a raw pragmatism can lead to political compromise. One can well understand why Berger wants to constrain plays of power, to limit individual notions of justice, and to temper claims of speaking for the people when there is neither the authority nor the capacity to do so.

Even if one were to accept the legal text as capable of constraining judges, which is something everyone engaged in the law has yet to agree on, it is not the text per se that is constraining but the authority granted it. It has in this sense always a symbolic dimension.[55] It is said, for example, to embody the voice—the intention—of the people, as Alexander Hamilton argued in the *Federalist Papers*: "[T]he Constitution ought to be preferred to the statute, the intention of the people to the intention of their agents."[56] However that authority is understood, it always governs the range of interpretive possibility. Judges do not normally read the Constitution through its imagery, as indicative of the collective unconscious of the Framers, or as reflecting historically specific attitudes toward the print media.[57] They read it within prescribed limits and argue within these limits. Indeed, their particular interpretive stance takes on a symbolic import. Berger's excoriation of the activists is more than an intellectual argument: it situates him, whether he likes it or not, in a certain socio-political context. It presupposes certain attitudes toward authority, tradition, and figuration as well as images or theories of human nature, society, and polity. To attempt to escape the social and political implication of these presuppositions through the word, the historical fact, "ugly" as it may be, bespeaks not only an innocence, real or feigned, in good faith or bad faith, but also an attitude toward the word, the historical fact, that can support such innocence.

In reading Berger and other legal scholars of his orientation, one is immediately struck by their traditionalism: their devotion to a text, the Constitution, to its original meaning. Though they may rationalize this devotion on all sorts of grounds, including the need for a stability they understand in terms of predictability, the intensity of their commitment to the Constitution suggests that other factors are at play: a desire to justify historically the status quo (and their position in it), a need for structure, a fear of change, disappointment with the present, a longing, a nostalgia, for the past. Who knows? They do privilege an originary moment—the moment in which the Constitution and its amendments were conceptualized, negotiated, written, argued, and ratified. I use "moment" to underscore the condensation of time (and, by extension, intention) in their understanding of its framing. It is a mythic moment in which the Framers, blessed with exceptional and perduring wisdom, are possessed of a single intention which somehow transcends earthly politicking and becomes, as if by magic, the intention of the people: we-the-people. It is this singular intention that is embodied in the text—the Constitution, its amendments. The text is read accordingly, rather than as an expression of or a compromise between multiple intentions and interests. It has to have a single meaning identified with a "singular" intention—not only because of its role in legal arguments that in the end have always to be decided but also because it has to preserve the "unity" of the people it has constituted, even when division among the people is recognized and exploited politically. It must, in another words, preserve the effective category "people" that unites the people who are divided.

Berger does recognize the negotiations, the history, of the framing. Indeed, he looks to it for evidence of the meaning of the text. He proclaims the need to contextualize (historically) the writing of the Constitution and its amendments; but paradoxically, as we shall see, he fails to evaluate the "contextual evidence" he brings forth in terms of *its* context. With respect to the Fourteenth Amendment, he writes:

> In reconstructing the past, historians generally are compelled to rely on accounts written after the event by participants and witnesses, or on the hearsay versions of those who learned at second-hand what had occurred. Such writings are subject to the infirmities of recollection, or of bias arising from allegiance to one side or another. The historical records here relied on—the legislative history of the Fourteenth Amendment—are of a far more trustworthy character, being a stenographic transcription of what was said in the 39th Congress from day to day by those engaged in framing the Amendment. It is a verbatim account of what occurred, recorded while it was happening, comparable to a news film of an event at the moment it was taking place and free from possible distortion of accounts drawn from recollection or hearsay. What men say while they are acting are themselves facts, as distinguished from opinions about facts. Such

statements constitute a reliable record of what happened as the
Amendment was being forged by the framers.[58]

Opinions about fact are, of course, facts too—distinct, to be sure,
from the facts that are their subject, but nevertheless facts that require critical evaluation. They are also, insofar as they are expressed, acts by Berger's own understanding. (He cites Oliver
Wendell Holmes on the relationship between words and acts: "a
'party's conduct' may 'consist in uttering certain words.' "[59]) Almost everyone recognizes that news films are not perfect renderings
of events, acts, and words: they always have a perspective, a point of
view. No doubt, a stenographic record of Congress is more accurate
than a recollected one or one derived from hearsay, but it is not
thereby free from distortion, if only because it is never comprehensive. It does not describe tone of voice, gesture, or audience response, nor does it include what is said behind the scenes. However
accurate a stenographic record may be, it has to be understood for
what it is and within its context. What is said publicly may in fact be
a coded reference to what cannot be said publicly.[60] Public utterance has always a rhetorical function, and must be evaluated in
terms of the circumstances—in this case, political—in which it was
uttered.

Contextualization is always a matter of convention. What is
thought relevant is determined not just by what is salient in the sur-
roundings, or by what is called forth by the text or object we are
considering. Disciplinary histories like those produced by legal
scholars have a different take on relevance than those written by political, economic, social, or cultural historians. Even the most superficial reading of any standard textbook on constitutional law reveals
this. Rarely do they consider explicitly the broader socio-
economic, political, or social circumstance of the cases they discuss, and when they do, it is usually in order to explicate the
particular meaning of the case. They do not try to explain why a
particular decision was reached in extralegal or extratextual terms.
There are, of course, "conventional" exceptions in these
textbooks—the cases concerned with slavery or the New Deal,

say—but even these are from a broader historical perspective severely limited.

There are also, of course, legal scholars who invoke broader socio-economic facts in their historical understanding. As Stanford's Robert Gordon notes, they have tended to be conservative, appealing to continuity and tradition.[61] Referring to the background assumptions about the relationship between law and history present in mainstream legal scholarship (and not necessarily in the work of professional legal historians), Gordon writes:

> Over the last 150 years or so, enlightened American legal opinion
> has adhered with remarkable fidelity to what, in broad conception,
> looks like a single set of notions about historical change and the re-
> lation of law to such change. Stated baldly, these notions are that the
> natural and proper evolution of a society . . . is toward the type of
> liberal capitalism seen in the advanced Western nations (especially
> in the United States), and that the natural and proper function of a
> legal system is to facilitate such an evolution.[62]

These histories are teleological, evolutionary in character, and assume an outdated functionalist sociology. Their basic presuppositions, according to Gordon, are shared by both formalist and the "Realist" scholars.[63] Formalists focus on the development of legal doctrine and consider extralegal phenomena irrelevant. Their hero is the judge or the treatise writer. The Realists, who see doctrine as a component of general, if not always coordinated, policy-making, stress the relationship between law and social development. Their hero is the social engineer. Their causal arguments tend to be quite simplistic, and, like the formalists, they are dismissive—at times defensively—of movements like Critical Legal Studies, which are more concerned with the ways in which particular and conflicting interests and desires of the members of any society come to be articulated as "impersonal social forces" from which the evolutionary-functionalists argue.

Legal purists, argue, or at least try to argue, strictly from within the law. They treat it as a relatively autonomous system, though—here they contradict themselves—one that is not immune to extralegal influence. Moral, social, and other extratextual factors are considered irrelevant, of secondary significance, even dangerous, for they can open the floodgates of subjectivism and "judge-made law." Notions of the social good, of economic efficiency, and of respect for life can be used to rationalize decisions that depart radically from the law as it is written. Purists argue among themselves about the relevance and authority of texts like the Congressional Record and the *Federalist Papers*, which are not, strictly speaking, the law. Berger makes use of them. Scalia would not, or in the event argues that certain of them, like legislative history, are irrelevant.[64]

What is of importance here is not the details of the rules of inclusion and exclusion, which vary from one domain of law to another, but, first, the way in which these rules privilege the text, whether of the law or of the documents in dispute; and, second, the way in which they exclude or render of secondary importance extratextual evidence that, to the outsider, often seems particularly relevant. Constitutional historians like Berger are willing enough to use extralegal texts to ascertain the meaning of the Constitution and its amendments, but they are reluctant if not downright hostile to any attempt to understand the Constitution, or any of its clauses, or even their own interpretations, in terms of prevailing social and political conditions. Berger himself seems reluctant even to consider the context of the sources he quotes. He simply rattles off citations and quotations without characterizing their authors or explaining the circumstances in which (and the purposes for which) they were uttered. They seem to have authority simply because they were uttered by lawmakers or judges. Quotations from the *Federalist Papers* are taken, for example, at face value, as expressions of the writer's belief or intention, rather than polemically, to convince the reader to ratify the Constitution.[65]

The citations and quotations are designed to give determinant, "original" meaning, understood as "intention," to the constitutional texts under consideration. The priority given to original intention is itself justified on citational grounds. Berger quotes James Madison: "If 'the sense in which the Constitution was accepted and ratified by the nation . . . be not the guide in expounding it, there can be no security for a consistent and stable [government], more than for a faithful exercise of power.'"[66] He quotes "traditional canons of interpretation": "A thing may be within the letter of a statute and not within its meaning, and within its meaning though not within its letter. The intention of the lawmaker is the law."[67]

Why should a common law maxim be given interpretive authority? Why should Madison be taken as an authority on legal hermeneutics? Why not a contemporary philosopher of interpretation? It may well be that the philosopher will have less of a political investment in his hermeneutics than Madison, who, despite his brilliance as a jurist, was a man of politics. It would seem that Berger's peculiar, decontextualizing way of reading history removes the Framers from any political engagement that would have had an impact on their law-making. And just as they are removed from politics, so is the Constitution: it comes to have a historically transcendent, timeless quality that is, or ought to be if read correctly, resistant to political abrasion. Of course, Berger is fully aware of this abrasion, indeed of the usurpation by the courts of legislative responsibility. His constitutional history, like those of so many conservatives (whatever their stated political sympathies), is a tale of decadence, of hermeneutic corrosion. It is only the Constitution, taken in its purity, like Holy Scripture, that offers—dare I say?—salvation from earthly corruption.

And yet we have to recognize that the idealization of a moment in time, Philadelphia in 1787, thrusts the Constitution back into history, one in which tradition is given greater weight than the present or future. However embarrassing this may be to the formalist, we would do well to remember Chief Justice John Marshall's words in *McCulloch v. Maryland* in which he argued that the national government must be given the means, under the Constitution, for the execution of its delegated powers—case in point, a national bank:

> This provision is made in a constitution intended to endure for ages
> to come, and, consequently, to be adapted to the various *crises* of
> human affairs. To have prescribed the means by which government
> should, in all future time, execute its power, would have been to

change, entirely, the character of the instrument, and give it the properties of a legal code. It would have been an unwise attempt to provide, by immutable rules, for exigencies which, if foreseen at all, must have been seen dimly, and which can best be provided for as they occur. . . .[68]

Berger describes this passage as a "mythical incantation" for those who arrogate a "living Constitution."[69] He would probably not go as far as Marshall's prescriptor, but the push in his jurisprudence and historical understanding is clearly toward fixity.[70] He reads the passage narrowly, in context (for once), arguing that it was "merely a plea for some freedom in the 'choice of means' to execute an existing power, not a license to create a fresh power in each new crisis."[71] He quotes Marshall's own pseudonymous defense of his decision without, of course, asking why Marshall felt compelled to justify it pseudonymously: "It does not contain the most distant allusion to *any extension by construction of the powers* of congress. Its sole object is to remind us that a constitution cannot possibly enumerate *the means* by which the powers of government are to be carried into execution."[72] He asserts that Marshall's defense, discovered only in the late sixties, shatters whatever use the above dictum may have for judicial activists.[73]

A text should not be construed strictly, and it should not be construed leniently; it should be construed reasonably, to contain all that it fairly means.

Antonin Scalia, 1997[74]

Textualism, as Justice Scalia defines it, appears to me to be as permissive and as open to arbitrary judicial discretion and expansion as the use of legislative intent or other interpretive methods, if the text-minded judge is so inclined.

Gordon S. Wood, 1997[75]

In 1995, Antonin Scalia, one of the most conservative members of the Supreme Court, delivered the Tanner Lecture at Princeton. His respondents were the historian Gordon Wood, the constitutional scholar Laurence Tribe; Mary Ann Glendon, a specialist in comparative law at Harvard, and the legal philosopher Ronald Dworkin. Tribe and Dworkin are longstanding critics of Scalia. Scalia's theme was the relationship between common law courts and the civil law system. He was distressed by what he takes to be the effect of the common law tradition on the way we read statutes and, by extension, the Constitution. Scalia tends to regard the Constitution as a sort of megastatute, subject to the restrictive readings characteristic of statutory law. As he sees it, common law by its very nature facilitates "judge-made" law. In extracting the relevant legal principles from previous cases, the common law judge is always redefining the law, expanding or contracting it, making or remaking it, in accordance with the particular case he is deciding. His decision, based on his engaging precedent with the situation on hand, becomes in turn precedent.[76]

Unlike civil law, which assumes the timelessness of its statutes, its law, the Law—particularly in those European versions where previous cases may be used in argument but are not published in the court's opinion—common law appears to be incremental and dynamic. It is this evolutionary push that Scalia associates with the judicial activism characteristic of the Warren and Burger courts, without recognizing, at least in his Tanner Lecture, that though the common law may in fact be incremental, even evolutionary, it has not always been taken that way. Indeed, it was understood in seventeenth-century England in static terms, as simply an uncovering of immemorial usage.[77] Reformers like David Dudley Field and Robert Rantoul, who were proponents of codified law saw, as Scalia notes, the dangers of judge-made law in the common law.[78]

Gordon Wood notes that Scalia's assumptions about the effect of the common law on statute and constitutional law are questionable from a historical point of view.[79] The discretion of the judiciary has deep roots in American legal culture. The tension between a static and dynamic view of the law is, I would argue, structural. It results from the application of a set of perduring, *textualized* principles to specific situations which they do not cover exactly and, therefore must be applied analogically. The tension lies in the fit between law and circumstance. To which do we give greater weight? For the Fundamentalists, as we have seen, there is no choice: as God's Word, Scripture has priority. In secular law, there can be no such certainty. Inasmuch as the written law cannot be ignored in the practice of the law, the legal conservative always has, if you will, an edge on the more policy-oriented, the more circumstance-sensitive lawyer or judge. The conservatives determine the *champs de bataille*, the legal texts, which becomes the symbolic field in which the battle for priority between law and circumstance, law and policy, is fought in terms of intratextual interpretation. There is a structural hypocrisy in the law which is masked by (ideological, though not altogether unjustifiable) notions of the independence, timelessness, and truth of the law as well as the putative need to eliminate the incursion of the judge's own interests, values, and outlook.

There is probably nothing in these observations that is specific to the American legal system. What *is* striking is the insistence on the original, on the oxymoronic identification of origin and timelessness. We can understand this equation, I suppose, in mythic terms, which give to the "moment" of origin an eternally determinative role. It founds the categories that not only define the world but may, like Platonic ideas, realize the world and its dynamic processes. We can recognize the relationship between originary moment, the moment of creation, and time in our various Christian theologies — some of which, unlike Fundamentalism, have a distinctly Platonic character. Change, by which time is marked and measured, always poses a problem (particularly in Platonic theologies) and is understood in terms of decadence, corruption, a falling from paradise. We can relate this originalism to the Romantic idealization of the source, the *Ursprung*, that which springs up in earliest of times, the origin, the original. (Of course we have to ask how current this Romanticism, this idealization of the original, was at the time the Framers were writing the Constitution and, one assumes, anticipating how it and the laws it generated would be construed. We also have to ask why legal theorists who stress origin — and thus historical reconstruction — ignore the cultural evaluation of origin in both their "historical" reconstruction and its anachronistic theorization.) We may also understand originalism in terms of a romantic traditionalism—I am tempted to write medievalism. Historical reconstructions of this sort would undermine, I believe, the kind of historical reconstructions—I would call them rhetorical—that are produced in legal argument. Though they claim to be neutral, objective, true to the "facts," they are often manifestly biased by the arguments and theories that underlie them and which—circularly—they support.

Scalia is not a promiscuous originalist like Robert Bork. In fact, he is extremely critical of arguments founded on original intent. Instead, he advocates a textualism based on the original meaning of statutes and the Constitution; and while he gives priority to the statute and the Constitution and, like other conservatives, is often critically suspicious of precedent, he does not hesitate to make positive use of it in his opinions. He claims to be critical of strict constructionism, which he characterizes as "a degraded form of textualism that brings the whole philosophy into disrepute."[80] The "good textualist," he argues, is neither a literalist nor a nihilist: "Words do have a limited range of meaning, and no interpretation that goes beyond that range is permissible."[81] Like other conservatives, he cites as the distinguished example of overextended interpretation the substantive understanding of the due process clauses in the Fifth and Fourteenth Amendments, which have been used by the Supreme Court to prevent the government from depriving people of liberties not specifically named in the Constitution. These amendments declare that no person shall "be deprived of life, liberty, or property without due process of law"—and that, according to Scalia, is exactly what they mean. Process is process: "Property can be taken by the state; liberty can be taken; even life can be taken; but not without the *process* that our traditions require—notably, validly enacted law and a fair trial. To say otherwise is to abandon textualism, and to render democratically adopted texts mere springboards for judicial lawmaking."[82] Like other conservatives, Scalia likes to point out that the first case to interpret the due process clause in substantive terms was *Dred Scott v. Sanford*, which denied the citizenship of blacks, even those living in "free states," and declared unconstitutional the Missouri Compromise of 1820, forbidding slavery in some federal territories.[83]

In the Tanner Lecture, Scalia opens his critique of "original-intent" interpretations by discussing *Church of the Holy Trinity v. United States*.[84] This gives him the opportunity to illustrate his own brand of textualism. In 1892, in *Church of the Holy Trinity*, the Supreme Court overruled a lower court decision that found the New York City church of that name guilty of violating a statute that made it illegal "to assist or encourage the immigration of any alien" into the United States by giving him a contract or making an agreement with him "to perform labor or service of any kind" before he had actually immigrated. The statute excepted only professional actors, artists, lecturers, singers, and domestic servants." Holy Trinity had made a contract with an English clergyman to come to New York to become its rector and pastor. On the face of it, and so Scalia insists, the church was in error, but the court argued that it could not "think Congress intended to denounce with penalties a transaction like that in the present case." "It is a familiar rule," the court observed, "that a thing may well be within the letter of the statute and yet not within the statute, because not within its spirit, nor within the intention of it makers." Where the language of the legislature, the court concluded, is so broad in its attempt to reach all aspects of an evil that it "unexpectedly" includes "cases and acts which the whole history and life of the country affirm could not have been intentionally legislated against," then it is the duty of the courts "to say that, however broad the language of the statute may be, the act, although within the letter of the law, is not within the intention of the legislature, and therefore cannot be within the statute."

For Scalia, the court's decision in *Church of the Holy Trinity* was simply wrong. By invoking legislative intent, it made use of one of the "subterfuges" by which the courts try to change and often succeed in changing the meaning of statutes that appear incorrect, irrelevant, or obsolete. It is an interpretive tack that, in Scalia's view, should be abandoned. "It is simply not compatible with democratic theory that laws mean whatever they ought to mean, and that unelected judges decide what that is."[85] With respect to this case, he makes his point even clearer.

> It may well be that the statutory interpretation adopted by the Court in *Church of the Holy Trinity* produced a desirable result; and it may even be thought (though I doubt it) that it produced the unexpressed result actually intended by Congress, rather than merely the one desired by the Court. Regardless, the decision was wrong because it failed to follow the text. The text is the law, and it is the text that must be followed.[86]

One would like to know on what grounds Scalia doubts that the Court produced "the unexpressed result actually intended by Congress." Such asides are not simply arrogant: they belie the very stance Scalia advocates. They have no textual, or, for that matter, any other support.

In the next chapter, I shall consider original intention. Here, I want to note Scalia's epistemological naiveté: his unquestioned assumptions that words are spiritless, that is, without figurative extension, that meaning can be divorced from intention, and that texts can have a context-independent meaning that is at least potentially immune from the interlocutory effects of reading and interpretation. Scalia's critics note that his textualism, his focus on the original, so privileges the text of the law, the written word, that he can bypass the human, humane, and social dimensions of the cases before him. Like other conservatives—Justice Story and Ohio's Judge Read, just before the Civil War—he dismisses these considerations by declaring them to be outside the judge's purview. But are they? In even the purest civil law systems like the French, where no cases are cited in the published decisions, there is always a creative dimension to the application of the law that defines and redefines the law if it does not make and remake it.[87]

Scalia claims, as I have noted, not to be a strict constructionist, and ironically, in a 1989 article on originalism, he described himself as a faint-hearted originalist.[88] He asks how an originalist would respond to a new state law that provided lashing or branding the right hand as a punishment for certain crimes, even if it could be demonstrated that in 1791, when the Eighth Amendment was ratified, such punishment was not considered to be cruel and unusual. (The Eighth Amendment reads: "Excessive bail shall not be required, nor excessive fines imposed, or cruel and unusual punishments inflicted.") He doubts that any federal judge, not even the originalists on the bench, would sustain these laws against the Eighth Amendment.

But, on what grounds does one draw the line between a strict and loose construction of original meaning? Or of any meaning? Do not personal values and interests enter into the determination? Does not desire play its role? Do not loose constructions, indeed strict constructions, always mask at some level personal values, interests, and desires? The strict constructionist would answer these questions in the affirmative—arguing, like the Fundamentalist, that by adhering as closely as possible to the plain, ordinary meaning of the text one can insulate one's interpretation and application of the law from personal interests, values, and desires.

Scalia is certainly conscious of the perils of loose interpretation and is in fact always ready to point out its wayward influences. Though he is not as hidebound a textualist as some—and is even given at times to an irony, however rhetorical, that is rare among lawyers and judges of any persuasion—he has, or at least professes, faith in the purificatory effect of his literalist hermeneutics. In his Tanner Lecture, he refers to two cases, *Maryland v. Craig* and *Smith v. United States*, in which he dissented.[89] *Craig*, which was decided in 1990, is cited as an example of the restrictive effect of most decisions based on the notion of an evolving or "living" Constitution. (Scalia argues that this approach to the Constitution has resulted in a dramatic reduction of the liberties Americans once had.[90]) His dissent in *Smith*, which was decided in 1993, is meant to illustrate the reasonableness of his textualism as opposed to the unreasonableness of strict constructionism. But his approach in *Craig* is that of a strict constructionist. In *Smith*, as he himself characterizes it, it is one of a reasonable textualist. A loose constructionist? He opts in *Smith* for ordinary meaning, in *Craig* for literal meaning. In both, he resists expanding meaning; in neither does he justify himself on the theoretical grounds he will proclaim in the Tanner Lecture. His position, like the position of most judges and lawyers, is in fact ad hoc and of the moment.

The Smith case reads like a thriller complete with drug sales, police informers, undercover agents, betrayal, and a high-speed chase. The Court's decision rests on the meaning of "use" in a section of the U. S. criminal code stating that if a firearm is used in a drug trafficking offense the sentence is five years' imprisonment, and if the firearm is a machine gun, or is equipped with a silencer, the sentence is thirty years.[91] John Angus Smith and a companion drove from Tennessee to Florida to buy cocaine through an acquaintance, Deborah Hoag. They planned to sell it later. After Hoag had obtained the cocaine, she introduced them to a drug dealer in her motel room. Smith discussed the possibility of selling his MAC-10, which was equipped with a silencer and had been modified to operate as an automatic weapon (and thus qualified as a machine gun) with the drug dealer, in the event his deal with another buyer fell through. Hoag, who turned out to be a police informer, told the sheriff's office. They sent an undercover agent, who posed as a pawnbroker and agreed to buy the gun for two ounces of cocaine. Before the agent returned with the cocaine, Smith fled the motel and, after a high-speed chase, was arrested. In addition to the MAC-10, police found a MAC-11, a loaded .45 caliber pistol, a .22 caliber pistol with a homemade silencer, and, in Smith's waistband, a 9 mm handgun. (Justice Sandra Day O'Connor, who wrote the court's opinion, evidently could not resist putting in the last details.) A grand jury indicted Smith, alleging, among other things, that he "knowingly used the MAC-10 and its silencer during and in relation to a drug trafficking crime." He was found guilty. Smith appealed, maintaining that the relevant statute applied only to using a firearm as a weapon during drug trafficking and not to using it as "a medium for exchange or barter."

The Supreme Court ruled that trading a firearm for drugs constitutes "use" of the firearm within the meaning of the statute.

"Surely petitioner's treatment of his MAC-10 can be described as 'use' within the everyday meaning of that term," O'Connor wrote, citing, among others, Webster's New International Dictionary ("to make use of; to convert to one's service; to employ; to avail oneself of; to utilize; to carry out a purpose or action by means of"). Arguing that the court "does not appear to grasp the distinction between how a word can be used and how it ordinarily is used," Scalia asserted in his dissent that "to use an instrumentality ordinarily means to use it for its intended purpose." One can say that one used a firearm in drug trafficking by trading it for cocaine, Scalia acknowledges, and one can also say that one used it to scratch one's head, but these examples say "nothing about whether the ordinary meaning of the phrase 'uses a firearm' embraces such extraordinary employments." Given the rule that ordinary meaning governs in the interpretation of a statute, Scalia concluded that "use" in the relevant section of the criminal code, refers only to use as a weapon:

> We are dealing here . . . with common words that are, as I have suggested, inordinately sensitive to context. Just as adding the direct object "a firearm" to the verb "use" narrows the meaning of that verb (it can no longer mean "partake of"), so also adding the modifier "in the offense of transferring, selling, or transporting firearms" to the phrase "use a firearm" expands the meaning of that phrase (it then includes, as it previously would not, nonweapon use). But neither the narrowing nor the expansion should logically be thought to apply to all appearances of the affected word or phrase. Just as every appearance of the word "use" in the statute need not be given the narrow meaning that word acquires in the phrase "use a firearm," so also every appearance of the phrase "use a firearm" need not be given the expansive connotation that phrase acquires in the broader context "use a firearm in crimes such as unlawful sale of firearms."

To this argument, O'Connor responds not by denying the ordinary use of "use a firearm" but by pointing out that an ordinary meaning of a word does not exclude any of its other uses. "That one example of 'use' is the first to come to mind when the phrase 'uses . . . a firearm' is uttered does not preclude us from recognizing that there are other 'uses' that qualify as well." Both O'Connor's and Scalia's argument are sophistic—Dickensian parodies of lawyers who in their quibbling seem to forget that a serious crime has been committed or that a man's life is in question. Thirty years' imprisonment is a long time. Of course, it is reasonable to assume that both justices are well aware of the seriousness of the crime and its punishment and are arguing as best they can from within the letter of the law for a decision they consider appropriate. Certainly, this can be said for O'Connor, but given Scalia's usual hard-nosed stance on crime, one must ask whether the pleasures of textual play and argument have not led him astray.

Craig, like *Smith*, rests on the meaning of a single word; "confrontation," as it occurs in the Sixth Amendment. "In all criminal prosecutions, the accused shall enjoy the right... to be confronted with the witnesses against him. . . ."[92] *Craig*, a child-abuse case, concerns the constitutionality of a Maryland statute, not dissimilar to those in many states, which permitted an allegedly abused child to testify through one-way closed-circuit television if it were demonstrated that the child's presence in the courtroom would result in the child's suffering such serious emotional distress that he or she could not reasonably communicate. Sandra Ann Craig was found guilty of abusing, among other children, a six-year-old girl who had attended a preschool and kindergarten she owned and operated. In accordance with the Maryland statute, the child witnesses testified through a closed circuit television after expert witnesses had testified that the children's confrontation with Craig would so distress them that they would be incapable of communicating. The children were not able to see Craig, but Craig, her lawyer, the judge, and jury were able to see them, and Craig, or her lawyer, was permitted to challenge the prosecutor and question the children. Craig objected to the procedure, arguing that the confrontation clause requires a face-to-face courtroom encounter between the accused and accusers. Despite Craig's objections, the trial court went ahead, and Craig was found guilty. Craig appealed. The Maryland Court of Appeals reversed and remanded for a new trial, not on Craig's grounds but on the grounds that the trial court had not reached "the high threshold" required for determining whether or not the children would have been able to communicate reasonably in front of the defendant. To resolve confrontation clause issues raised by the case, the Supreme Court agreed to review it. Justice O'Connor, who argued that the purpose of the clause was to ensure the reliability of evidence given by witnesses, wrote the opinion. She concluded that

> where necessary to protect a child witness from trauma that would be caused by testifying in the physical presence of the defendant, at least where such trauma would impair the child's ability to communicate, the Confrontation Clause does not prohibit use of a procedure that, despite the absence of face-to-face confrontation, ensures the reliability of the evidence by subjecting it to rigorous adversarial testing and thereby preserves the essence of effective confrontation.

Scalia vigorously objected.[93] He begins: "Seldom has this Court failed so conspicuously to sustain a categorical guarantee of the Constitution against the tide of prevailing current opinion. . . ." He insists that "confrontation" in Sixth Amendment means face-to-face confrontation: it stipulates and requires a procedure. Given its guarantee in the Constitution, the Court has no more right to say that it is dispensable than it has to say that trial by jury, also guaranteed by the Sixth Amendment, is dispensable. "The Court makes the impossible plausible by recharacterizing the Confrontation Clause, so that confrontation (redesignated 'face-to-face confrontation') becomes only one of many 'elements of confrontation.'" Scalia's refusal to expand the meaning of confrontation here is reminiscent of his refusal to expand the meaning of "use" in *Smith*, at least when it was followed by "firearms." There, however, he argued on the basis of ordinary meaning. Here he simply asserts meaning. "'To confront' plainly means to encounter face to face, whatever else it may mean in addition." Indeed, Scalia's adhesion to the face-to-face essence of "confrontation" is philological. Confrontation is derived from the Latin, *cum*, "with" and *frons, frontis*, "forehead," "front," "face."

Although Scalia insists on an unquestionable constitutional requirement for the face-to-face confrontation, he also argues that, given the suggestibility of children and their frequent inability to separate fantasy from reality, it is all the more important for them to testify in front of the accused. He cites events in a Jordan, Minnesota case, clearly exceptional, in which twenty-four adults were charged with molesting thirty-seven children primarily on the basis of the children's testimony. One of the adults pleaded guilty, two were acquitted, and charges against the others were finally dropped.

> Is it difficult to imagine how unconvincing such a testimonial admission might be to a jury that witnessed the child's delight at seeing his parents in the courtroom? Or how devastating it might be if, pursuant to a psychiatric evaluation that "trauma would impair the child's ability to communicate" in front of his parents, the child were permitted to tell his story to the jury on closed-circuit television?

Clearly, Scalia worries about adults being falsely charged. Already, in the opening paragraph of his dissent, he hypothesizes cases of children's falsely accusing their parents of abuse.[94] No doubt, Scalia's worries are real, but so are the worries of those concerned with children's welfare. Scalia appears not to believe that abuse can so terrorize a child that the child is incapable of communicating in front of his or her abuser. He writes as if this is simply a matter of will. The child's "unwillingness" to testify "cannot be a valid excuse under the Confrontation Clause, whose very object is to place the witness under the sometimes hostile glare of the defendant," Scalia writes. In his comments on the case in the Tanner lecture, he shows even less sympathy for the child. He notes that one of the major purposes of the confrontation clause

> was to induce *precisely* that pressure upon the witness which the little girl found it difficult to endure. It is difficult to accuse someone to his face, particularly when you are lying. Now no extrinsic factors have changed since that provision was adopted in 1791. Sexual abuse existed then, as it does now; little children were more easily upset than adults, then as now; a means of placing the defendant out of sight of the witness existed then as now (a screen could easily have been erected that would enable the defendant to see the witness, but not the witness the defendant). But the Sixth Amendment

nonetheless gave *all* criminal defendants the right to *confront* the witnesses against them, because that was thought to be an important protection. The only significant things that have changed, I think, are the society's sensitivity to so-called psychic trauma (which is what we are told the child witness in such a situation suffers) and the society's assessment of where the proper balance ought to be struck between the two extremes of a procedure that assures convicting 100 percent of all child abusers, and a procedure that assures acquitting 100 percent of those falsely accused of child abuse. I have no doubt that the society is, as a whole, happy and pleased with what my Court decided. But we should not pretend that the decision did not *eliminate* a liberty that previously existed.[95]

Scalia's opinion has an inordinate intensity. He idealizes and idolizes a moment in time and surrenders himself (and us) to the values and structures, the laws, produced in that moment. He takes these laws as literally as possible, at least in the cases we have discussed, resisting any expansion of meaning, any metaphorization, any translation, and thereby freezes meaning—the meaning *he* claims, often on scant evidence, was the original (and therefore only valid) meaning. He scorns (to quote his *Craig* dissent) "the tide of prevailing current opinion" that insinuates itself into the interpretation of the Constitution. He assumes, rhetorically at least, that it is possible to resist such an intrusion and that such resistance is admirable. He asserts, again in *Craig*, that "the Constitution is meant to protect us against, rather than to conform to, current 'widespread belief.'" He insists, as we have noted, that more open-ended readings of the Constitution, those associated with the notions of a living or evolving Constitution, readings that facilitate this intrusion of current beliefs, often deprive us of liberties we once had. He so idealizes such liberties that they seem to end up having greater importance for him than many humane values which the society at large holds and for which it is willing to sacrifice some of its freedom.

A constitution is, in fact, and must be regarded by the judges as, a fundamental law.

Alexander Hamilton, 1788[96]

It is our rock and our redeemer, the civil religion of society that has no state church. It is a unifying symbol as powerful in our diverse Republic as the queen in a monarchy. It is history: roots for a country with little sense of the past. For a restless people, it is the prime source of stability, of certainty.

The Constitution of the United States is all these things. But to state them is to recognize a profound irony. For there is no certainty in the Constitution, and there never has been. It was born in controversy. Its purposes were contradictory: to create a governmental power and to limit that power. Its framers did not make clear and very likely did not agree on what they intended in particular provisions. Through all its history, the meaning of the Constitution has been subject to ferocious argument, and to change. . . .

In the end the distinctive character of the American Constitution does not lie in this particular clause or that. It lies in our willingness to accept the Constitution, interpreted by judges, as law. Other people look to pageantry or history or ethnic identity or ideology. Our national sense of legitimacy rests on law.

Anthony Lewis, 1987[97]

The absolute finality of [Supreme] Court decisions — barring constitutional amendment or subsequent reversal by the Court itself — does more than give gravity to that body's pronouncements on constitutional matters; it makes constitutional arguments and determinations count, in a way that they would not count if each government official were bound only by that person's own opinion of the Constitution's meaning.

Laurence H. Tribe[98]

It is analytically possible to distinguish between the constitutive and the foundational role of the Constitution, although such a distinction tends to mask the rhetorical play between the two. The *constitutive* refers back to the inaugural moment of the new order produced by the Constitution. That moment is, in principle, historically specifiable; its effect is coextensive with the polity it has created. The *foundational* refers to the paramount authority of the Constitution as the "final citation" for the order — government and laws—it has authorized. It is valid so long as the Constitution is taken to be constitutive of that order. For example, a particular governmental agency has its own rules purporting to govern all of its actions. It is these rules that determine the validity of a particular action. The agency's rules themselves are judged to be valid in terms of some "higher" law—that is, an authorizing act of Congress, which in turn must be authorized by or consistent with the Constitution. What we have in effect is a total system of law, which can be pictured as a hierarchical cone, encompassing all the laws and regulations of the government, which are subsumed under the final authority of the Constitution.

It can be asked, if one accepts the hierarchical model of law, what gives final authority to the Constitution. The question reflects the thinking imposed by a hierarchical model, one coupled to a particular sense of history that gives authority to the original. Although such a view seems perfectly natural to us, it is by no means universal. As Louis Dumont and other anthropologists have attempted to show, many societies—for Dumont, India—do not conceptualize social reality in terms of a hierarchy that we in the West would recognize as such.[99] While we understand hierarchy as a "ladder of command" in which lower ranks are encompassed in higher ones in regular succession, in "traditional" India, at least according to Dumont, "the elements of a whole are ranked in relation to the whole." Other, usually simpler, societies do not understand themselves in hierarchical terms at all. They may be organized genealogically in terms of moieties, sections, lineages, and clans of equal status but differentiated power, which bear little relationship to anything we might call a social whole. Certainly, the weight Americans give to the "original" is not universally shared.[100]

Within our hierarchical model, in any case, the question of who or what gives the Constitution its foundational value has been answered in several ways. We have already considered the Constitution's constitutive role—the symbolism, the ritual, attached to it—which supports its foundational function in legal argumentation. But this is a view from the outside; from the inside, it becomes tautological. The Constitution is constitutive of the political and legal order; therefore, it is foundational; therefore, it is paramount. Its position in the legal system can of course be justified, rationally, logically, from within our hierarchical understanding. It is our final appeal. It parallels our appellate system and it articulates our most basic values. To some, it gives expression in positive form to natural law, or, at least presupposes that law.[101] To others, its authority results from the very institutions it established, their coerciveness, or, paradoxically, from the precarious order it has created—from the fear of what could happen if we betrayed it through misinterpretation and manipulation. And to still others, as naive as this may sound, to its perfection.

Whatever the classical beauty of this hierarchical picture of the law, it is not necessarily an accurate picture of the law as it is in fact displayed and performed. We can imagine other models of legal organization in which there is no single final authority. The most obvious, though perhaps not the most interesting, are those in countries in North Africa and the Middle East, where there are two or more different systems of law—a secular one based largely on European civil law, a religious one, the *sharia*, and then, in some places, a customary one—whose jurisdictions and authority often conflict.[102] To the continental European, whose legal system is succinct, codified, and highly centralized, the American system, with its complex of significantly different laws in different states and municipalities and its admixture of common and statutory law, seems baroque if not simply confused. It is likely that there are rules and regulations in the United States that are only at the most tenuous level subsumable to constitutional authority. After all, given the fact that our laws are not subject to judicial review before they are promulgated, their constitutionality is not necessarily questioned— that is, until they are challenged. Consider the fact that so much of American constitutional history has been a struggle between the federal government and the states over the limits of constitutional authority. Under what circumstances can one appeal from a state court to a federal one? Must states adhere to the Bill of Rights? Indeed, it can be argued that the Civil War was fought over the Constitution. A more accurate picture of the legal system might well be more baroque than classical.

As the great Austrian jurist Hans Kelsen, who taught at Harvard and Berkeley, observes in his *General Theory of Law and State*, many laws (including constitutions) contain elements or dicta that unlike holdings, do not have a specific legal, that is normative, character.[103] These might include theoretical views, the motives of the legislators, or policy considerations. For a legal purist like Kelsen, the elements are "legally irrelevant products of the law-creating process." However, they *do* play a role in the justification and interpretation of the law, appealing, for example, to some external raison d'être, such as natural rights, God's will, or, for that matter, Reason. They do figure in court decisions and are so entangled in "issues of law" that it is in practice often difficult to distinguish between normative and justificatory propositions. Indeed, justificatory or otherwise peripheral propositions—at any rate, those which do not have immediate normative effect in one court decision—may be picked up as normatively effective in another.

For example, in *NAACP v. Alabama*, in which the Supreme Court reversed a decision allowing the attorney general of Alabama to ban the NAACP, Justice John Marshall Harlan observed:

> It is hardly a novel perception that compelled disclosure of affiliation with groups engaged in advocacy may constitute [an effective] restraint on freedom of association. [There is a] vital relationship between freedom to associate and privacy in one's association. [Inviolability] of privacy in group association may in many circumstances be indispensable to the preservation of freedom of association. . . .[104]

Seven years later, in *Griswold v. Connecticut*, in which the court ruled that a statute prohibiting the use of any birth control device was an infringement of the constitutional right to privacy, Justice Douglas invoked *NAACP v. Alabama* as precedent for establishing the right to privacy.[105] (The Constitution does not mention the right to privacy—a point that the literalist Hugo Black emphasized in his dissent.[106]) Douglas stated that the right was a "peripheral

First Amendment right" and has a "penumbra where privacy is protected from government intrusion." He went on to say, much to the
horror of conservative interpretivists, that *NAACP v. Alabama*
(along with *NAACP v. Button*[107]) suggests "that specific guarantees
in the Bill of Rights have penumbras, formed by emanations from
those guarantees that help give them life and substance." This is
certainly an extraordinary set of metaphors for a case dealing with
birth control![108] He argued further that other rights, like the Third
Amendment right involving the quartering of troops, create zones
of privacy. Thus, privacy (whatever it might mean) became a constitutionally protected right and has figured in such controversial
cases as *Roe v. Wade*[109] and *Bower v. Hardwick*,[110] which upheld a
Georgia sodomy statute.

Kelsen, who like all positivists wants to keep legal understanding
and adjudication free of moral and political considerations, finds
constitutional validity in what he calls a *Grundnorm*, or basic
norm.[111] He argues for a "pure theory" of law, one that is logically
self-supporting and independent of extralegal values. The legal order is, for him, a system of norms or "ought" propositions. The validity of a norm, he points out, lies in another norm, and not in
reality, as a statement purporting to be factual does. The basic norm
is one whose validity cannot be derived from a superior norm; and
from which flows the entire normative, or legal, order. Kelsen is not
particularly clear about the status of this basic norm. At times he
speaks of it as a transcendental reality, at other times, as a presupposition, an unconscious one even, an authority, or a first constitution. Most often, he seems to mean the presupposition that the first
constitution is the binding legal norm. In a manner reminiscent of
the inevitable circularity postulated by Cornelius van Til's presuppositionalism (see Chapter One), he states that the basic norm is
valid because it is presupposed to be valid. "And it is presupposed
to be valid because without this presupposition no human act could
be interpreted as a legal, especially a norm-creating, act."

> By formulating the basic norm, we do not introduce into the science
> of law any new method. We merely make explicit what all jurists,

mostly unconsciously, assume when they consider positive law [roughly, man-made law as opposed to, say, natural law] as a system of valid norms and not only as a complex of facts, and at the same time repudiate any natural law from which positive law would receive its validity. That the basic norm really exists in the juristic consciousness is the result of a simple analysis of actual juristic statements. The basic norm is the answer to the question: how—and that means under what condition—are all these juristic statements concerning legal norms, legal duties, and so on, possible?[112]

It is not altogether clear that one can restrict the law to normative propositions. It would appear that at least in the common law—certainly in Supreme Court decisions, which are often extremely elaborate and at times almost preposterously wordy—no strict line between norm and justification, can be drawn. This is particularly true if one takes into account the subsequent history of these decisions. We need not invoke "penumbras" and "emanations" to appreciate this. Ronald Dworkin, perhaps the most reputed legal philosopher writing today, argues that judges are (or always ought to be) making use in their decisions, particularly the hard ones, of principles of law that are not given direct expression in the law.[113] They are not expressed, as I understand Dworkin, because they are presupposed by the law. They are of a different logical order. Once determined, they can of course be stated as normative though not narrowly construed legal propositions. By introducing such principles, Dworkin brings into the law the moral and political, which positivists and textualists, like Scalia and Berger, want to keep out and therefore eschew.

Kelsen not withstanding, it is in my view impossible to find within a legal system, indeed within any system of thought, its own ground. One accepts the system, its presuppositions, either on faith, as van Til urges us to accept the Bible's self-proclaimed authority, or by coercion, or out of desire, or through fear. Kelsen himself regards all norms, including, I presume, the basic norm, as intrinsically coercive.[114] He recognizes that it is possible to question the source of validity of the basic norm and to answer in terms, say, of a god who authorized the first legislator or fathers of a first constitution, but he denies the relevance of such a religious justification to a positivist theory of the law like his own.[115]

Whatever philosophical reasons Kelsen may have had for arguing for a "pure theory of law," he also had political ones. As the author of the 1920 Austrian constitution and a judge on the Austrian Supreme Constitutional Court from 1920 to 1930—he managed to emigrate to the United States in 1940—Kelsen was well aware of the way in which a legal system could be politicized and manipulated. In his Preface to *General Theory of Law and States*, he argues that a pure theory of law exposes the political ideology within traditional jurisprudence.

> It is precisely by its anti-ideological character that the pure theory of law proves itself a true science of law. Science as cognition has always the immanent tendency to unveil its object. But political ideology veils reality either by transfiguring reality in order to conserve and defend it, or by disfiguring reality in order to attack, to destroy, or to replace it by another reality. Every political ideology has its root in volition, not in cognition; in the emotional, not in the rational, element of our consciousness; it arises from certain interests, or, rather, from interests other than the interest of truth. This remark, of course, does not imply any assertion regarding the value of other interests. There is no possibility of deciding rationally between opposite values. It is precisely from this situation that a really tragic conflict arises: the conflict between the fundamental principle of science, Truth, and the supreme ideal of politics, Justice.[116]

Kelsen observes that especially in troubled times—he was writing toward the end of World War II—legal science, in fact any social science, cannot counteract "the overwhelming interest that those residing in power, as well as those craving for power, have in a theory pleasing to their wishes. . . ."[117] He hopes, nevertheless, that the fruits of a pure science of law will be appreciated in the Anglo-American world, where "freedom of science continues to be respected" and "ideas are in greater esteem than power" (!), and eventually in a Europe liberated from tyranny.

Kelsen's commitment to a pure science of law as a way of preserving law from political consideration and manipulation seems naive today when the ideological independence of any science—even the hard sciences like physics and chemistry—is in question. Kelsen is writing in the tradition of a conservative Germanic or, more generally, European jurisprudence, which unlike the more rough-and-ready, pragmatic approach of most American adjudication and theorizing, stresses the rational, systemic quality of the law and its independence from the political, economic, social, moral, and cultural domains. His commitment to scientific positivism, though dated, reminds us of one of the hopes positivists of his generation saw in their philosophy—a means by which one could separate truth from ideology, cognition from volition, reason from emotion. What they did not appreciate was that, by insisting on the independence of the law, they in fact opened it to all sorts of political manipulation. A positivist stance toward the law, its isolation from the social and political, coupled with what Richard Weisberg calls a "desiccated Cartesian logic," enabled French lawyers to argue narrowly, literally, in terms of the racial laws promulgated by the Vichy government, the fate of countless Jews; and to do it with a diligence that surprised even the Germans.[118]

As I read through literally thousands of pages of theorizing legal interpretation, I was struck by an insistent, indeed obsessive, concern about the relationship between law, politics, and morality. To even the sophisticated layman, this concern seems at once obvious and bizarre. How can one possibly separate the law from moral and political considerations? How can a judge possibly bracket off his or her political and moral beliefs in coming to a legal decision, in interpreting the Constitution or a statute? Our psychologies, our personal experience, the way we learn to read literature, the way we evaluate what others say—all this tells us that we are not fully in command of ourselves; that we are subject to all kinds of influences of which we are never fully aware; that desire, including the desire for power, is neither pure nor transparent; and that our ability to rationalize in anticipation of a decision or retrospective to it can blind us brilliantly to the obvious. In any case, we know that judges are known for their political and moral positions, and that, despite their claims to be true to the law, those political and moral positions are frequently manifested in their decisions. Indeed, it is for these positions that they are usually appointed.

Of course we strive or ought to strive to be objective, neutral, fair, and just. Of course we strive, with sincerity and in good faith, to disengage ourselves "when the situation calls for it" from our personal moral and political commitments or, if we think it best, to lay those commitments on the table. But we know that only a fool would assume that we are fully capable of such transcendence. A degree of skepticism has always been a prerequisite of social survival, unless one happens to be a Forrest Gump. But too much skepticism can be as socially dysfunctional as none at all. We are capable, to a surprising degree, of disengaging ourselves from personal interest; but, with the possible exception of the saints, the pure and selfless altruists among us, we require an external referent, distinct and commanding, to achieve disengagement and personal transcendence. It may be a God, an idol, a religious text, a law, a constitution, a principle, an ideal, even a person. Insofar as this referent, this "Third" as I have called it, facilitates our transcendence, our disinterest, or our disengagement, it seems to take on a sacred aura.[119] It has, it would seem in our social-symbolic calculus, to be transcendent, at the very least extraordinary, in order to bring about our own transcendence.

But here our, or at any rate my own, skepticism returns. We have to be wary of attributions of sanctity and specialness, for they figure easily in our rationalizations and mystifications. We may consider texts like Holy Scripture or the Constitution sacred or near-sacred, as containing truths that enable us to bypass or overcome our own situationally determined interests. But while the quality, the authority we give those texts, may enable us to achieve what we take to be disengagement and disinterest, how we interpret them (for they are never so obvious) is always, despite our hermeneutics, subject to our desire and to the plays of power that are inevitably attached to it.

Yes, we act *as if* we can bracket off or transcend our own moral and political commitments and adhere to the letter of the law, or more broadly, to its spirit; but we must recognize the artifice of that position. Those positivists, like Kelsen, who proclaim the purity of the law (at least its needful separation from the moral and political) or those narrow interpretivists, particularly of a literalist orientation, like Black, Berger, Bork, and Scalia (who claim one can obtain *the* meaning of the law by some hermeneutic, independent of personal political and moral consideration), fail to realize, or prefer to ignore, that their stances inevitably have moral and political consequences and *therefore are moral and political.*

Their delusion (or preference) is facilitated by the way they construe and evaluate the text. It is not simply a question of the particular style of interpretation they adopt. What seems clear to any outsider who reads law is that those of opposing interpretive orientations still frame texts in the same way. Though they argue with one another over meaning, they assume the possibility of determinate meaning. That a decision has to be made, with important and, by some accounts, violent implications, gives them no choice: they must find determinate meaning.[120] It is this fact, far more than the normative quality of the law, that distinguishes legal from literary, philosophical, and theological interpretation, where a final decision is not normally expected. In the legal setting, the determinate meaning of the law is constantly argued by lawyers and judges; but, given their dedication to the text, its facticity, its continuance, its possession of determinate meaning, the literalists tend to ignore the fact that the determination of that meaning results less from any meaning inherent in the text than from highly ritualized argument and negotiation. I do not mean that there is no meaning in the text but rather that this meaning, whatever it is, serves to constrain argument and negotiation, desire, and plays of power. It is, however, only one constraint; a second is the real or imagined interlocutor. Meaning has then both semantic and rhetorical value, and yet its rhetorical value has to be denied if it is to be effective both in argument and decision. Meaning has, in other words, to be in the text. Though my emphasis on argument and negotiation might suggest an indeterminate notion of meaning—the "determination" of which depends upon extratextual factors like coercion and seduction—I would argue that it is precisely the nature of legal argument that requires focus on the word and ideally preserves that focus, and the understanding that comes with it, from being merely a product of self-interest or an expression of one's own moral and political views. I write "ideally," for a dramatic hermeneutics like the law produces its own blindness, distortion, and complicity. These are controlled, if they are controlled at all, not by the letter but by the institutions of the law and, by extension, the polity that has vested and is vested in that law.

6—Intention

JUDGE BORK I think the American people want judges to interpret the law and not to make it. I think that is pretty clear.

SENATOR SPECTER Well, I agree with you about that. But the interpretation of the law does not depend upon an understanding of original intent. . . .

JUDGE BORK Well, when I say original intent . . . what I mean is really original understanding, because law is a public act, and it is really what was understood generally at the time the Constitution was framed, not the subjective intentions of James Madison.

And when I say original understanding, when I sit down and look at the Bill of Rights, and it says "freedom of the press," right away, I know what they are driving at. I may not know exactly what they mean, but I know what they are driving at. I know the central freedom, or the core of the freedom, that they are driving at. When they say "no unreasonable searches or seizures," not from the language but from the history of the British and the way they behaved in this country with their searches and seizures and general warrants, I know what they are driving at.

So I do not think there is any difficulty in understanding the basic principles of the powers granted to Congress or of the freedoms preserved in the Bill of Rights and the Civil War Amendments.

SENATOR SPECTER Well, Judge Bork, this theme has run through the hearings and I think is a central theme, and I think there is some difference of opinion as to whether you can really find original intent, whether the tradition of U.S. constitutional interpretation looks to specific constitutional rights as, for example, privacy, which we have talked about so often, or whether in a more generalized context, justices who advocate restraint, like Frankfurter, talk about values rooted in the conscience and tradition of a people, and that the history of U.S. constitutional jurisprudence, as I see it, has in many, many cases not been grounded on original intent—sometimes, yes, but frequently not. . . .

In 1968 . . . in *Fortune Magazine*, where you set forth a theory of constitutional law, you had written this at page 141: "The text of the Constitution, as anyone experienced with words might expect, is least precise where it is the most important. Like the Ten Commandments, the Constitution enshrines profound values, but necessarily omits the minor premises required to apply them."

So that, from that statement, it seems to me a fair reading is that it is pretty hard to find intent of the Framers.

Then, you go on on the same page: "History can be of considerable help, but it tells much too little about the specific intentions of the men who framed, adopted and ratified the great clauses. The record is incomplete. The men involved often had vague or even conflicting intentions." . . .

Now, in that context, where I think you are exactly right in what you have written and said, because of the great difficulty of finding intent, how much validity is there in searching for original intent as a necessary prerequisite for a constitutional decision, without which the Court has no legitimacy?

JUDGE BORK Well, I think that is right, Senator; there is a lot of difficulty. But let me discuss this. . . . The Constitution and the Bill of Rights . . . have a similar generality, but we are closer in history, and we have a lot of evidence about the Bill of Rights now. . . .

But we do have, in the case of the Constitution — I referred to the fact that we cannot know the Framers' specific intentions; I think you read that in one of those pieces, that we cannot know their specific intentions, and indeed we cannot. And indeed, their specific intentions would not help us a great deal because our task is to apply their public understanding of what they were protecting to modern circumstances as to which they could have not specific intentions. . . .

Now, we have the text. For example, the First Amendment tells us that it deals with religion, no establishment, free exercise. Right away we know that we are in an area, so that we know it is not just a free-floating liberty; we know what we are talking about. They are talking about not establishing religion, and they are talking about free exercise of religion.

Then they say Congress shall make no law abridging the freedom of speech or of the press. So I know now that I am talking about speech and press, and the freedom of those two, so I know that I am not talking about a generalized liberty; I am talking about a freedom of the press.

Now, when you want to flesh that out, for example, you have a lot of contemporary debate about what was going on. You have, in the case of the main body of the Constitution, the *Federalist Papers,* the *Anti-Federalist Papers,* and many debates. In the case of the Bill of Rights, we are a little short on debate in Congress, but you have some contemporary discussion; you have actions by the early Congresses which show what they understood themselves to have proposed; and you have actions by the early courts, which show what they understood to have been done, and some of those courts for people who were at the convention or at various ratifying conventions. . . .

Now, judges who look for original understanding and look at the same evidence and think as hard as they can, will, in the borderline cases, often come out differently. I do not mean to say that original understanding gives anybody a mechanical way to approach a problem. It does not; but it gives them a pretty firm starting point.

Bork Hearings, September 19, 1987[1]

The centerpiece of Robert Bork's jurisprudence is his belief that the only way, or at least the most desirable way, to understand the Constitution is in terms of "original intent" or, as he sometimes puts it, "original understanding." In his opening statement to the Judiciary Committee, he asked, "How should a judge go about finding the law?"[2] To which he answered: "The only legitimate way is by attempting to discern what those who made the law intended. The intentions of the lawmakers govern, whether the lawmakers are the Congress of the United States enacting a statute or those who ratified our Constitution and its various amendments." He added, as if this were not clear enough, "If a judge abandons intentions as his guide, there is no law available to him and he begins to legislate a social agenda for the American people."

The theory of original intent or intention was the hallmark of Ronald Reagan's jurisprudence, if one can speak of Reagan's determination to undo the decisions of the Warren and Burger courts as a jurisprudence. His attorney general, Edwin Meese III, outraged the liberal—in fact, not just the liberal—establishment when he proclaimed his particular philosophy of original intent in a speech before the American Bar Association in July 1985. "The text and intention of the Constitution must be understood to constitute the banks within which constitutional interpretation must flow," he wrote; and in words that Bork anticipated in his earlier writing and echoed during the Hearings, he went on:

> In the main, a jurisprudence that seeks to be faithful to our Constitution—a jurisprudence of original intention, as I have called it—is not difficult to describe. Where the language of the Constitution is specific, it must be obeyed. Where there is demonstrable consensus among the framers and ratifiers as to a principle stated or implied by the Constitution, it should be followed as well. Where there is ambiguity as to the precise meaning or reach of a constitutional provision, it should be interpreted and applied in a manner so as to at least not contradict the text of the Constitution itself.[3]

Meese's words, ridden as they are with the clichés of originalism, frame the "intellectual" setting in which the debate on originalism proceeded in the Bork Hearings.

As Stanford's Paul Brest noted, there are two extreme forms of originalism: *strict textualism*, or literalism, in which the words and phrases of the Constitution are construed narrowly and precisely; and *strict intentionalism*, which attempts "to ascertain and give effect to the intent of its framers and the people who adopted it."[4] In both their extreme and more moderate forms, the textualist and intentionalist positions blend with each other and are often confounded at a theoretical level. Bork's switch from original intent to original understanding in his exchange with Senator Specter, however politically motivated it may have been, is a example of this confusion: "When I say original intent . . . what I mean is really original understanding, because law is a public act, and it is really what was understood generally at the time the Constitution was framed, not the subjective intentions of James Madison." Bork's identification of intention and understanding is not unique: lawyers and judges frequently translate the one into the other with little reflection. But surely there is a difference between intent and understanding (even when understanding is conceived in intentional terms).[5] Understanding, like intent, can be understood subjectively as well as publicly. What merits study is why the switch is made in legal argument and theory.

It is noteworthy that in his book *The Tempting of America* Bork does not refer to original intent but to original understanding. "What is the meaning of a rule that judges should not change?" he asks.

> It is the meaning understood at the time of the law's enactment. Though I have written of the understanding of the ratifiers of the Constitution, since they enacted it and made it law, that is actually a shorthand formulation, because what the ratifiers understood themselves to be enacting must be taken to be what the public of that time would have understood the words to mean. It is important to be clear about this. The search is not for a subjective intention. If someone found a letter from George Washington to Martha telling her that what he meant by the power to lay taxes was not what other people meant, that would not change our reading of the Constitution in the slightest. Nor would the subjective intentions of all the members of a ratifying convention alter anything. When lawmakers use words, the law that results is what those words ordinarily mean. If Congress enacted a statute outlawing the sale of automatic rifles and did so in the Senate by a vote of 51 to 49, no court would overturn a conviction because two senators in the majority testified that they really had intended only to prohibit the *use* of such rifles. They said "sale" and "sale" it is.[6]

Bork's argument here is rather more textualist, naively so, than intentionalist. It rests on several strawmen that enable him to sidestep the philosophical problems his position raises. The first of these is that there are serious, competent readers of the law who believe that one can understand a text without understanding what it meant at the time it was written. To my knowledge no serious readers of the law or any other text, for that matter, would actually make such a claim. Some might argue, for instance, that the meaning of a text is always somewhere in tension between what it meant at the time of writing and at the time of reading. They might refuse to differentiate between original meaning and present significance, arguing that an interpretation is always a compromise between the two.

The second strawman is that intent or intention is necessarily subjective. To be sure, there are original intentionalists who speak this way, but many of them, the more sophisticated ones at least, hold that intention is deduced from the text and has little if anything to do with its author's internal ruminations at the time of writing.[7] Some argue that text-deduced intention can be complemented by extratextual data, such as letters written at the time. Others deny the relevance of extratextual information.

Bork's argument is addressed to his critics: the liberal law professors, judges, and justices of the Supreme Court. Since his rejection by the Senate, these liberal activists have become the enemy against whom he has morally positioned himself as he spins out his increasingly extreme and acrimonious views.

Several of Bork's former colleagues who opposed his nomination reminded me that he had not always been an extremist—he had once been a Democrat and had even flirted with Marxism—and recommended that I ignore his postnomination writings, or at least be cautious in using them. Old-boyism and possible guilt of betrayal aside, they did have a point. Bork's recent books are the books of a wounded man; yet they must be taken into account. Given his desire to rid interpretation of the personal views of the interpreter, they underscore not only his personal failure but the ultimate failure of his project. Objective meaning does not lie only in the words of a text. "They said 'sale' and 'sale' it is." Meaning arises out of and is always—up to a point—an artifice of the dialogical or, as I would prefer with regard to the law, the *dramatic* context in which the text's, the words', meaning is sought. Meaning is always constrained by grammar, deeper language structures, and prevalent interpretive conventions. These conventions are not just the product of "containing" interpretive communities, as some theorists would have it, but are evoked by the words, the texts, themselves.[8] Words, texts, the written law, are never inert, though as we have seen they may be read that way and deadened.

Whether Bork's evaluation of the intellectual life of the legal academy is right, there is no doubt that very considerable—one could say, obsessive—thought has been devoted to the question of original intention, understanding, and meaning. Here I will restrict myself to the consideration of original intention. I should point out that the relationship between intention and meaning does not feature in all interpretive theories and methodologies. Their consideration is culturally and historically specific. Samoans, for example, rarely, if ever, consider a speaker's intentions, motives, or psychological condition; rather, they are concerned with "the responsibility speakers must assume (or be forced to assume) for the state of affairs created by their own words."[9] No doubt, with romanticism, intention acquired an *Innerlichkeit*, an innerness, a psychological dimension that it had not had earlier, when it was understood more rhetorically. English legal theorists focus on "objective" semantic meaning whereas Americans, whose idiom is more psychological, look to intention. In 1980 in an important article on original intention, Paul Brest claimed that, from the eighteenth through at least the mid-nineteenth century, American lawyers and judges were more textualist than intentionalist.

> The plain meaning rule was frequently invoked: judicial recourse to legislative debates was virtually unknown and generally considered improper. Even after references to extrinsic sources became common, courts and commentators frequently asserted that the plain meaning of the text was the surest guide to the intent of the adopters.[10]

In March 1985, several years after Brest had published his article and several months before Meese's Bar Association speech, H. Jefferson Powell, a professor of law and divinity at Duke, elaborated

Brest's historical argument. Powell asked how "intention" was understood at the time the Constitution was written and ratified. Did the Framers assume that future interpreters of the Constitution would seek its meaning in the intentions of the delegates to the Constitutional Convention in Philadelphia? Behind Powell's question was another, implicit one: By their own argument, ought not proponents of original intention like Meese, Berger, and Bork adhere to the Framers' hermeneutics? To *their* view of intention? It was one of those questions that the ancient logicians would have adored. If it can be shown that the Framers shared the original intentionalists' views on intention, then the intentionalists are, by their own argument, correct in advocating it; but if it can be shown that the Framers did not share the intentionalists' views, then the intentionalists can neither maintain nor abandon their stance on intention without contradiction. If they maintain it, they are contradicting their intentionalism, for the Framers did not intend intention to count. If they abandon it, they are in fact clinging to their intentionalism since they are doing precisely what the Framers intended. Of course, one can try to avoid the argument by asserting, for example, that the Framers' hermeneutics, their particular approach to intention, is beside the point—how one conceives what one is doing and what one is in fact doing are not necessarily coordinate. But wouldn't the same argument apply to today's originalists? For the most part, originalists have simply sidestepped the problem by ignoring it, or by declaring intentionalism so "natural" that no one could possibly interpret a text without taking into consideration its authors' intentions.

Since the Framers neither developed a theory of interpretation nor explicitly incorporated one in the Constitution, Powell looks to the interpretive "resources" at their disposal: namely, Enlightenment rationalism and British Protestantism, whose "unlikely alliance," he claims, engendered a suspicion of any sort of interpretation, and the rich interpretive tradition of English common law. He notes then a tension between "a global rejection of any and all methods of constitutional construction and a willingness to interpret the constitutional text in accordance with the common law principles that had been used to construe statutes."[11] He argues that at the time the Constitution was written, the intent or intention of a statute and, by extension, of the Constitution was to be discovered in the text itself, and not in extratextual material such as legislative history or political and social context. Wholly textual, intention was not then about an author's subjective purpose. Powell remarks that in none of the debates over the language of the Constitution did any of the Framers suggest that future interpreters could resolve textual ambiguities by consulting evidence for the Framers' intentions.[12] It was only later, during John Adams's administration, when federalists and republicans fought over their respective understandings of the Constitution, that extratextual material was resorted to for determining "original intent."[13] Federalists like Hamilton derived an expansive view of federal power from the Constitution's generalizations by applying traditional tools of statutory construction, whereas the republicans "took up the cudgels of the religious and philosophical opposition to interpretation and warned that the 'wiles of construction' could be controlled only by a narrow reading of the Constitution's expansive language."[14] After an extensive historical review, Powell concludes that a notion of intention which resembles the contemporary one was only incorporated into constitutional interpretation at the time of the Civil War.[15]

"Intention" is a troubling word. Its ambiguity was already apparent in medieval usage, where *intentio* could refer either to an individual's subjective purpose (however subjectivity was then conceived) or to an observer's determination of the purpose of another's action.[16] Aside from its special usages today (as in surgery, where it refers to the healing process) it signifies both a mental determination or predisposition to bring about some action or result and to that result, action, or purpose, at least as it is mentally conceived. In its ordinary usage, it presupposes a psychology, mentalism, interiority, subjectivity, volition, desire—though strictly speaking it need not. It describes a performative act, "I intend," and like other, stronger performatives, "I promise" or "I vow," it carries, or can carry, considerable moral weight—commitment and engagement.[17] We speak of a suitor with good intentions, or we distrust his matrimonial intentions. In phenomenology, intention describes the structure of consciousness, which always aims at, or intends, in a specific way—imaginatively, perceptually, volitionally, lovingly—its object. Sometimes, frequently in the law, we speak of collective intentions, as when we speak of the Framers' or the legislature's intention, and evoke, paradoxically, or at least metaphorically, individual (though collectivized) psychological presuppositions. We-the-people . . .

In everyday usage, certainly in the law, intention has very considerable rhetorical power. It is what I would call a "term of epistemological dubiety," whose doubtfulness has in most social exchanges to be denied. Pragmatically, I accept for the most part my interlocutor's attestation of intention: I assume his or her sincerity, firmness of purpose, realism, integrity. I support my assumption, inferentially, on the basis of evidence of various sorts and authority. I ignore, up to a point, my own desire that what my interlocutor tells me he intends is in fact his intention and will be carried through. I grant him the "mental space" those words demand. It is only when there is reason to doubt—a breakdown in communication or commitment, a failure to act, the revelation of duplicity—that I allow myself epistemological skepticism. "How do I ever really know what another intends?" How indeed do I know what I intend? I may say I have the intention, I intend to go to the circus, even as I doubt consciously, or perhaps less than consciously, that I will ever find the time, the will, the means, to go. And when I say that I have the intention to go to the circus, what am I in fact referring to? A disposition? A determination? A desire? To do what? Make a reservation? Hail a taxi? Buy a ticket? Enter the big top? Does "intention" really have a mental referent? Is this mental referent nothing more than an artifact of the denomination, the *description*, of the performative "I intend . . ."? Or does the insertion of that performative into a space—call it "mental," "subjective," or "psychological"—give it added force? By evoking precisely that interiority that we identify with the moral?

In my reading of the law, despite the countless pages devoted to it, I have not found its treatment to be satisfactory simply because intention has been treated if not wholly from within a legal perspective (as perhaps it should be) then without regard to its— persuasive, argumentative—rhetorical potential. Despite their sophistication, many lawyers appear to me to be so caught in the semantics of intention—even when, like Dworkin, they regard it as an invention—that they fail to appreciate fully its primarily rhetorical function.[18] What we may be judging when we evaluate a person's declaration or description of intention is not a referentially describable mental condition but the success or failure of a certain rhetorical maneuver masked by that declaration or description. We may be deciding whether it meets the criteria of acceptance within a certain, say, legal argument; but what needs to be worked out, at least in the case of evaluating arguments based on intention, is what these criteria are. We are not interested in whether a certain disposition in fact exists but in whether the declaration or description of that intention meets our criteria of acceptance and allows that "intention" to figure successfully in our argument. The postulation of the existence of an intention—supported, for example, by evidence in letters or a confidant's diary—should be evaluated in terms of whether such evidence meets the criteria for figuring in a certain kind of argument—and not in terms of whether that intention, whatever it was or is, actually existed or exists.[19]

This argument may strike many readers as skeptical as to the point of nihilism. This is not because it leads inevitably to nihilism (it does not) but because it goes against the epistemological naiveté that is demanded in ordinary social life. There we bracket off such epistemological considerations and believe, insofar as we can without being duped or duping ourselves, that when someone says they have the intention of doing something they not only intend to do it but have the appropriate mental disposition that we call "intention." The question is: Ought the law, ought a theory of jurisprudence, ought a legal hermeneutics, also bracket off these epistemological considerations? I don't propose to answer this question. But I will make one observation: If the law abandons socially mandated epistemological naiveté with regard at least to intention, its arguments in the courtroom, in briefs, and at times in law review articles, will be less persuasive, for despite their specialized language the arguments are cast in and presuppose the conventions of everyday communication and relationship.

———————

v.c. I have often wondered why lawyers haven't considered the relationship between intention in criminal law and in their theories of interpretation.

c.l. (laughing) I wouldn't want to get into that, if I were you.

Conversation with a constitutional lawyer, 1998

The Socratic command runs deeply through our hermeneutics. It runs counter, however, to our modernist psychology and to its postmodernist elaborations, which are preoccupied—at times ironically, at times with tragic seriousness—with man's incapacity to know himself. Indeed, they question the very possibility of a self, any self, let alone a fully knowing self. They are concerned with the self's alienation and fragmentation, its refractory nature, its multiplicity, its embeddedness, indeed, its loss in the interpersonal relations, dialogical exchanges, narrative structures, or grammars that, paradoxically, give rise to it, to its illusion. They stress the role of the other—generalized and often harrowingly abstract, or else specified as a father, a mother, a peer, a stranger of the opposite sex (or gender, if you prefer), a member of another race or ethnicity. They speak at times of the self's "incorporation" of that other, those others, as if it were spirit possession or a viral infection. They stress split consciousness, the failure of reason, its artifice and irrationality, and even when they offer techniques, like psychoanalysis, which are said to give insight, they recognize the insufficiency of those techniques—their ultimate failure.

Modern psychology challenges the psychological assumptions implicit in traditional legal hermeneutics and embedded in the Constitution. Though immensely shrewd, and certainly well aware of the human capacity for subterfuge and self-delusion, the Framers did not share our passion for dispossessing ourselves of reason and certainty. They were men of the Enlightenment and partook, however cautiously and with what little confidence they ultimately had in the common man, in their era's faith in reason, progress, and human perfectibility. The Constitution they wrote did not, however, depend on their psychological assumptions. For the most part, the law has avoided probing the recesses of the human mind. Very much in the spirit of the Enlightenment, Oliver Wendell Holmes argued that as the law comes increasingly to reflect scientific knowledge, it will have less and less need for mental constructs.[20]

Consideration of the mental condition, the "internal" state, of the actor is often said to distinguish morality from law. Criminal law is the primary exception, but only up to a point. Here, with considerable conceptual embarrassment, at least for the formalists, the law appears to depart from its focus on external evidence, be it behavioral or textual, to take into account the mental state, the *mens rea*, of the actor in attributing responsibility and casting blame.[21] As every reader of detective fiction knows, questions of premeditation, motivation, and intention feature in the description of crimes and the determination of punishment. The defendant's sanity, his capacity to understand the meaning and/or consequences of his actions, is in principle necessary for conviction. "In any developed legal system," the Oxford philosopher of law, H. L. A. Hart wrote,

> the general requirement of *mens rea* is an element in criminal responsibility designed to secure that those who offend without carelessness, unwittingly, or in conditions in which they lacked bodily or mental capacity to conform to the law, should be excused. A legal system would be open to serious moral condemnation if this were not so, at any rate in cases of serious crimes carrying severe punishment.[22]

The law, particularly the law of torts, uses (implicitly if not always explicitly) a "normal" or "reasonable" man or woman as the standard for attributing responsibility when it does not simply deny the relevance of the actor in adjudication, as in most contract and inheritance law. Is this standard a legacy of the Enlightenment? To the modernist, who would insist on distinguishing between normal and reasonable, the standard is fictive, and its determination in any particular situation no doubt reflects the norms of the dominant—at least of the judge's or jury's—culture. Of course, in everyday intercourse even the modernist ends up applying some sort of reasonable-man standard in predicting or appraising the conduct of those with whom he engages. It is in reflective moments, after some breakdown in expectation or communication, that one tends to invoke a more sophisticated psychology. The law has for the most part opted for the "everyday" standard and not for the exceptional one, even though the cases it treats are, if not in law, then in everyday life, of necessity exceptional.

Something like this normal or reasonable man standard is implied in most legal hermeneutics, of course, where it is assumed that the interpreter, the judge, is in fact normal or reasonable. We usually speak not in these terms but in terms of the judge's commitment to the law and his personal integrity. We may also praise him, as Bork was praised by his supporters, as a scholar and intellectual. Frequently, we refer to the law school where he was trained. Although law professors and other legal professionals complain about the failure of today's law schools to develop a sense of moral and legal integrity in students, they do not usually consider the relationship between integrity and interpretation. There is, as Gregory Leyh observes, "a jurisprudential void" in most legal education today.[23] Unlike the Fundamentalists, who believe that correct interpretation depends on the moral and spiritual condition of the interpreter, legal scholars take a fully secular stance, which stresses correct methodology and ignores the condition of the interpreter.

I deny not the existence of mental phenomena but the utility for law of the concept of mind in which intentions and free will figure.

Richard Posner, 1990[24]

With the publication in 1946 of W. K. Wimsatt and Monroe Beardsley's "The Intentional Fallacy," an essay that has had considerable influence in the law, authorial intention became an important issue in American literary interpretation. The essay can be taken as a manifesto of what the critic John Crowe Ransom called the "New Criticism," a technique of close reading, popular in the forties and fifties, which was inspired by scientific positivism and bears striking parallels with the legal positivism of the time.[25] Just as the legal positivists insisted on the text-centered autonomy of the law, the New Critics took the literary work to be an autonomous, aesthetic artifact that was best understood without reference to the historical and biographical conditions in which it was produced. The work was said to have an ontological status of its own. Wimsatt and Beardsley questioned the role of authorial intention in the interpretation of a literary work and argued that it was "neither available nor desirable as a standard for judging the success" of that work.[26] The meaning of a literary work, they insisted, is independent of its author's (stated) intention; and that intention, in any case, is realized in a successful work and revealed through it and not by external evidence, whose relevance is always questionable. Although the poet may say he wanted to write, or that he wrote, a love poem, the poem may be about the relationship between love and hate, the ambivalence, the impossibility, of relationship, or the failure of language to describe human sentiment.

Though "The Intentional Fallacy" was still de rigueur when I was an undergraduate at the end of the fifties, it was soon to be attacked by the conservative literary critic E. D. Hirsch, who gave primacy to authorial intention in interpretation.[27] Arguing against those critics who held that the meaning of a text changes over time, Hirsch insisted that the permanent meaning of a text, its only objective meaning, is what its author meant: it is the "content" of the author's intention. For Hirsch, the interpreter's greatest problem is distinguishing between what a text implies and what it does not. The interpreter must reconstruct the author's aims and attitudes in order to get at a text's meaning and its plausible implications. He or she must take account of the typical expectations and probabilities—the horizon proclaimed by the text, by its genre, for example. Within this horizon, Hirsch argued, the process of explication is unlimited. Hirsch tends at times to confuse a perspectival approach to authorial intention, its horizon—the horizon announced by the text—with the author's psychological condition, or subjectivity, which (to do Hirsch justice) he derives largely from the author's text. The important point is that Hirsch refuses to disengage a text's meaning from its author's intention. Meaning is thus fixed in time, the time of origin, and is not what a reader makes of it at some later date. Relevance—the concern, according to Hirsch, of the critic—can change but meaning cannot.

In more recent years, the debate over intention in the law has been pursued in an almost ritualized fashion by the Santa Cruz philosopher David Hoy, who is attached to Hans-Georg Gadamer's anti-intentionalist hermeneutics, and by two professors of English, Steven Knapp at Berkeley and Walter Benn Michaels at Johns Hopkins.[28] Knapp and Michaels argue, against Hoy—and Gadamer—that the only plausible object of interpretation is the author's intended meaning: "what the interpreter wants to know, if she wants to know the meaning of 'equal' in the equal protection clause [of the Fourteenth Amendment], can only be what its authors meant."[29] Hoy, like Gadamer takes the position that a text is not an expression of authorial intention but a "common object" whose meaning is always in tension between authorial intention and interpreter's understanding. Knapp and Michaels worry that, if this were the case, what would determine the text's identity? Put simply: Can text and meaning be so separated that the text remains constant while its meaning changes? They answer no. The question is of critical importance in the law, theology, and other areas of normative presumption, which on pragmatic grounds demand constancy. For law to be socially serviceable—a point Bork made frequently in the hearings—it has to have a determinant and determinable meaning; it cannot be subject to the whims of whoever is interpreting. Unlike Hirsch and his followers, though, Knapp and Michaels do not claim that an intentionalist approach provides an interpretive methodology. "For if interpretation is just a matter of figuring out what some author or authors intended on some particular occasion, then interpreting can amount to nothing more than finding out whatever one can, by whatever means possible, about what the authors in question are likely to have intended."[30] One can show, *but not for sure*, Knapp and Michaels insist, that an interpretation is correct. What their free-wheeling pragmatic stance fails to take into account is what determines what evidence is relevant and when an interpretation is deemed correct. Considerations of power and desire, however problematic, must be brought into the account.

As Hirsch and other critics were attacking anti-intentionalism in America, the French poststructuralists, most notably Roland Barthes and Michel Foucault, were questioning the very notion of authorship.[31] In his essay "Death of the Author," Barthes claimed that noninstrumental writings like literature demand the extinction of the writer. "As soon as a fact is *narrated* no longer with a view to acting directly on reality but intransitively, that is to say, finally outside any function other than that of the very practice of the symbol itself, this disconnection occurs, the voice loses its origin, the author enters his own death, writing begins."[32] The author, his voice, disappears in the ever-thickening tissue of literary language or discourse. He is, Barthes postulated, nothing more than the instance of writing.

> We know that a text does not consist of a line of words, releasing a single "theological" meaning (the "message" of the Author-God), but a multi-dimensional space in which a variety of writings, none of them original, blend and clash. The text is a tissue of quotations drawn from innumerable centres of culture.[33]

Extravagantly, Barthes argues that no text has precedence over any other and, even more extravagantly, that once the "author" has disappeared, it is futile to try to "decipher" a text. "To give a text an Author is to impose a limit on that text, to furnish it with a final signified, to close the writing."[34] There is, at least in literature, no final meaning. Barthes claims that literature is "countertheological" because "to refuse to fix meaning is, in the end, finally to refuse God and his hypostases—reason, science, the law." But, ironically, as I see it, Barthes's "author" is destined to perform a near-sacred act. He sacrifices himself to the reader who can then take pleasure in the text, in the indeterminate play of meaning. We might ask, why privilege the reader? Why allow him to retain the independence and individuality denied the author?

Of course, Barthes's theology, or antitheology, of writing and reading is anathema to conservative legal scholars like Bork and Scalia, whose position in Barthes's terms would be preeminently theological. They search for authorship—rather, for the position of authorship, since the author himself need not be named or characterized—intention, origin, *the* meaning, if not the final meaning, of the law. Reluctantly, they have to acknowledge that, given the contestatory nature of legal practice, there can never be a final meaning. Yet the law is still for them an hypostasis of God. When Barthes and Foucault speak of the death of the author, they are of course making reference to Nietzsche's proclamation of the death of God. Barthes's declaration takes place in the no-place of a literary discourse which seems to have no grounding in reality. Being a French intellectual of the sixties, he dutifully acknowledges a relationship between capitalism and the value we give to authorship but not to the reader. That is as far as his "history" goes.

Foucault's position is more subtle. He understands that the notion or even the invention of authorship as well as the privilege and authority vested in that role are historically conditioned. Authorship—or as he sometimes calls it, the "author-function,"—is neither universal nor constant. "It results from a complex operation whose purpose is to construct the rational entity we call an author."[35] He notes that as books, articles, and speeches became real property with the development of strict copyright rules (toward the end of the eighteenth and the beginning of the nineteenth century), the author was incorporated into the order of property.[36] In line with his argument, we could and perhaps should ask what are the historical—the social, political, and economic—determinants of a legal discourse that privileges, or at least takes seriously, the notion of authorial intention. We should note that this concern for authorial intention, whether of the Framers of the Constitution or the congressmen and congresswomen who enact a statute, personalizes a discourse, the law, whose authority is supposed to lie in its impersonality. We might ask why legal and political conservatives seem partial to intentionalist arguments. Why do they seek "theological" authority in an intentionality that, however abstract, however collectivized, tends to be understood in (individual) psychological terms?

I do not have much faith in most sociological or psychological answers to these questions. They tend to be tautological: to replicate and reinforce on another register—the sociological, the psychological—what they claim to explain. I do believe, however, that as irresponsibly extravagant as Barthes's and Foucault's proclamations of the death of the author are, they do point out that "authorship" and by extension "intention" are constructs that reflect prevalent social and cultural values, such as individualism, personalized creativity, and originality, and concurrent psychologies. They call attention to the fact that the author of a literary work, indeed of any text, any utterance, is never fully in command of his communication, never entirely conscious of its meaning. He—or she—writes, speaks, in a medium that always exceeds him or her. This author is caught in his cultural assumption, in tradition, in the discursive and interpretive strategies of his time, and in language, his language, its grammar, its deep structure, its self-understanding, and its history. He will always speak and write more than he knows and intends, and thus, at some level, however trivial, he gives voice to his society and culture. We might call this the oracular dimension of discourse. It certainly figures in normative discourses—law, for example.

The personalization of authorship in law is in fact more complicated than I have indicated. Legal discourse is at once personal and impersonal, fateful, we might say, abstract. A law, a decision, is removed from the circumstances in which it was written because, paradoxically, it is embedded and interpreted within *conventional limits* in terms of those circumstances. Although original intent arguments personalize the law, they do so abstractly: they focus on authorship even as they deny personality to the author. Rarely is the name of the judge who wrote a decision given when that decision is cited in later opinions, and when he (less often she) is named, it is because of his or her special reputation and authority. It is a John Marshall, a Joseph Story, an Oliver Wendell Holmes, a Louis Brandeis, a Benjamin Cardozo, a Felix Frankfurter, or another of the justice heroes. Their names are indices of authority the way the names of authors like Aristotle, Pliny, or Galen, were indices of authority in the "scientific" treatises of the later Middle Ages. They do not serve the lawyer or the judge, as they do the historian, as sources for understanding why a particular law was promulgated or decision made.

Whatever interpretive pleasures Barthes's author may have given the reader through his "sacrifice," he has also aggrieved that reader by depriving him of the surety of the text. The author has left the reader with only an occasion for interpretation. I suppose, one can make a case for such liberality in literature (that is, if one believes like the eighteenth-century critics that literature exists primarily to please and entertain), it is harder to make one for other, instrumentalist texts, like law, theology, and science, whose offer of pleasure is secondary to a "serious" purpose. As I noted in my discussion of Knapp and Michael's intentionalism, what is demanded of the text in these fields is constancy—meaning, a core of meaning, that somehow transcends time and the vicissitudes of interpretive practice.

It is the denial of this constancy that has distressed many readers of Barthes and the postmodernists and led them to declare postmodernists nihilists. Those few Fundamentalists I met who actually knew about postmodernism were particularly critical. They said it exalted man over God and played obscenely with His word. Posner, a friend of neither postmodernism nor of literalism, describes the effect of the denial of the author's interpretive authority on the law:

> Foucault dethrones him; deconstruction denigrates the intelligibility and coherence of texts and joins Derrida in undermining authorial authority. The net effect—a kind of reader's and critic's rebellion—gives aid and comfort to the advocates of free interpretation of legal texts. If statutes and constitutions lack definite author-given meanings, then judges in "interpreting" these texts must

actually be exercising discretion. So the attack on interpretability and authors' authority is an attack on "ruledness" as well.[37]

Less subtly, Bork sees the denial as justifying an interpretive free-for-all that permits "judge-made law." He finds, as we would expect, the "impetus" for the postmodernists' "attack on reason, on the concept of truth, and on the idea that there is an objective reality to which we must attempt to make our words and theories correspond" to come from the political left.[38] He deplores, for example, Sanford Levinson's flirtation with a Nietzschean approach to constitutional interpretation,[39] and he is appalled by his observation that there are "as many plausible readings of the United States Constitution as there are versions of *Hamlet*."[40] "There is nothing," Levinson tells us, "that is unsayable in the language of the Constitution."[41]

The question is not how many plausible readings of the Constitution there are—or how many versions of *Hamlet*. (Incidentally, what kind of versions? Plausible? Successful? Faithful?) The relevant questions are: What constitutes "plausible" in reading the Constitution? What are the criteria of plausibility? Are there any? Can there be any? Different readers will have different criteria of plausibility. I may read the Constitution from, to simplify, a "legal" point of view. I may read it historically, as, for example, an indication of the Framers' political ideology? I may read it from a historical-psychological point of view, trying to uncover the psychological theory the Framers presumed. Or I might even read it psychoanalytically, as an indication of the Framers' defenses against, perhaps, unconscious wishes to perpetuate their will over their "sons," over future generations who threaten to slay them.

The important question, which I wouldn't presume to answer, is this: Is it possible in a domain like the law, which lays some claim to being systemic, to discover criteria of plausibility? I say that I wouldn't want to answer this question precisely because, while it may make sense from within the law, it does not necessarily make sense from outside the law—from, say, an anthropological perspective. From the outside, the law's presumption of systematicity is an empirical question. From the outside, criteria of plausibility as they are enunciated (if they are) must be measured against what appear empirically to be the criteria of what I earlier called *acceptance*. (The criteria of plausibility, as enunciated, may mask the "real" criteria of acceptance.) They presuppose privileging the text—the Constitution, a statute—and a certain style of reading that follows from that privileging. From within the law the fact that the meaning of the text is negotiated in a ritual-dramatic fashion—in briefs, oral arguments, and among the deciding judges—has to be denied. Such a view can, of course, be expressed by lawyers in private, outside the court, or in law reviews even, but it cannot be expressed in the court, in legal argument, and in decisions. Imagine a lawyer before the Supreme Court saying, "Come on now, let's face it, the meaning of the due process clause in the Fourteenth Amendment has always been negotiated. It's always a political compromise. Doubly so among you guys up there on the bench and between you and what you think the American people or the President or Congress would tolerate. So in the present case, let's cut the crap and read it this way. . . ." Whatever the truth of our lawyer's observations, the mere description of such a scene strikes all of us, outsiders and insiders, as not only ludicrous but blasphemous. The aura of the law always flows beyond its boundaries. Therein lies much of its power.

In one of his exchanges with Knapp and Michaels, Hoy asks the reader to imagine a set of propositions imprinted in the sand by retreating ocean waves.[42] He says that its meaning would not be affected by the fact that it was produced by chance by the waves. But would whoever discovered the pattern in the sand regard it as a communication? As meaningful? Interpretable? It seems to me that much of the confusion in arguments over intention results from a failure to recognize that all "communications," including the written, the Constitution—have to be taken as intentional if they are to be regarded as communications and, therefore, potentially meaningful and interpretable.[43] (I except scientific interpretations of natural phenomena. They are taken not as communications—except, at times, metaphorically, as in, What is nature telling me?—but, rather, as natural occurrences to be explained by one theory or another.) Hoy assumes a distinction philosophers like to make today between "sentence meaning" and "utterance meaning"; that is, roughly, between the meaning coded in words, here carried by the letter marks in the sand, and the meaning that the author (here the nonauthor, the waves, the ocean) intended those words to mean. He argues that the marks can be read as propositions. I would argue that they can't be read this way, that they wouldn't be read this way, unless some communicative intention was assumed. In order to be read, the reader would have to assume some, even empty, intention. He might well construct or project an "author" endowed with the intention to communicate something. That "author" might be a god, Poseidon, a spirit, Nature, or more likely today (except maybe in New Age circles) an ironic personification of contingency, or fate, that enables the reading.

No doubt philosophers like Hoy would argue with me. My point is that, at least in the case of incontestably human-authored utterances and texts, thought to be communications and interpretable, there is always an assumption of intention.[44] Let us call this basic assumption "communicative intention." What has immediately to be recognized is that that communicative intention, and the concurrent assumption of authorship (itself problematic) lacks all content: they are simply positional prerequisites, real or fictive, for meaningful communication and interpretation. They may be elaborated in all sorts of ways. Ronald Dworkin would call this "construction" or "invention." We will call this filling-in of communicative intention "constructive intention." It is with this intention that lawyers and critics are primarily concerned.

Unlike communicative intention, constructive intention is not a prerequisite for interpretation: it need not figure explicitly in an act of interpretation. British lawyers and judges tend to ignore intention, for example, and focus on semantic meaning. Hoy's discoverer of the sand proposition has to assume, as I have argued, communicative intention if he is to take its marks as meaningful signs, but he need not elaborate that intention or incarnate its author.[45] We may describe these constructed intentions in many different ways: psychologically, mentally, collectively, or in personifying terms, as we do when we say, "The Constitution tells us. . . ."

The authority of our constructions of intention depends upon the authority of the idiom in which we cast them.[46] By describing intention in psychological terms, for example, our argument profits from the persuasive force of that idiom in our culture. It benefits from the prevalent, one could even say Cartesian, notion of inner certainty, from the association of innerness and consciousness, and from a sense of interiority as an undefilable "space" of independence, integrity, and (despite the capriciousness of desire) self-knowledge. By expressing intention in textual or text-derivable terms, we strengthen our faith in the written word—in its objectivity, in the fact that it can be ascertained by others. We can imagine other idioms, alien to our own tradition, in which intention may be authoritatively cast as originating in a god, demon, or muse who has somehow, through spirit possession perhaps, been given human voice. Whatever their truth, however strong our desire to accept that "truth," our constructions of intention serve circularly and rhetorically to support and give authority to the interpretation we make on their basis. Of course, we must deny the rhetoric in serious legal argument; for were it accepted, the argument would collapse. Serious arguments appear to demand a literalism or perhaps a metaliteralism, a literalist framing.[47]

More authoritative perhaps than intention is the *original* in original intention: it seems to give authority to most intentionalist arguments. However important it is to discover the original meaning of a text, discovery need not be the end of interpretation. Philosophers of interpretation like Gadamer insist that it is not and cannot be an end. For them, an interpretation is the result of a continuing and mutually enriching encounter between text and reader: it cannot be divorced from the significance, the application the reader gives it. "Original" as it is used by Bork and other originalists detemporalizes and sacralizes meaning: it becomes fixed at the moment of origin and, as such, is given exceptional privilege in argument. It becomes *the* point around which the originalist can spin his argument rhetorically, politically, morally, and personally as well as "legally." At the same time, though, cut off from the vicissitudes of history, it provides a way to deny precisely the incursion of the rhetorical, political, moral, and personal into legal argument. This privileged meaning is for the originalist enshrined in the Constitution, which becomes a bulwark against history. Constitutional history itself, embodied in precedent, threatens that bulwark, that privileged meaning. No doubt the extreme pressure of the hearings led Bork to make no reference to the Constitution when he answered Senator Arlen Specter's question of why, given the difficulty of determining original intent, the Constitution was sacrosanct: "Well, Senator, you are making a very powerful argument from a very strong tradition. I hope—I think what I was saying also comes from a very strong tradition in our constitutional law, going back to Joseph Story and the first Marshall Court. . . ." Perhaps no one has ever known better the value of rhetoric, serious rhetoric, in constitutional interpretation, than Chief Justice Marshall.

7—Precedent

THE CHAIRMAN [SENATOR BIDEN] Judge Bork, I am sure you know the one question to be raised in these hearings is whether or not you are going to vote to overturn Supreme Court decisions, which is obviously your right as a Supreme Court Justice, if you are confirmed.

In 1981 in testimony before the Congress, you said, "there are dozens of cases" in which the Supreme Court made a wrong decision. This January, in remarks before the Federalist Society, you implied that you would have no problem in overruling decisions based on a philosophy or a rationale you rejected.

In an interview with the *District Lawyer* magazine in 1985, you were asked if you could identify cases that you think should be reconsidered. You said, and I again quote, "Yes, I can but I won't."

Would you be willing for this committee to identify the "dozens of cases" that you think should be reconsidered?

JUDGE BORK Mr. Chairman, to do that I am afraid I would have to go out and start back through the casebooks again to pick out the ones.

I do not know how many should be reconsidered. I can discuss with you the grounds upon, the way in which I would reconsider them.

So there is, in fact, a recognition on my part that *stare decisis* or the theory of precedent is important. In fact, I would say to you that anybody who believes in original intention as the means of interpreting the Constitution has to have a theory of precedent, because this Nation has grown in way that does not comport with the intentions of the people who wrote the Constitution—the commerce clause is one example—and it is simply too late to go back and tear that up.

I cite to you the *Legal Tender* cases. These are extreme examples admittedly. Scholarship suggests that the framers intended to prohibit paper money. Any judge who today thought he would go back to the original intent really ought to be accompanied by a guardian rather than be sitting on the bench.

Bork Hearings, Sept. 15, 1987[1]

Paradoxically, most constitutional law is concerned not with the Constitution but with previous decisions. "[I]t is primarily in the interpretation of prior cases that the battle for constitutional meaning is joined," Laurence Tribe and Michael Dorf note.[2] What then is the role of the Constitution in these arguments? It is, substantively, the document of last instance; it is restrictive, constraining the flights of judicial imagination; it is also rhetorical insofar as it provides the authoritative reference point for legal arguments, including, most notably, the choice of precedent. As we might expect, there are divergent approaches to the doctrine of precedent—the strict, at one pole, and the relaxed, on the other.[3] The strict doctrine, the exact form of which is different in the United States and Britain and in the "several states," obliges a judge to follow earlier decisions made, most often, in higher courts, even if he or she believes them to be wrong. Bork insists correctly (though this has been challenged) that a judge in the federal courts is bound to follow Supreme Court decisions.[4] The relaxed position requires the judge to give weight to prior decisions but does not oblige him to follow them if they seem wrong. The Supreme Court can overturn previous decisions.

Joseph Biden, the Delaware Democrat and, as the Chairman of the Judiciary Committee the first senator to question Bork immediately raised the issue of precedent. It was to become one of the major concerns in the hearings. Bork was known for his virulent and extravagant attacks on many significant Supreme Court decisions, particularly those of the Warren Court. As late as January 1987, six months before his nomination, he told a group of conservative law professors and students at the Federalist Society that he would think "an originalist judge would have no problem whatever in overruling a non-originalist precedent, because that precedent by the very basis of his judicial philosophy has no legitimacy. It comes from nothing the framers intended."[5] It was to this speech that Biden referred when he said Bork had implied that he "would have no problem overruling decisions. . . ."

Bork had anticipated his opponents' objection in his opening statement:

> The past, however, includes not only the intentions of those who first made the law, it also includes those past judges who interpreted and applied it in prior cases. That is why a judge must give great respect to precedent. It is one thing as a legal theorist to criticize the reasoning of a prior decision, even to criticize it severely, as I have done. It is another and more serious thing altogether for a judge to ignore or overturn a prior decision. That requires much careful thought.[6]

Bork went on to note, portentiously, that "Times come, of course, when even a venerable precedent can and should be overruled." He cited as a positive example *Brown v. Board of Education*,[7] the 1954 decision outlawing racially segregated schools. *Brown* had overruled *Plessy v. Ferguson*,[8] which fifty-eight years earlier had decided in favor of a doctrine of "separate but equal." "Yet *Brown*, delivered with the authority of a unanimous court, was clearly correct and represents perhaps the greatest moral achievement of our constitutional law," Bork observed with political care.[9] He had, after all, been accused of favoring racially discriminatory legislation. If Bork were to become a justice of the Supreme Court, Kennedy had claimed, "Blacks would sit at segregated lunch counters."

Throughout the hearings, Bork was always as evasive as he had been in his initial exchange with Biden about those cases an originalist would have grounds to overturn. He cited again and again the commerce clause and the *Legal Tender* cases, which legalized paper money, as being so rooted in American society that they could not be overruled despite their misreading of the Constitution. Pushed by Biden, he mentioned *Shelley v. Kraemer*, a 1948 decision against racially restrictive covenants.[10] Since *Shelley* is considered to be "one of the most controversial decisions in all of constitution law," criticized both by conservatives and liberals, Bork had in effect insulated himself from attack.[11] Behind Biden's question was the fear that Bork, along with the other conservatives justices, would try to overturn some of the most socially progressive, rights-oriented decisions the court had made, most notably *Roe v. Wade*. During hearings on a human life bill in 1981, Bork had said: "*Roe v. Wade* is, itself, an unconstitutional decision, a serious and wholly unjustifiable judicial usurpation of state legislative authority."[12]

Certainly, something like (if not quite so vehement as) Bork's sentiments has fueled American conservatism and no doubt given to conservative legal argument its emotional tenor. Our law is structurally oriented toward the past: we find stability in the past.[13] We give precedence to past decisions, to the Constitution, and to statutes whose present interpretation is mediated and authenticated by previous interpretations. The doctrine of precedent requires "that decisions of earlier cases sufficiently like a new case should be repeated in the new case."[14] We maintain continuity thereby. *Stare decisis* ("to abide by or adhere to decided cases"), as the doctrine of precedent is called, is derived from the common law maxim *stare decisis et non quieta movere* ("to adhere to precedents and not to unsettle things which are established"). We apply the test of time. We tend to give greater value to older precedents, those which have had long histories and are, so we say, ensconced in our tradition, than to newer ones.[15] We, even the liberals among us, look askance at decisions based less on articulated law than on future effect.[16] We refer to these as policy decisions and would prefer that they were the result of legislation and not of adjudication. The "past" serves—rhetorically, I would say, but others would say substantively—to guard ourselves from present political and policy considerations.

In constitutional law, particularly as it is read by originalists, there is always a tension between the Constitution and precedent, a tension that replicates the tension between statute and common law. This is the tension that so troubled Scalia in his Tanner Lecture.[17] Theoretically, the Constitution always has priority. It is the final reference point: the *Grundgesetz*, as the Germans say, the fundamental law. But to speak of the Constitution that way, as if it has *a* final meaning, is in a certain sense a diversionary tactic. The literalists notwithstanding, the Constitution is always a locus for interpretation. From a literalist viewpoint, and from the viewpoint of many if not most practicing lawyers and judges, precedents are (or at least can be) at once illuminating and authoritative interpretations of the Constitution and distortions of its "original" meaning. They are by nature divergent: there is always a gap between them and the Constitution, and, I should add, a gap between their textual expression and our reading of them. By inserting history—that is, the effect of changing circumstances—into the interpretive process, precedent challenges the originalist's detemporalized notion of meaning by calling attention to its artifice. And yet in practice, *it is said* to bring about a convergence of interpretation: "The practice of precedent, which no judge's interpretation can wholly ignore, presses toward agreement: each judge's theories of what judging really is will incorporate by reference, through whatever account and restructuring of precedent he settles on, aspects of other popular interpretations of the day."[18] Does it? One doesn't have to be as cynical as the nineteenth-century legal reformer Robert Rantoul to answer this question in the negative. Rantoul said in his 1836 Fourth of July oration at Scituate, Massachusetts:

> The judge makes law, by extorting from precedents something which they do not contain. He extends his precedents, which were themselves extension of others, till, by this accommodating principle, a whole system of law is built up without authority or interference of the legislator.[19]

Or, as Jerome Frank, a leading Legal Realist, put it in the thirties:

> Lawyers and judges purport to make large use of precedents; that is, they purport to rely on the conduct of judges in past cases as a means of procuring analogies for action in new cases. But since what was actually decided in the earlier cases is seldom revealed, it is impossible, in a real sense, to rely on these precedents. What the courts in fact do is manipulate the language of former decisions.[20]

Less passionately, I will simply note that precedents themselves have to be read and interpreted and, therefore, are subject to "each judge's theories of what judging really is."

But what does it mean to follow a precedent? To be sure, there are easier and harder cases — cases for which one can find a decision that closely matches the cases but also cases where there are no clearly relevant precedents. In both, one is said to argue from analogy, but in the latter the analogy is often so stretched as to be completely questionable. In 1971, Bork, who read the First Amendment as applying only to political speech, was unwilling to extend it analogically to art, science, or pornography.[21] "I agree," he wrote,

> that there is an analogy between criticism of official behavior and the publication of a novel like *Ulysses*, for the latter may form attitudes that ultimately affect politics. But it is an analogy, not an identity. . . . If the dialectical progression is not to become an analogical stampede, the protection of the First Amendment must be cut off when it reaches the outer limits of political speech.

Where then and on what basis does one stop the "analogical stampede"? Can one find a basis in the law? Of course, Bork and other originalists are convinced that if one can be true to the Constitution by adhering to its original intent or literal meaning, one can be true to precedent as well. Ideally, they would accept only precedent that is true to original intent of the Constitution.

It can be argued — as Jerome Frank has argued it — that for all cases except perhaps the easiest, precedents are simply justifications for decisions made on other grounds: consequential, political, moral, economic, or on just simply a plain, unreflected and perhaps even unreflectable sense of fairness. He would have judges give clearer expression to how they arrive at decisions.[22] Others, like Dworkin, find the answer in political morality.[23] In a 1977 essay, "Hard Cases," Dworkin argued that the jurist "must develop a theory of the constitution, in the shape of principles and policies that justify that scheme of government."[24] A judge must refer "alternatively to political philosophy and institutional details." Later,

Dworkin argued that "a proposition of law is sound if it figures in the best possible justification that can be provided for the body of legal propositions taken to be settled."[25] Are there any? He noted two dimensions of this justification. The first is the dimension of fit—roughly, that one political theory is better than another if the person holding that theory is able to enact more of what is already settled in law than someone who holds the other. The second is the dimension of political morality, which supposes that "if two justifications provide an equally good fit with the legal materials, one nevertheless provides a better justification than the other if it is superior as a matter of political or moral theory." By moral or political theory, Dworkin seems to mean a theory that "comes closer to capturing the rights that people in fact have." Aside from this circularity—on what basis other than "settled" law do we determine the rights a "people in fact have"?—he can be challenged on the value he places on "settled." What is settled may not provide the best (whatever the best is) basis for a moral or political theory. Dworkin's argument, here as elsewhere, assumes that an interpreter always aims at giving the best possible interpretation, or construction, to the text its genre permits. This assumption is questionable on psychological and political grounds. It presumes the interpreter's integrity, self-knowledge, and self-mastery. Dworkin's argument also fails to take into account the contestatory and apologetic dimensions of interpretation, which are particularly evident in the law, and the way defensive argumentation can convert "best" into "rhetorically efficacious"—an equivalence that a moralist like Dworkin would find unacceptable.

Still other legal theorists, Richard Posner for example, adopt a ruthlessly realistic, pragmatic stance toward precedent. Posner observes:

> Citations of previous cases are also used to disguise fiat as reason, to establish propositions not in dispute and therefore not in need of support, and as sources from which to quote general language that either is truistic or is contradicted by general language in other

cases, which the opinion does not cite. Case citations often are used, in other words, to make an opinion look more solid than it really is.[26]

The decision of difficult cases, he argues, "is very often a form of policy analysis rather than the product of a distinctive methodology of legal reasoning."[27] Ultimately, for Posner, the ground of any legal holding is political.

Precedents themselves are evaluated in many different ways. Most often and most seriously, they are judged in terms of their fidelity to the Constitution or the statute to which they relate and by the quality of their argument. There are cases like those involving privacy (which I discuss in the next section) where, according to the originalists, the court has read into the Constitution values or concepts that are either not there or not derivable in any responsible way. Of course, anyone who has read court decisions, particularly those dealing with hard cases, realizes how difficult it is to work through their argument or arguments, to discover their intention or intentions, and to determine what ought to be read literally. Though lawyers distinguish between holdings and dicta, holdings and dicta are rarely as independent as the distinction suggests.[28] As I have noted, most opinions, even the best, are complex, multi-leveled texts, combining legal arguments, whatever a legal argument may be (inductive? deductive? analogical?) with citations, the relevance and meaning of which is not always clear; with factual and counterfactual examples; legal and moral maxims; anecdotes; supporting material from various sources (historical, sociological, or economic); and, most important, concluding or summary statements that, when carefully read, may be shown to deviate significantly from what has been said and argued in the decision they purport to summarize and to which they belong. It is these conclusions and summaries that are most often cited as the court's holding.

In discussing precedent, Posner acknowledges that precedents are applied analogically (in his view, inductively) to the case at hand.[29] He distinguishes the use of cases as informative analogies and as authorities.

> Analogies, viewed simply as instances similar to the problem at hand (examples, anecdotes) rather than as steps in a logical demonstration or even as pieces in a regular pattern . . . on which inductive inferences might be based, provide a fund of ideas and information on which to draw in deciding what to do. Previously decided cases supply lawyers and judges with a wealth of facts, reasons, and techniques pertinent to how a new case should be decided.[30]

The dicta do not necessarily have any legal authority. True, but only up to a point. What Posner fails to take into sufficient analytic account is that informative analogies are not just wells of information but also framing devices. Let me give a nonlegal example. When one casts the I Ching or reads tarot cards or visits a seer, ones does not learn exactly what will happen in the future—that can always be tested against empirical reality, usually to the detriment of the diviner—but one is given an analogizing "text" that counters present, usually fuzzy understanding, thereby crystallizing a new, "clearer" understanding that may influence subsequent understanding and behavior. In the law, though informative analogies have no necessary legal authority, they may underwrite the choice of authoritative precedents by helping to frame a case in such a way as to make those authoritative precedents relevant.[31]

The selection of precedent is never as clear-cut as lawyers and judges like to assume. Rarely are precedents reducible to the simple holdings their citations imply. The genre of opinion is simply too complicated. Obviously, as I noted in my discussion of Fundamentalism, there are different styles of reading in different disciplines: lawyers and judges cannot, nor ought they, read opinions the way a literary critic does. It is a question of the role they play in argument. What literary critical or other philosophical and linguistic readings can do is point to the way in which the peculiar genre and style of opinion writing permits and restricts legal readings and the arguments they support. Whether these readings have any practical application to the law—for example, in teaching judges how better to write opinions and lawyers to argue from them—is an open question.[32] From the outside, they may reveal the way in which plays of power are facilitated and masked. Though failing to take full account of the formative and framing function of precedent (that is, of the past), Posner takes a pragmatic, future-oriented stance toward precedent:

> [I]n a system of precedent it is the later court that has the whip hand, not the earlier court, the court that created the precedent. The later court decides whether to read the earlier decision broadly or narrowly and, if it cannot be narrowed sufficiently to distinguish the present case, whether to overrule it. The court has the power, and it also has the information, just by virtue of coming later. The decision of how much weight to give the earlier precedent— whether to apply it at all, and if so how broadly—is a pragmatic decision in which the uncertainty that will be created by too casual an attitude toward past decisions—and the additional work that such an attitude will create for the courts both by requiring more time on each case and, as a result of the greater uncertainty, engendering more cases—are compared with the increased risk of error that an uncritical view of past decisions will create. . . . Reasoning by analogy is not a technique for striking a balance.[33]

However realistic Posner's argument is, it's an argument that gives the originalist and the literalist nightmares. And it gives the judge too much freedom.

THE CHAIRMAN Well, let's talk about another case. Let's talk about the *Griswold* case. Now, while you were living in Connecticut, that State had a law—I know you know this, but for the record—that it made it a crime for anyone, even a married couple, to use birth control. You indicated that you thought that law was "nutty," to use your words, and I quite agree. Nevertheless, Connecticut, under that "nutty" law, prosecuted and convicted a doctor and the case finally reached the Supreme Court.

The Court said that the law violated a married couple's constitutional right to privacy. You criticized this opinion in numerous articles and speeches, beginning in 1971 and as recently as July 26th of this year. In your 1971 article, "Neutral Principles and Some First Amendment Problems," you said that the right of married couples to have sexual relations without fear of unwanted children is no more worthy of constitutional protection by the courts than the right of public utilities to be free of pollution control laws.

You argued that the utility company's right or gratification, I think you referred to it, to make money and the married couple's right or gratification to have sexual relations without fear of unwanted children, as "the cases are identical." . . .

JUDGE BORK I was making the point that where the Constitution does not speak—there is no provision in the Constitution that applies to the case—then a judge may not say, I place a higher value upon a marital relationship than I do upon an economic freedom. Only if the Constitution gives him some reasoning. . . . I was objecting to the way Justice Douglas . . . derived the right. It may be possible to derive an objection to an anti-contraceptive statute in some other way. I do not know.

But starting from the assumption, which is an assumption for purposes of my argument, not a proven fact, starting from the assumption that there is nothing in the Constitution, in any legitimate method of constitutional reasoning about either subject, all I am saying is that the judge has no way to prefer one to the other and the matter should be left to the legislatures who will then decide which competing gratification, or freedom, should be placed higher.

THE CHAIRMAN Then I think I do understand it, that is, that the economic gratification of a utility company is as worthy of as much protection as the sexual gratification of a married couple, because neither is mentioned in the Constitution.

JUDGE BORK All that means is that the judge may not choose.

THE CHAIRMAN Who does?

JUDGE BORK The legislature.

THE CHAIRMAN Well, that is my point, so it is not a constitutional right. I am not trying to be picky here. Clearly, I do not want to get into a debate with a professor, but it seems to me that what you are saying is what I said and that is, that the Constitution—if it were a constitutional right, if the Constitution said anywhere in it, in your view, that a married couple's right to engage in the decision of having a child or not having a child was a constitutionally-protected right of privacy, then you would rule that that right exists. You would not leave it to the legislative body no matter what they did.

JUDGE BORK That is right.

THE CHAIRMAN But you argue, as I understand it, that no such right exists.

JUDGE BORK No, Senator, that is what I tried to clarify. I argued that the way in which this unstructured, undefined right of privacy that Justice Douglas elaborated, that the way he did it did not prove its existence. . . . What I was doing was criticizing a doctrine the Supreme Court was creating which was capable of being applied in unknown ways in the future, in unprincipled ways. . . .

THE CHAIRMAN Does a State legislative body, or any legislative body, have a right to pass a law telling a married couple . . . that they can or cannot use birth control? Does the majority have the right to tell a couple they cannot use birth control?

JUDGE BORK There is always a rationality standard in the law, Senator. I do not know what rationale the State would offer or what challenge the married couple would make. I have never decided that case. If it ever comes before me, I will have to decide it. All I have done was point out that the right of privacy, as defined or undefined by Justice Douglas, was a free-floating right that was not derived in a principled fashion from constitutional materials. That is all that I have done.

THE CHAIRMAN Judge, I agree with the rationale offered in the case. Let me just read it to you. . . . It said, in part, "Would we allow the police to search the sacred precincts of marital bedrooms for telltale signs of contraceptives? The very idea is repulsive to the notions of privacy surrounding the marriage relationship. We deal with the right of privacy older than the Bill of Rights. Marriage is a coming together for better or worse, hopefully enduring, and intimate to the degree of being sacred. The association promotes a way of life, not causes. A harmony of living, not political face. A bilateral loyalty, not a commercial or social projects." [*sic*]

Obviously, that Justice believes that the Constitution protects married couples, anyone.

JUDGE BORK I could agree with almost every—I think I could agree with every word you read but that is not, with respect, Mr. Chairman, the rationale of the case. That is the rhetoric at the end of the case. What I objected to was the way in which this right of privacy was created and that was simply this. Justice Douglas observed, quite correctly, that a number of provisions of the Bill of Rights protect aspects of privacy and indeed they do and indeed they should.

But he went on from there to say that since a number of provisions did that and since they had emanations, by which I think he meant buffer zones to protect the basic right, he would find a penumbra which created a new right of privacy that existed where no provisions of the Constitution applied, so that he. . . .

THE CHAIRMAN Judge, let's go on. There have been a number of cases that flow from the progeny of the *Griswold* case, all relying on *Griswold*, the majority view, with different rationales offered, that there is a right of privacy to the Constitution, a general right of privacy, a right of privacy derived from the due process, from the 14th Amendment, a right of privacy, to use the Douglas word—the penumbra, which you criticize, and a right [Justice] Goldberg suggested in the *Griswold* case, from the ninth amendment. It seems to me, if you cannot find a rationale for the decision of the *Griswold* case, then all the succeeding cases are for grabs.

JUDGE BORK I have never tried to find a rationale and I have not been offered one. Maybe somebody would offer me one. I do not know if the other cases are up for grabs or not.

THE CHAIRMAN Wouldn't they have to be if they are based on the same rationale?

Bork Hearings, Sept. 19, 1987

As I noted earlier, lurking behind the questions about cases that Bork would want to overrule was his position on abortion, specifically on *Roe v. Wade*. As Senator Biden told the *New York Times*, it was critical that the opponents of Bork's nomination not focus on so controversial an issue as abortion because doing so could weaken their opposition.[34] Of course, Bork's position was well known. In a fashion virtually unparalleled in American history, the Reagan administration had set as a precondition to any judicial appointment the candidate's willingness to overrule *Roe*. Only in 1870 had Ulysses S. Grant imposed such a condition on nomination to the Supreme Court: in case in point, to uphold the Legal Tender Act.[35] Both Bork's supporters and opponents avoided the issue, although they danced around it in their questions on *Griswold v. Connecticut* and the constitutional right of privacy. Senators Orrin Hatch and Howell Heflin did raise it, and Bork did admit that he had written (as Heflin quoted him): "*Roe v. Wade* is in itself an unconstitutional decision, a serious and wholly unjustifiable usurpation of eight legislative authorities."[36] They could not pursue their questioning because the right to abortion was a live issue in the court and Bork would be revealing his position.

Roe v. Wade rested in part on the right to privacy, which was developed in *Griswold* from prior decisions that had to invoke it because it was not specifically mentioned in the Constitution. The privacy cases that led up to *Griswold* and *Roe* have been more than amply debated in books, articles, and subsequent court decisions.[37] What concerns me here is the position that Bork and other strict constructivists take on what are technically called "unenumerated rights." Their literalism is manifest: if a right like privacy—one could add family autonomy, reproductive freedom, and marital choice—is not literally mentioned in the Constitution, it has, according to them, no legal standing no matter how compelling or cherished it is or how widespread its appeal. These rights simply do not have what Bork has referred to as "textual support." Of course, as even Bork had to admit, the Constitution does acknowledge certain rights that can be construed as privacy. Justice Douglas put them this way in *Griswold*:

> Various [constitutional] guarantees create zones of privacy. The right of association contained in the penumbra of the First Amendment is one. . . . The Third Amendment in its prohibition against the quartering of soldiers "in any house" in time of peace without the consent of the owner is another facet of that privacy. The Fourth Amendment explicitly affirms the "right of the people to be secure in their persons, houses, papers, and effects, against unreasonable searches and seizures." The Fifth Amendment in its Self-Incrimination Clause enables the citizen to create a zone of privacy which government may not force him to surrender to his detriment. The Ninth Amendment provides: "The enumeration in the Constitution, of certain rights, shall not be construed to deny or disparage others retained by the people."

Whether we accept all of Douglas's instances of the right of privacy in the Constitution, we have to admit that he makes a reasonable, certainly an arguable, case for reading the cited amendments in terms of privacy. It is Douglas's derivation of a generalized right of privacy that Bork objects to, since, as he put it in the hearings, it is "free-floating" and can be extended indefinitely in unprincipled ways. In *The Tempting of America* Bork put his concerns angrily, revealing the moral and political stance he pretended to bracket in the hearings.

> Judges and lawyers live on the slippery slope of analogies; they are not supposed to ski it to the bottom. *Roe* became possible only because *Griswold* had created a new right, and anyone who reads *Griswold* can see that it was not an adjustment of an old principle to a new reality but the creation of a new principle by *tour de force* or, less politely, by sleight of hand. When we say that social circumstances have changed so as to require the evolution of doctrine to maintain the vigor of an existing principle we do not mean that society's values are perceived by the judge to have changed so that it

would be good to have a new constitutional principle. The difference is between protecting the privacy guaranteed by the fourth amendment—the "right of the people to be secure in their persons, houses, papers, and effects against unreasonable searches and seizures"—by requiring a warrant for government to listen electronically to what is said in the home and expanding that limited guarantee of privacy into a right not only to use contraceptives but to buy them, into a right to have an abortion, into a right, as four Justices of the Supreme Court would have it, to engage in homosexual conduct, into rights, as a number of professors would have it, to smoke marijuana and to engage in prostitution. If one cannot see where in the progression the adjustment of doctrine to protect an existing value ends and the creation of new values begins, then one should not aspire to be a judge or, for the matter of that, a law professor.[38]

We are confronted here with the by-now familiar distrust of precedent and the mistrust of analogical—or, as I prefer, metaphorical—reasoning both in the interpretive process (if that can be separated from application to a specific case) and in application itself.

Jerome Frank reminds us of what we often forget: that lawyers are always seeking to change the law. Depending on our view of the law, as timeless or evolving, as static or dynamic, we may view alteration as a corruption of the law or as its further declaration, as a revelation, or indeed as an actualization of its potential. What the originalists of today fail to realize, or prefer to ignore, is that adjudication, at least in hard cases, is both a declaration and an alteration of the "existing" law. It is both law-giving and law-making. However evaluated, alteration is a given in adjudication. It may be masked, as it is in the French syllogistic decision, but it is manifest in those legal systems, like the American, which rest on authoritative, published precedent.[39] Unlike interpretations of literature, which can be ignored, interpretations in a precedence-based system of law cannot be ignored—though, as we know, they are in fact often ignored. With respect to *Griswold*, Bork would have preferred to have had a "nutty" statute ignored rather than found unconstitutional on what he took to be unprincipled grounds. Just as there is a danger in inventing new constitutional principles, so there is a danger in preserving old, nutty laws: they, too, can be used and misused, as they were in Connecticut, in preventing birth control counseling. A judge has also to be aware of that progression and the dangers it can pose.

The Constitution, its Framers and ratifiers, never claimed that it specifically covered every contingency that was ever likely or, for that matter, unlikely to occur. Maybe the Framers knew better. The Constitution never specified that a right not literally mentioned had no standing. On the contrary, the Ninth Amendment presumes that the enumeration of constitutional rights is incomplete. The people retained others that could neither be denied nor disparaged. The Ninth Amendment does not create any rights of its own but is, as Laurence Tribe and Michael Dorf note, a rule of interpretation, the only such rule in the Constitution.[40] It has been relied on only twice, once by Justice Arthur Goldberg in his concurring opinion in *Griswold*: "[to] hold that a right so basic and fundamental and so deep-rooted in our society as the right of privacy in marriage may be infringed because that right is not guaranteed in so many words by the first eight amendments to the Constitution is to ignore the Ninth Amendment and to give it no effect whatsoever. . . ." Of course, what is frightening to the literalist, and not just the literalist, about the Ninth Amendment—particularly if it is read as a sort of delimiting metacommentary on the Bill of Rights and by extension on the Constitution—is precisely it lack of content. It can serve to justify the court's consideration "in constitutional terms" of just about any right so long as it is "retained by the people."

Who can determine what rights are retained by the people. The judge? If so, in what capacity? As a social observer? As an oracle of the people? (Since the rights are unenumerated, he cannot derive them from the Constitution.) The legislature? Again, in what capacity? As the people's representative? Or should it be the people themselves? Through their representatives? Through their judges chosen by an elected president and confirmed by an elected Senate? However we answer these questions, there is a more fundamental one that reveals some of the epistemological presuppositions of our understanding of rights and undergirds our literalism. I am reminded of an interview I once had with an applicant to graduate school in anthropology. He was a Maya, the first person in his village ever to go to high school and college. We were talking about anthropological methods, of which he was quite critical. "An anthropologist comes to my village," he said "and having read somewhere that there are people who believe in more than one soul, he asks us how many souls we believe in. 'How many souls?' we ask ourselves. 'What can he mean?' We don't understand, but we think he's a good guy so, just to answer him, we say thirteen. He writes down thirteen in his notebook, and then we know how many souls we believe in." He paused. I was caught in his terrible irony. And then, after a long minute had passed, he added, "Of course, it never occurred to the anthropologist to ask us whether or not souls can be counted." So, can rights ever be enumerated? Fully enumerated? The question is by no means trivial. It calls attention to our particular "arithmetic" attitude toward social and legal categories: to a certain static referentiality we presuppose and upon which our law has of necessity to rely. We must, it would seem, recognize that although we enumerate rights, giving them at least minimal semantic fixity, they can never be fully enumerated or defined. They are embedded in history, subject to change, which our legal system must at once recognize and deny this. While James Madison, I am quite confident, never entertained this train of thought (in this respect he was more a Horatio than a Hamlet) his words in the Ninth Amendment call attention not just to the Constitution's limitations but to all that it must account for but could not foresee. They underscore, unwittingly perhaps, the incompleteness and the insufficiency of any codification of the law. On both social and epistemological grounds, the law must always be surpassed as it is relied on and transmitted.

Bork is, of course, quite correct: the right of privacy elaborated by Douglas has no (I would say few) contours. But then, have any of the great and noble values the Constitution was designed to create and preserve fixed contours? Union? Justice? Tranquillity? Welfare? Liberty? Are all of the rights proclaimed in the Bill of Rights so clear and delimited? To freedom of religion, speech, press, assembly? To bear arms? To be secure from unreasonable searches and seizures? To due process of law? To speedy and public trial? To be free from excessive bail and fines? From cruel and unusual punishments? Obviously not. They are general rights and values, the delimitation of which has been argued and given authorized (though never permanent and unquestionable) expression in the course of constitutional history. Is this not the function of the court? They are, to use Bork's expression, textually identified, and yet they *still* require definition. Their application demands elaboration—and that elaboration, the legal reasoning behind it, its creativity, should not be hidden behind a stony literalism that claims to deny that it serves a political and moral agenda. This is clearly exemplified in the blatant contradiction between what Bork said in his hearings and what he had written and said prior to and since those hearings.

The danger is in the masking. None of us can successfully bracket off our political and moral concerns. This is recognized in the political process by which judges and justices are chosen. To hide behind the literal word, as if that word protects us from political and moral machinations, is in fact to deprive the word of precisely the protection it can give us. It is to cheapen it. It is to deny its symbolic quality. What is so fascinating about the law is that its words both give expression to the law and convey the authority of the law they express. This commingling of expression and authority effect legal argumentation, interpretation, and self-understanding. In my earlier discussion of Fundamentalism, I explored the epistemological turmoil caused by the Fundamentalist's derivation of the authority of the Bible from the Bible itself, from 2 Peter 1:20–21 and 2 Timothy 3:15–16. Although Fundamentalists cling to a literal interpretation of the Bible and, therefore, believe its every word (including its proclamation of its own authority), in the end they had to rest their case on a change in their spiritual condition which gave rise to, or was coincidental with, faith, complete and undying faith in the Word of God. But in the law—which, despite its religious roots, purports to be entirely secular—there can be final appeal to neither God nor faith. There is appeal to the Constitution as grounding the law of the republic. Some choose to speak of "constitutional faith," but they are speaking metaphorically: the Constitution is man-made, not God-breathed. Yet some approach the Constitution with almost religious veneration. They give to its words the authority of the Word.

I am not claiming that what I have described is true of all, or even of any particular originalists. I am evoking what one might call the cognitive and affective undersong—or, if you prefer, the cultural presuppositions—of a certain approach to the Constitution and the laws said to derive from or authorized by it. What the legal literalists share with the Fundamentalists and other literalists is not only an adherence to plain meaning and original intention but a divorcing of the word from the context in which it occurs. In the name of verbal purity, in the quest to immunize the word, the law, from self-interested moral and political contamination, they deny the inevitable role the word, the law, plays in precipitating and defining that context. They deny as well the enrichment that the word, the law, receives from its only partially precipitated context. They ignore the insufficiency of the word, indeed the law, taken in isolation. Application cannot be separated from the interpretation any more than it can be collapsed into interpretation. The two stand in tension as word and context stand in tension. Although there is no stability, no final word, no final interpretation, hopefully there is, as those of us who are not literalists must believe, the creative possibility I call the power of figuration. Without it, without risking it, there is only the dead letter of the law.

Conclusion

Therefore I do not much like the opinion of the man who thought by a multiplicity of laws to bridle the authority of judges, cutting up their meat for them. He did not realize that there is as much freedom and latitude in the interpretation of laws as in their creation. And those people must be jesting who think they can diminish and stop our disputes by recalling us to the express words of the Bible. For our mind finds the field no less spacious in registering the meaning of others than in presenting his own. As if there were less animosity and bitterness in commenting than in inventing!

Montaigne, On Experience, 1588[1]

The reader will have noticed a discrepancy between my chapters on Fundamentalism and those on the law. I treat the Fundamentalists far more gently than I do the lawyers and judges, with whom I engage in more heated argument. My reasons for this are complex, as I will try to show; but first I should say that I share a frame of reference, a culture, a discursive mode, with the lawyers that I did not share with the Fundamentalists. In working with the Fundamentalists, I was often struck, as was Henry James in reading Charles Nordoff's book on communistic societies in America, by "the existence in human nature of lurking and unsuspected strata, as it were, of asceticism, of the capacity for taking a grim satisfaction in dreariness."[2] I find that the Fundamentalists have, for their salvation, sacrificed and condemned aspects of social and cultural life from which I gain a sense of meaning, satisfaction, and pleasure. Working with them, I was saddened by the restrictions they imposed on their lives, by a puritanism for which I could find no justification, by a spiritual and moral discipline that turned, at times selfishly, upon itself, by an uncritical and rote allegiance to a reading of the Bible that deprived it of what many have found to be its deepest meaning, its beauty and truth, and by a pervasive fear of imaginative and figurative possibility, which stifled creativity. I have tried to understand *their* reasons for cutting themselves off from so much of what I find valuable in life; and though I have failed to appreciate them as I am sure they would have wanted, I respect their decision to live the life they have chosen. I am, however, affronted by their effort to impose their way of life, their values, on other people, including myself.

I was fortunate in working with what I would call Fundamentalism's conservative elite. Although they preached their values with often chilling effectiveness, they were neither the political activists who dictate right-wing policies in the name of religion nor the extremists who identify their opponents with Satan or argue for a return to Old Testament laws like stoning homosexuals. As Ron Saywell, one of the seminarians whose Bible classes I attended, put it, "Politics is not a church matter. A pastor is trained to preach the word of God—and not to be a politician." Nor were the Fundamentalists I worked with the exploitative radio and television revivalists, the media barkers, who count the souls they have converted in terms of the tithes they collect, or the irresponsible faith healers who blame their failures on their clients' faulty faith. For the most part, they disapproved of mixing religion and politics, of exploitative and hate-provoking preaching, and of irresponsible healing. They looked askance at organizations like the Christian Coalition (though I suspect most of them vote along coalition lines). They were so certain of their values—and so isolated, morally and spiritually, from mainstream America—that they could not understand why anyone with different values would be angered by their incapacity, their unwillingness, to engage in dialogue or debate. I was frustrated by their failure to acknowledge the possible validity of another point of view, including my own. I was incensed by their effort to deprive me and people like me of liberties as vital to me as their convictions are to them. Theirs was a preclusive discourse: they had the truth. Either I accepted their terms or I didn't. If I didn't, they ultimately had nothing to say to me, nor I to them. I found their dismissal of all other points of view profoundly divisive.

The lawyers were more open to argument, though the conservatives among them were probably no more flexible than the Fundamentalists. Their pretense was different; their styles of argument freer and in my view more sophisticated; their terms of reference broader and seemingly more tolerant. Their textual allegiance did not lead them to dismiss other readings on the grounds of transcendent certainty. By the nature of the law, they had no choice but to engage with those who held positions contrary to their own, and as a result they had to anticipate those positions. This demanded a certain creativity, admittedly limited by the law, which often verged on rhetorical hairsplitting and manipulation. They may have believed in their arguments, their way of reading the Constitution, but they had to respect the procedures of the law and the consequences—the decisions—of those procedures. They could not responsibly drop a case or dismiss their opponents with a name. They often disagreed with me, but they did not see the fact of our differences as branding me one of the unchosen. Theirs was not a salvationalist discourse. They were for the most part willing to ignore differences on social occasions, for their commitment was never as complete, as consummate, as the Fundamentalists'. They could detach themselves from their positions, ironize, and even be amused by them. (There were obviously some who couldn't, but I did not meet them. I never met Bork.) They had an etiquette; one that, I'm afraid, often facilitated a hypocrisy, a cynicism, a semantic nihilism concealed behind protestations of sincerity, goodwill, and loyalty to the word and its truth. Many of the literalists, people in high places with enormous power, used their literalism as an alibi to mask personal and political interests and agendas.

I am more restrained—more ethnographic—in my discussion of Fundamentalism than I am when writing about the law. I was disturbed by this asymmetry and thought seriously of rewriting the law chapters, or even the chapters on religion. But I could find no single, sustainable authorial position from which to write (or even edit) the two. This may be a failure, but I do not think so. I have come to see my inability to view the two literalist discourses from the same vantage point as a telling symptom of the demands they each make on those who read them from the outside. I cannot presume to know how either would be read from the inside.

As an anthropologist, I am by profession a straddler. I struggle as best I can to enter the world of those I study even as I try to remain outside that world, preserving, as it were, the necessary distance to translate it for myself and my readers. This isn't the place to agonize over the impossibility of this position. Like most of my colleagues, I have done that countless times, producing one epistemologically morbid reflection after another, if not confessing to a "betrayal" of those studied. Nor is this the place to describe the feelings of always being an outsider, at home as well as in the field. I find arguments like Ronald Dworkin's—that law, for jurisprudential purposes, must be (or can even be) understood from within—as too safe.[3] At the same time, I have to acknowledge a certain envy of that position. Anthropologists are, of course, less prone to discuss the advantages of straddling: the vicarious pleasures, the adventure without the burden of commitment, it gives us. Up to a point, we can have our cake and eat it too. We have had the privilege of experiencing otherness without becoming other or, most of the time, without even accepting the challenge that otherness poses. We justify our disengagement, the dishonor of refusing a challenge, to use a metaphor of a moribund but perhaps not entirely defunct chivalry, on scientific grounds; and we find relief from this morally awkward position in its transfer to our even more removed readers.

This straddling accounts for part, but only part, of the discrepancy in my writing about religion and law. The Fundamentalists and their world were always distinctly other for me in ways the originalists and their world was not. I came to understand something of that world, however limiting and wrongheaded I found it, to appreciate the interpretive if not the intellectual energy with which they responded to it, and to have considerable respect for the integrity their faith demanded. I made a great effort not to treat the Fundamentalists as, in Susan Harding's words, "repugnant cultural others" or to dismiss them as "know-nothings," as Harold Bloom has.[4] Although I was never tempted by their worldview or transported by their attempts to convert me, I was often confused after an interview that edged on their witnessing me and more often embarrassed by the disappointment I must have caused. For the most part, as I have noted, the Fundamentalists had enormous patience with me—a patience, however, that bordered on a judging if not judgmental impatience. I could appreciate its transformative power. I felt as though I were a participant in a story, theirs, of which I had only an inkling.

I liked many of the Fundamentalists I came to know. I did not really become friends with any of them—I couldn't. It was as though God came between us. Theirs is an either/or world: either one has been chosen or not; either one has given oneself to Jesus or one has not; either one has truth or one has not. Their world is riven, if not by God then by their faith in God. Those like myself who do not have their faith are simply other—condemned to a depraved life and finally to the fires of Hell. With the exception of the extreme separatists, like those at Bob Jones University, Fundamentalists are not always dividing everyone into the saved and unsaved and acting in accordance with this division. For the most part, they lead ordinary lives, associating at work and on other occasions with all sorts of people. Like most Americans, most of the time, they are able to bracket ideas and values that conflict with those of the people they meet in their daily lives. They are, as I have said, a friendly, practical people, whose "retreat" from continual evangelical engagement is justified, if they justify it at all, by their belief in God's inscrutable will. Despite their friendliness and even their evangelical commitment, they are, finally, indifferent to those who do not care enough about their own salvation to join them. I believe they are no more comfortable with the unsaved than the unsaved are with them. It was this division that I found particularly disturbing. I no more liked being other than I liked declaring others other. Of course, I often did, inevitably. But the way I responded—at least the way I think one should respond—to otherness is with a respect that seeks neither to condemn it nor to incorporate it. It was the Fundamentalists' and other evangelicals' determination to incorporate the unsaved, through conversion, or to abandon them if they did not respond to their evangelizing that I found particularly un-Christian, at least as I understand Christianity. It seems to me that their separatist tendencies, their concern with the individual's spiritual rebirth, and their stress on Christ's Second Coming and the end of time, have led them to underplay Christ's message of love, which I take to be at the heart of Christianity.

I write this with the hope that any evangelicals who might read it will take it as a challenge and not as dismissive criticism. It is one thing to criticize a religion from the inside, where one participates in the discourse one is criticizing, and another to do so from the outside, where such criticism can easily be taken as condescending, even when it is not meant to be so. This point is one that those who advocate religious criticism like Harold Bloom usually fail to realize. We take belief to be a privileged domain, so deeply personal as to be untouchable. From the inside, it is permissible for John MacArthur to criticize Charles Ryrie's view of sanctification, but it is not permissible for him to criticize the quality of Ryrie's faith. Even MacArthur's attack on Pentecostalism in *Charismatic Chaos* is considered by some Fundamentalists to be insensitive to the Pentecostalists' faith. Criticism by an outsider, like me, of a theological or hermeneutic position can easily be taken to be a criticism of personal faith. It is, I suppose, the effect of our own particular chivalry toward belief and faith that accounts for some of the differences between my chapters on religion and law. The law, even when it is taken in the manner of a Sanford Levinson as a confession of faith, is not protected by an etiquette of belief.

Of course, Fundamentalists are always ready to attack other Christian churches, particularly the Catholics and the liberal Protestants. I have heard some of them thunder against any entente with the Catholic Church as if they were combatants in the wars of religion, even when the subject—abortion, say—is one in which they are in substantial agreement. (I should add that Fundamentalists who are affiliated with the Christian Coalition or similar organizations of the religious right have, as one preacher I know put it, "sacrificed the purity of faith for worldly, political concerns" in their attempt to bring about such an entente.) For the most part, Fundamentalists view other religions like Islam and Buddhism as Satanic cults, and their deities and spirits as devils. They make no effort to understand these religions in their own terms, and they feel God-bound to save their adherents. The Jews present a special problem because Jews are biblically and therefore undeniably a chosen people. However, this special status does not preclude the occasional anti-Semitic slur. But it would be a mistake to privilege this as or reduce it to anti-Semitism, for it must be seen as part of a larger condemnation—or at least dismissal—of those who are not "Christian." The conviction of being chosen, of being saved, of having a special relationship with Jesus, can easily lead to ignorance and bigotry.

We are no longer living in the age of a Frank Norris, whose anti-Catholicism and anti-Semitism could draw enormous unembarrassed crowds and incite them to defeat a presidential candidate like Al Smith on the grounds of his Catholicism.[5] But it would be a mistake to dismiss the possibility that this kind of mass bigotry could recur. The structures of thought that were responsible for it are still with us. They are manifest right now in our Congress, and we saw them displayed in Kenneth Starr's pursuit of President Clinton. They are exhibited in the various fringe groups, white supremacists, for example, or those militias who proclaim the literal word of God as they plot to overthrow the government—we see it in those "Christians" who promote a particular telephone company because it does not hire homosexuals or boycott Disneyland because it does. We have to ask about the consequences of their religious belief on their politics. Can they separate the two? Ought they to separate them in their own terms? I am less concerned about their specific issues—abortion, homosexuality, school prayer—than about the way in which their beliefs lead them to frame and understand political and social issues. How does the belief that only reborn Christians will be saved affect their politics—their position on social welfare programs, for example? How can they conduct a reasonable and realistic foreign policy if they are convinced that religions like Islam and Buddhism are Satanic? I do not know the answers to these questions. Obviously, they disturb me.

It is not the particular positions taken up by the Fundamentalists that I find most troubling; nor is it even the way they frame those positions. Rather, it is their refusal to question these positions.

They have, they are preached, they are taught, the right answers, Frances FitzGerald notes for Jerry Falwell's Thomas Road congregation. They "always seem to know exactly what God wants."[6] Theirs is an authoritarian discourse. FitzGerald remarks, "But just as fundamental theology posits the absolute authority of the Bible, fundamentalist moral doctrines posit the absolute authority of pastors, teachers, fathers, 'civil authorities,' and so on."[7]

Although authoritarianism runs through legal literalism, perhaps through all literalism, it is not normally so consuming as it is among the Fundamentalists. I write this advisedly, for in the impeachment proceedings of Bill Clinton we saw how absolutism and literalism were pitted against relativism and "looseness" of meaning in a moralistic drama of purportedly transcendent import. It was as though the fate of the nation — certainly its moral and spiritual condition, its innocence — was at stake. Despite the pretense to uncover the truth and debate the legal and moral questions that "uncovered truth" would pose, the exposition of tawdry and no doubt legally unnecessary details of an already-admitted truth replaced real and perhaps necessary investigation. There was no debate, only diatribe. Political considerations were poorly masked by legal and moral pretense. Literalism, absolutism, and moralism became figures in precisely the politicking they were "designed" to combat.

As I often have to remind my students, "debate," "dialogue," and "resolution" are historically specific cultural categories. They, or the faith we have in them, are by no means universal. With the exception of the resolution of problems in mathematics, physics, and the other sciences, resolutions and solutions are rarely more than compromises. Debate and dialogue — talking it through — may help to clarify a problem, position, or difference of opinion, but they are also arenas for the exercise of power and desire. The Fundamentalists' conviction of the God-given truth of their position in effect reduces any exchange over that truth to its assertion; any response, even one cast as open-minded exploration of other possibilities, is taken as a counter-assertion that must immediately be denied. To relinquish a point, even for the sake of argument, is as dangerous as raising the possibility that even a single word of Scripture is not God-breathed and inerrant. This is not to say that Fundamentalists are not skilled in arguing with those who do not share their views. They are, but always, at some level, in an evangelizing mode. Their first aim is to find a chink in their "opponent's" armor, to show up the artifice, the wrongheadedness, of his or her presuppositions. Having laid bare these defective presuppositions, having elicited some acknowledgment of their questionableness, the evangelist then proceeds with relentless logic and insistent rhetoric to their only possible conclusion—the truth of his or her position. The opponent is given no chance to escape.

I have stressed the logic of evangelizing, as if that logic, that rationality, were what it is all about. But it is more than that. There is a dramatic side to evangelizing, of which the logical maneuver is only part. By finding fault in the evangelized's presuppositions, by shifting all levels of discourse from the logical to the biographical, from argument to prayer, from the impersonal to the personal—the intensely personal in which vulnerabilities are revealed—by constantly, rhythmically, citing Scripture, by posing ultimate questions concerning contingency, death, and salvation, the experienced evangelists so disorient (reorient, they would say) the evangelized that their logic becomes inexorable, their truth a dead certainty, and Jesus's embrace becomes simple, loving fact. I have likened this condition to the semantic vertigo that shamans and other curers produce in their patients, heightening a patient's suggestibility to the point where the stories the shamans tell, the pictures of the world they draw, become the only possible reality.[8] I have seen it among the Navaho in this country, as well as in Morocco, South Africa, and Brazil. As I mentioned earlier, I experienced something of the same vertigo when I was witnessed. I came to appreciate the long drives between my appointments in Los Angeles. They gave me time to reorient myself.

For any conversation, dialogue, or debate to move in a meaningful way, its participants must share, or at least have the illusion of sharing, a set of assumptions about language, communication, interpersonal relations, the nature of their world of reference, the way to make sense of it, and how to evaluate divergent understandings and to adjudicate differences. We don't have to be in perfect accord; we probably never will be. But there are requirements. Like any non-evangelical American, I shared many of the prerequisites for dialogue and debate with the Fundamentalists. The problem was that I did not share with them what they found most essential. Obviously, we could talk about many other things, but the fact that I was not saved underlay all our conversations. Their belief—their version of God, their special relationship to Him, the way they supported that version and that relationship through the Bible—put a stop to any real communication. It symbolized difference, our difference, *the difference that privileged them.* It was the constant if not always manifest focal point for their discrimination of the world, its people, its past and future. It is why they say that with rebirth comes a new way of seeing the world—one no longer measured directly by the individual but, rather, by God's Word.

In the law, the situation is at once simpler and more complex. It is simpler because the immediate stakes (for the judges and the lawyers, not necessarily for the clients) are not as great. Though the law can affect most aspects of one's life, it does not demand the same life commitment as biblical commandment does for the Fundamentalist. One's personal salvation is not in question—at least, it isn't the direct concern of the law. Interpretation carries a burden, but certainly not the same burden. It must insulate the law from moral and political interests and concerns from which, as we all know, it cannot in fact be separated, for the law founds and maintains an order that, despite all the mechanical analogies we use to describe the relation between individuals and that order, is profoundly human. It is steeped in self-concern and concern for others, in self-interest and interest in others, and in concern and interest for the whole. Whether it in fact embodies the ideals and aspirations of its community, the law is nevertheless taken to do so, metaphorically perhaps, in moral and political as well as legal argument. The fact that the law cannot divorce itself fully from the moral and the political is evidenced by its rhetorical and often impassioned appeal to the moral and the political, even as it denies their relevance or insists that they be removed from consideration. Taken to be a purgative, hermeneutics, especially in its literalist mode, can serve to perpetuate the illusion of the purity of the law. I do not mean that hermeneutics is bunk (we cannot do without interpretation) or unilluminating; I mean that, as we saw so dramatically in the impeachment proceedings, it can also mask those impurities of the law—the moral and the political—that effectuate it.

I have raised the question of the relationship between literalism and democracy several times in this book. Is there an incompatibility between the principles of democratic engagement and the absolutist standpoint of the Fundamentalist? Of the legal originalist? Of the literalist more generally? Obviously there is no one answer to these questions. Despite their obvious similarities, there are, as we have seen, important differences among literalisms. Just as obviously there are several versions—several visions—of democracy. It is certainly more complicated than the one-man-one-vote principle that America and other countries in the West have taken as the hallmark of democracy, ignoring that this is only a prerequisite for democracy, necessary to be sure but not sufficient. There are popular democracies, representational democracies, parliamentary, presidential, multi-party, and single-party ones. Indeed, as we have seen in some countries in Africa, Asia, and South America as well as in several of the former Soviet republics, one-man-one-vote, taken alone, can easily mask anti-democratic practices and jeopardize precisely the liberties that it is meant to safeguard.

Democracy is not just a procedure; it demands a culture that recognizes the dignity and integrity of the individual and respects—for lack of a better term—the sacral dimension of human relationship. It is easy to talk about the rights of citizens. The guarantee of citizen's rights is obviously central to any democracy, but casting human relations solely in these terms, however necessary this is or seems to be, can easily lead to such an instrumental understanding of the relations that bind, or ought to bind, men and women in any political community that the quality I am calling sacral is forgotten. Its roots lie deep in our history. The stories of secularization we tell and the countless benefits we have accrued from secularization often justify—in the name of historical objectivity—political self-interest. My point is that our secularization is not as complete as we pretend, nor can it be, and that the languages by which we describe political behavior (those of political science, for example) give support to this somewhat—I stress somewhat—falsified view. I believe that the Fundamentalism I have discussed in this book (and other movements popularly called fundamentalist but better called simply religious) support my point. Certainly, even a superficial analysis of political rhetoric points to the ways in which the most naked, cynical political strategies evoke the sacred to effect their aims. This alone should tell us something. Our languages of commentary (including my own) perpetuate our inevitably partial—our mystified—understanding of the social world in which we find ourselves. We distinguish Fundamentalism and other religious movements from the political. When they have political import, we tend to see them as exceptional, arising out of special circumstances by which we explain them away. We focus on the way religion masks power. We think of the corrupt mullahs in Iran; the violent Hindu nationalists in India; the fanatic ultra-orthodox in Israel; and the religious right in Congress, whose self-interest is barely masked by its appeals to American values (by which the politicians mean *Christian* values, as of course they understand "Christian").

Secularization notwithstanding, there is—call it primitive, call it sentimental—a quality in human relations that bypasses the instrumental, and it seems to me that the recognition of this is necessary in any society that aspires to democracy. First, I should point out that this quality of relationship cannot be reduced to any particular religious understanding. This is why I prefer simply to evoke the idea of the sacral here, instead of giving it a definition which would be deceptively easy to incorporate into one or another of our ready-made socio-political or religious understandings. Second, I should note that, as history has attested again and again, the sacrality of relationship is easily ignored or abused. Indeed, its abuse seems rather more commonplace than its respect.

One prerequisite for democracy is an openness to the position of the other. We may be convinced that we have truth, but—if only to maintain democracy, however defined—it is incumbent upon us to recognize the truth, the possible truth, of the others. (By this, I do not mean that we should assume naively that the truths proclaimed by the other are not self-interested. They often, and perhaps at some level always, are. We have to maintain a critical attitude.) Where we believe, as the Fundamentalists do, that we have special access to *the* truth, then we have no choice but a stubborn proclamation of that truth. Such a position is absolutist. As Ron Saywell said in one of his classes, "God is no democrat." We cannot engage in dialogue; we cannot arrive at compromise. There can be no compromise, since compromise, for the Fundamentalist, amounts to blasphemy—a betrayal of truth. There can be no dialogue—at most only a pretense to dialogue that covers an evangelizing discourse. I have the truth. You don't. I have, therefore, to convert you. Where there is an unwillingness to convert, there can only be combat. We see this, most dramatically, in the dispute over abortion, but it occurs frequently over other less dramatic issues in the United States today. I am speaking not just of school prayer, homosexuality, and the right to bear arms, but in the way these and other issues are argued by the absolutists. Theirs is simply an assertive discourse. "I have the right to. . . . " (This is why I hesitated to discuss democracy in terms of rights.)

A corollary of the openness to the other's truth is of course the ability to represent that truth, that position. In my discussion of Lino Graglia's assumption that a community is "fully capable of speaking for itself through the representatives it elects," I noted some of the contradictions in the notion of representation in complex democracies. Here I want to call attention to one important prerequisite for dialogue, itself a prerequisite for democracy: the ability, or at least the attempt, to represent the other's truth (if only to oneself in order to respond to it). Is the literalist, who has surrendered to the absolute truth of a text, capable of such representation?

The Fundamentalist would argue that we cannot relate to others in a biblical way except through the mediation of God's word. In a more formal fashion, the Constitution is the ultimate mediator in legal dispute. Obviously, I do not want to deny the role of a mediator in any relationship. Quite the contrary. I am arguing that all exchanges are mediated by a set of communicative and interpersonal conventions, which may be located, symbolically and in fact, in a special, often sacred or near-sacred texts. What concerns me here is the attitude one takes to those conventions—to the texts that contain and embody them. One can accept them unquestioningly as the literalists do. Or one can take them pragmatically, acknowledging only that they are necessary for the creation and maintenance of relationship. Both these positions are extreme: they challenge the basic principles of democracy. The one precludes dialogue and engagement; the other reduces dialogue and engagement to opportunism. Fortunately, between complete surrender and pragmatic engagement, there is a range of attitudes toward convention and authority that are more flexible than the literalist's position and less instrumental than the pragmatist's. It is in this in-between that democracy flourishes. The mediating conventions and authority have, I believe, to be taken not as given, not as once-and-for-all, but as aspirational—as future-oriented—if a vital and creative political community is to survive and not simply reiterate traditional virtues and procedures. It was to this arid traditionalism that Thomas Jefferson responded in his letter to Samuel Kercheval that I quoted when he wrote that "laws and institutions must go hand in hand with the progress of the human mind." We have to recognize that there is always a contradiction between claims to eternal truth and the subsequent history of these claims. They are recontextualized and, as such, something of their truth is surrendered to rhetorical manipulation.

It seems to me that today in the United States we—at least in our political rhetoric—are caught between the two extremes. On the one hand, we have the Fundamentalists' and originalists' intransigent adherence to the letter of the text. On the other, we have the instrumentalists' dedicated self-interest. The instrumentalists' position is reflected in the promiscuous extension of a market metaphor to just about every domain of human life as well as to the social policies that follow from that metaphorization. Money, rather than social and cultural value, becomes the engine of American democracy—a democracy that has come to resemble more a competitive plutocracy than the republic envisioned by the Framers of the Constitution. As I write this, I read in the papers more about the amount of money a particular candidate for the presidency or the Senate has collected than about that candidate's views. It is assumed, perhaps accurately, that whoever has the greatest cache will win the election. Vision and policy are simply rhetorical covers for the *real* dynamic for winning: money. Of course we tell ourselves that money is only part of the equation, that the issues do count. But do they? The majority of Americans may claim they do, but the fact that so many Americans no longer vote suggests they feel otherwise. We seem to have engendered a political cynicism that goes precisely against the democratic values that we claim are quintessentially ours. Of course, we also pride ourselves on our pragmatism. The two appear to be in contradiction. But need they be?

What we forget is that our conception of the "market" has deep theological roots and that our attitude toward it, our faith in it really, verges on the religious. We take Adam Smith's invisible hand as a metaphor, as we should, but often enough we act as if it, or something like it, exists: a homeostatic mechanism which will make everything work out in our best of all possible worlds. Not only have we faith in the market, but we preach its virtues with complacency and satisfaction. There have been moments when President Clinton, talking foreign policy (but not the politics behind it), has sounded like an evangelical preacher. He produces resentment in "less fortunate countries" not only because of envy but because no one wants to be preached to.

Yes, we have been successful. We have had our century. We pride ourselves on the progress we've made, but unless I am mistaken "progress" now refers less to the security of our citizens than to technological miracles and economic success. As stupendous as these are, technology, like money, is never more than instrumental.

Both require vision—political and social vision—for their potential to be realized. They require at once realism and naive faith. The Fundamentalists and the originalists offer one vision, but it is a nativistic one, a re-assertion of traditional values that have lost the force of ideals they may once have had and have become a set of imperatives, biblical and legal, that demand discipline rather than aspiration, repetition rather than creation. They can only be asserted, and as such they precipitate precisely the instrumental politics they are meant to overcome. We have certainly seen this in Congress in the 1990s. The religious right, asserting its values and its "vision," is at least as rhetorical as its pragmatist opponents. It is to this rhetoric that those don't-mix-politics-and-religion Fundamentalists with whom I worked were responding. They found it blasphemous. But then they themselves were caught in a separatism that is hardly conducive to democracy.

Are we then entrapped, as a country, in complacency? Has puzzlement given way to platitude, dialogue to preaching? Has our creativity been reduced to *bricolage*—to the mere manipulation of the tried and true? It would seem so—and not only among Fundamentalists and originalists, but among those who prefer the "security" of the status quo over the risks of change without seeming to ever recognize that the status quo itself is in history. Americans like to say democracy is the best political system human beings have managed to come up with, so let it alone. To me, such observations sound a death knell to democratic understanding.

As I have suggested, the dominant idiom by which Americans describe and evaluate their social and cultural reality is moral, not political. We do not usually understand our circumstances in terms of social and political structure. Though we continually evoke class, through personal style, dress, language, and assumptions, we do not think in terms of class. Nor do we think of ourselves, our circumstances, in terms of economic—that is, capitalist—formations. When we have lost a job, failed to be promoted, or believe our potential is not recognized, we tend, if not always in full consciousness, to blame ourselves, or those (a boss, for example) whom we hold directly and usually personally responsible for our situation. When we are successful, we tend, with requisite modesty, to give ourselves and those who have supported us credit. We prefer miniaturized and personalized understanding, in which moral and character evaluations predominate, to large-scale, impersonal, and abstract understanding, which is too intellectual, too ideological, rhetorical, foreign. I remember returning from Germany a few years ago and telling a class I was teaching about my trip. The students were undergraduates, adults mainly, primarily working-class or lower-middle-class, who were working and borrowing as they studied for their degrees. When I told them about the minimum wage in Germany, which was very much higher than the American, about unemployment insurance, which was a substantial percentage of the unemployed's last income, whatever that income was, about national health insurance, and about students' protesting not over tuition (which was negligible) but over a living allowance, they listened at first with interest, then with envy, and finally in disbelief. I watched them sink into themselves, asking themselves (I could not help thinking) what they, or their parents, had done wrong. When I tried to get them to discuss their reaction, they could not frame it, however hard I pressed them, in critical, social, political, and economic terms. The closest any one of them came was the oldest student in the class, a man in his late forties, who said, "And to think they lost the war. . . ."

I finally told them how I thought the French, the Brazilians, or the Germans, for that matter, would have understood what I had described. I stressed class, social position, economic organization, political parties, unions, and the obligation of the state to its citizens, to its youth. The students understood what I said, but somehow they could not frame their own circumstances in the same terms. The terms were too alien; their premises too different. Even the most cynical of the students centered their comments on the self, the other-taken-as-a-self, on moral condition, blame, guilt, and on a generalized and barely ironical sense of "something had gone wrong somewhere." They asserted, defensively, a moral superior-ity, tinged with xenophobia, as they recited the virtues of American society. They seemed to take solace, or at least to situate themselves, in a morally superior but fatalistic resignation—a passivism I found terrifying and yet revealing of the engine of the American economy. Isolated, separated from one another in their ambition, they were able to imagine their success only in terms of work and more work. Immediate and particular in context, their sense of work was coupled with a self-enhancing opportunism. Their realism was tempered both positively and negatively by a notion of chance.

They were not a particularly religious group of students—they did not, at any rate, talk about religion, salvation, good works, predestination, or even God's will. At least in class, they had no such solace. In fact, there was something lonely and grim about their vision of the world. And there was something admirable about their ascesis, their discipline—its expression, its focus on the individual, its fatalism coupled, paradoxically, with possibility, had a religious quality, one of innocent faith, which seemed so far from the political understanding of the French, Brazilians, and Germans I had projected. Though the latter had the advantage of a transcending idiom, one that removed some of the burden of individual responsibility, they were often lost in political rhetoric, squabbling, and excuses. Their understanding seemed an indulgence by contrast to these American students.

———

There is probably nothing particularly exceptional, particularly American, about literalism taken narrowly, taken as simply a focus on what philosophers like Donald Davidson call "first meaning"—that is, roughly, what the literalists mean by "plain, ordinary meaning."[9] I want to suggest that what characterizes American literalism is its moral commitment. This is clear in Fundamentalist thought, where literalist interpretation is the only means for uncovering the meaning of God's word and thus serving it as faithfully as possible, but also the key to living a correct, biblical life. Any deviation from that interpretive mode is dangerous, for it can lead to sin by facilitating the insinuation of desire, self-interest, depraved imagination, power, and egocentric cognition into the understanding of the Word. For the Fundamentalist, the commitment to literalism becomes a discipline that, in its own way, is not altogether different from many other spiritual disciplines—though, for the most part, they do not place the same stress on interpretation.

Legal literalists do not in most circumstances have the same total and consuming commitment to their hermeneutics. Their literalism tends, as I have observed, to the instrumental. However, many appear to be morally committed to it—at least if we take them at their word. But even if we do not take that word at face value, we must nevertheless recognize the way it is used in argument. We must also recognize the moral outrage—or the pretended outrage—that the rhetorical manipulation of this commitment produces. As Trenholme Junghans, an anthropologist with whom I discussed literalism, pointed out, Americans, even the pragmatists and instrumentalists among them, are not particularly comfortable in revealing their strategies of argument and persuasion. This is particularly true when they are talking about moral and spiritual matters, but it is also true, I believe, in many other areas. Unlike many people—in eastern Europe, for example, or the Mediterranean—we are often so embarrassed by strategy and rhetoric that we have to justify their use pragmatically, on moral grounds, when we do not simply ignore it. Obviously, as I pointed out in my discussion of the law, we cannot reveal our argumentative strategies in our arguments, for then those arguments would collapse. There is, as Henry James so often described, a willful innocence in Americans, and this willfulness extends to limiting knowledge. Like everyone at some level, we may choose not to know—but, unlike some, we tend to deny our willfulness. We mask it behind methodologies and hermeneutics like literalism. They have an authority that is often dangerous, in my view, because they promote ignorance in the name of truth and innocence. As James well knew, wittingly or unwittingly, innocence, like truth, can be manipulated.

Several years ago, I was discussing some of my findings on American literalism with Brazilian colleagues at the National Museum in Rio de Janeiro. One of them asked, apologetically, why I focused only on literalism in religion and the law. "To me, to us Brazilians, you Americans are all literalists," he said. I was taken aback. I had nicely compartmentalized the literalisms I was studying, treating them as important but somehow exceptional. I did not realize how pervasive and authoritative the literalist style is in even those domains of American thought, like literary criticism and science, that we do not normally associate with it. Literalism is by no means restricted to bounded areas like Fundamentalism and originalism, which self-consciously elaborate their hermeneutics.

Let me give you one small example. In an article in *The New Yorker* in 1994, James Park Sloan assumed a literalist stance in his discussion of the Polish reception of Jerzy Kosinski's novel *The Painted Bird*. A Polish journalist, Joanna Siedlecka, had accused Kosinski of falsifying his wartime experiences in that book, which many of its readers took for a thinly disguised autobiography. Admittedly, Kosinski had done little to discourage this view. But even the most superficial reading of *The Painted Bird* leaves no doubt that, whatever basis in fact there may be, it flees for grueling, expressionistic fantasy. There may be autobiographical truth in Kosinski's delirium but by no means any full historical "reality." (Years ago, in a book on a demon-ridden Moroccan, I suggested that Americans tend to conflate autobiographical truth and reality where others separate them.[10]) But it was not the fact of a Polish journalist trying to make a scandal over Kosinski's life that struck me as odd—there were reasons enough for that, most of them unpleasant—but, rather, it was Sloan's attitude. Instead of merely pointing to the absurdity of Siedlicka's argument on the grounds of Kosinski's style, he also added "two lines of reasoning" that "might have suggested that 'The Painted Bird' was something less—and therefore more—than straightforward autobiography."[11] The first of these, Sloan tells us, is a matter of statistics: the odds that members of a Jewish family separated during the war would survive were one in ten thousand. The second concerns "episodic intensity." I cannot resist quoting Sloan here:

> Kosinski's protagonist has a knack for riding into town just as the local pot of trouble is about to boil over. He arrives in one village just in time to see the brutal murder of Stupid Ludmila, and at the miller's house just in time to witness the plucking out of eyeballs. Unless one is prepared to believe that a woman is assaulted and eyeballs plucked out at least, say, once every month or two, it follows that the experiences described in the book are heightened to some degree.[12]

"To some degree"! Either Sloan is spoofing scientific argument applied to literature—something Kosinski himself might have done—or he is a sort of Forrest Gump of literary biography. His conclusion to the paragraph quoted above suggests the latter: "Why didn't these arguments occur to the readers at the time?" he asks—and answers, because "people hear what they want to hear."

I have no desire to impugn Sloan. Others, as he notes, have taken Kosinski's book as autobiographical fact—among them Elie Wiesel. *The Painted Bird*, Sloan tells us, became "the cornerstone of reading lists in university courses on the Holocaust where it was often treated as an historical document." It is of course, but only the poorest historians would accept it (or any other document for that matter) at face value. Like other teachers of literature, I have received research proposals that seem to forget literary artifice—that propose, for example, to do "demographies" of novels by Austin, Brontë, Balzac, or Gaskell and compare these demographies with the actual population of the towns and cities on which the novelist based his or her descriptions! That a writer like Sloan, who clearly has a fine sense of style (something he demonstrates elsewhere in his article), should relinquish arguments over the truth of a representation based on style for probabilistic ones that would embarrass any statistician, is in my view, a dramatic example of the way in which literalism can insinuate itself even into as figuratively sensitive field as literary criticism.

I could cite many examples of literalism in other, "harder" domains, like science. Indeed, as the historian of science David Noble has recently written, science and religion are not necessarily opposed discourses.[13] He argues that they share a common history, and that our faith in technology is in many respects coordinate with evangelical millenarianism. We could probably extend Noble's argument to include literalism. As we have seen, Fundamentalist interpretation shares many of the presuppositions of empiricism and positivism. Certainly, many of the scientists Noble describes, especially those who specialize in "Artificial Intelligence" (AI) and "Artificial Life" (A-Life), appear to take the word at face value as they dream of cognitive immortality by downloading their brains into some computer or transferring genetic instruction into a machine. American psychologists, linguists, and specialists in communication have attempted to operationalize what the Russian literary historian and philosopher Mikhail Bakhtin says about language, without realizing that his formulations are loose, evocative, and not meant to be systemic. An even more dramatic example is the attempt by some Americans to systematize the writings of the French psychoanalyst Jacques Lacan, whose language is self-consciously ambiguous and provocative. Indeed, Lacan's purpose was to call attention to the limits of all linguistic formulations, including his own.

Though I have chosen not to discuss in detail these other manifestations of literalism in America, I do want to look further at two, briefly, to underline its reach. The first is in psychoanalysis—a field, like literary criticism, so sensitive to symbolic and figurative expression that one would assume it was immune to literalist influence. To be sure, the psycho-mechanical theorizing that has always been characteristic of some of its practitioners verges on literalism. These analysts take, or at least refer to, the unconscious as something somewhere out there rather than as a hypothetical construct. But it is in the traumatic experience, which has become a key concept, a *causa universalis*—at least in popular accounts of, say, multiple personality, serial murder, and child abuse—that literalism has most visibly insinuated itself. What is striking about these accounts is the assumption that the trauma, as described or, better, elicited, actually occurred. I don't want to deny the reality of abuse or trauma; nor do I want to deny its role in the development of all kinds of mental pathologies or draw attention yet again to the ways in which some therapists have induced memories of traumas that never occurred or were at the very least exaggerated, then exploited them for sensation or profit. That has been amply discussed. Rather, I want to point out that by the very structure of memory, at least as it is understood by psychoanalysis, the delimitation of a single, definable memory is always at some level a fiction, an artifice, because the memory of any event (the event itself, some might argue) immediately draws in other real and fantasized experiences in the individual's life. These are not just events or memories of events that preceded the "traumatic event" but also of those which followed it, and were drawn back into it in later conscious or unconscious remembrances. I have suggested elsewhere that what makes an event, or more accurately an event ensconced in memory, traumatic is often precisely its lack of definition and location. It is the aura of uncertainty, the doubt attached to it, that is so wrenching.[14] I should note in this regard that of all the countries in which psychoanalysis is popular, it is the United States that has devoted the most attention to the question of the reality of the fatherly seductions that Freud's female patients so frequently reported.

The second example I want to mention, again very briefly, is the way many of us talk about genes. I am not referring to genetics here or to the genome project, with its mandate to map the entire repertory of human genes. Genes for eye color, for one kind of dwarfism or another, for beauty, less often for ugliness, for alcoholism, cancer, homosexuality, violence, and even adultery are proclaimed. How often have we heard, or said, "After all, it's in the genes." Sometimes this is said in humor, with irony, with longing even, but at other times it is said uncritically, in seriousness, without any consideration of the implications. We know that gene talk has become a way of talking about race and ethnicity without ever having to say "race" or "ethnicity." I have a friend, a quite brilliant psychotherapist, who now attributes, privately at least, just about every human ailment to genes. This no doubt alleviates the anxiety and frustrated sense of responsibility which any therapeutic encounter generates, by giving my friend a simplifying edge on his patients, his therapy, and perhaps even on himself. Who knows? We do know that the way some of us, some of the time, attribute cause—sole cause—to genes relieves us of all kinds of social responsibility. The gene is today's equivalent of the "bad seed." It underlies, silently for the most part, opposition to welfare, support for public education, and government-funded health care. It is in turn underlaid by a social Darwinism that has never quite left us, being so intertwined by now with our notions of masculinity, success, progress, the frontier, and what we call "seizing the moment." Ironically, it often seems to inflect the thought of precisely those, the religious right, who oppose evolutionary theory. We take the gene to be a given, like a word that can be read literally. We ignore the fact that genes are potentials whose actualization depends on complex factors. They are environmentally sensitive, some more than others. We prefer to see their effects as inevitable. They give us a new theology as deterministic as any the Reformed churches produced, but read in the Book of Genome.

It is extraordinary that when Christian and other fundamentalisms were on the rise, they were ignored by the would-be social prophets of the academy, who were heralding a new "postmodern" age. This was to be, and no doubt is in some ways, an age of play, artifice, impermanence, surface, speed, byte, buzz, and figuration, in which representations, symbols, and signifiers count more than whatever they represent, symbolize, or signify. Meaning would be seen as a momentary cessation of rhetorical ploys, destined in its turn to a rhetorical career. There would be no history, or merely a history of obsolescing presence; no allegiance to any single narrative, sacred or otherwise; no stock in philosophical foundations; no credence in those great, encompassing explanations—Marxism, Darwinism, Freudianism—that were born in the late nineteenth and early twentieth centuries and governed us through the long moments of irrationality, iconoclasm, and nihilism that have punctuated this century. I needn't rehearse these descriptions of postmodernity any further. They are too well known, too easy. They fuel their own vision. What is remarkable is that they are Fundamentalism's mirror image: no sacred texts, no literal meanings, no foundational stories, no history, no depth. . . . Like all mirror images, they occur in the same frame—trapped, one might say, in the same metalanguage. They play on each other in an endless dialectical drama of exposure and condemnation. Can they ever escape from each other? Can they ever slip out of their same insistent presuppositions? The questions are worth asking. I think of the *contadino* and the *padrone*, the peasant and the landowner, born the same year, 1900, friends and enemies ever since then, fighting like two old satyrs on a railroad track at the end of Bernardo Bertolucci's movie *1900*. No doubt Bertolucci wanted to create a cinematographic replay of Hegel's and Marx's master-slave dialectic. Here I would focus on the railway tracks extending into the infinite horizon over which the same train rolls, and the same fight occurs.

———————

When I was doing my research on the Fundamentalists (though not when I was researching on the law), I was bombarded with questions by friends and strangers, some of whom were religious. They all wanted to know about Fundamentalism. I was astonished by how little they in fact knew about evangelical Christianity. They often confused Fundamentalism and Pentecostalism. Some of the Catholics and Jews, and many people who claimed to have no religion, assumed that all Protestants were the same. Some of the people who had in fact been brought up in an evangelical church did not know much about its relationship to other Protestant churches. Some were surprised to learn how indebted their church was to Calvin. Despite their real and professed ignorance, many of them launched into diatribes against the Fundamentalists— diatribes they would have condemned as prejudice and bigotry if somebody else were addressing another religion in the same terms. Some were all too ready to draw parallels with Islamic fundamentalism; some Jews were disappointed because I wasn't treating Jewish fundamentalism. A surprising number of people confessed, often with embarrassment, that they had Fundamentalists in the family.

Often, I invited the most curious to go to church with me to see what it was all about. No one accepted; some even asked if they would be welcome.

Nearly everyone who showed interest in my research asked me, sheepishly, apologetically, but with consuming curiosity, whether or not I had ever been tempted—that was the word they most frequently used—by Fundamentalism. They wanted to know how I withstood the evangelizing. I felt that for some of them I had become a test case on resistance. Others were genuinely interested in the appeal Fundamentalism had. One of them, a liberal United States senator, referred to the sense of community, the hominess, he felt when he visited evangelical churches in his state. I agreed with him. I said that Robert Duvall's film *The Apostle* captured this sense beautifully, but that many of the churches I had attended were not so warm and friendly. I referred to their enormous range in style and to the fact that some of the megachurches had different services, of differing severity, for different age groups. What impressed him most—indeed, what impressed most of the people I talked to—was the scholarly approach that many of the largest churches had. They were like old-fashioned schoolrooms. You were given a pencil and paper to take notes. There was nothing flashy about their pedagogical methods. You had to understand the Bible as best you could— that was your first responsibility. If it meant learning Greek, then it meant learning Greek. If it meant learning hundreds or thousands of verses by heart, then it meant learning those verses.[15] While good works did not lead to salvation, leading a biblical life was work— joyous work. I often found myself in the odd position of defending the Fundamentalists' commitment and dignity and underplaying their faults and all that I found wrong with their religion. I did this less out of any loyalty to them than to ruffle those who wanted to preserve a pat understanding.

I was asked time and again how I explained Fundamentalism's dramatic rise. I could have invented explanatory stories, but the fact is that none of them seemed to hold. "Yes, but . . ." was the most frequent response to my refusal to try to explain—which was frequently followed by my interlocutors' telling *me* why. Although they knew little enough about Fundamentalism, they seemed to have no difficulty in finding explanations for it. They talked about the need for structure, the need for meaning, the need for community. They referred to the loss of values, the loss of certainty, the loss of perspective. They blamed the media, the schools, the information explosion, market uncertainty, the uncaring nature of the government, poor parenting, drugs and alcohol, promiscuity, the absence of love. . . . They cast their arguments in sociological and psychological terms and they spoke of the challenges of modernism and postmodernism. They referred to class—but were surprised when I said that Fundamentalism could no longer be attached to any one class in the United States. They mentioned personality type. I said I found all sorts of personality and character types among the Fundamentalists I had interviewed. I have to admit that I took a certain perverse delight in refusing them explanations. Their own impressed me as being strongly projective. I said that the only irrefutable explanation, provided that you accepted its terms, was the Fundamentalists': "Jesus is responsible." A few laughed at that. A couple looked at me carefully to see whether or not I was being serious. I usually ended these conversations with the same observation I have made in this book: I preferred the disquieting effect of description to the complacency of explanation.

The gap between literalists and non-literalists is great. Do we need formal arenas like that of the law to bring about encounters? Is there something so terrifying about meeting in an authentic way someone who understands the world in so radically a different way that we require some kind of superior governance? We are preoccupied with the problem of "going native" (if, indeed, that is ever possible)—of losing our control. Relativism is one of the lurking conspiracies conservatives imagine. They do not bother even to differentiate between different kinds of relativism (cognitive, moral, or argumentative); they fail, as I earlier found that many white South Africans fail, to recognize that any understanding requires a suspension of your own view in order to grasp the other's. This does not mean that you abandon your own view; ideally, you have sufficient confidence to entertain someone else's view and to accept the challenges it poses. Any democracy presupposes this confidence. Perhaps it is the evangelical's exclusionist emphasis, indeed Christianity's emphasis, on conversion as a total self- and world-transformation that colors our stance, our fear of relativism, of going native.[16]

I remember meeting my wife in a shoe store in Pasadena where she was buying a pair of running shoes. Her salesman was young and handsome, and he used all his charm to sell her shoes. I had a Bible commentary with me, and when he caught sight of it he asked me if I were a Bible reader, by which he meant an evangelical Christian. As he continued selling my wife shoes, he managed to warn me of the dangers of most Bible commentaries, to discuss the various Greek words for love used in the New Testament, and to ask how important we thought it was for a Christian to know Greek. He said that he had so little time to study because the commute between Pasadena and his home in Orange County was so long. My wife asked why he didn't find a job closer to home (he hadn't been able to, he said) and why he didn't move closer to Pasadena. He looked tortured, as he silently wrapped my wife's shoes, and then, smiling, he said, the Holy Spirit was "much stronger" in Orange County than in Pasadena.

For me, this story exemplifies how we manage to live with one another without realizing or having to cope with our often radically different ways of understanding and evaluating the world around us. It was only because I was carrying a Bible commentary with me that the shoe salesman's world was open to us. Neither my wife nor I had ever thought of Orange County (or anywhere else, for that matter) in terms of the Holy Spirit, though we had driven through it, visited friends, and even gone to the theater there. We tend to shy away from challenges to our outlook. Maybe that's why the people who were so curious to learn about Fundamentalism from me, at a safe remove, were unwilling to attend a church service. I think they were afraid, although they would not admit it. Had they been in Japan, I am sure they would have attended a Buddhist or Shinto ceremony without hesitation. Far from home, foreign, exotic, it would not have challenged or shamed them in the same way. The Fundamentalists are particularly sensitive to the problems of engaging with others. I have stressed their evangelizing, but they are practical people who know where and when not to intrude their religion. They know better than to witness their co-workers; yet given their commitment, they are troubled by this.

Although we guard ourselves (and are guarded) from disruptions in our daily lives, there are always certain issues that are of such moral or intellectual significance to us, so defining of our position or outlook that we are compelled to risk disruption for their sake. When that happens, we move from the merely ordinary to the dramatic. We are willing to violate the social etiquette that preserves us from confrontation. I have been particularly fascinated by how certain of the most significant of today's divisive issues—abortion, school prayer, homosexual marriage, gun control, capital punishment—are given condensed, often iconic representation. By iconic representation I mean some verbal or visual image so intensely identified with the issue or principle that its representational status falls away. Such icons are intensely visual in themselves or evoke a visual image. It is this quality that facilitates their turning in on themselves, their involution, giving them a self-sufficiency, an independence, factualness. In its isolating particularity, the icon comes to stand for the general principle or issue, taken at times, almost magically, for the principle itself. The debate over flag-burning is a case in point.

Iconic representation coordinates with our rampant sloganism and the endless manufacture of advertising logos. Like the catch phrases that politicians invent—"trickle-down economics," for example—icons mark *prêt-à-porter* stances and frequently preclude critical, creative thought. No one notes for example that the poor do not want a trickle-down but a downpour economy. They act as signals, giving rise to monologues, diatribes, riffs, spiels that end only from exhaustion—I would suggest because they are not dialogically engaged. Show someone a picture of an electric chair or of a gay marriage ceremony; describe one of those "pro-life" bank checks with a matted image of a fetus on the lower left-hand side and a pretty little blond girl on the upper right-hand side; say "Brady Bill" or mention Ralph Reed (of Christian Coalition fame) or, at least as I'm writing, William Jefferson Clinton—do any of these things and one is immediately—how shall I put it?—blown away by the ensuing monologue. There is no stopping it: it ends when it does, regardless of what one does. Bring up a second icon for another issue: the same thing will happen. The two monologues may be contradictory: a pro-life lecture that invokes the sanctity of life will easily be followed by a lecture in favor of capital punishment, in which no mention of life's sanctity is made. Point out the contradiction between the two positions and elicit a third lecture in which you become the icon of the liberal intellectual. Rarely have I heard people given to this sort of iconic reaction attempt to reconcile conflicting positions. Like the icons turning in on themselves, the monologues are independent of one another. I have stressed the conservative diatribes, but there are liberal ones as well. Ralph Reed, Newt Gingrich, the National Rifle Association's logo of an eagle perched on two crossed rifles—these icons can trigger a liberal monologue just as contradictory as any conservative one. I am exaggerating here, but only a little, and I am doing it to point out a pattern.

These observations on iconic representation lead to a distinction I would like to make between literalism and essentialism. Essentialism has been much discussed in contemporary social and cultural theory. Indeed, many postmodernists rail against it. It is seen as conducive to racism and ethnic, class, and gender stereotyping. It has certainly been exploited for political ends by multiculturalists on both the right and the left. I myself have no argument with these critiques, though I confess to an inability to imagine thinking that is fully free from essentialism. What troubles me is the confusion of essentialism, literalism, and iconic representation. However offensive some of its implications may be, essentialism presupposes a level of analysis, of deciphering, that is absent from iconic representation, which rests fully and uncritically on the force of the image. Essentialism, it has been argued, has analytic depth; iconicism is surface. Iconic representation has an immediacy that essentialism does not necessarily have. It is certainly translatable, one image coming quickly to substitute for another. Essentialism is less easily translated; it suggests fixity, permanence. This is not to say that iconic thought is any less fixed. Its substitutions may give the illusion of change, the same sort of rapid change that some postmodernists proclaim, but the substitutions may simply mask their constant referent.

I would suggest that literalism occupies a position midway between essentialism and iconic representationalism. The focus in literalism is on the relationship between word and meaning rather more than on any essential feature of meaning carried by the word. The relationship is simply asserted: it is neither analytically derived nor based iconically on similarity. Literalism stresses fixity, but behind that stress is a sense of impending change, a loosening, a falling-away of meaning that can only be sustained by a moral commitment to preserve in its singularity the relationship between word and meaning. It resists the easy translation characteristic of iconic representation, particularly when that translation is founded on metaphor and promotes through allegory departure from the word's primary meaning. It is in figurative language that danger lurks for the literalist; and so then, in language terms, is he or she destined to uphold a moral, spiritual, legal (or other) world order by preserving and serving the literal word. Although, as I have said, a case can always be made for a literalist reading of a text, the transfer of that text's meaning, its significance, to the real world—its application, as the hermeneuticists say—has always to be figurative. Despite all efforts to preserve the original meaning of the word, the world, which is after all the the word's context, goes on changing.

We must not underestimate the power of metaphor. In this one respect, the literalists have reason to worry. In thinking they can do without metaphor, they end up serving it—though without the richness of possibility it offers. Who knew this better than Mark Twain, America's great satirist of literalism? Remember his hero David Wilson. Before Wilson could even start his practice as a lawyer in

Dawson's Landing, that outpost of pure Mississippi River Americana, he was "elected" by a fatal remark he made, and for twenty years he never had a client.

> He had just made the acquaintance of a group of citizens when an invisible dog began to yelp and snarl and howl and make himself very comprehensively disagreeable, whereupon young Wilson said, much as one who is thinking aloud—
> "I wish I owned half of that dog."
> "Why?" somebody asked.
> "Because I would kill my half."

Wilson's words filled the group with curiosity, with anxiety even. They could not read his expression. They went away to discuss him. One said he appeared, another that he *was*, a fool.

> Said he wished he owned *half* of the dog, the idiot," said a third. "What did he reckon would become of the other half if he killed his half? Do you reckon he thought it would live?"
> "Why, he must have thought it, unless he *is* the downrightest fool in the world; because if he hadn't thought it, he would have wanted to own the whole dog, knowing that if he killed his half and the other half died, he would be responsible for that half just the same as if he had killed that half instead of his own. Don't it look that way to you, gents?"

The group went on to discuss—in a way that would surely please the literalist lawyer—the niceties of general versus front-to-back ownership and the ways they might effect responsibility for the dog's death. One of them concluded that Wilson was out of his mind; another that he hadn't got a mind; a third said he was a lummox; a fourth that he was a labrick—"just a Simon-pure labrick, if ever there was one"; and a fifth, "a dam fool." It was the sixth, however, who "elected" him.

> "I'm with you, gentlemen," said No. 6. "Perfect jackass—yes, and it ain't going too far to say he is a pudd'nhead. If he ain't a pudd'nhead, I ain't no judge, that's all."

Within a week, the narrator tells us, Wilson lost his name. "Pudd'nhead took its place," and he was "not able to get it set aside or even modified." It was, in fact, only after Pudd'nhead proved the marvelous power of detection through fingerprinting, some twenty years later, that he lost his nickname. "And this is the man the likes of us have called a pudd'nhead," one of the villagers remarked. "He has resigned from that position, friends." "Yes, but it isn't vacant," said another. "We're elected."[17]

One wonders if any of the men in Dawson's Landing, including Wilson, ever realized that "pudd'nhead" is a metaphor. We should recall with Wallace Stevens, himself a master of the metaphor, that the absence of imagination has itself to be imagined.[18]

Notes

PREFACE

1. Eliot 1986:5.
2. Fitzgerald 1986:131.
3. Boone 1989:11.
4. Horwitz 1973; Perry 1985.
5. Crapanzano 1985.
6. See Heidegger 1967:95ff.
7. Noll 1994. "Secular humanism" is a catch-all phrase that was first publicized by Francis Schaeffer, an American conservative evangelist who lived and worked out of Switzerland. Secular humanism was picked up by Tim and Beverly LaHaye and other conservative evangelical activists with a political agenda. See Martin 1996:194–97. Hugo Black included secular humanism among "religions in this country which do not teach what would generally be considered a belief in the existence of God" (*Torcaso v. Watkins*, 367 U.S. 488, 495 [1961]).

INTRODUCTION

1. Carroll 1960:269.
2. Wittgenstein 1958:17.
3. Barthes 1970:19.
4. Levinson 1988:32. Levinson tells the Severeid-Black anecdote.
5. Messick 1993:26.
6. Nilsson 1949.
7. Crapanzano 1992:43–45.
8. Connolly and Keutner 1988:4–6.
9. Ibid:7.
10. Gadamer 1985:154.
11. Compare Schleiermacher's observation that "every act of understanding is the reverse side of an act of speaking" (1977:97).
12. Schleiermacher 1977b:181.
13. Gadamer 1985:158.
14. Schleiermacher 1977a:98–100.
15. Heidegger 1971:112.
16. Ott 1972:170.
17. Saussure 1966:82.
18. Ironically, in their exuberance for a positive science of language, Saussure and his followers failed to incorporate into their new science the study of prescriptivism itself. Prescriptivism, after all, is a universal fact of language. Of all human disciplines, none is as exacting as that of language. None demands as thorough and lengthy an education—an education, curiously, that is almost always successful. There is, in fact little choice: either one speaks correctly (within the "prescribed" limits of transgression) or one fails to speak—to communicate.
19. Naturalization itself is a consequence of a theory of language which views signification in terms of convention and words as tools for designating objects out there, which are

independent of them. Gadamer (1985: 366–78) finds the roots of the instrumental view of language in the *Cratylus*—a view that ignores the being of language (discourse, *logos*) itself and its revelatory nature.

20. Saussure 1966:14.
21. 111 LTR. 869 (1915).
22. Austin 1970.
23. Quoted in Ramm (1970:121).
24. Chafee 1981:41.
25. Davidson 1986.
26. Bloom 1992:222.
27. Bendroth 1993.
28. Eliot 1958:121.
29. Yeats 1959:184–85; Robert Bork (1996) picks up on Yeats's poem and, as we shall see, distorts it for his own political purposes.

CHAPTER 1: ELECTION

1. Gallup 1981; Time Logo 149 (18), May 5, 1997.
2. Gallup 1983; 1995. Roper puts angel believers at 76 percent (Roper Angel Survey, 1997).
3. Though there appears to be an increase in evangelical Christianity, Gallup polls show that most patterns of religious belief and practice have held steady since the early seventies, when America's religious commitment was slightly higher. Church attendance has been stable for the last sixty years. Recent polls show that nine out of ten American adults have a religious preference and attend church on some occasions. Two thirds are affiliated with a church or synagogue. Sixty percent consider religion to be important in their lives, but only 40 percent percent attend church regularly.

   Eighty-seven percent of Americans say they belong to one of four major Christian groups: 58 percent Protestant; 27 percent Roman Catholic; 1 percent Mormon; 1 percent Eastern Orthodox. Of the Protestants, 19 percent claim affiliation with one or another Baptist church; 9 percent are Methodist; 6 percent Lutheran; 5 percent Presbyterian; 3 percent Church of Christ; and 2 percent Episcopalian. Three percent are Jews. Five percent say they have no religious preference whatsoever. Church pews seat more blacks, elderly, and Republicans (Newport and Saad 1999). These figures contradict claims that there are as many as seventy million evangelicals in the United States today.
4. Ibid.:131.
5. I would like to note a parallel between the hero in a world destined by God and "America" as it was conceived of in nineteenth-century Protestant historical consciousness. George Bancroft, a well-known historian, was able to maintain a sense of Providence as an active force in shaping history at the same time that he acknowledged human causation and historical contingency. Contingency and human causation were, for him, woven into Providential design and heightened the awareness of divine over human power (Ross 1984:915). Many Fundamentalists hold something like this view of history until they are questioned, at which point they express an even more distinctly premodernist view in which the ultimate cause and meaning of historical events simply lies in God's hands.
6. Marsden 1980:4.

7. Ibid.:55–62. Marsden has noted the influence of Francis Bacon, Thomas Reid, and other Scottish Common Sense philosophers on Fundamentalism.

8. Fundamentalists are adamantly opposed to Arminians, who, like Methodists, stress free will over divine election.

9. Noll 1994:8

10. A 1997 Barna poll ("How Pastors View the Church") found that only one out of three evangelical churchgoers "had shared his/her faith in Christ with a non-Christian within the past 12 months."

11. Ammerman 1988:5.

12. Quoted in Marsden 1980:86.

13. Noll 1992:365.

14. Ibid.:227.

15. Bendroth (1993:20–21) quotes from Willard F. Mallalieu's article "Mr. Moody's Ministry to Men" which was published in Davenport's *Dwight L Moody: His Life and Labors*.

16. Marsden 1980:50.

17. Stocking 1987:12. See Ross (1984:924–25) for changes in historical understanding after the Civil War.

18. Marsden 1980:54.

19. Sandeen (1974;1970) argues that doctrinally the two movements were identical.

20. Marsden 1980:118–23.

21. The Stewarts founded the Bible Institute of Los Angeles (BIOLA) in 1908 and managed the massive free distribution of William E. Blackstone's *Jesus is Coming*.

22. Martin 1996:10.

23. This and the preceding quotation are quoted in Bendroth 1993:24.

24. Martin 1996:9.

25. Dayton 1987; Sandeen (1970).

26. Cox 1995a. Cox has been criticized for a simplistic separation of Pentecostalism from Fundamentalism, as well as for not giving sufficient attention to Pentecostal theology (LeMasters 1995).

27. Acts 2:1–4.

28. Dayton 1987:23.

29. Barna poll 1997 ("How Pastors View the Church").

30. Mark 16:17–18.

31. Anderson 1992:28.

32. Cox 1995:xv. According to the 1997 Barna poll ("How Pastors View the Church"), six out of ten pastors who described their churches as Fundamentalists described themselves as charismatic.

33. Most historians, like Anderson (1992), trace Pentecostalism back to an outbreak of speaking in tongues at the Topeka Bible College at the turn of the century. Dayton (1987) argues that its roots are much deeper.

34. Anderson 1992:66.

35. Ibid.:69.

36. Ibid.:68.

37. Cox 1995a.

38. MacArthur 1992:29–30 and passim.

39. Ibid.:30.

40. There are Pentecostalists like Russell Spittler, the provost of Fuller Theological Seminary, who argue for the development of a rigorous Pentecostalist theology.

41. Quoted in Martin 1996:11.
42. Ibid.:14.
43. Carpenter 1997:11.
44. Ibid.:9.
45. Hankins 1996.
46. Carpenter 1997:161–76.
47. Ibid.:24. Fuller's coverage jumped from 152 stations in 1939 to 456 in 1942. By 1925 ten percent of the more than 600 radio stations in the United States were owned and operated by religious organizations (Martin 1996:18).
48. Martin 1996:17–18.
49. Ibid.:16.
50. For comparison with black churches in South Africa, see Sunkler 1948.
51. Carpenter 1997:233–34.
52. Accurate figures are hard to obtain since many churches measure their membership in terms of church attendance, and often include one-time visitors in their figures.
53. Cox 1995b.
54. Ibid.
55. Bahnsen 1984:31;183.
56. Sandlin 1997.
57. Sandeen 1974:293–94.
58. FitzGerald 1986:163.
59. Robbin 1996.
60. Barr 1981:36.
61. Jakobson 1960.
62. Quoted in Smith 1920:165.
63. Several important Fundamentalist theologians of Ockenga's generation attended Harvard Divinity School (Carpenter 1997:190–92).
64. Barr 1981:40.
65. Enns 1989:167–68.
66. Barr 1981:290.
67. Johnson 1996.
68. Enns 1989:149.
69. Kaiser, in Kaiser and Silva 1994:203.
70. Ibid.:201–202.
71. McCartney and Clayton 1994:34.
72. Matt. 21:10–17; Mark 11:15–19; Luke 19:45–48.
73. John 2:13–17.
74. Ramm 1970:298.
75. Ramm 1970:123, emphasis added.
76. Ibid.:119. Kaiser and Silva (1994:9) note that since Ramm wrote *Protestant Biblical Interpretation* in 1956, "the changes in the way texts are understood have been nothing less than catastrophic."
77. Rosscup 1992:129.
78. John 10:1–6.
79. Thomas 1991:94.
80. Rev. 7:4.
81. Thomas 1991:95–96.
82. See Chapter Six of this volume for a discussion of original intentionalism.

83. Ramm 1970:115.
84. Thomas 1992:148.
85. Ramm 1970:128.
86. McCartney and Clayton 1994:115.
87. Ibid.
88. See, for example, Bultmann 1957a and 1857b.
89. Luke 11:38.
90. 1 Kings 20:31–32.
91. Ramm 1970:157.
92. Matt 18:21–35.
93. 2 Cor. 2:10.
94. FitzGerald 1986:158.
95. Barr 1981:67.
96. Ibid.
97. Paul's words occur in a letter to Timothy that has a strong imperative tone. He refers to Scripture in verse 3:16. Does he consider his own letters to be part of Scripture? Most scholars, Barr (1981:78–79) for one, argue that he is writing about the Old Testament and perhaps a few books of the New. In 2 Timothy 3:16, he is commenting on Scripture (as he understood it) with considerable performative force. He is saying something like, "I proclaim, I assert, I declare, I promise you that, that Scripture is inspired by God. . . ." Both by his qualification of Scripture, as inspired by God, and by the structure of his performative utterance (by the covert prefixes like "I proclaim" or "I promise that") he differentiates his words from "Scripture." Even if his words are included in Scripture, as inspired by God, as they were later, they would still have to be distinguished from "Scripture" (as he uses it in Timothy), for there they are metascriptural. They comment on Scripture, including, under the circumstances, his own words.
98. Like the Epistles to Timothy, Peter's epistles are marginal and his authorship questioned (Barr 1981:67).
99. See Ramm (1970:269–72) for a conservative discussion of these verses.
100. Enns 1989:154.
101. 1 Cor. 14:37; 1 Thes. 2:13.
102. 1 John 4:6. It is difficult to reconcile Enns's literalism with his paraphrase of this verse: "John too recognized that his teaching was from God; to reject his teaching was to reject God."
103. Jer. 11:21, 12:6.
104. Jer. 23:21, 32; 28:1–17.
105. Enns 1989:155.
106. Idem.
107. Van Til 1967:3.
108. Van Til 1967:77.
109. Ibid.:90; he cites Rom. 1:18–20.
110. Ibid.:108.
111. Ibid.:94.
112. Ibid.:99.
113. Ibid.:105; 94.
114. Ibid.:105n3.
115. FitzGerald 1986:164.

116. Van Til :101.
117. Ibid.:92–93.
118. Ibid.:101.
119. Idem.

CHAPTER 2: SANCTIFICATION

1. See McCartney and Clayton (1994:75–76) for discussion of these verses.
2. Ramm 1970:13. He refers to John 3:3 and to Angus and Green's *Cyclopedic Handbook of the Bible* 179.
3. Pink 1972:14, MacArthur 1993:256; see also Murray 1981 for Pink's biography.
4. Pink 1972:15.
5. Ibid.:14.
6. Ibid.:15–16; 1 Cor. 8:2.
7. Pink 1972:15–19.
8. Troeltsch 1992, vol. 2: 586.
9. Van Til 1967.
10. Keller 1985.
11. Rom. 7:14; 17–25.
12. Ryrie 1972:111.
13. Rom. 3:11–13.
14. MacArthur 1993:65.
15. Ibid.:58.
16. Ibid.:59–60.
17. Ibid.:61.
18. Some Fundamentalist theologians such as Adams distinguish between "need" and "desire" (1970:65n1). (Desire is sometimes equated with "drive.") Needs, they argue, must be fulfilled, while desires have to be subjected to biblically authorized self-control.
19. Col. 1.
20. Gal. 5:22.
21. Morris and Clark 1987:204–205.
22. 2 Peter 1.
23. MacArthur 1993:192.
24. Mat. 18:15–17.
25. Rom. 12:2.
26. MacArthur 1993:62.
27. Ibid.:261.
28. Enns 1989:332.
29. Lévi-Strauss 1967.
30. Enns 1989:150.
31. Hodge 1960, vol. 1:21, quoted in Enns 1989:147.
32. Enns 1989:151. He refers to Lewis Sperry Chafer's *Systematic Theology* and Millard J. Erickson's *Christian Theology*.
33. Enns 1989:149.
34. MacArthur 1993:62.
35. Foucault 1970.
36. Stromberg 1993.

37. Enns 1989:639.
38. Ibid.:175.
39. Pink 1972:97.
40. Stone 1992.
41. Hirsch 1976:79.
42. Zuck 1996.
43. Deut. 4:2.
44. Pink 1972:97.
45. Virkler 1996.
46. Ibid.:235–37.
47. Ibid.:237–38.
48. Eph. 4:24, cf. Col. 3:10–11.
49. Unlike Methodists, Fundamentalists insist that there can be no entire sanctification, or Christian perfection, in this world. See Dayton 1987 for a discussion of sanctification in Methodism, the Holiness movement, and Pentecostalism.
50. MacArthur 1993:89.
51. Ibid.:89–90.
52. Ibid.:109.
53. Rom. 6:17–18.
54. Ryrie 1969, 1989; Hodges 1989.
55. MacArthur 1993:87–121.
56. Ibid.:108.
57. 2 Pet. 2:4 and Rev. 19:20, respectively.
58. Rom 12:2; 8:29.
59. MacArthur 1993:130.
60. Rom. 7:15.
61. Miller 1961:56.
62. Billheimer 1977:89, quoted in Carter and Narramore 1979:30.
63. MacArthur 1994:132–33.
64. Some Fundamentalists argue that American Christians have lost touch with the practical wisdom — "the Shepherd's discerning love" — necessary for the cure of souls that had characterized earlier Protestant writers. They cite Thomas Brooks's *Precious Remedies Against Satan's Devices* (1652), Richard Baxter's *Christian Directory* (1672, 1673), John Bunyan's *Pilgrim's Progress* (1678, 1684), and Jonathan Edwards's *A Treatise Concerning Religious Affections* (1746). They are particularly impressed by the Puritans' insistence on man's depravity, their constant war against sin, and their commitment to Scripture as the source of all counseling. They echo Richard Sibbes's (1577–1635) observation "There is not anything or any condition that befalls a Christian in this life but there is a general rule in the Scriptures for it, and this rule is quickened by example." J. I. Packer, one of the most literate of conservative evangelical theologians, contrasts the Puritans favorably with contemporary evangelicals with respect to their "passion for spiritual integrity and moral honesty before God, their fear of hypocrisy in themselves as well as in others, and the humble self-distrust that led them constantly to check whether they had not lapsed into play-acting."
65. The biographical information that follows is from Powlison 1994.
66. Carter and Narramore 1979:133.
67. Adams 1970:xi–xxii.
68. Idem.

69. Adams 1970:128. Adams is referring here to Genesis 1:28 in the King James Version, where God tells Adam and Eve to "subdue" and "have dominion" over "every living thing that moveth on the earth." Fundamentalists frequently quote Genesis 1:28, but I have never heard them use it to justify social and political engagement or activism. Noble 1997 notes that evangelical scientists often refer to it to justify their research.
70. Adams 1970:128–29.
71. Ibid.
72. Ibid.:133–34.
73. Adams 1974.
74. Ibid.:30–31.
75. Morris and Clark 1987.
76. Adams 1970:48.
77. Ibid.:58.
78. Ibid.:46; 2 Sam. 11–12.
79. Powlison 1994:51n19.
80. Adams 1970:199.
81. Ibid.:231–36.
82. Ibid.:18; 59–62.
83. Rom. 15:15–16.
84. Adams 1970:117n1.
85. Mack 1994a.
86. Mack is referring to 1 Sam. 21:10–15.
87. Mack 1994b.
88. Ibid.:200.
89. Adams 1970:199n1.
90. Ibid.:213.
91. Ibid.:131–37.
92. Mack 1994b:205.
93. Adams 1970:216.

CHAPTER 3: HISTORY

1. Kaiser and Silva 1994:197–98.
2. Bacon 1937:144.
3. Ong 1982:119.
4. Augustine 1961:114.
5. Ong 1982:119.
6. Lindsey 1977:48–60.
7. Kaiser and Silva 1994:156.
8. Payne 1973:631–82, quoted in Kaiser and Silva 1994:139–40.
9. Von Rad 1965:77–88. Von Rad's notion of cultic time, based on W. F. Otto's analysis of the Greek festival, is from a contemporary anthropological perspective questionable. His recognition of different coexisting and potentially conflicting notions of time in ancient Israel is, however, important. In stressing Christ's Second Coming over his first, do Fundamentalists give greater allegiance to linear time than do Christians who focus on His first historical appearance, commemorating it "cultically" in communion services?
10. Brueggemann 1978.

11. Ramm 1970:244–45.
12. Girdlestone 1955:48.
13. Ramm 1970:255.
14. McCartney and Clayton 1994:220.
15. Ibid.:219.
16. Ibid.:219–20.
17. Ibid.:220.
18. Ramm 1970:247–48.
19. Liberal theologians often understand the events recounted in the historical books of the Bible to be at once "verifiably historical" (*historisch*) and historical (*geschichtlich*); that is, they are at once events that have actually occurred and "events" that figure in a redemptive understanding of history (Cullmann 1964:99, referring to Martin Kähler's 1892 *Der sogenannte historische Jesus und der geschichtliche biblische Christus*). Given their literalism, the Fundamentalists would not be able to make this distinction.
20. Mat. 24:30–31.
21. McCartney and Clayton 1994:221.
22. Ibid.:220.
23. They list and often count the occurrence of formulaic expressions that mark the presence of prophecy: for example, "in the latter days," "the Lord comes," "the dwelling of God is with man," or "the kingdom of God" (Kaiser and Silva 1994:151–52).
24. Harding 1992a.
25. Ibid.:43.
26. Ibid.:54.
27. Ibid.:43.
28. Ibid.:44.
29. Ibid.:51.
30. Harding 1992. See pp. 60–61 for the account of witnessing Susan.
31. Ibid.:63–64; 66–72.
32. Ibid.:72.
33. Ibid.:73.
34. Coleridge 1907:6.
35. Frei 1974, Boone 1989:50.
36. Sowers 1965:89, quoted in McCartney and Clayton (1994:153). See Ross 1984:918) for the way in which typological thinking affected the nineteenth-century American conception of history. She relates this to Bercovitch's (1978) understanding of the role of types in the Puritan thought about mission.
37. Pink 1972:29.
38. Luke 24:44.
39. John 5:39.
40. Heb. 10:1.
41. Rom. 5:14; Peter 3:21.
42. Ramm 1970:217–18. He mentions among other typologically suggestive words *hupodeigma* (a sign suggestive of anything, a representation, a figure, a copy), *tupos* and *tupikos* (the mark formed by a blow, an impression), *skia* (from *skene*, a tent, meaning a shade, sketch, an adumbration), *parabole* (a likeness), *eikon* (an image); and *antitupon* (a repelling blow, an echoing, a reflecting, a counterpart). He even mentions *allegoreo*, which he glosses as "to tell a truth in terms of a narrative."
43. Ramm 1970:223. Stanley Fish (1980:272–73) puts it this way: typology "is not, at least

in its Protestant version, allegorical because it insists on respecting the historical reality of the type who is unaware of his significance as an anticipation of one greater than he."

44. Ramm 1970:231.
45. Ibid.:216. Torm lived 1870–1953.
46. McCartney and Clayton 1994:153–54.
47. Pink 1972:28.
48. Eric's observation is a version of an oft-repeated aphorism in Fundamentalist circles: "The prophets wrote better than they knew." Among others, Kaiser criticizes it as he ends up admitting its truth (Kaiser and Silva 1994:146). See Gadamer (1975:484ff.) for a discussion of the reader's superior knowledge to that of the author.
49. McCartney and Clayton 1994:154.
50. Tolstoy 1970:1.
51. Ibid.
52. Carol Greenhouse suggests that the two visions of time are always intertwined. The linearity of time "reproduces both the cry for redemption and redemption's form in the fundamental proposition that the individual can find completion only by participating in a cosmic order—through social institutions that award the end of time" (Greenhouse 1989:1636). She notes, however, that linear time cannot fulfill its redemptive completion without borrowing from the cyclical. See also Greenhouse 1996.
53. Cullmann 1964:52–54, 81–93.
54. Eliade 1971:111.
55. Morris and Clark 1987:333.
56. Both this citation and the following one are from the King James Version.
57. Morris and Clark 1987:334.
58. Ibid.:334–36.
59. Ibid.:82.
60. Hugh Ross, the founder of Reasons to Believe, a creationist think tank near Pasadena, California, who has a doctorate in astronomy from the University of Toronto, argues the extradimensionality of the God's wisdom from a literalist reading of the Bible. He cites, for example, 2 Timothy 1:9 (New International Version [NIV]): "This grace was given us in Jesus Christ before the beginning of time . . ." and Titus 1:2 (NIV), "God who does not lie, promised [the hope of eternal life] before the beginning of time." He comments: "Paul states here that our time dimension had a beginning and implies that God created our time dimension. These verses tell us that God engaged in cause and effect behavior before our time dimension existed. Thus, there must be at least the equivalent of a second dimension of time for God" (Ross 1996:42). Elsewhere he (1996:13) speaks of "God's mind-boggling capacities" to grasp the "mind-boggling eleven (the newly proven *minimum*) dimensions of reality."
61. The Fundamentalists I talked to did not speculate about the nature of eternity; they stressed our inability to grasp it. They spoke at times of eternity as timeless, as outside time, and at others, more frequently in my experience, as in unending time. See Cullmann (1964:61–68) for a discussion of the difference between primitive Christianity's notion of eternity as within time but of unlimited duration and the Greek (at least Platonic) notion in which, as timelessness, it is qualitatively different from time.
62. Strictly speaking, dispensationalists understand the unity of Scripture in terms of the glorification of God. Covenant theologians stress salvation—a position the dispensa-

tionalists find man-centered. Covenant theology teaches that God made a covenant of works with Adam, which promised him eternal life for his obedience and death for his disobedience. Because of Adam's disobedience, God made a second covenant, that of grace, through which sin and death would be overcome. Dispensationalists argue that covenant theology simplifies God's changing relationship with man.

63. Booth 1984.

64. Frei 1984.

65. Enns 1989:517.

66. Ibid.:516.

67. Barr 1981:191. I have been told that Oxford University Press, which published the Bible, has no reliable record of its sales.

68. Scofield's dispensations are: (1) innocence (before the Fall); (2) conscience (between the Fall and the Flood); (3) human government (between the Flood and Babel); (4) promise (with the call of Abraham); (5) law (with Moses receiving the law); (6) grace (roughly with the death of Christ); and (7) the personal reign of Christ (with the Second Coming).

69. Dispensationalism was not always confined to premillennialism. According to Walvoord (1959:223), Augustine was an amillennial dispensationalist and Charles Hodge, the nineteenth-century conservative theologian, whose influence is still felt in Fundamentalist circles, a postmillennialist one.

70. Ladd 1956. They are often called "historic premillennialists."

71. Ibid.:5.

72. Walvoord 1959:134.

73. See Boone 1989:53, 57–60, for a discussion of Falwell's and Pat Robertson's premillennial stance.

74. See also Walvoord 1959:159–73.

75. MacArthur 1994:219.

76. Lindsey 1970:111.

77. God's progressive revelation through history and deed parallels the reader's progressive understanding of the Scripture.

78. Kaiser and Silva 1994:143.

79. Ryrie 1995:161–81.

80. Ladd 1967:184.

81. The German philosopher of history, Karl Lowith (1949:18, 183–84) recognizes an implicit cicularity in the future orientation of Christian philosophies of history. The future, the *eschaton*, is understood as a return to the beginning, the *arche*. "Everything is from God and to God through Jesus Christ as mediator."

82. Greenhouse (1996:181) probably does not make enough of the difference between infinity and eternity in her otherwise quite brilliant discussion of time and history and their relationship to the political and social orders.

83. The level of anxiety concerning the year two thousand is well illustrated by the fact that as of January 1999 there were 761,039 websites devoted to the millennium (Martin 1999).

84. Friedrich 1982:12.

85. I am deriving this picture from what people say and do in everyday life and how they describe temporality. I have no doubt that their secular sense of history slips into a providential mode in moments of crisis, remorse, and prayer, even those "secular prayers" uttered by unbelievers when they wish intensely for something to happen.

86. Greenhouse 1989:1633.
87. See Ross (1984:910) for a discussion of historicism.
88. *McLean v. Arkansas* is cited in Numbers (1993:351n10), who refers to its reprint in LaFollette, *Creationism, Science, and the Law*, pp. 45–73.
89. Numbers 1993:x, 41–44.
90. Frair and Davis 1983:57–58.
91. In his foreword (p. 7) to Frair and Davis 1983.
92. Morris 1984:261.
93. Ibid.:260.
94. These presuppositions contrast with the gradualism of traditional theories of evolution. Indeed, as much as they differ from him, creationists sometimes support their position by invoking Gould's (1965; see also Morris 1984:305–306) "punctuated equilibrium" approach to evolution. They contest the uniformitarian assumptions of geology and all datings based on them. Morris (1984:261) lists the following three uniformitarian assumptions: (1) the process used must always have operated at the same rate at which it functions today; (2) the system in which the process operates must always have functioned as a closed system throughout its history; (3) the initial condition of the various components of the system, when it first began to function at a constant rate in a closed system, must be known.
95. Morris insists that dating according to geological strata is questionable because we have no way of knowing that the formation of geological strata proceeded at a uniform rate. In any event, he argues, its justification is based on circular reasoning: the age of the strata, which determines the sequence of fossils, is itself determined by the stage of evolution of the fossils found in it!
96. Frair and Davis 1983:67.
97. Morris 1984:91.
98. Ibid.
99. Ibid.:189.
100. Ibid.:204–10.
101. Ibid.:190–91.
102. Ibid.:214–15.
103. Ibid.:215.
104. See Numbers 1992 for a discussion of Morris's significance among creationists.
105. Koselleck 1985:3–20.

CHAPTER 4: THE CONSTITUTION

1. September 15, 1987, pp. 180–82. Hereafter all references to these Hearings will be given as Bork Hearing with appropriate pagination.
2. See Adler (1987:17) for a discussion of the multiple uses of "judicial restraint" (as well as "judicial deference," "original intent," "laissez-faire," and "conservative") at the time of the Hearings.
3. Bronner 1989:352.
4. Ibid.:80.
5. Adler 1987:20; see also Adler 1987a.
6. Bronner 1989:348.
7. The Marshall quote is from *Marbury v. Madison* (5 U.S. [1 Cranch] 137 [1803]). See Adler (1987a) for a more detailed critique of Bork's position on these issues.

8. Quoted in Bronner 1989:98–99.
9. Pertschuk and Schaetzel 1989:5–6.
10. *Oil, Chemical, and Atomic Workers International Union v. American Cyanamid Company* (741 F. 2nd 444 [D.C. Cir. 1984]).
11. All quotations are from Greenhouse 1997.
12. Pertchuck and Schaetzel 1989:15.
13. The clear and present danger doctrine, which was first formulated in *Schenk v. U.S.* (249 U.S. 47 [1919]), provides that government restrictions on "First Amendment freedoms of speech and press will be upheld if necessary to prevent grave and immediate danger to interests which the government may lawfully protect" (Black's Law Dictionary, 6th ed.).
14. Senate Judiciary Committee Executive Report 100–7 (1987):93. See Greenhouse (1996:175–210) for a fascinating analysis of the multiple temporalities in which Bork situated himself and was situated by the Hearings.
15. Bronner 1989:232.
16. See Kerenyi 1959:100 and passim for a discussion of the mythic association of the doctor, curing, and death.
17. Cover 1995.
18. All references in this paragraph are to Greenhouse 1996:185–87. See also Adler (1987a), commenting on Rehnquist's *The Supreme Court: How It Was, How It Is.*
19. Greenhouse also notes that, unlike presidents, justices are not inaugurated. No emphasis is given to their "becoming," their passage into justiceship. I would argue that the congressional hearings serve and have always served as a rite of passage.
20. Brennan 1998:15.
21. Posner 1990:12.
22. Graglia 1990:45.
23. Graglia's phrasing — the community speaking for itself through its representatives — calls attention to the ambiguities inherent in "representative" and by extension "representation," to democracy's Achilles' heel. Do representatives in fact speak for their community? Do they represent the "community speaking for itself"? What does "a community speaking for itself" mean? Graglia confuses two different but intertwined senses of representation, the cognitive and the political. The members of a legislature may well represent us politically, that is, vote in our stead for what *they* take to be our will, without re-presenting, or speaking, our views — our will — in any way we would recognize. Any representation of a people's view or will is always an artifice if only because it collectives the views of many with often startling different points of view. We may try to justify this collectivization on numerical grounds, through polling or counting letters, or on exemplary grounds, by allowing a "representative" individual to speak for the people, but polling always preframes its answer and is therefore presumptive, and exemplification is usually simply a displacement. Every writer, journalist, and politician knows the rhetorical advantages of uttering his or her opinions through another. Projection and personification are old rhetorical devices. Legislators as well as judges inevitably speak oracularly. The difference is, as Graglia and other conservatives worry, that judges — at least justices in the Federal courts — are not elected but appointed for life. But does that necessarily make them less capable of voicing the "people"? Graglias, Borks, and Scalias notwithstanding, an equally sound case can be made that, removed from politicking if not politics, they may be more sensitive to the "people" and less subject, as the Framers thought, to political pressure. See Pitkin 1967 for a brilliant discussion of representation.

24. Black 1969:66.

25. Jefferson 1984:1401–02.

26. Horwitz 1993:34.

27. Ibid.:33.

28. Brisbin 1997; Bork 1996.

29. Stone et al. 1996:785–86. See, among others, Powell 1990, Lofgren 1990, and Rakove 1990 for the discussion of Framers' versus ratifers' intention.

30. Posner 1990:140.

31. Stone 1996:786.

32. Cover 1995, Ackerman 1991; Unger 1986; Minow 1990; Cornell 1992. Many feminist legal theorists have taken far more radical and socially sensitive positions than the advocates of Critical Legal Studies and postmodernist approaches to the law. See, for example, Binion 1991; Frug 1992; Smart 1989; West 1988; Young 1990.

33. Posner 1990.

34. Black 1960:874.

35. Ibid.:879.

36. 381 U.S. 479 (1965).

37. Ibid.:522.

38. Black 1960:881.

39. Ibid.:879–80.

40. For a readable account of change in the interpretation of common, statutory, and constitutional law, see Levi 1949.

41. See, for example, *Duncan v. Louisiana* (391 U.S. 145 [1968]) for a summary of decisions to that date. In an important dissent in *Adamson v. California* (332 U.S. 46 [1947]), Black argued that the first section of the Fourteenth Amendment made the entire Bill of Rights applicable to the states. That section reads: "No State shall make or enforce any law which shall abridge the privileges or immunities of citizens of the United States; nor shall any State deprive any person of life, liberty, or property, without due process of law; nor deny to any person within its jurisdiction the equal protection of the laws." Black's total incorporation argument has never been accepted by the court. Interestingly, Frankfurter argued against Black in *Adamson* on literalist grounds: "The short answer to the suggestion that the [due process clause of the Fourteenth Amendment] was a way of saying that every State must thereafter initiate prosecutions through indictment by a grand jury, must have a trial by jury of twelve in criminal cases, and must have a trial by such a jury in common law suits where the amount in controversy exceeds twenty dollars, is that it is a strange way of saying it. *[Those] reading the English language with the meaning which it ordinarily conveys [would] hardly recognize the Fourteenth Amendment as a cover for the various explicit provisions of the first eight Amendments . . .*" (emphasis added). See Berger 1997.

42. 5 U.S. [1 Cranch] 137 (1803). Ackerman (1991) argues that certain of the court's decisions, those surrounding the New Deal, for example, are of such magnitude that they are equivalent to amendments.

43. Jefferson's position in his letter to Kercheval seems on first consideration to contradict his originalist approach to the law. He was critical of dynamic conceptions of English law and argued for a "plain meaning" understanding of constitutional language (Horwitz 1993: 48–49). No doubt he would have argued that it is precisely because of the need to follow the original intent of the Framers that periodic review and revision are necessary.

44. Little is known of Kercheval. He was a deputy sheriff in Frederick (now Clarke) County, Virginia, a member of the Virginia House of Deputies, and an unsuccessful candidate for Congress (Wayland 1925).
45. Jefferson 1984:959–64.
46. Horwitz (1971) argues that in eighteenth-century America common law was not regarded as an instrument of legal change.
47. Arendt 1973:232.
48. Quoted in ibid.:23.
49. Ibid.:145.
50. Quoted in ibid.:300f8.
51. Quoted in Wood 1969:127.
52. Ibid.:128.
53. Ibid.:306–43; Rakove 1990. See Caplan (1988) for the history of constitutional and other constitutive conventions.
54. Preston 1893:252.
55. Roche 1987.
56. Ibid.:179.
57. Arendt 1973:84.
58. See Kay 1987:57–58, for example. Levinson (1988:130) likens the Founders' act to Abraham's smashing idols and rejecting traditional understandings.
59. Greenhouse (1996:181) understands kingly succession in terms of the conflict between time and eternity. She notes (via Kantorowicz 1957) that secular monarchies resolved the contradiction between an enduring kingship and a mortal king with the notion of "the king's two bodies"—with the distinction between the office of the king and the occupant of the office. "When both the king's mortal person and the enduring kingship were embraced within a single institutional form, the state's claim to constitute in itself a body of enduring principles were insulated from the most unpredictable aspects of succession."
60. See Arendt's *On Revolution* (1973), which initiates the debate; Derrida's (1986) "Declarations of Independence," which is provoking but superficial; Honig's (1991) comparison of Arendt and Derrida; and Lee's (1997:321–45) analytic synopsis of the debate. Fliegelman's (1993) discussion of orality and the Declaration of Independence and Warner's (1990) of the contemporary understanding of print media and the writing of the Constitution are also of interest. Maier (1997:47–59) has recently observed that the Declaration of Independence was not as unique a document as it has come to seem. It was part of a tradition of declarations and declarations of independence, including state and local ones. My own discussion is indebted to all of these writers, though I part company with all of them insofar as they focus on discursive practices and texts without giving them sufficient contextualization. None of them has attempted to relate the paradoxes of constituting a government or an independent people to the sacralization of the ensuing document, the Constitution or the Declaration of Independence, and the heroizing of the authors of such a document.
61. In reaction to the expanding power of Tudor and Stuart monarchies, there arose in seventeenth-century England the idea that England had had an ancient but lost constitution that restricted monarchical power. It was at this time that the Magna Carta was resurrected and given prominence. It was also assumed, by Whig originalists, that the Normans had corrupted the just system of Anglo-Saxon common law (Horwitz 1993:44–45).

62. See Maier (1997:59 – 96) for the history of the mobilization of the people — and for the diversity of concerns about the declaration and independence. I am restricting my argument to the textual as it determines the way the declaration came to be read and used rhetorically.

63. For a concise, relevant statement of this position, see the opening paragraphs of Hamilton's *Federalist 31* (Madison et al. 1987:216 – 17).

64. Wood 1969: 18.

65. Quoted in idem.

66. Ibid.:329 – 30.

67. Ibid.:607.

68. Madison et al. 1987:124.

69. Wood 1969:608.

70. Ibid.:606 – 13.

71. Ibid.:612.

72. Quoted in ibid.:613.

73. Lutz 1995:238 – 39.

74. Caplan 1988:14.

75. Lutz 1995:240.

76. Ibid.:240.

77. Griffin 1995:49 – 50.

78. Caplan 1988:27 – 32; Vile 1993:127 – 28.

79. Weber and Perry 1989:55.

80. Ibid.

81. Ibid.:105 – 25.

82. It was the threat of such a convention that finally moved a recalcitrant Senate to approve an amendment, the Seventeenth, for the direct election of senators. Between 1893 and 1911, thirty states (one shy of the required two thirds majority) filed seventy-three petitions for a convention to propose such an amendment. Finally, on May 13, 1912, responding to public pressure, the Senate gave in (Weber and Perry 1989:61).

83. Rovere 1979:137.

84. Vile 1993:130-31.

85. Ibid.

86. Quoted in ibid.:131.

87. Ibid.

88. Ibid.:132 – 33.

89. Madison et al. 1987:313 – 14.

90. Quoted in Caplan 1988:34.

CHAPTER 5: FOUNDATIONS

1. Grey 1984:17.

2. Leary (1999:34) gives the full year figure.

3. Levinson 1988:13.

4. These examples are all taken from ibid.:9 – 14.

5. I use one of the many self-characterizations that Henry James used in *The American Scene* (1993). Though his description of America is rife with stereotypes, unlike many students of American society, he had the good sense to recognize their tentativeness and the instability of his own stance.

6. Levinson 1988:4.
7. Ibid.:6–7.
8. Ibid.:193.
9. Ibid.:16–17. Levinson is playing on Matthew 16:18–19. See, among others, Goebel (1931) for a discussion of the relationship between Puritanism's biblicism and the law.
10. Perry 1985:558. See also p. 562: "[T]he sacred text is normative for a religious community, and the foundational text [the Constitution] for a political community, in a way that the literary text is not normative for an interpretive community."
11. Ibid.
12. Ibid.:559.
13. The literalist looks back, according to Perry (ibid) to past normative judgments. This may be true of legal fundamentalists, but it is not necessarily true for Fundamentalists who look behind, prophetically, as they look forward.
14. Ibid.:564.
15. Ibid.:567–68.
16. Grey 1984:16.
17. Ibid.:14.
18. Technically, I am stressing the appellative dimension of the pragmatic function of language. I am arguing that the felicity conditions of performative, or constitutive, acts are not as autonomous as Austin's examples suggest. His favored examples (marriage, christening) are highly ritualized, relatively infrequent, and resistant to change. Most performatives do elicit conditions felicitous of their performance—up to a point.
19. Weber and Perry 1989:81.
20. Grey 1984:23.
21. Ibid.
22. Tribe and Dorf 1991:9.
23. 5 U.S. (I Cranch) 137 (1803).
24. I recognize that my observations are inevitably determined by my linguistic understanding, which is necessarily "contemporary." I will make no attempt to discuss Jacques Derrida's notion of writing, *écriture*, as encompassing, indeed precipitating, speech. I do note, however, the anxiety that derives from the "absence" of a "live and present" interlocutor in writing, as well as from the author's loss of connection with what he has written. Derrida 1967; Blanchot 1955:13–32.
25. 517 U.S. 620, 636 (1996).
26. Hearings before the Committee of the Judiciary, U.S. Senate, 99th Congress, 2d session, on the Nomination of Judge Antonin Scalia to be Associate Justice of the U.S. Supreme Court: 1987; p89.
27. 413 U.S. 528, 534 (1973).
28. 17 U.S. (4 Wheat) 316 (1918).
29. See Chapter Six for a discussion of precedent.
30. 250 U.S. 616 (1919).
31. Justice Clarke who wrote for the court based his argument on two of Holmes's earlier opinions that year: *Schenck v. United States* (249 U.S. 47 [1919]) and *Frohwerk v. United States* (249 U.S. 204 [1919]).
32. Levi 1949:32.
33. See Lasser 1998 for comparison between the two systems at the appellate level.
34. Quoted in Schell 1973.

35. *Oregon v. Mitchell* (400 U.S. 112, 202–203 [1970]). Both Santarelli (in part) and Harlan are from Berger (1997:351, 352, respectively).

36. Even in their theoretical writing, legal scholars seem always to be arguing against someone, in some (imagined) context. This is noteworthy and jarring to the literary critic in their writings about literature. See particularly Posner 1998, where the literary text is often little more than a figure for some argument between critical approaches, most notably between deconstruction and New Criticism.

37. Quoted in Cover 1975:119.

38. 2 Western L. J. (Ohio, 1845), quoted in Cover 1975:120–21.

39. Legal Realists like Frank (1950:157–64) stressed the "psychological element" in a judge's decision. They did not suggest, to my knowledge, that "deep readings" of opinions are a way to uncover these elements

40. Quoted in Berger (1997:21) from *Table Talk: Being the Discourses of John Selden, Esq.* (1606).

41. Berger 1997:339.

42. Ibid.:457.

43. The privileges or immunities clause reads: "No State shall make or enforce any law which shall abridge the privileges or immunities of citizens of the United States." The due process clause is: "nor shall any State deprive any person of life, liberty, or property, without due process of law." It relates back to a similar clause in the Fifth Amendment.

44. The equal protection clause is a continuation of the due process clause: "nor deny to any person within its jurisdiction the equal protection of the law."

45. 347 U.S. 483 (1954).

46. 369 U.S. 186 (1962).

47. 377 U.S. 533 (1964).

48. 410 U.S. 113 (1973).

49. Berger 1997:457.

50. Ibid.:428.

51. Quoted in ibid.:23–24, n24.

52. Ibid.:11.

53. Ibid.:11n34.

54. Ibid.:12.

55. "One never has more power than when one has so successfully appropriated the symbols of authority that one's actions are not seen as exercises of power at all, but simply expressions of sound pragmatic common sense"(Gordon 1984:112, quoting S. Lukes, *Power: A Radical View*).

56. Madison et al. 1987:439.

57. Warner 1990.

58. Beger 1997:7.

59. Ibid.:7n20. The distinction between fact and opinion plays an important role in the law—in terms of what is permissible evidence, for example, in cases involving defamation. In *Hustler Magazine v. Falwell* (485 U.S. 46 [1988]), the respondent argued (in Chief Justice Rehnquist's words) that so "long as the utterance was intended to inflict emotional distress, was outrageous, and did in fact inflict serious emotional distress, it is of no constitutional import whether the statement was a fact or an opinion, or whether it was true or false. It is the intent to cause injury that is the gravamen of the tort, and the State's interest in preventing emotional harm simply outweighs whatever

interest a speaker may have in speech of this type." That the distinction between fact and opinion may function one way in the law does not mean that it should function in the same way in history.

60. See my discussion of court speech in Crapanzano (1992:292ff.).

61. Gordon 1984:57. Gordon ignores Critical Legal Studies, whose position is influenced by Marxism.

62. Gordon 1984:59.

63. Ibid.:67. Legal realism refers to a school of jurisprudence popular in the thirties and forties of this century, which sought to view the law through the social and psychological sciences — and to develop therefrom more "realistic" bases for legal argumentation and decision.

64. Scalia 1997:29–37. Scalia (1997:38) says that he uses the *Federalist Papers* to determine not intent but the way the Constitution was originally understood.

65. See Jakobson (1981:66–69) for a discussion of the way in which Berger has misread Hamilton.

66. Berger 1997:4.

67. Ibid.:8n24.

68. 17 U.S. (4 Wheat) 316 (1819).

69. Berger 1997:428.

70. Berger (ibid.:313) quotes, favorably, a letter the Massachusetts House wrote to Lord Shelbourne in 1768: "There are, my Lord, fundamental rules of the Constitution . . . which neither the supreme Legislative nor the supreme executive can alter. In all free states, the *constitution is fixed*; it is from thence, that the legislative derives its authority; therefore it cannot change the constitution without destroying its own foundation."

71. Ibid.:430.

72. Ibid.:431.

73. It is noteworthy that Marshall's words occur after a discussion of the meaning of "necessary and proper" in Article I, Section 8, of the Constitution: "The Congress shall have the power . . . to make all law which shall be necessary and proper for carrying into execution the foregoing powers. . . ." In this often-quoted discussion, Marshall observes: "Such is the character of human language, that no word conveys to the mind, in all situations, one single definite idea; and nothing is more common than to use words in a figurative sense. Almost all compositions contain words which, taken in their rigorous sense, would convey a meaning different from that which is obviously intended. . . ." He goes on to compare the use of "necessary" in the above-cited clause with its use in Article I, section 10: "No state shall, without the consent of Congress, lay any imposts or duties on imports or exports, except what may be absolutely necessary for executing its inspection laws. . . ." "Necessary," qualified by "absolutely" here, clearly increases "the impression the mind receives of the urgency it imports" in ways that it does not in Section 89. "This word, then, like others," Marshall concludes, "is used in various senses; and, in its construction, the subject, the context, the intention of the person using them, are all to be taken into view." Though Berger would probably have to agree with Marshall, he would emphasize the textual rather than the situational context in which the disputed word occurred. He is certainly in greater sympathy with Marshall's equally often-cited affirmation of "the plain import of words" in *Marbury v. Madison*, [(5 U.S. (1 Cranch) 137 (1803)] in which Marshall argued "that all those who have framed written constitutions contem-

plate them as forming the fundamental and paramount law of the nation." (Berger (1997:432–33 and elsewhere) quotes other of Marshall's dicta concerning language in which Marshall stresses literal and intentional meaning: *Ogden v. Saunders* (25 U.S. [12 Wheat.] 213 [1827], dissenting opinion); *Gibbons v. Ogden* (22 U.S. [9 Wheat.] 1 [1824]); *Osborn v. Bank of the United States* (22 U.S. [9 Wheat.] 738 [1824]); and *Providence Bank v. Billings* (29 U.S. [4 Pet] 514 [1830]).

74. Scalia 1997:23.

75. Wood 1997:63.

76. The process, at least in hard cases, is considerably more complicated than I have indicated here, for, the "preselection" and selection of precedent determines the way in which the circumstances of the case at hand is framed for interpretation. It is at this level of framing that the judge's personal views, his desires, can insinuate themselves "most unconsciously" into the decision process.

77. Horwitz 1993:46–48. By the last third of that century, however, a more dynamic view of the common law developed, which was dramatically halted in 1861 for a time when the House of Lords declared unconstitutional the court's overruling a prior case.

78. Scalia 1997:10–11.

79. Wood 1997:58–63.

80. Scalia 1997:23.

81. Ibid.:24.

82. Ibid.:24–25.

83. 60 U.S. (19 How.) 393 (1857). What I find ironic in the conservatives' obsessive citation of this most disastrous of Supreme Court decisions as an example of the abuses of the due process clause is their failure to see it also as an example of an abuse of the literalism they advocate. We must note, however, that aside from interpreting the due process clause in substantive terms, *Dred Scott* was the second case (*Marbury v. Madison* being the first) in the history of the Supreme Court in which the court exercised judicial review, by invalidating an act of Congress: the Missouri Compromise (Stone, Seidman, et al. 1996:504). There is apparently no limit to the ironic impurities of the law.

84. 143 U.S. 457 (1892); Scalia 1997:18–21. All quotations from the court's opinion are from Scalia's discussion.

85. Scalia 1997:22.

86. Ibid.

87. See Levi 1949 for examples.

88. Scalia 1989. See pp. 861–62n10 for Scalia's hypothetical case of cruel and unjust punishment.

89. *Smith v. U.S.* 508 U.S. 223 (1993) and *Maryland v. Craig* 497 U.S. 836 (1990). Harry Blackmun concurred with Scalia's dissent in *Smith*. Scalia was joined by William J. Brennan, Thurgood Marshall, and John Paul Stevens in his dissent in *Craig*. It is ironic that Scalia's literalism in these cases led him to a position that was supported by liberal members of the court, to whom he is usually opposed.

90. Once, Scalia notes (1997:41–42), we could elect one of the two houses of a state legislature the way the United States Senate is elected. Once we could admit in a state criminal trial evidence of guilt that was obtained by unlawful search; invoke God at public school graduations; terminate welfare payments as soon as evidence of fraud was given; impose property right as a condition of voting; prohibit anonymous campaign literature and prohibit pornography.

91. 18 U.S.C. 924(c)(1).

92. Strictly speaking, the Sixth Amendment does not specify that the confrontation take place in a courtroom during the trial, nor does it describe the nature of the confrontation. The full text reads: "In all criminal prosecutions, the accused shall enjoy the right to a speedy and public trial, by an impartial jury of the State and district wherein the crime shall have been committed, which district shall have been previously ascertained by law, and to be informed of the nature and cause of the accusation; to be confronted with the witnesses against him; to have compulsory process for obtaining witnesses in his favor, and to have the Assistance of Counsel for his defense."

93. I am addressing here, as in other cases I mention, only those arguments that are relevant to the author's hermeneutics.

94. "Because of this subordination of explicit constitutional text to currently favored public policy, the following scene can be played out in an American courtroom for the first time in two centuries: a father whose young daughter has been given over to the exclusive custody of his estranged wife, or mother whose young son has been taken into custody by the State's child welfare department, is sentenced to prison for sexual abuse on the basis of testimony by a child the parent has not seen or spoken to for many months; and the guilty verdict is rendered without giving the parent so much as the opportunity to sit in the presence of the child, and to ask, personally or through counsel, 'It is really not true, is it, that I — your father (or mother) whom you see before you — did these terrible things?' Perhaps that is a procedure today's society desires; perhaps (though I doubt it) it is even a fair procedure; but it is assuredly not a procedure permitted by the Constitution."

95. Scalia 1997:44.

96. Madison et al. 1987:439.

97. Lewis 1987.

98. Tribe 1987.

99. Dumont 1970:65–66 and passim.

100. See Crapanzano 1997 for a discussion of the original translation and certain Amerindian languages.

101. Jacobsohn 1981; Habermas 1973:82–120.

102. See Weaver 1998 for the discussion of an Egyptian case in which jurisdiction was manipulated in such a way as to declare a university scholar apostate. Muslim "fundamentalists" who were responsible for the charges found that by reading certain references in the Koran to angels, devils, genies, and the throne of God as metaphors, the defendant denied that the Koran was the word of God.

103. Kelsen 1945a:123.

104. 357 U.S. 449 (1958).

105. 381 U.S. 479 (1965).

106. See also Justice Stewart's dissent.

107. 371 U.S. 415 (1963).

108. In *Carey v. Population Services International* (431 U.S. 678 [1977]), in which the court invalidated a New York law prohibiting any person other than a licensed pharmacist to distribute contraceptives, Justice Brennan used another birth image: "Read in light of its progeny, the teaching of *Griswold* protects individual decisions in matters of childbearing from unjustified intrusion by the State" (p. 687). Whatever such imagery says about the individual psychology of the justices writing these decisions, it points to a symbolic-affective dimension of decision-making and writing that has to be

ignored in legal argument but certainly questions a judge, any judge's, ability to bracket off fully his own particular values in his allegiance to the letter of the law.

109. 410 U.S. 113 (1973).

110. 478 U.S. 186 (1986).

111. Kelsen 1945a:110ff. See also Hart's 1961 comparable notion of a rule of recognition.

112. Kelsen 1945a:116–17.

113. Dworkin 1985:72–103.

114. Kelsen 1945a:28–30.

115. In fact, Kelsen (ibid.:116) speaks of "the first constitution as a binding norm" in this context. Though he denies to his positivism a religious (or any other extralegal) justification, he argues in a fashion that parallels the religious, certainly the mythic, one. "The ultimate hypothesis of positivism is the norm authorizing the historically first legislator." That basic norm is equivalent to the presuppositions taken on faith by the religious. "The whole function of this basic norm is to confer law-creating power on the act of the first legislator [read, God] and on all the other acts based on the first act" (1945a:116). The same "patriarchal" style of argument is made whether we speak of God, the father of the Constitution, the first legislator authorized by God, and so on. One figure substitutes for another. The acceptance of the basic norm as a presupposition is equivalent to the acceptance of ultimate religious authority, or truth, as a presupposition. Acceptance in both instances rests on something like faith the justification for which — the clarity, the certainty — comes only after the acceptance. Do pure, formalistic theories of the law, like Kelsen's, have to have a theological structure?

116. Ibid.:xvi.

117. Ibid.:xvii.

118. Weisberg 1996. Weisberg (ibid.:xx) argues that one cannot understand the lawyers' passion for executing these laws simply in terms of anti-Semitism or entirely from their understanding of *the* law. Rather they were responding to a particularly (French) Catholic anti-Talmudism that combined traditional xenophobia with "the sense that the Jew's choice of a peculiar and 'non-French' approach to law somehow made reasonable and even necessary laws dealing with the Jew."

119. Crapanzano 1992; see espec. Introduction and Chapters Three and Four.

120. Cover 1995:203–38; Tribe 1987.

CHAPTER 6: INTENTION

1. Bork Hearings 1987:816–20.

2. Ibid.:107.

3. Meese 1990:17.

4. Brest 1980: 204.Lofgren (1990:118) notes that historians would not normally use "intention" in the contexts in which lawyers do but in its stead "understanding" or "expectation." Lofgren sidesteps the question of the difference between intention and understanding — and, here, expectation.

5. Note that Specter insists on referring to Bork's approach as original intent even after Bork describes it as original understanding.

6. Bork 1990:144.

7. See Hugo Black (quoted in Brest 1980:206): "It is a cardinal rule in the interpretation of constitutions that the instrument must be so construed as to give effect to the inten-

tion of the people, who adopted it. This intention is to be sought in the Constitution itself, and the apparent meaning of the words employed is to be taken as expressing it, except in cases where that assumption would lead to absurdity, ambiguity, or contradiction." Intention as a psychological condition or mental state may, of course, play a role in the consideration of the validity of legal transactions and criminal responsibility. In these cases, external measures of intention are often used because of the difficulty of proof or as a matter of social policy. They "treat certain forms of outward behavior as conclusive evidence of the existence of mental states or impute to an individual the mental state that the average man behaving in a given way would have had" (Hart 1983:96). Legal theorists do not usually compare intention in the interpretation of the law and in the execution of legal documents or criminal behavior.

8. Fish 1994, for example.

9. Duranti 1993.

10. Brest 1980:215–16.

11. Powell 1990:54.

12. Ibid.:62.

13. "Intentions" referred not to the aims of the Framers, Powell insists, but to those of the sovereign parties to what was then conceived of as a constitutional compact.

14. Powell 1990:73.

15. I am not doing justice to Powell's complex argument. The reader is referred to his discussion of the Alien and Sedition Acts, the Virginia and Kentucky Resolutions, and Madison and Jefferson's reformulation of the Constitution as a compact or contract between states. See Lofgren 1990 for a critical expansion of Powell's argument. For expository convenience, I have referred to the Framers' intentions in this summary of Powell's argument. It applies as well to the ratifiers' intentions.

16. Powell 1990:58, referring to Langton's *Fragments on the Morality of the Human Act* (ca. 1200 A.D.).

17. Dworkin (1986:345) argues that a statement of intention is "mainly a report rather than a performance." A promise has "mainly performative character and therefore a life of it own." I would take issue with Dworkin here. Neither a promise nor an intention is, strictly speaking, a performative. They describe or refer to the performatives: "I promise" and "I intend." There is no question that various kinds of performatives have different performative force. A vow is stronger than a promise, and a promise is stronger than an intention. It is true that an intention may be considered, in technical terms, a stative, referring to the mental or subjective condition of the intender, but I would argue that there is also a stative dimension to promises and vows, which support the performative force of the utterance, "I promise" or "I vow."

18. Dworkin 1985:34–57.

19. See Dworkin (1985:34–57) for his distinction between institutionalized and collective (psychological) intention.

20. Holmes 1963 [1881].

21. Posner (1990:168–86) proposes a behaviorist model that he claims would do away with mentalist considerations in criminal law. His argument rests on an altogether debatable means—ends, essentially economic rationalism, which fails to take sufficient account of the symbolic dimension of criminal cases and the moral outrage accompanying them.

22. Hart 1997:178.

23. Leyh 1992:277–82.

24. Posner 1990:176.
25. Ransom 1941.
26. Wimsatt and Beardsley 1992:945.
27. See Hirsch 1960.
28. See Hoy (1992:197nn1,2) and Knapp and Michaels (1992:197n1) for relevant bibliography.
29. Knapp and Michaels 1992:187.
30. Ibid.:196
31. Barthes 1977; Foucault 1977.
32. Barthes 1977:142.
33. Ibid.:146.
34. Ibid.:147.
35. Foucault 1977:127.
36. Ibid.:124–25.
37. Posner 1998:216–17. However, Posner (1998:382) invokes Foucault's notion of the author as a cultural artifact in his discussion of authorship and the law.
38. Bork 1996:268.
39. Bork (1990:217), who refers to Levinson (1988a:162).
40. Levinson 1988a:166.
41. Levinson 1988:191.
42. Hoy 1992:178.
43. I share this position with Searle (1969) though I recognize that our understanding and evaluation of intention reflects our person-centered culture. See Du Bois (1993), who challenges the assumption that intention is necessary criterion for meaningful language.
44. I exclude literary and philosophical denials of the assumption of intention, for their denial always presupposes the assumption they put into question.
45. Of course, we would have to examine exactly how British lawyers and judges and Hoy's sand-reader express their interpretations. We cannot simply accept what they say they do and say as what they in fact do and say.
46. By acknowledging the construction of intention, we avoid some of the difficulties concerning collective intention. We do not have to assume a group mind or spirit. We do not have to discover exactly what each framer thought the meaning and consequences of a particular clause in the Constitution were. We still do have to decide how we construct a collective intention. Do we take a head count, as Paul Brest suggested, and decide "democratically"? Do we construct it textually? Extratextually? That collective intentions are often cast in mental terms attests to the rhetorical power of our psychological idiom.
47. The above argument applies also to what Brest (1980:212) calls "interpretive intent," that is, the author's or Framer's stipulation of the canons by which the text should be read. Such instruction has to be regarded as part of the author's rhetoric, though, as in many legal codes which specify interpretive intent, it may be legally binding.

CHAPTER 7: PRECEDENT

1. Bork Hearings 1987:112–13.
2. Pertschuk and Schaetzel 1989:17.
3. Bork Hearings 1987:108.

4. Brown I:347 U.S. 483 (1954); see also Brown II:349 U.S. 294 (1955).
5. 163 U.S. 537 (1896).
6. See Bork (1971:12–15) for extensive comment.
7. 334 U.S. 1 (1948). See Bork (1971:15–17) for more extensive comments.
8. Stone, Seidman, et al. 1996:1717.
9. Bronner 1989:256.
10. I would maintain an illusory (or at least fragile, rhetorical) stability not only because the "past" is always shifting, despite its declared fixity, in our reinterpretations but because, in the (common) law at least, precedents can under certain, usually troubling circumstances be overturned. Greenhouse (1996:184) suggests that one of the several temporalities she attributes to the law is, like mythic time, reversible. I would argue that whatever the effect of the possibility of reversing a precedent is on our understanding of time, it is time's irreversible linearity — another of law's temporalities — that gives force to precedent. It is why its overturning is always so disturbing. This is reflected in the committee's reaction to Bork's raising its possibility. Such reversals are, in any case, never complete because they are rarely retroactive.
11. Dworkin 1986:24.
12. Given the often greater relevance of recent decisions, they may in fact prove more authoritative.
13. Even Jerome Frank (1970: 166–67), a leading Legal Realist, argued that as we cannot imagine the future except in terms of the present, we had better know the present as thoroughly as possible. "If the decision of a particular case takes the form of the enunciation of a rule with emphasis on its future incidence, the tendency will be to connect the past by smooth continuities with the future, and the consequence will be an overlooking of the distinctive novelties of the present." Frank notes that in focusing on the past (or the future), the law often neglects the case at hand.
14. In a series of articles, Lawrence Lessig (1993, 1995, 1997) attempts to articulate the relationship between original and contemporary meaning of a text in terms of translation. His argument is more refined than that of most of the originalists — or, for that matter, most aspirationalists — for it provides a model for how the relationship can be processually articulated. However, because Lessig's notion of fidelity of translation is not particularly rigorous, questions of fidelity of risk becoming a new idiom for the same old arguments between originalists and aspirationalists.
15. Dworkin 1986:88.
16. Quoted in Scalia 1997:11.
17. Frank 1970:159. For a more sober account of how lawyers manipulate precedent, see Frank 1950:275–82.
18. Tribe and Dorf 1991:72.
19. Dworkin 1996:24–26.
20. For challenges, see Dworkin 1996:25n21.
21. Bork 1971:27.
22. Frank 1970:159–66.
23. Dworkin 1985:1986.
24. Dworkin 1977:107.
25. Dworkin 1985:143.
26. Posner 1990:93.
27. Ibid.:133.
28. Ibid.:94–95.

29. Ibid.:88–98.
30. Ibid.:89.
31. In line with his distinction between informative and authoritative analogies, Posner distinguishes between precedent and *stare decisis*—a distinction that is not generally followed in the law.
32. See Fish 1994, where this argument is repeated at numerous points.
33. Posner 1990:98.
34. *New York Times*, July 23, 1987:A21.
35. Horwitz 1993:37n30.
36. Bork Hearings, 1987:289–90.
37. See Tushnet 1996 for a recent example, with bibliography.
38. Bork 1990:169–70.
39. It often tends to be masked in Anglo-American decisions. Hart (1983:133) notes, for example, that "when courts overrule some past decision, the later new decision is normally treated as stating what the law has always been, and as correcting a mistake, and is given a retrospective operation."
40. Tribe and Dorf 1991:54.

CONCLUSION

1. Montaigne 1958:815.
2. James (1984:563), from his review in *The Nation* (Jan. 14, 1875) of Charles Nordhoff's *The Communistic Societies of the United States, from Personal Visit and Observation.*
3. Dworkin 1986:11–15.
4. Bloom 1992; Harding 1991. See also Rosenberg 1989.
5. Hankins 1996.
6. FitzGerald 1986:158.
7. Ibid.:157.
8. Crapanzano 1992:293–95.
9. Crapanzano 1980.
10. Sloan 1994:52.
11. Ibid.:52.
12. Noble 1998.
13. Crapanzano 1996.
14. Malcolm 1997.
15. Compare FitzGerald's (1986:158–61) brief but telling description of education at Falwell's church.
16. See Nock (1961) for a discussion of the relationship between conversion and the exclusionist outlook of monotheism, of Christianity.
17. Twain 1982. Quotations are from pp. 920–21 and 1055.
18. From Stevens (1957: 502-503): "A Plain Sense of Things."

References

Abrams, M. H.
  1971 *Natural Supernaturalism: Tradition and Revolution in Romantic Literature.* New York: Norton.

Ackerman, Bruce
  1991 *We the People: Foundations.* Cambridge: Harvard University Press.

Adams, Jay E.
  1970 *Competent to Counsel: Introduction to Nouthetic Counseling.* Grand Rapids, Mich.: Zondervan.

  1974 *The Christian Counselor's Casebook.* Grand Rapids, Mich.: Zondervan.

Adler, Renata (Anonymous)
  1987 "Notes and Comment." *New Yorker* (Aug. 3):17–20.

  1987a "Coup at the Court." *The New Republic* (Sept. 14, 21):37–48.

Ammerman, Nancy Tatom
  1988 *Bible Believers: Fundamentalists in the Modern World.* New Brunswick: Rutgers University Press.

Anderson, Robert M
  1992 *Visions of the Disinherited: The Making of American Pentecostalism.* Peabody, Mass.: Hendrickson. [1979]

Arendt, Hannah
  1973 *On Revolution.* Harmondsworth: Penguin. [1963]

Augustine, Saint
  1958 *On Christian Doctrine.* New York: Macmillan.

  1961 *Confessions.* Hammondsworth: Penguin.

Austin, J. L.
  1970 *How to Do Things with Words.* New York: Oxford University Press.

Bacon, Francis
  1937 *Essays, Advancement of Learning, New Atlantis, and Other Pieces.* New York: Odyssey.

Bahnsen, Greg L.
  1984 *Theonomy in Christian Ethics.* Expanded ed. Phillipsburg, N.J.: Presbyterian and Reformed Publishing Company.

Barr, James
  1981 *Fundamentalism.* 2d ed. London: SCM Press.

Barthes, Roland
  1970 *Writing Degree Zero.* Boston: Beacon.

  1977 "The Death of the Author." Pp. 142–48. *Image, Music, Text.* New York: Hill and Wang. [1968]

Bendroth, Margaret Lamberts
  1993 *Fundamentalism and Gender, 1875 to the Present.* New Haven: Yale University Press.

Bercovitch, Sacvan
1978   *The American Jeremiad*. Madison: University of Wisconsin Press.

Berger, Raoul
1997   *Government by Judiciary: The Transformation of the Fourteenth Amendment*, 2d ed. Indianapolis, Ind.: Liberty Fund.

Billheimer, P.
1977   *Don't Waste Your Sorrows*. Fort Washington, Pa.: Christian Literature Crusade.

Binion, Gayle
1991   "Toward a Feminist Regrounding of Constitutional Law." *Social Science Quarterly* 72:207–20.

Black, Hugo
1960   "The Bill of Rights." *New York University Law Review* 35:865–81.

1969   *A Constitutional Faith*. New York: Knopf.

Blanchot, Maurice
1955   *L'Espace littéraire*. Paris: Gallimard.

Bloom, Harold
1992   *The American Religion: The Emergence of the Post-Christian Nation*. New York: Simon and Schuster.

Boone, Kathleen C.
1989   *The Bible Tells Them So: This Discourse of Protestant Fundamentalism*. Albany: State University of New York Press.

Booth, A. E.
n.d.   *The Course of Time*. Neptune, N.J.: Loizeaux Brothers.

Bork, Robert H.
1971   "Neutral Principles and Some First Amendment Problems." *Indiana Law Review* 47:1–35.

1990   *The Tempting of America: The Political Seduction of the Law*. New York: Free Press.

1996   *Slouching Towards Gomorrah: Modern Liberalism and American Decline*. New York: Regan Books (HarperCollins).

Brennan, William J., Jr.
1988   "The Constitution of the United States: Contemporary Ratification." Pp. 13–24. *Interpreting Law and Literature: A Hermeneutic Reader*. Ed. S. Levinson and S. Maillous. Evanston, Ill.: Northwestern University Press.

Brest, Paul
1980   "The Misconceived Quest for Original Understanding." *Boston University Law Review* 60:204–38.

Brisbin, Richard A., Jr.
1997   *Justice Antonin Scalia and the Conservative Revival*. Baltimore, Md.: Johns Hopkins University Press.

Bronner, Ethan
1989   *Battle for Justice: How the Bork Nomination Shook America*. New York: Norton.

Brueggemann, Walter
    1978   *The Prophetic Imagination.* Minneapolis: Fortress Press.

Bultmann, Rudolph
    1957a   *Kerygma and Myth: A Theological Debate.* Ed. Hans Werner Bartsch. London: SPCK.

    1957b   *Primitive Christianity in its Contemporary Setting.* New York: Meridian.

Caplan, Russell L.
    1988   *Constitutional Brinkmanship: Amending the Constitution by National Convention.* Oxford: Oxford University Press.

Carpenter, Joel A.
    1997   *Revive Us Again: The Reawakening of American Fundamentalism.* New York: Oxford University Press.

Carroll, Lewis (Charles Lutwidge Dodgson)
    1960   *The Annotated Alice: Alice's Adventures in Wonderland and Through the Looking Glass.* New York: Bramhall House. [1865]

Carter, John D. and Bruce Narramore
    1979   *The Integration of Psychology and Theology: An Introduction.* Grand Rapids, Mich.: Zondervan.

Chafee, Zechariah, Jr.
    1981   "The Disorderly Conduct of Words." Pp. 35–56. *Freedom's Prophet: Selected Writings of Zechariah Chafee, Jr.* Ed. E. D. Re. New York: Oceana Publications. [1941]

Coleridge, Samuel Taylor
    1907   *Biographia Literaria,* vol. 2. Oxford: Oxford University Press.

Connolly, John M. and Thomas Keutner, eds.
    1988   *Hermeneutics versus Science?* Notre Dame, Ind.: University of Notre Dame Press.

Cover, Robert
    1975   *Justice Accused: Antislavery and the Judicial Process.* New Haven: Yale University Press.

    1995   *Narrative, Violence, and the Law.* Ann Arbor: University of Michigan Press.

Cox, Harvey
    1995a   *Fire from Heaven: The Rise of Pentecostal Spirituality in the Twenty-first Century.* Reading, Mass.: Addison-Wesley.

    1995b   "The Warring Visions of the Religious Right." *The Atlantic Monthly*: 276 (Nov. 5):59–69.

Crapanzano, Vincent
    1980   *Tuhami: Portrait of a Moroccan.* Chicago: University of Chicago.

    1985   *Waiting: The Whites of South Africa.* New York: Random House.

    1992   *Hermes' Dilemma and Hamlet's Desire: On the Epistemology of Interpretation.* Cambridge: Harvard University Press.

    1994   Kevin: On the Transfer of Emotions. *American Anthropologist* 96(4):866–85.

1996   "Riflessioni, frammentarie sul corpo, il dolore, la memoria." Pp. 156–81. *Perchè il corpo: utopia, sofferenza, desiderio.* Ed. M. Pandolfi. Rome: Meltemi.

1997   "Translation: Truth or Metaphor. *RES* 32:45–51.

Cullmann, Oscar
1964   *Christ and Time: The Primitive Christian Conception of Time and History.* Rev. ed. Philadephia: Westminster Press.

Davidson, Donald
1986   "A Nice Arrangement of Epitaphs." Pp. 433–46. *Truth and Interpretation: Perspectives on the Philosophy of Donald Davidson.* Ed. E. Lepore. Oxford: Blackwell.

Dayton, Donald W.
1987   *Theological Roots of Pentecostalism.* Metuchen, N.J.: Hendrickson Publishers/Scarecrow Press.

Derrida, Jacques
1967   *L'Ecriture et la différence.* Paris: Seuil.

1986   "Declarations of Independence." *New Political Science* 15:7–15.

Du Bois, John
1993   "Meaning Without Intention: Lessons from Divination." Pp. 48–71. *Responsibility and Evidence in Oral Discourse.* Ed. J. H. Hill and J. T. Irvine. Cambridge: Cambridge University Press.

Dumont, Louis
1970   *Homo Hierarchicus: The Caste System and its Implications.* London: Weidenfeld and Nicolson.

Duranti, Alessandro
1993   "Intentions, Self, and Responsibility: An Essay in Samoan Ethnopragmatics." Pp. 24–47. *Responsibility and Evidence in Oral Discourse.* Ed. J. H. Hill and J. T. Irvine. Cambridge: Cambridge University Press.

Duxbury, Neil
1995   *Patterns of American Jurisprudence.* Oxford: Clarendon Press.

Dworkin, Ronald
1977   *Taking Rights Seriously.* Cambridge, Mass.: Harvard University Press.

1985   *A Matter of Principle.* Cambridge, Mass.: Harvard University Press.

1986   *Law's Empire.* Cambridge, Mass.: Harvard University Press.

Eliade, Mircea
1954   *The Myth of the Eternal Return or, Cosmos and History.* New York: Pantheon (Bollingen Series 64).

Eliot, George
1986   *The Mill on the Floss.* New York: Avenel Books.

Eliot, T. S.
1958   *The Complete Poems and Plays: 1909–1950.* New York: Harcourt Brace.

Enns, Paul
1989   *The Moody Handbook of Theology.* Chicago: Moody Press.

Esterbrook, Frank H.
   1997   "What Does Legislative History Tell Us?" Pp. 230–37. *Judges on Judging: Views from the Bench*. Ed. D. M. O'Brian. Chatham, N.J.: Chatham House.

Fish, Stanley
   1980   *Is There a Text in this Class? The Authority of Interpretive Communities*. Cambridge: Harvard University Press.

   1994   *There's No Such Thing as Free Speech . . . and It's a Good Thing Too*. New York: Oxford University Press.

Fischer, Michael, and Mehdi Abedi
   1990   "Qur'anic Dialogues: Islamic Poetics and Politics for Muslims and for Us." Pp. 95–149. *Debating Muslims: Cultural Dialogues in Postmodernity and Tradition*. Madison: University of Wisconsin Press.

FitzGerald, Frances
   1986   *Cities on a Hill: A Journey Through Contemporary American Cutures*. New York: Simon and Schuster.

Fliegelman, Jay
   1993   *Declaring Independence: Jefferson, Natural Language, and the Culture of Performance*. Stanford: Stanford University Press.

Foucault, Michel
   1970   *The Order of Things: An Archeology of the Human Sciences*. New York: Pantheon.

   1977   "What is an Author?" Pp. 113–38. *Language, Counter-Memory, Practice: Selected Essays and Interviews*. Ithaca, N.Y.: Cornell University Press.

Frair, Wayne, and Percival Davis
   1983   *A Case for Creation*, 3d ed. Lewisville, Tex: Accelerated Christian Education.

Frank, Jerome
   1950   *Courts on Trial: Myth and Reality in American Justice*. Princeton, N.J.: Princeton University Press.

   1970   *Law and the Modern Mind*. Gloucester, Mass.: Peter Smith. [1930]

Frei, Hans
   1974   *The Eclipse of the Biblical Narrative; A Study in Eighteenth- and Nineteenth-Century Hermeneutics*. New Haven: Yale University Press.

Friedrich, Otto
   1982   *The End of the World: A History*. New York: Coward, McCann, and Geoghegan.

Frug, Mary Jo
   1992   *Postmodern Legal Feminism*. New York: Routledge.

Gadamer, Hans-Georg
   1985   *Truth and Method*. New York: Seabury Press. [1965]

Gallup, G. H.
   1981   *Public Opinion 1980*. Wilmington, Del.: Scholarly Resources.

   1983   *Public Opinion 1982*. Wilmington, Del.: Scholarly Resources.

   1995   "It Was a Very Bad Year: Belief in Hell and the Devil on the Rise." *The Gallup Organization Beliefs Poll Newsletter Archive*: January.

Girdlestone, Robert B.
  1955   *The Grammar of Prophecy: Guide to Biblical Prophecy.* Grand Rapids, Mich.: Kregel.

Goebel, Julius, Jr.
  1931   "King's Law and Local Custom in Seventeenth-century New England." *Columbia Law Review* 31:416–48.

Good, Byron J.
  1994   *Medicine, Rationality, and Experience: An Anthropological Perspective.* Cambridge: Cambridge University Press.

Gordon, Robert W.
  1984   Critical Legal History. *Stanford Law Review* 36:57–125.

Gould, Stephen Jay
  1965   "Is Uniformitarianism Necessary?" *American Journal of Science* 263:463–79.
  1997   "Darwinian Fundamentalism. Evolution: The Pleasures of Pluralism." *New York Review of Books.* June 12, pp. 34–36, and June 26, pp. 46–52, respectively.

Greenhouse, Carol J.
  1989   "Just in Time: Temporality and the Cultural Legitimation of the Law." *Yale Law Journal* 98:1631–51.
  1996   *A Moment's Notice: Time Politics Across Cultures.* Ithaca, N.Y.: Cornell University Press.

Greenhouse, Linda
  1997   "Why Bork Is Still a Verb in Politics, 10 Years Later." *New York Times*, Oct. 5:WK-3.

Grey, Thomas C.
  1984   "The Constitution as Scripture." *Stanford Law Review* 37:1–25

Griffin, Stephen M.
  1995   "Constitutionalism in the United States: From Theory to Politics." Pp. 37–61. *Responding to Imperfection: The Theory and Practice of Constitutional Amendment.* Ed. S. Levinson. Princeton: Princeton University Press.

Habermas, Jürgen
  1973   *Theory and Practice.* Boston: Beacon.
  1985   "On Hermeneutics Claim to Universality." Pp. 294–319. *The Hermeneutics Reader.* Ed. K. Mueller-Vollmer. New York: Continuum.

Hankins, Barry
  1996   *God's Rascal: J. Frank Norris and Southern Fundamentalism.* Lexington: University Press of Kentucky.

Harding, Susan
  1991   "Representing Fundamentalism: The Problem of the Repugnant Cultural Other." *Social Research* 58:373–93.
  1992   "The Afterlife of Stories: The Genesis of a Man of God." Pp. 60–75. *Storied Lives.* Ed. R. Ockberg and G. Rosenwald. New Haven: Yale University Press.

1992a   "The Gospel of Giving: The Narrative Structure of a Sacrificial Economy." Pp. 39–56. *Vocabularies of Public Life: Empirical Essays in Symbolic Structure.* Ed. R. Wuthnow. London: Routledge.

Hart, H. L. A.
1961   *The Concept of the Law.* Oxford: Clarendon.

1983   *Essays in Jurisprudence and Philosophy.* Oxford: Clarendon.

Heidegger, Martin
1967   *Being and Time.* Oxford: Blackwell. [1927]

1971   *On the Way to Language.* New York: Harper and Row. [1959]

Hancher, Michael
1988   "Dead Letters: Wills and Poems." Pp. 101–14. *Interpreting Law and Literature.* Ed. S. Levinson and S. Maillous. Evanston, Ill.: Northwestern University Press.

Hirsch, E. D., Jr.
1960   "Objective Interpretation." *PMLA* 75:463–79.

1976   *The Aims of Interpretation.* Chicago: University of Chicago Press.

Hodge, Charles
1960   *Systematic Theology.* 3 vols. London: Clarke.

Hodges, Zane
1989   *Absolutely Free!* Grand Rapids, Mich.: Zondervan.

Holmes, Oliver Wendell
1963   *The Common Law.* Cambridge: Harvard University Press. [1881]

Honig, B.
1991   "Declarations of Independence: Arendt and Derrida on the Problem of Founding a Republic." *American Political Science Review* 85:97–113.

Horwitz, Morton J.
1973   "The Emergence of an Instrumental Conception of American Law, 1780-1820." *Perspectives in American Legal History* 5:275.

1993   "Foreword: The Constitution of Change: Legal Fundamentality without Fundamentalism." *Harvard Law Review* 107:30–118.

Hoy, David Couzens
1992   "Intention and the Law: Defending Hermeneutics." Pp. 173–86. *Legal Hermeneutics: History, Theory, Practice.* Berkeley: University of California Press.

Jacobsohn, Gary J.
1981   *The Supreme Court and the Decline of Constitutional Aspiration.* Lanham, Md.: Rowman and Littlefield.

Jakobson, Roman
1960   "Closing Statement: Linguistics and Poetics." Pp. 350–77. *Style in Language.* Ed. T. Sebeok. Cambridge, Mass.: MIT Press.

James, Henry
1984   *Literary Criticism: Essays on Literature, American Writers, English Writers.* New York: Library of America.

1993   "The American Scene." Pp. 353–36. *Collected Travel Writings: Great Britain and America.* New York: Library of America. [1907]

Jefferson, Thomas
1984   *Writings.* New York: New American Library.

Johnson, Elliot E.
1996   "Dual Authorship and the Single Intended Meaning of Scripture." Pp. 171–79. *Rightly Divided: Readings in Biblical Hermeneutics.* Ed. R. B. Zuck. Grand Rapids, Mich.: Kregel.

Kantorowicz, Ernest H.
1957   *The King's Two Bodies: A Study in Medieval Political Theology.* Princeton: Princeton University Press.

Kay, Richard
1987   "The Illegality of the Constitution." *Constitutional Commentary* 4:57–80.

Kaiser, Walter C. and M. Silva
1994   *An Introduction to Biblical Hermeneutics: The Search for Meaning.* Grand Rapids, Mich.: Zondervan.

Keller, E. Fox
1985   *Reflections on Gender and Science.* New Haven: Yale University Press.

Kelsen, Hans
1945a   *General Theory of Law and State.* New York: Russell and Russell.

1945b   "Natural Law Doctrine and Legal Positivism." Pp. 389–446. *General Theory of Law and State.* New York: Russell and Russell.

Kerenyi, C.
1959   *Asklepios: Archetypal Image of the Physician's Existence.* New York: Pantheon (Bollingen).

Knapp, Steven, and Walter Benn Michaels
1992   "Intention, Identity, and the Constitution: A Response to David Hoy." Pp. 187–99. *Legal Hermeneutics: History, Theory, and Practice.* Ed. G. Leyh. Berkeley: University of California Press.

Koselleck, Reinhart
1985   *Futures Past: On the Semantics of Historical Time.* Cambridge, Mass.: MIT Press. [1979]

Kuhn, Thomas
1970   *The Structure of Scientific Revolutions.* 2d. edition. Chicago: University of Chicago Press.

Ladd, George Eldon
1956   *The Blessed Hope: A Biblical Study of the Second Advent and the Rapture.* Grand Rapids, Mich.: William B. Eerdmans.

1967   *The New Testament and Criticism.* Grand Rapids, Mich.: William B. Eerdmans.

Lasser, Michel de S.-O.-l'E
1998   "'Lit. Theory' Put to the Test: A Comparative Literary Analysis of American Judicial Tests and French Judicial Discourse." *Harvard Law Review* 111: 689–770.

Leary, Warren E.
1999 "New Framers of the Declaration of Independence Act to Save it in Parchment." *New York Times,* Feb. 2:A34.

Lee, Benjamin
1997 *Talking Heads: Language, Metalanguage, and the Semiotics of Subjectivity.* Durham: Duke University Press.

LeMasters, Carol
1995 "From Ragged Empowerment to Naked Power. A Review of Harvey Cox's *Fire from Heaven: The Rise of Pentecostal Spirituality and the Reshaping of Religion in the Twenty-first Century."* *Cross Currents* 45. 2:257–61.

Lessig, Lawrence
1993 "Fidelity in Translation." *Texas Law Review* 71:1165–1268.
1995 "Understanding Changed Readings: Fidelity and Theory." *Stanford Law Review* 47:395–472.
1997 "Fidelity and Constraint." *Fordham Law Review* 65:1365–1443.

Levi, Edward H.
1949 *An Introduction to Legal Reasoning.* Chicago: University of Chicago Press.

Lévi-Strauss, Claude
1967 "The Structural Study of Myth." Pp. 202–28. *Structural Anthropology.* Garden City, N.Y.: Doubleday Anchor.

Levinson, Sanford
1988 *Constitutional Faith.* Princeton: Princeton University Press.
1988a "Law as Literature." Pp. 155–73. *Interpreting Law and Literature.* Ed. S. Levinson and S. Mailloux. Evanston, Ill.: Northwestern University Press.

Levinson, Stephen C.
1983 *Pragmatics.* Cambridge: Cambridge University Press.

Lewis, Anthony
1987 "An Ingenious Structure." *New York Times Magazine.* Sept. 13:39–42.

Leyh, Gregory
1992 "Legal Education and the Public Life." Pp. 269–94. *Legal Hermeneutics.* Ed. G. Leyh. Berkeley: University of California Press.

Lindsey, Hal, with C. C. Carlson
1977 *The Late Great Planet Earth.* Grand Rapids, Mich.: Zondervan. [1970]

Llewellyn, Karl N.
1971 *Jurisprudence: Realism in Theory and Practice.* Chicago: University of Chicago Press.

Lofgren, Charles A.
1990 "The Original Understanding of Original Intent?" Pp. 117–50. *Interpreting the Constitution: The Debate over Original Intent.* Ed. J. N. Rakove. Boston: Northeastern University Press.

Löwith, Karl
1949 *Meaning in History.* Chicago: University of Chicago Press.

Lutz, Donald S.
    1995   "Toward a Theory of Constitutional Amendment." Pp. 237–74. *Responding to Imperfection: The Theory and Practice of Constitutional Amendment.* Ed. Sanford Levinson. Princeton: Princeton University Press.

McCartney, Dan, and C. Clayton
    1994   *Let the Reader Understand: A Guide to Interpreting and Applying the Bible.* Wheaton, Ill.: Victor Books (Bridge Point).

MacArthur, John F., Jr.
    1992   *Charismatic Chaos.* Grand Rapids, Mich.: Zondervan.

    1993   *Faith Works: The Gospel According to the Apostles.* Dallas: Word Publishing.

    1994   "The Work of the Spirit and Biblical Counseling." Pp. 131–41. *Introduction to Biblical Counseling: A Basic Guide to the Principles and Practice of Counseling.* Ed. J. A. MacArthur and W. A. Mack. Dallas: Word Publishing.

Mack, Wayne
    1994a "Developing a Helping Relationship with Counselees." Pp. 173–88. *Introduction to Biblical Counseling: A Basic Guide to he Principles and Practice of Counseling* Ed. J. A. MacArthur, Jr., and W. A. Mack. Dallas: Word Publishing.

    1994b "Instilling Hope in the Counselee." Pp. 189–209. *Introduction to Biblical Counseling: A Basic Guide to the Principles and Practice of Counseling.* Ed. J. A. MacArthur, Jr., and W. A. Mack. Dallas: Word Publishing.

Madison, James, Alexander Hamilton, and John Jay
    1987   *The Federalist Papers.* Hammondsworth, Eng.: Penguin. [1787]

Maier, Pauline
    1997   *American Scripture: Making the Declaration of Independence.* New York: Vintage.

Marcus, George, and Michael Fischer
    1986   *Anthropology as Cultural Critique: An Experimental Moment in the Human Sciences.* Chicago: University of Chicago Press.

Marsden, George M.
    1980   *Fundamentalism and American Culture: The Shaping of Twentieth-Century Evangelicalism, 1870–1925.* Oxford, Eng.: Oxford University Press.

Martin, Douglas
    1999   "The Sound of 2000? Ka-ching: Millennial Schlock Merchants Count Down to Payday." *New York Times,* Feb. 3:B1–B2.

Martin, William
    1996   *With God on Our Side: The Rise of the Religious Right in America.* New York: Broadway Books.

Marty, Martin E., and R. Scott Appleby
    1993   *Fundamentalism and Society: Reclaiming the Sciences, the Family, and Education.* Chicago: University of Chicago Press.

Meese, Edwin
    1990   "Interpreting the Constitution." Pp. 13–21. *Interpreting the Constitution: The Debate over Original Intention.* Ed. J. Rakove. Boston: Northeastern University Press.

1987   "The Law of the Constitution." *Tulane Law Review* 61:979 – 90.

Messick, Brinkley
1993   *The Calligraphic State: Textual Domination and History in a Muslim Society.*
        Berkeley: University of California Press.

Miller, Geoffrey P.
1990   Pragmatics and the Maxims of Interpretation. *Wisconsin Law Review*
        1990:1179 – 1225.

Miller, Perry
1961   *The New England Mind: The Seventeenth Century.* Boston: Beacon Press.
        [1930]

Minow, Martha
1990   *Making All the Difference: Inclusion, Exclusion, and American Law.* Ithaca,
        N.Y.: Cornell University Press.

Montaigne, Michel de
1958   *The Complete Essays of Montaigne.* Stanford: Stanford University Press. [1588]

Morris, Henry M.
1984   *The Biblical Basis for Modern Science.* Grand Rapids, Mich.: Baker Book
        House.

Morris, Henry M., and M. E. Clark
1987   *The Bible Has the Answer.* Rev. ed. El Cajon, Calif.: Master Books.

Mowrer, O. Hobart
1961   *The Crisis in Psychiatry and Religion.* Princeton: Van Nostrand.

Murray, Iain H.
1981   *Arthur W. Pink: His Life and Thought.* Edinburgh, Scotland: Banner of Truth.

Newport, Frank, and Lydia Saad
1999   "Religious Faith Is Widespread but Many Skip Church." Princeton: Gallup
        Pool Archives.

Nilsson, M.P.
1949   *History of Greek Religion.* 2d ed. Oxford: Oxford University Press.

Noble, David F.
1998   *The Religion of Technology: The Divinity of Man and the Spirit of Invention.*
        New York: Knopf.

Nock, A. D.
1961   *Conversion.* Oxford: Oxford University Press. [1933]

Noll, Mark A.
1992   *A History of Christianity in the United States and Canada.* Grand Rapids,
        Mich.: William B. Eerdmans.

1994   *The Scandal of the Evangelical Mind.* Grand Rapids, Mich.: William B. Eerd-
        mans.

Numbers, Ronald L.
1992   *The Creationists: The Evolution of Scientific Creationism.* Berkeley: University
        of California Press.

Ong, Walter J.
1982   *Orality and Literacy: The Technologizing of the Word.* London: Routledge.

Ott, Heinrich
  1972   "Hermeneutic and Personal Structure of Language." Pp. 169–93. *On Heidegger and Language*. Ed. J. Kockelmans. Evanston, Ill.: Northwestern University Press.

Packer, J. L.
  1990   *A Quest for Godliness: The Puritan Vision of the Christian Life*. Wheaton, Ill.: Crossway Books.

Payne, J. Barton
  1973   *Encyclopaedia of Biblical Prophecy: The Complete Guide to Scriptural Predictions and their Fulfillment*. New York: Harper and Row.

Perry, Michael J.
  1985   "The Authority of the Text, Tradition, and Reason: A Theory of Constitutional 'Interpretation.'" *Southern California Law Review* 58:551–602.

Pink, Arthur W.
  1972   *Interpretation of the Scriptures*. Grand Rapids, Mich.: Baker Books.

Pitkin, Hanna Fenichel
  1967   *The Concept of Representation*. Berkeley: University of California Press.

Posner, Richard A.
  1990   *The Problems of Jurisprudence*. Cambridge: Harvard University Press.
  1998   *Law and Literature*. Rev. ed. Cambridge: Harvard University Press.

Powell, H. Jefferson
  1990   "The Original Understanding of Original Intent." Pp. 53–114. *Interpreting the Constitution: The Debate over Original Intent*. Ed. J. N. Rakove. Boston: Northeastern University Press.

Powlison, David
  1994   "Biblical Counseling in the Twentieth Century." Pp. 44–60. *Introduction to Biblical Counseling*. Ed. J. F. MacArthur, Jr., and W. A. Mack. Dallas: Word Publishing.

Preston, Howard W.
  1893   *Documents Illustrative of American History: 1606–1863*. New York: G. P. Putnam's Sons.

Rakove, Jack N.
  1990   "Mr. Meese, Meet Mr. Madison." Pp. 179–94. *Interpreting the Constitution: The Debate over Original Intent*. Boston: Northeastern University Press.

Ramm, Bernard
  1970   *Protestant Biblical Interpretation*. 3d rev. ed. Grand Rapids, Mich.: Baker Book House.

Ransom, John Crowe
  1941   *The New Criticism*. Norfolk, Conn.: New Directions.

Robbin, L. Katherine
  1996   "Befriending the Bible: Bible Reference Update." *Christianity Today* 40 (April 8):4–10.

Roche, John P.
1987   "The Convention as a Case Study in Democratic Politics." Pp. 175–212. *Essays on the Making of the Constitution.* 2d ed. Ed. L. W. Levy. Oxford, Eng.: Oxford University Press. [1961]

Rommetveit, Ragnar
1988   "Of Literacy and the Myth of Literal Meaning." Pp. 13–40. *The Written World: Studies in Literate Thought and Action.* Ed. R. Säljö. Berlin: Springer-Verlag.

Rosenberg, Ellen M.
1989   *The Southern Baptists: A Subculture in Transition.* Knoxville: University of Tennessee Press.

Ross, Dorothy
1984   "Historical Consciousness in Nineteenth-century America." *American Historical Review* 89:909–28.

Ross, Hugh
1996   *Beyond the Cosmos: The Extra-Dimensionality of God.* Colorado Springs: Navpress.

Rosscup, James E.
1992   "Hermeneutics and Expository Preaching." Pp. 119–36. *Rediscovering Expository Preaching.* Ed. J. MacArthur, Jr., and the Master's Seminary Faculty. Dallas: Word Publishing.

Rovere, Richard
1979   "Affairs of State." *New Yorker Magazine* (March 19):136–43.

Ryrie, Charles C.
1969   *Balancing the Christian Life.* Chicago: Moody.

1972   *Survey of Bible Doctrine.* Chicago: Moody.

1989   *So Great Salvation.* Wheaton, Ill.: Victor.

1995   *Dispensationalism.* Chicago: Moody.

Sandeen, Ernest
1970   *The Roots of Fundamentalism: British and American Millenarianism, 1880–1930.* Chicago: University of Chicago Press.

1974   "Fundamentalism and American Identity." Pp. 287–99. *The Social Meanings of Religion.* Ed. W. M. Newman. Chicago: Rand McNally. [1970]

Sandlin, Andrew
1997   *Crucial Distinctive of Christian Reconstruction: Christian Libertarianism.* Vallecito, Calif.: Chalcedon Foundation.

Sarles, Ken L.
1994   "The English Puritans: A Historical Paradigm of Biblical Counseling." Pp. 21–43. *Introduction to Biblical Counseling* Ed. J. F. MacArthur, Jr., and W. A. Mack. Dallas: Word Publishing.

Saussure, Ferdinand de
1966   *Course in General Linguistics.* New York: McGraw-Hill.

Scalia, Antonin
1989   "Originalism: The Lesser Evil." *Cincinnati Law Review* 57:849–65.

1997 "Common-law Courts in a Civil-law System: The Role of United States Federal Courts in Interpreting the Constitution and Laws." Pp. 3–47. *A Matter of Interpretation: Federal Courts and the Law.* Princeton: Princeton University Press.

Schell, Jonathan (Anonymous)
1973 "Notes and Comment." *New Yorker.* April 28:29–34.

Schleiermacher, Friedrich
1977a "The Compendium of 1819 and the Marginal Notes of 1828." Pp. 95–151. *Hermeneutics: The Handwritten Manuscripts.* Ed. H. Kimmerle. Missoula, Mont.: Scholars Press for the American Academy of Religion.

1977b "The Academy Addresses of 1879." Pp. 175–214. *Hermeneutics: The Handwritten Manuscripts.* Ed. H. Kimmerle. Missoula, Mont.: Scholars Press for the American Academy of Religion.

Scofield, C.I.
1945 *The Scofield Study Bible.* New York: Oxford University Press. [1909]

Searle, John R.
1969 *Speech Acts: An Essay in the Philsophy of Language.* Cambridge, Eng.: Cambridge University Press.

1983 *Intentionality: An Essay in the Philosophy of Mind.* Cambridge, Eng.: Cambridge University Press.

1985 *Expression and Meaning.* Cambridge, Eng.: Cambridge University Press.

Silva, Moisé
1987 *Has the Church Misread the Bible: The History of Interpretation in the Light of Current Issues.* Grand Rapids, Mich.: Zondervan.

Silverstein, Michael
1979 "Language Structure and Linguistic Ideology." Pp. 193–247. *The Elements: A Parasession on Linguistic Units and Levels.* Ed. P. Cline, W. Hanks, and C. Hofbauer. Chicago: Chicago Linguistic Society.

Sloan, James Park
1994 "Kosinski's War." *New Yorker* (Oct. 10):46–53.

Smart, Carol
1989 *Feminism and the Power of the Law.* London: Routledge.

Smith, Preserved
1920 *The Age of the Reformation.* New York: Henry Holt.

Sowers, S.G.
1965 *The Hermeneutics of Philo and the Hebrews.* Richmond, Va.: Knox.

Stevens, Wallace.
1957 *The Collected Poems.* New York: Knopf.

Stocking, George W., Jr.
1987 *Victorian Anthropology.* New York: Free Press.

Stone, Geoffrey, L. M. Seidman, C. R. Sunstein, and M. V. Tushnet
1996 *Constitutional Law.* 3d ed. Boston: Little, Brown.

Stone, Jerry H.

1992 "Christian Praxis as Reflective Action." Pp. 103–26. *Legal Hermeneutics: History, Theory, and Practice.* Ed. G. Leyh. Berkeley: University of California Press.

Stromberg, Peter G.

1993 *Language and Self-Transformation: A Study of Christian Conversion Narrative.* Cambridge: Cambridge University Press.

Sundkler, B. G. M.

1948 *Bantu Prophets in South Africa.* London: Lutterworth.

Thomas, Robert L.

1991 "Literary Genre and Hermeneutics of the *Apocalypse.*" *Master's Seminary Journal* 2:79–91.

1992 "Exegesis and Expository Preaching." Pp. 137–53. *Rediscovering Expository Preaching.* Ed. J. MacArthur, Jr., and the Master's Seminary Faculty. Dallas: Word Publishing.

Tolstoy, Leo

1970 *Anna Karenina.* New York: Norton Critical Editions. [1878]

Tribe, Laurence H.

1987 "The Final Say." *New York Times Magazine.* Sept. 13:68–72.

Tribe, Laurence H., and Michael C. Dorf

1991 *On Reading the Constitution.* Cambridge: Harvard University Press

Troeltsch, Ernst

1992 *The Social Teaching of the Christian Churches.* 2 vols. Louisville, Ky.: Westminster/John Knox Press. [1912]

Tushnet, Mark V.

1996 *Abortion: Constitutional Issues.* New York: Facts on File.

Twain, Mark (Samuel Langhorne Clemens)

1982 *Pudd'nhead Wilson.* Pp. 913–1056. *Mississippi Writings.* New York: Library of America. [1894]

Unger, Roberto Mangabeira

1986 *The Critical Legal Studies Movement.* Cambridge: Harvard University Press.

Van Til, Cornelius

1967 *The Defense of the Faith.* 3d ed. Phillipsburg, N.J.: Presbyterian and Reformed Publishing Company.

Vile, John R.

1993 *Contemporary Questions Surrounding the Constitutional Amending Process.* Westport, Conn.: Praeger.

Virkler, Henry A.

1996 "A Proposal for the Transcultural Problem." Pp. 231–44. *Rightly Divided: Readings in Biblical Hermeneutics.* Ed. R. B. Zuck. Grand Rapids, Mich.: Kregel.

Von Rad, Gerhard

1965 *The Message of the Prophets.* New York: HarperCollins.

Warner, Michael
   1990   *The Letters of the Republic: Publications and the Public Sphere in Eighteenth-century America.* Cambridge: Harvard University Press.

Walvoord, John
   1959   *The Millennial Kingdom.* Grand Rapids, Mich.: Zondervan.

Wayland, John W.
   1925   "Samuel Kercheval." N.p. *A History of the Valley of Virginia.* 4th ed. Strasburg, Va.: Shenandoah Publishing House.

Weaver, Mary Anne
   1998   "Revolution by Stealth." *New Yorker* (June 8):38 – 48.

Weber, Paul J., and Barbara A. Perry
   1989   *Unfounded Fears: Myths and Realities of a Constitutional Convention.* New York: Greenwood.

Weisberg, Richard H.
   1996   *Vichy Law and the Holocaust in France.* New York: New York University Press.

Wimsatt, W., Jr., and M. Beardsley
   1992   "The Intentional Fallacy." Pp. 944–51. *Critical Theory Since Plato.* Rev. ed. Ed. H. Adams. Fort Worth, Tex.: Harcourt Brace Jovanovich. [1946]

Wittgenstein, Ludwig
   1958   *The Blue and Brown Books.* New York: Harper Torchbooks.

Wood, Gordon S.
   1969   *The Creation of the American Republic: 1776 – 1787.* Chapel Hill: University of North Carolina Press.

   1997   "Comment." Pp. 49 – 63. *A Matter of Interpretation* by A. Scalia. Princeton: Princeton University Press.

Yeats, W. B.
   1959   *The Collected Poems.* New York: Macmillan.

Young, Iris Marion
   1990   *Justice and Politics of Difference.* Princeton: Princeton University Press.

Zuck, Roy B.
   1996   "Application in Biblical Hermeneutics and Exposition." Pp. 278 – 96. *Rightly Divided: Readings in Biblical Hermeneutics.* Grand Rapids, Mich.: Kregel.

Index

400 — INDEX